Cybertext Poetics

International Texts In Critical Media Aesthetics

Volume #2

Founding Editor
Francisco J. Ricardo

Associate Editor
Jörgen Schäfer

Editorial Board
Roberto Simanowski
Rita Raley
John Cayley
George Fifield

Cybertext Poetics

The Critical Landscape of New
Media Literary Theory

MARKKU ESKELINEN

continuum

The Continuum International Publishing Group

The Tower Building
11 York Road
London
SE1 7NX

80 Maiden Lane
Suite 704
New York
NY 10038

www.continuumbooks.com

Library of Congress Cataloging-in-Publication Data
Eskelinen, Markku.
  Cybertext poetics : the critical landscape of new media literary theory / by Markku Eskelinen.
    p. cm. – (International texts in critical media aesthetics ; v. 2)
  Includes bibliographical references and index.
  ISBN-13: 978-1-4411-2438-8 (hardcover : alk. paper)
  ISBN-10: 1-4411-2438-1 (hardcover : alk. paper)
  ISBN-13: 978-1-4411-0745-9 (pbk. : alk. paper)
  ISBN-10: 1-4411-0745-2 (pbk. : alk. paper) 1. Literature and technology. 2. Digital media–Social aspects. 3. Literature and society. 4. Communication and technology. 5. Narration (Rhetoric) I. Title.

  PN56.T37E85 2012
  809'.93356–dc23

2011038964

ISBN: HB: 978–1–4411–2438–8
PB: 978–1–4411–0745–9

Typeset by Fakenham Prepress Solutions, Fakenham, Norfolk, NR21 8NN
Printed and bound in the United States of America

CONTENTS

ACKNOWLEDGMENTS

There are eight people without whom this book would have been either pointless or impossible for me to write: Espen Aarseth, John Cayley, Julianne Chatelain, Gonzalo Frasca, Raine Koskimaa, Stuart Moulthrop, Francisco Ricardo, and my wife. I remain in debt and you all know why.

I feel lucky. Fifteen years ago I decided to stop writing fiction and essays in Finnish and to do something completely different instead. I didn't ever expect to find myself belonging to a wonderfully open and welcoming international community of scholars and artists just a few years later, but that is exactly what happened to me after the first Digital Arts and Culture conference in Bergen in 1998. Ever since that magical event I have enjoyed having intense and inspiring discussions with an evergrowing number of people on top of their profession. Among those friends, colleagues, artists, and researchers who and whose work have shaped my thinking the most are Simon Biggs, Philippe Bootz, Laura Borrás Castanyer, Serge Bouchardon, Eliza Deac, Maria Engberg, Mary Flanagan, Peter Gendolla, Loss Pequeno Glazier, Anna Gunder, Cynthia Haynes, Jan Rune Holmevik, Fotis Jannidis, Michael Joyce, Jesper Juul, Aki Järvinen, Eduardo Kac, Lisbeth Klastrup, Michael Mateas, Talan Memmott, Nick Montfort, Jason Nelson, Katherine Parrish, Mariusz Pisarski, Jill Walker Rettberg, Scott Rettberg, Jim Rosenberg, Jörgen Schäfer, Roberto Simanowski, Janez Strehovec, Patricia Tomaszek, Rui Torres, Susana Tosca, Ragnhild Tronstad, Piret Viires, and Noah Wardrip-Fruin. Thank you all, it was fun.

To be honest, I was also genuinely inspired by several scholars whose work I despise, but me being me, they are way too numerous to be listed here.

Markku Eskelinen
Helsinki, 1 August 2011

$250 I am updating &
Finessing Trattnicts

These are not new items but by
adding hyperlinks & focusing
on ann I recalibrints
discussions started by
Trattnicts.

*In H intro I suy Mene in a cnin q rendng —
du nd hnun hau ta rend, du nd hnun hen t mnnage
into — med attempt t encode hau t rend in H text.
Nt a rew nlea. I waad nd Mn burt q inc a
hystry q th nla — Trotter; Eco. I Men updite it
with cylurtext,
hr exampli, or
Parteka.
So ... I
am pincessing renlng encoded idea. ✱ 2
nck as respung t hau t rend - inder
q cmin*

CHAPTER 1

Introduction

1.1 Points of departure

Cybertext Poetics has three different points of departure:
theoretical, strategic, and empirical. It uses ludology and modified
cybertext theory as a cross-disciplinary perspective to solve four
persistent and strategically chosen problems in four separate, yet
interconnected fields: literary theory, narratology, game studies,
and digital media.[1] The problems in the first three fields stem
from the same root: hegemonic theories are based on a subset of
possible media behaviors that is far too limited, and this limitation
seriously undermines their explanatory and analytical power. The
cumulative effects of this lack also obscure our understanding of
transmediality, media ecology, and digital media. An example may
perhaps help demonstrate what I mean.

If we take an ordinary printed and bound book, what are the
facts that we just might agree about? The color of its cover, the
number of its pages and words if we bother to count, but all this
is deemed banal for a good reason: the rest and with it everything
that really interests us is up to interpretation. By now we know very
well to where that road leads: irreducible differences in reception,
contexts and communities and also in competence and skill. But
let's try another kind of book, B.S. Johnson's *The Unfortunates*:
it comes with simple instructions allowing the reader to decide in
which order to read the bundles of text. Here we can also agree, in
addition to those banal facts, on a certain operational procedure of

is value
is a query what is uncs — how ish — how
is I new
is new

*This is how I use dry lit t finesse
rendr conshul argument — encoded into MhL/MM etc
is abo a specisin operational procedure — hau t
rend*

how we should make this literary work function. The whole range of existing media behavior naturally goes far beyond this simple operation of choosing paths, as is evident in such dynamically ergodic digital works as *Book Unbound* (Cayley 1995a) or *The Impermanence Agent* (Wardrip-Fruin et al. 1998–2002).

Two aspects are essential here: we have established a range of media behavior that is easily verifiable. Luckily, for the last 15 years we have had a theory that takes into account the dimension that is lacking and ignored in contemporary and hegemonic theories of literature, Aarseth's cybertext theory, which is capable of situating every text, based on how its medium functions, into its heuristic but empirically verifiable map of 576 media positions. Before going any further into this it is important to understand that similar theories of media functioning do not exist in neighboring scholarly fields (including those centered on audiovisual presentations) – in this respect cybertext theory is a unique achievement.

If currently hegemonic literary theories are viewed from the perspective of cybertext theory, it quickly becomes evident that these theories cover and are valid only in a very limited range of media positions. In practice, they are based on only one position and therefore on literary works that are static, determinate, intransient, featuring random access and impersonal perspective, no links and only interpretative user function, while pretending to be general theories of literature applicable to every literary work in every possible medium. Similar limitations also affect classical and postclassical literary (and film) narratologies and the behavioral scope of their favorite objects of choice.

The clash between the claims of hegemonic literary and narrative theories and their actual explanatory and analytical power is by no means only theoretical and cybertextual: empirically verifiable anomalies and counterexamples to the basic assumptions, premises, and presuppositions of these theories abound in digital and ergodic works of literature and film. In short, in the first half of the book we'll see what happens and what can be made to happen when sophisticated theories of reading and text are supplemented by an equally advanced theory of media.

However, those are not the only benefits of adopting the cybertextual perspective on media behavior. It is also relevant in ludology and game studies, because it can be used to introduce and justify the existence of comparative game studies as a paradigmatic alternative and extension to digital game studies and to suggest the shift of focus from what a game medium is to what it does in terms of ludic media positions. Finally, because cybertext theory is ultimately based on a study of media, it is also applicable to the problems of transmediality and media ecology that become somewhat easier to crack after expanding literary and narrative theories to cover a fuller range of media positions and constructing one possible basis for comparative game studies.

With cybertext theory, we are not limited to speculations on what a medium supposedly is and what it can or cannot do, which usually only result in long-lasting, hype-ridden, and counter-productive dichotomies (such as print vs. digital for example) excluding overlaps and the actual media behavior. We also don't need to limit our observations to loosely or poorly defined genres, but are able to look beyond them from a more unified perspective constructed from the full range of media positions (a theoretical entity that is necessarily open to change). Therefore this is not a study of hypertext fiction, poetry generators, first-person shooters or MMOGs, even though examples of these and many other "genres" are used in building the argument for more compre-hensive literary theory, narratology, and game studies. Following the inherent tension in cybertext theory between what is (the empirically verifiable behaviors) and what could be (myriad combi-nations), this project is necessarily oriented towards poetics as well.

1.2 Orientation: the uses of theory

Ultimately, this treatise is a theoretically oriented enterprise that aims at constructing several heuristic models. This necessitates a conscious move away from past debates while applying perspec-tives and conceptualizations that have explanatory power and analytical potential beyond the schisms in question. Thus, while applying McHale's theories of postmodernism (McHale 1987; 1992; 2004), we are not interested in being stuck with the all too familiar problems of how to discern postmodernism from modernism or how to maintain (if one so wishes) or draw a clearcut and inviolable boundary line between them. Instead, it is much more important to us to lift the useful distinction between epistemological and ontological problems from McHale's discourse and to graft it onto our constructions that have nothing to do with the already automated discourses on modernism and postmodernism. The ample empirical evidence of both epistemological and ontological problems that remain alien and unknown to modernist and postmodernist fiction and poetics is more than enough to justify this move.

Likewise, in theorizing and modeling the textual whole (a material-theoretical-ideological entity perhaps under erasure), the Oulipian distinction between objects and operations is lifted from its original context and applied as a heuristic model of how to best think about that totality, its behavior and reception.

Generally speaking, theories and theoretical constructions are mostly seen as heuristic tools, perspectives and frameworks that can be modified, revised, abandoned and supplemented should the need and evidence arise. This brings us close to Todorov's definition (1977, 33) of poetics as "a sum of possible forms: what literature can be rather than what it is." Thus, for example, in the context of expanding literary narratology from one to several available media positions, we are not stifled by the lack of the literary works to exemplify some positions, as long as they can be deduced or inferred from empirical examples through sound theoretical categorizations.

Should we require authoritative justification for our efforts in poetics, we could do worse than to quote Genette twice on what is certain and what is important: "What is certain is that poetics in general, and narratology in particular, must not limit itself to *accounting for* existing forms or themes. It must also explore the field of what is possible and even *impossible* without pausing too long at the frontier, the mapping out of which is not its job ... what would theory be worth if it were not also good for *inventing practice*" (Genette 1988, 157); and: "What is important about it is not this or that actual combination but the combinatorial principle itself, whose chief merit is to place the various categories in an open relationship with no a priori constraints" (Genette 1988, 129).

In short, what we have here are constellations, along with the principle that is also at work in Aarseth's open model of seven dimensions combining into hundreds of media positions, and as long as the values of the variables are found in our research objects, an empty slot or 10 in the combinatory system do not constitute a problem. On the contrary, such empty slots give us a valuable and very rare glance at several new frontiers of literature, narrative and games that may also help us formulate new research questions. The flexible modularity and temporality of digital media makes this combinatory principle even stronger and the resulting constellations much less permanent both in theory and in practice.

To resist hype and speculation, there usually is an empirical point of departure and a corresponding need for theoretical elaborations and revisions in every chapter. To take three examples: whatever one thinks of transtextuality and intertextuality, it is hard to deny that networked and programmable media have brought with them new relations and types of relation between and among texts (discussed in Chapter 3); whichever definition of narrative one prefers there is a strong connection between narratives and (re)presentation of events and time and it is hard to deny that digital media have added new means to manipulate time (theorized mostly in Chapter 8); and however one wishes to see the relations between games and narratives, it is hard to deny that current narrative theories cannot explain (and were never set to explain) such key features of games as rules, goals and player effort (as discussed in Chapters 12 to 17). Similarly, it is very hard to imagine a comprehensive literary theory that would not include theories of intertextuality, narrative theories ignoring narrative temporalities, or ludologies excluding the study of the dominant formal features of games.

The scope of this project is much less ambitious than it may sound. Even though one of the main thrusts is to revise, expand, and integrate theories in several scholarly fields, the aim is not to construct yet another grand theory, but to make several small steps away from the doxa of the day, mostly by following and being guided (and constrained) by an eclectically and pragmatically selected variety of empirically verifiable counterexamples. This is also reflected in the modular structure of the book, within which each chapter, and each section of each chapter comes with its own (yet mutually compatible) focus and agenda. The open arrangement should also convey the feeling that new, exciting, and unexplored possibilities are within one's grasp and there is no need or reason to limit one's theoretical appetites and practical interests to traditional zones of comfort.

1.3 Disciplinary contacts and contexts

1.3.1 Literary studies

Even though the dichotomy between paper- and digital-based media is false and breaks down under closer scrutiny, it still seems to divide the scholarly field of literary studies. Even (and sometimes especially) the most prominent literary scholars usually avoid digital and ergodic texts and stay firmly with printed and non-ergodic works. There are exceptions, most notably Brian McHale's (2004) recent probes into postmodernist poetry, but even in these cases the digital-ergodic realm is barely touched on and when it is, the results are not very convincing. As just one example, McHale's labeling John Cayley and Jim Rosenberg as postmodernist poets may well raise their cultural status from obscurity to marginality, but it also misses significant features of their oeuvre that run counter to various constructions of postmodernism, including McHale's own.

On the other side of that divide, scholars of digital literature tend to focus only on digital specimens, even though a limited selection of print literature is usually mentioned and included in discussions, most likely as "predecessors" (for example as proto-hypertexts) to the main objects of study providing a tradition and all the other benefits that come with that territory. Similar reliance and discourse on predecessors often occurs during theoretical construction when theories of print literature or Aristotelian drama are extended and mildly modified to better explain the theorists' digital objects of choice. At its most extreme these "new" objects are seen as embodiments of the ideas of recent literary-philosophical theories (as in Bolter's and Landow's influential but ill-informed attempts to conflate poststructuralism and hypertext literature in the early 1990s).

In many ways, this is just business as usual in the academy, as scholars have to specialize and prefer to stay within their primary areas of expertise. Still, there is no reason for boundaries or barriers of specialization to exist between the studies of print literature and digital literature. Our problem with that boundary is that the print side, which, for historical reasons, has the upper hand (culturally, economically, institutionally, educationally, theoretically etc.), still sees print literature as the one and only literature with any value.

This is not only an aesthetic problem, but a theoretical one. Digital and ergodic literature contain specimens that run counter to a wide variety of basic assumptions and presuppositions that ground an equally wide variety of sophisticated theories of print literature that pretend or are taken to be general theories of literature (in whatever medium). In other words, several implicit and explicit generalizations these theories make about literature either are or may be valid *only in the context* of print literature. Print scholars seem to be blind to this, and if digitally and ergodically oriented scholars do not challenge them with insights and perspectives derived from digital and other anomalies, the implicitly print-biased paradigms of literature will remain in power.

My aim is not to hint at revolutionizing literary studies (not even at palace revolution inside departments of comparative literature if and where such ineffective islets are still allowed to exist), but to set selected paradigms of hegemonic literary theory in dialogue with digital and ergodic anomalies, much to their own benefit, and most of all to the benefit of the enterprise of literary theory that has for quite some time now (after various "post" movements and cultural studies) existed without fresh challenges, new openings or remarkable advances. The nature of these challenges is grounded in empirically observable textual behavior, which makes these challenges easily verifiable even though we may (and are very likely to) disagree on how to best theorize them.

More generally then, we will cross the unnecessary divide between traditional literary studies of mainly non-ergodic texts and digital literary studies of mainly ergodic texts. This divide still has its institutional basis, but it is getting harder and harder to see the actual benefits (if willful ignorance doesn't count) of maintaining the split in any theoretically oriented scholarly work. The usual interpretative orientation could go on as unaffected as before, as from the vantage point of the humanistic-interpretative industry digital and ergodic literary texts are neither appealing nor canonized enough to become career-making cases.

1.3.2 Media studies and literary studies

Schematically, we can draft at least four partly overlapping stages in theoretical discussions and developments around literary media and more generally around digital media. First, various poetics of individual practitioner-theorists working in text generation (Bense 1962), digital poetry (Glazier 2002), intermedia (Higgins 1966), hypertext fiction (Joyce 1995), holopoetry (Kac 1995), video poetry (Melo e Castro 2007), and "interactive fiction" (Montfort 2005), to name but a few, who were usually content to explore the potentials of one particular medium, genre or material technology without generalizing their findings to other areas and without any attempt at constructing a theoretically valid comparative and comprehensive perspective. Second, the rise of hype contrasting the digital and new with the print or the analog and old (cf. the main bulk of hypertext theory) resulting in various lists of the supposedly novel or key properties of the new media or medium (cf. Manovich 2001; Murray 1997) that break down under closer scrutiny. Third, introduction of a comparative theory of media functioning and textual communication within which any literary text could be situated, shifting emphasis away from media essentialism (what a medium is or is supposed to be) to what a medium does (Aarseth 1991; 1994; 1997). Fourth, approaches trying to go beyond the textual surface and communicative models in general into operations, operational logics, and processes of various digital media (Bogost 2006; Bootz 2003; Wardrip-Fruin 2009).[2] So far these approaches are not fully developed and their explanatory power and heuristic value is still unclear. Moreover, to fully assess their value and usability, at least at this point in time, one needs to be considerably more familiar with research in artificial intelligence and computer science than I am. Still, in what follows we abandon only the second type, and apply mainly the third, while trying to be informed by the first and fourth.

1.3.3 Ludology and game studies

The importance of the section (Chapters 12–17) on first-generation ludology is at least fourfold. First, without ludology addressing and studying the defining and core features of games, the whole field of game studies would be left to what could be called overlap studies, more interested in connecting games to other phenomena, and thus ultimately eroding the justification for the existence (not to mention future) of game studies as a distinct academic discipline.

As always such distinctiveness would not exclude interdisciplinarity; one simply needs to have a discipline before it is possible to
become truly interdisciplinary.

Second, the necessary ontological question (what is a game?)
begs additional questions concerning the constituents of narrative
as well. The blind spot or imbalance among various contemporary definitions of narrative is that that they mostly predate
the emergence of representational video games and certainly
the recognition of the latter's cultural and aesthetic importance.
Perhaps the most significant consequence of this historical fact is
that narrative scholars still take for granted that narratives have
an absolute monopoly for representing events, i.e. that every kind
of representation of events is necessarily or potentially a narrative
or at least contains narrativity. This type of thinking makes sense
only in an environment, cultural context, or scholarly field that
excludes or is not aware of simulations and representational
games, and within which the closest competitors and points of
comparison to narrative are other text types such as argument and
description. Compared to these, digital and other games constitute
a much stronger challenge to the cultural and theoretical hegemony
of narratives, and may even provide a welcome alternative to the
lesser blessings of the narrative turn.

Third, ludology is much more than yet another anti-narrative
movement, as its opponents often take it to be. The third section
could therefore have been titled "In defense of radical ludology",
not only because it counters the serious and unproductive misunderstandings and both scholarly and non- or semi-scholarly
misrepresentations in the famous debate between ludologists and
narrativists that is also the founding debate of (digital) game
studies, but also because it brings to the fore several forgotten
heuristic suggestions for further research in the early ludological
work. In other words, the point is to point to the paths not yet
taken or followed to their logical conclusions, and to the ludological
project as being far from complete, and its role as a necessary
countermeasure to the current fetishizing of both players and game
cultures that causes the field to gravitate towards an interpretative
and meaning-oriented synthesis of cultural studies and social
sciences. With some justification these two could be seen as moving
game studies to the state and status of normal science, but as the
section tries to show, the road there is less straightforward and

perhaps also less rewarding than the prevailing consensus among the interested parties in academia and industry seems to assume. Perhaps the most important of the half-forgotten ludological paths leads from digital game studies to comparative game studies.

Fourth, constructing a more unified ludology creates a heuristic perspective that can be applied far beyond games and game studies. As games are, unlike literature and art, a dominantly configurative practice,[3] ludology is useful in situating the wide variety of ergodic forms, modes and genres within a double perspective. In other words, we will have a fuller view if the current dyad of art and ergodic (or "interactive") art is replaced with the triad including games.

1.4 Structure and brief outline of the book

The four chapters that try to come to terms with the multiplication of literary media (Chapter 2), transtextual relations and connections (Chapter 3), and challenges to reading and to the notions of the textual whole (Chapter 4) as well the enigma of the ergodic (Chapter 5), are primarily concerned with constructing a conceptual map that could include both ergodic and non-ergodic literature.

The existence of an ever widening variety of literary media is inherently challenging to mainstream literary theories that still avoid close encounters with the trend that has been around for 50 odd years (or more) and perhaps even more importantly exclude from consideration the growing multitude of literary works that run counter to what such theories of literature still take for granted and as universal conditions and limitations of literature. Needless to say we take an opposite view, and formulate the main challenges and revisions through slightly revised cybertext theory and its heuristic notions of media positions, textonomical genres, non-trivial traversal, and the ergodic as a series of modes, genres, and discourse levels. On top of them, the main connecting line or frame is another notion that is implicit in Aarseth's theory: literature as dominantly interpretative practice.

After these four chapters, we move on to the problems of narratology and narrative theory, first to solve one remaining problem from the first section: the status of so-called anti- or non-narratives that seem not to belong to any recognized text type except narrative but are for various reasons excluded from more or less sophisticated late 20th century narratologies. Without integrating postmodernist, Oulipian and experimental narratives into the narratological framework we cannot embark on studying the interplay between ergodic and narrative layers, and therefore prospects for a more inclusive narratology are discussed in Chapter 7, which is also the first of the three intermissions in this study. These intermissions designate specific borderline or fuzzy areas that cause problems for standard approaches and require new or revised conceptualizations. Chapters 6 and 7 complement and supplement one another as the former one negotiates its way around the contested concepts of narrative and story and discusses several competing narratologies to ground the investigation in the following four chapters.

As the manipulation of temporality and the double logic of time are core features in almost any given narratology, Chapter 8 expands theories of narrative tense. The categories of narrative order, simultaneity, repetition (frequency), speed and duration are extracted from the context of their two media positions (in literary and film narratology respectively) and situated in the much wider variety of both non-ergodic and ergodic media positions.

Chapters 9 and 10 revise the categories of narrative mood and voice following similar procedures that were applied in Chapter 8, and thus we finally have a fully revised and expanded literary narratology at our disposal as well as a well-grounded conceptual frame capable of taking into account the main differences and similarities between literary narratives, on the one hand, and dramatic, filmic, and other audiovisual presentations, on the other.

Chapter 11 concludes the narratological section, discussing the interplay of narrative and ergodic discourses not only in terms of user functions but also in relation to the discourse layers of negotiation and progression. In particular, the presence of the former is shown to be a strong indication of the presence of game structures that are capable of dominating narrative structures, pointing thus to modal differences between games and narratives, which is one of the topics of Chapter 12.

Chapter 12 counters and confronts the limits of expanded narratologies and bears witness to the exhaustion of their explanatory power in the theoretical debate or semi-debate between ludologists and narrativists in the emerging scholarly field of (digital) game studies. This chapter marks the beginning of and the transition to the third part, which attempts to synthesize a first-generation paradigm of ludology from the theories and insights put forward by Espen Aarseth, Markku Eskelinen, Gonzalo Frasca and Jesper Juul. This paradigm is also a paradigm of dominantly configurative practices of gaming and play that will later be used to situate ergodic literature and art between interpretative and configurative practices.

Chapter 13 continues to chart ludological groundwork and takes as its point of departure Jesper Juul's classic game model while trying to construct a preliminary game ecology, an inter- and transludic system that both functions and is contextualized differently from narrative and other transmedial ecologies. The construction of game ecology counterbalances theories of transmediality that are usually centered on stories and narratives as if they were the only modes possessing transmediality. The recognition and construction of game ecology is also necessary for situating games in relation to other transmedial ecologies and for making valid comparisons between games.

Chapter 14 focuses on game ontology and builds on Aarseth's pioneering work while combining it with insights derived from Jesper Juul, Elliot Avedon, and Brian Sutton-Smith. Game ontology and game ecology supplement and support one another: only by combining diachronic and synchronic perspectives can we see the whole scope and depth of comparative game studies and locate the most important elements circulating and being transformed within game ecology.

After coming to better terms with what games are and how they relate to one another, it is time to move on and balance system-centric and player-centric approaches to games and play. Therefore in the next two chapters the focus is on the player's rule-based and goal-oriented manipulative action. Chapter 15 builds on Gonzalo Frasca's pioneering work on game rules, discussing the role of different types of rule in guiding and constraining player effort on micro- and mesolevels of gameplay. Chapter 16 shifts the focus towards the macrolevel while theorizing the complexities of time in games. A preliminary model of game time is constructed by synthesizing dimensions from the models of Elverdam and Aarseth, Juul, Eskelinen, and Mateas and Zagal.

Chapter 17 constitutes the third intermission. It combines the loose ends from various discussions in section three, and tries to circumscribe and contextualize games as configurative practices in relation to other configurative practices. The chapter specifies the differences between two partly overlapping conceptualizations of players, the implied player(s) of ludology and the real player(s) of social sciences, and highlights the inevitable shortcomings in the kind of game research that dismisses the former as formalism.

In Chapter 18, ludological thinking is applied to transmediality, which is now viewed from the perspectives constructed in section three. Transmediality is anchored in two types of mode, representation and action, which constitute two basic ways of articulating events and existents. Chapter 18 also locates several modal ecologies and various ergodic practices cutting across them. In Chapter 19, ergodic literature is situated within the latter while its actual and potential connections to ergodic art and various forms of play are foregrounded.

Finally, in Chapter 20, this investigation leads us to theorizing textual instruments, and to a lesser degree instrumental texts, arguably the most important genres of ergodic literature that have emerged since the publication of *Cybertext* in 1997. At stake here is the middle space between ergodic practices and computer games (as dominantly ergodic practices) as well as finding a balance between interpretation and configuration.

I need to be able to say persuasively in th intro: I'm not discussing old lit directly + how to why. This is difficult because I am discussing old lit (Aters - P'tchn, etc. or am I? This = what I need to decide. How in hyp used + how do I use old lit.

CHAPTER 2

Cybertext theory revisited

2.1 Introduction: the problem with media plurality

In this chapter, we begin with a review of the problems media plurality has caused for literary studies, revisit cybertext theory, and discuss its critical reception and alternatives while teasing out its implications and presuppositions.

The fact that poets in the 20th century were aggressive in using all available material alternatives to the printed page is not a great secret. During this period there have already been several types of new media; as recently as in the 1980s and 1990s "new media poetry" included not only digital but video and holopoetry as well (cf. Kac [ed.] 1996) not to mention the predecessors of video poetry from Marcel Duchamp's *Anemic Cinema* (1926) to Paul Sharits' *Word Movie* (1965). It has also become obvious in the light of visual, concrete, sound, and kinetic poetries that poetry has ceased to be a merely verbal art (in fact, given the long history of illustrated books and mixed-media performances, it can be argued that it never was). Moreover, each of these poetic "movements" can employ a wide variety of media for their purposes, as the following quote from Eduardo Kac makes clear:

> Between 1982 and 1983 I was very unsatisfied by what I then considered as a blind alley of visual poetry. Aware of the multiple directions the genre had taken in the twentieth century, I experimented with different media ... billboards, Polaroid cameras, artists' books, fine graffiti, electronic signboards, video, mail art, photocopiers, videotex, and finally holography. (Osthoff 1994)

As far back as the mid–1960s Dick Higgins (1982, 414–15) tried to untangle the pluralities of media by separating intermedia from mixed media. In the latter, the spectator can "readily perceive" the separation of different media (for example musical, literary, and visual aspects in opera) while in the former, they cannot be resolved in the combination of older media, as the elements are in much tighter fusion. Higgins used the concept of intermedia to connect (or fuse) poetry to various other arts and technologies. His list of fusions includes visual poetry, video poetry, sound poetry, conceptual poetry (fusion of poetry and philosophy), object poetry (fusion of poetry and sculpture), postal poetry (fusion of poetry and mail art), and action poetry (fusion of poetry and happenings), while remaining open for countless other fusions. Higgins also notes that through familiarity any intermedium may become a new medium existing in between the old ones.

The introduction of personal computers and computer networks added yet another wave of multiplication and diversion to this already rich tradition of moving away from literature as verbal signs printed on paper. From the perspective of the media history of poetry, the paralyzing theoretical dichotomy of printed versus digital works seems to have originated from a narrow scholarly focus on narrative fiction and prose literature, in which context the digital seems to mark the shift from one major medium to the competition (and coexistence) between two. In any case, literary theory chose to ignore the existing and increasing multitude of literary media, its behavioral variety, and its theoretical and methodological implications, until the emergency of cybertext theory in the 1990s (Aarseth 1991; 1994; 1995;1997), despite the fact that cybernetic thinking was there in the very beginning of digital literature (Bense 1962; Gendolla 2010).

Compared to the other new media mentioned earlier, digital media attracted much more scholarly attention and many more attempts to conceptualize its most important properties and aspects. Among the most influential of these have been the general models and conceptualizations of Jay David Bolter and Richard Grusin (1999), Lev Manovich (2001), and Janet Murray (1997), all of which seem to assume (albeit to varying degrees) that digital media (or medium) are uniquely different from its predecessors. We'll take a quick look at each of these attempts before going into more literary matters.

2.2 The problem with digital media

In *Hamlet on the Holodeck* (1997, 71) Murray listed four main properties of the digital medium seemingly equal to digital environments: they are procedural (i.e. programmable), participatory (i.e. interactive), spatial, and encyclopaedic. Perhaps because Murray's focus is on speculative development of virtual worlds, and not on myriad other forms and genres of digital media, she seems to have missed both literary and audiovisual works that are neither participatory nor encyclopaedic (for example, many kinetic texts and textual movies) and in which spatiality plays a minimal or even non-significant role (as in *Eliza*). We are therefore left with only the first property which, if not further specified, is almost tautological. Instead of specifying further, Murray only speculates on the possibilities of a hypothetical technology for fiction which was not around in 1997 and is still not available today. As Murray's focus is limited to narrative (conceptualized in prenarratological fashion), her discourse is more speculative than analytical, and her definitions and distinctions fail (including the major presupposition that there is only one unified digital medium), her model cannot be used in comparisons among literary (or other) media.

In *The Language of the New Media* (2001, 29–48), Lev Manovich identifies not four but five key features of digital media (numerical representation, modularity, automation, variability, and transcoding), while stating that the last three are dependent on the first two. However, these two core features turn out to be problematic. As Aarseth notes:

> Numerical representation is much older than computer representation (it is as old as writing), so it is not a principle exclusive

to computing, while computer representation does not have to be linked to a numerical value … the binary codes used by computers only make sense as part of a sequence of such codes, unlike, again a binary number, which would have the same value in any system. (Aarseth 2006, 845)

Modularity, at least as defined by Manovich (separate and independent components assembled at run time by the program that displays them), is not exclusive to computers either as it

[S]eems to be a principle covering too many non-digital phenomena (Peter Cook's *plug-in city*, inspired by the automobile industry, springs to mind) – while not covering all the digital ones – an HTML page with links and formatting, or an SMS message – so the primacy of this principle is less than apparent. Isn't the principle of modularity at work in any industrial process, starting with the types, lines, pages and folded sheets of printing? (Aarseth 2006, 845)

Moreover, there are several other unsolvable problems and limitations in Manovich's discourse. It wavers too often between the literal and the metaphorical; to take just one example he uses Dziga Vertov and his groundbreaking film *A Man with a Movie Camera* (1929) as an example of what he calls database aesthetics, although Vertov's work has neither interface nor database. Manovich also reduces his new media to the realm of the audiovisual, and there the scope of his research is very limited if compared to the media historical depth of Siegfried Zielinski's work (Zielinski 1999; 2006). Within that scope Manovich (2001, 314–26) has trouble seeing beyond the supposed return of the features that were suppressed after the early cinema: the loop and spatial montage. Thus it seems that nothing that exceeds the means and ends already inherent in film history can enter the field of new media. In short, although Manovich provides a more sophisticated discourse on digital media than Murray, the limited scope of his theory and problems at the heart of his definition of "new media" bring us no closer to satisfyingly (or at the very least non-contradictorily) theorizing and comparing digital and non-digital media.

Last but not least, Manovich's main distinction between interface and database largely corresponds to Aarseth's distinction between storage and interface media and their arbitrary (programmable) relations, which is at the heart of Aarseth's detailed typology of textual communication. As Manovich is unable to produce similar heuristic models covering the variety of audiovisual media, his theory does not help us in constructing a comparative perspective on media behavior (i.e. functioning).

Jay David Bolter and Richard Grusin give two definitions of media in *Remediation*. The first definition, "that which remediates" (Bolter and Grusin 1999, 65), is circular; the second more complex definition, "the formal, social and material network of practices that generates a logic by which additional instances are repeated or remediated, such as photography, film or television" (Bolter and Grusin 1998, 273), leaves out communication and, as Aarseth (2003a, 437) noted, "seems to describe material, artifact-producing processes (e.g. the car industry) better than signifying ones (e.g. telephony)."

Remediation can be better or more accurately employed to describe certain relationships within media ecologies, but remediation as "a process of cultural competition between or among technologies" (Bolter 2001, 23) doesn't affect every medium the same way or to the same degree. Also, Bolter's list of values that are negotiated, debated, and struggled for in the processes of remediation raises questions: "This debate turns on the question: which form is better at constituting the real, the authentic, or the natural? Remediation is always an attempt to redefine these key cultural values" (Bolter 2001, 43). Whatever the value of these supposedly key cultural values in other scholarly fields and discourses, it is safe to say that they have been criticized, undermined, and more or less abandoned during the last 50 to 90 years in the fields of literature and literary studies, and especially so in postmodernist and poststructuralist critical theory and practice.

Finally, if the concept of remediation is not defined more rigorously to include more detailed differences between technologies, media and aesthetic practices, it lacks explanatory and analytical power, and remains at best a vague umbrella term under which an ever increasing plenitude of media remediate each other and we are in principle free to pick any of myriad possible relationships for closer inspection as they are seemingly all equal. For example, in *Remediation*, computer games are seen as remediated cinema (and not once as remediated games), and in the second edition of Bolter's *Writing Space* (synthesizing the first edition and *Remediation*) "electronic writing" is seen as a singular medium remediating print (as if textual movies didn't remediate other kinds of movie at all). For his part, Grusin (2005, 498) seems to acknowledge the conceptual limitations of remediation that was primarily "designed to account for the visual genealogy of contemporary digital media."

The failures of Murray and Manovich in trying to pinpoint the key properties of digital media/medium, and the vagueness of remediation as a concept, point to perhaps insurmountable difficulties in trying to define and conceptualize digital media as uniquely different from all the other media. As digital media continue (despite loudly predicted and heavily marketed convergences) to be legion, and new devices, gadgets and applications pile up in the market, while almost every surviving "old" medium has already been or is being digitalized, the heuristic question may no longer be what a medium is, but what a medium does and is used for. Espen Aarseth's *Cybertext: Perspectives on Ergodic Literature* (1997) made the crucial move away from media essentialism to functional differences among the wide variety of literary media. As Aarseth's model allows significant functional overlaps between media, it frees us from assuming there have to be absolute differences between digital and non-digital media and that we already know what any given medium is capable of (as if it has somehow already exhausted its possibilities).

2.3 Cybertext theory: a summary

In cybertext theory, the elementary idea is to see a text (or a work of art) as a concrete (and not metaphorical) machine for production and consumption of signs, consisting of the medium, the operator and the strings of signs (Aarseth 1997, 19). The last are divided into *textons* (strings of signs as they are in the text) and *scriptons* (strings of signs as they appear to readers/users). The mechanism by which scriptons are generated or revealed from textons[1] is called a traversal function, which is described as the combination of seven variables[2] (dynamics, determinability, transience, perspective, links,[3] access, and user function) and their possible values) This combinatory approach gives us a heuristic map of 576 different media positions into which every text could be situated based on how its medium functions, but independently of what that medium is[4] (Aarseth 1997, 58–67).

I quote Aarseth's typology of textual communication almost in full as we are going to use these categories, distinctions and definitions extensively:

> The following variables allow us to describe any text according to their mode of traversal: *Dynamics*. In a *static* text the scriptons are constant whereas in a *dynamic* text the contents of scriptons may change while the number of textons remains fixed (*intratextonic* dynamics, or IDT), or the number (and content) of textons may vary as well (*textonic* dynamics). [...]
>
> *Determinability* concerns the stability of the traversal function; a text is *determinate* if the adjacent scriptons of every scripton are always the same, and *indeterminate* if not. [...]
>
> *Transiency*. If the mere passing of the user's time causes scriptons to appear, the text is *transient*, if not, it is *intransient*. [...]
>
> *Perspective*. If the text requires the user to play a strategic role as a character in the world described by the text, then the text's perspective is *personal*; if not, then it is *impersonal*. [...]
>
> *Access*: If all scriptons of the text are readily available to the user at all times, then the text is *Random* access (typically the codex), if not, then access is *controlled*. [...]
>
> *Linking*: A text may be organized by *explicit* links for the user to follow, *conditional* links that can only be followed if certain conditions are met, or by *none* of these (no links). [...]
>
> *User-functions*. Besides the *interpretative* function of the user, which is present in all texts, the use of some texts may be described in terms of additional functions: the *explorative* function, in which the user must decide which 'path' to take; and the *configurative* function, in which scriptons are in part chosen and/or created by the user. If textons and/or traversal functions can be (permanently) added to the text, the user function is *textonic* (...) If all the decisions a reader makes about a text concern its meaning, then there is only one user function, here called "interpretation." (Aarseth 1995, 70–2)

Cybertext focuses on ergodic literature, where the user has to do non-trivial work in order to traverse the text (Aarseth 1997, 1). Thus in ergodic literature there are other necessary tasks for the user in addition to mere interpretation, and there necessarily exists a feedback loop between the user and the text.[5] Traditional problems of literary theory and interpretation are not foregrounded in *Cybertext*, as the focus of Aarseth's theory is on textonomy (the study of the textual medium) rather than on textology (the study of the textual meaning). This is also clearly stated in the first chapter (Aarseth 1997, 15). After constructing his model, Aarseth applies it to hypertext fiction, adventure games, text generators, and MUDs, arguably the main generic examples of ergodic literature in the early and mid–1990s. Although cybertext theory is explicitly presented as an extension of contemporary literary theory (Aarseth 1994, 83–4; 1997, 17), there is no attempt at systematic integration of the theories of ergodic and non-ergodic literature in *Cybertext*.

The useful inclusiveness of cybertext theory results from its almost standard deconstructive strategy. It lays its emphasis on an understudied and marginalized area of literary scholarship (despite some previous efforts, most notably those of Brian McHale and the Tel Quel group):[6] the material diversity of the textual media from which Aarseth then deduces[7] the functional differences in his typology (1997, 67–75). This way the existing field of textuality is both expanded and dynamically rearranged, and the previously dominant forms are reinscribed back into a considerably changed field of study as mere subsets of cybertexts. Unlike many hypothetical and utopian models of digital media (along the lines of Murray's Aristotelian Holodeck and Bolter and Landow's claims of hypertexts embodying the ideas and ideals of poststructuralism), the resulting non-media-specific[8] map of functional possibilities is fully empirical and based on observable differences: all the values its seven variables can have are already operational in existing textual objects.

In the context of discussions, debates, and definitions of the new or digital media, the usefulness of Aarseth's theory is based on its focus on detailed functional differences, which frees it from making essentialist claims and chasing absolute differences and clearcut dividing lines between various textual media. Relative historical differences among textual media are a different matter, and in helping to recognize these, cybertext typology is of great heuristic value. For example, if one tries to find print examples of the given 576 media positions, it becomes evident that the history of print literature has been able to utilize only 2 or 3% of them. Therefore it becomes clear that literary theories have been and are based on literary objects that are static, intransient, determinate, impersonal, random access, solely interpretative and without links. In the first half of this book we'll be drawing several consequences and insights from this severe "media blindness." But before going deeper into that direction, we'll take a closer look at more recent alternatives to cybertext theory.

2.4 Literary alternatives

Several theoretical alternatives to *Cybertext* have emerged during the decade after its publication: Philippe Bootz's procedural model (1996; 2003; 2006), N. Katherine Hayles' technotext and media-specific analysis (MSA) (2002) and intermediality (2008), and Noah Wardrip-Fruin's expressive processing (2007; 2009). With the exception of Hayles' MSA, their main or sole focus is digital literature or fiction, which makes their scope considerably more limited than Aarseth's. By the same token, they are not as caught up with essentialist claims on media as the scholars of digital media discussed earlier in this chapter. Bootz, Hayles, and Wardrip-Fruin also explicitly situate their theories in relation to cybertext theory, which gives us a chance to see it from multiple perspectives.

2.4.1 Hayles

For N. Katherine Hayles (2007) Aarseth's method presents limita-tions, "notably that it is blind to content and relatively indifferent to the specificity of media" despite which "it has the tremendous virtue of demonstrating that electronic texts cannot simply be shoved into the same tent with print without taking into account their different modes of operation." The former "limitation" is based on Aarseth's explicitly stated (1997, 15) focus on textonomy (the study of textual medium) instead of textology (the study of textual meaning), although it would be hard to claim Aarseth's readings of individual works in *Cybertext* are blind to content. Aarseth's focus is on theory and not on content analysis, and these two tasks should not be confused with one another. Hayles' second claim is not well grounded either, because the functional differences in Aarseth's model are deduced from material ones (in Chapter 3 of *Cybertext*) – a deduction that Hayles (2001b; 2002; 2007) makes no comment on.

Hayles' conceptual contributions to the field of "electronic literature," media-specific analysis (MSA) and technotext (Hayles 2002), are not yet fully developed as conceptual tools, and her insistence on materiality that supports and necessitates media-specific analysis has yet to prove its more general theoretical validity. This is mostly due to digital works foregrounding and utilizing different aspects of their medium while emulating, simulating, modifying, and combining the aspects, traditions, and practices of various other, both digital and non-digital, media; in short, they exhibit a staggering spectrum of "original" or idiosyncratic and borrowed behavior. This makes it very difficult to assess what exactly is to be done in MSA: how far to go into the matters of materiality and medium and where the general properties of a medium end and the specific properties of an individual work begin. The problem is to some degree acknowledged by Hayles:

> The physical attributes constituting any artifact are potentially infinite. ... From this infinite array a technotext will select a few to foreground and work into its thematic concerns. Materiality thus emerges from interactions between physical properties and a work's artistic strategies. For this reason, materiality cannot be specified in advance, as if it pre-existed the specificity of the work. (Hayles 2002, 32–3)

Taking this statement as a guideline, we can only move from one media-specific analysis to another, without a valid and coherent theoretical framework guiding the selection of properties to be thematized and analyzed. As such and at best MSA is then good for what it claims to be good for: analysis (or singular readings), but not theory.

Hayles' definition of technotext (2002, 25) further clarifies her thematic orientation: "Literary works that strengthen, foreground, and thematize the connections between themselves as material artifacts and the imaginative realm of verbal/semiotic signifiers they instantiate." One could say that this definition is both too broad, not to say unspecific, as in one way or another literary works can always be interpreted as doing this, and also too limited, as it excludes other (perhaps less novelty- and modernism-oriented) thematizations and connections. Moreover, compared to Hayles' thematic limitations of materiality, Aarseth's typology of media positions gives us an empirically verifiable and nuanced map of media behavior that can be connected to whatever thematizations one may prefer, while maintaining its use value as a conceptual tool in comparisons between literary works and between literary media. For the purposes of this study, that will be sufficiently media specific.

Later, Hayles (2008, 163–5) listed four features character- izing digital text: layered text, multimodality, the separation of storage from performance, and fractured temporality. Although she sees her list as a modification of Manovich's five features, three of her four features also carry a strong cybertextual flavour. Layered text implies the division into textons and scriptons as Hayles recognizes, the separation of storage from performance mirrors not only Manovich but also Aarseth's division of storage and interface media, and finally the reader's possible loss of control over temporal processes of textual presentation evokes the distinction between transient and intransient texts. This leaves us with multimodality, which is a weaker feature, as in Hayles' words "computer-mediated text tends to be multimodal" (Hayles 2008, 164). Hayles' further description roots this in the binary code and ultimately in the computer's capability to contain all other media within itself. Although Hayles attributes this notion to Manovich, we can go much further back to Allan Kay's notion of computer(s) as metamedium (Kay and Goldberg 2003).

2.4.2 *Wardrip-Fruin*

Noah Wardrip-Fruin (2009, 161) sees *Cybertext* as a predecessor that has created "the conditions of possibility" for his theory. Wardrip-Fruin identifies two major problems with cybertext typology that are related to its underlying distinction between scriptons and textons, and especially the generative relation between them:

First, many textual systems are difficult to describe in these terms. For example, the natural language generation system *Mumble* ... does not contain any easily-identified textons. Certainly surface texts are produced, but it is hard to see the process of their production as one of being revealed or generated from underlying textons (or, as Aarseth puts it "strings as they exist in the text)." This, in turn, points toward the second, more fundamental reason that this book will not employ Aarseth's model: many of digital media's (and digital fiction's) most important processes are not well described by the process of revealing or generating scriptons from textons. To return to the example of *Tale-Spin/Mumble,* many of the work's processes are focused on the simulation of character behavior ... This simulation is carried out entirely independently from any natural language generation, and it is best examined as a process of simulation rather than as a means of generating or revealing scriptons. (Wardrip-Fruin 2009, 161)

However, the case with cybertext theory seems to be more complex. First, there's no reason why textons should be easily identified. Second, as far back as "Non-linearity and literary theory" (Aarseth 1994), computation was included as one of the possible methods of producing scriptons, and the same paper also states that "A traversal function ... might be a complex set of instructions (for example a computer program such as *Eliza*) that compiles a scripton from textons" (Aarseth 1994, 61). One could argue that the difference between what is presented to the user and what is (as data and processes or textons and traversal functions) in the text is of key importance, and that the latter could be defined in a more detailed way if necessary to also include mechanisms of simulation. This way we could have the following threesome: data as it is in the text, processes operating on those data, and data as presented to the user (or a foursome should we separate operations as they are from the way they are presented or available to the user – a dimension that could be further specified by Wardrip-Fruin's three effects). Fourth, Wardrip-Fruin (ibid.) equates textons with textual data, but that is not necessarily the same as Aarseth's strings of signs as they exist in the text, because the definition of textons could be interpreted to include programming as written instructions. This is also supported by Aarseth's (1995, 72) example of the textonic user function: "The users can extend or change the text by adding their own writing and programming." Fifth, cybertext typology with 576 media positions is a typology of textual communication and as such necessarily oriented towards users and audiences. Because the typology's area of application is different from the model constructed by Wardrip-Fruin, the more logical point of comparison would be another model presented in *Cybertext*, "a schematic model of internal structure" (pp. 103–5) that describes the layers of indeterminate cybertexts (including MUDs, and textual and graphic games) and their interplay. As we'll see this four-layer model comes much closer to Wardrip-Fruin's objectives and orientations, not to mention the model he proposes.

Wardrip-Fruin's (2009, 13) model of digital media consists of six elements: data, processes, surface, interaction, author, and audience. The surface of a work is "what the audience experiences: the output of the processes operating on the data, in the context of the physical hardware and setting, through which any audience interaction takes place" (Wardrip-Fruin 2009, 10). In cybertextual parlance, Wardrip-Fruin's surface could be called the interface medium and thus this part of the model is not in conflict with Aarseth's scriptons as strings of signs that are presented to the user (on the surface) and the variety of user functions available to the audience(s).

Wardrip-Fruin (2009, 11) defines interaction in his model as "a change to the state of the work – for which the work was designed – that comes from outside the work." This definition has one important consequence: "digital media works interact with more than audiences – which is why the revised diagram also notes the possibility of interaction with outside processes and data sources" (Wardrip-Fruin 2009, 12). Changes of state coming from the outside are still part of the work, as long as they are designed to be allowed (and not uninvited or sanctioned acts of vandalism), and thus make no difference from the audience's point of view, neither do they affect the distinction between data and processes. Still, by stressing "outside" sources, Wardip-Fruin may be on to something important,[9] but that remains to be seen.

Finally, data and processes exist beyond surface, and as already argued Aarseth's textons are not necessarily in conflict with Wardrip-Fruin's data and processes, with which they could be seen to consist. Moreover, Aarseth's model of internal structure (Aarseth 1997, 103–5) also includes the layers of data and processes with two other layers (interface and users). If we compare it to Wardrip-Fruin's model, we can find several overlaps and correspondences between the two.

Wardrip-Fruin's processes may well correspond to the interplay of Aarseth's simulation engine in which "the course of action is decided, based on the user's input, the cybertext's idiosyncratic rules, and the current state of the simulated world" (Aarseth 1997, 104) and the representation engine presents "the results of the event to the user by providing a personal perspective on the simulated world" (Aarseth 1997, 105). Wardrip-Fruin's data match Aarseth's database and the latter's interface the former's surface. Seen in this light, Wardrip-Fruin's only addition is author, but that element is not in any way central or even necessary in Wardrip-Fruin's subsequent and superb analysis of three separate effects, named after *Eliza*, *Tale-Spin*, and *SimCity*, that "can arise in the relationship between audience, surface, and system processes" (Wardrip-Fruin 2009, 418).

Therefore this model seems to provide more support for literary analysis and creation than for literary theory, by stressing the importance of underlying processes mostly hidden from the audience. The same trend is in operation in many other potentially promising approaches such as software studies (Fuller 2008) and platform studies (Bogost and Montfort 2009). Still, as past discussions around code, codeworks, and critical code studies already show, to cross the bridge from computer science and artificial intelligence to the humanities (and social sciences) with heuristic conceptualizations of networked programmability and code is more easily promised than delivered.

2.4.3 Bootz

The point of departure for Philippe Bootz's procedural model (Bootz 1996; 2003; 2006) is also different from the communicative orientation of what he calls "standard theories":

> Thus, though the concepts of ergodic literature, of cybertext[10] and of technotext are useful, they do not allow us to apprehend

the fact of digital poetry in its entirety. Their limitations are contained in their premises; they address literature by locating themselves exclusively from the point of view of the reader, as if he was the focal point of the work ... In limiting themselves to this single point of view, the standard theories do not correctly describe the role that the machine plays, nor the exact purpose of reading. (Bootz 2006)

As we have already seen, this is not the case with cybertext theory that includes several models and not just the typology of textual communication that theorizes the triad of operator, medium and text and not just the reader as Bootz seems to believe. In Bootz's model, there is a semiotic gap that separates the *texte-auteur* from the *texte-à-voir* as follows:

The fact that the program cannot be seen by the reader once it is executed constitutes another important technical fact. What results is that the author of the program has an overarching view of the work whereas the reader can only have a local understanding of it. This difference would not be present in a non-computer programmed work which calls on the reader to execute its instructions. It is thus important to distinguish the "texte-auteur" ("author-text") from the "texte-à-voir" The "texte-auteur" is constituted by what is written by the author, in a format that he can understand and manipulate. It contains, in a programmed work, the program he writes himself in the programming language (and not in the compiled binary file) and the givens that the author adds. The "texte-à-voir" is the part of the transitoire observable that the reader considers "the" text. For the same transitoire observable, it could differ from one reader to the next by virtue of the archetypes and mental schemes brought into play by the reader. (Bootz 2006)

In cybertextual terms, this stems from the distinction between textons and scriptons and the user's lack of complete access to the former. In short, at least in this important respect Bootz's procedural model is compatible with Aarseth's typology of textual communication. Bootz's second point of departure, the incompleteness of program, addresses cybertext theory more directly:

> The theories of digital literature usually think of the computer as a simple calculating tool that transforms algorithms implemented by the author in the program into what is then seen and read by the reader. In the vocabulary of Espen Aarseth, the textual layer of a program is thus composed of textons and "what is read" – scriptons. From this perspective, the role of the program consists of calculating what is scripted onto the screen. (Bootz 2006)

In Bootz's procedural model, this is not all:

> The computer does not act like a Turing machine in relation to its user. The program that the author writes contains only a part of the instructions used for its execution: the author is only a co-author of what happens on the screen, even if his program is only a description of what he wants to see appear on the screen. The transitoire observable changes with time. The same program produces a different transitoire observable when it is executed in a different technical context or on a different machine, and this is true even when it consists of just a basic description of what can be seen on the screen ... One must take into account the incompleteness of that program, which acts as the unvoiced for the machine. (Bootz 2006)

If this aspect boils down to slight variations in output based on differences in hardware, Aarseth's omission doesn't seem too significant, as even in these situations the difference between textons and scriptons and the semiotic gap remains intact, however one wishes to rename it. Moreover, in light of Bootz's description and his later references to unreadable signs, adaptive generators, and the aesthetics of frustration it is hard to see what (if any) aesthetic or communicative importance these differences in machinic concretizations carry.

2.5 Cybertext theory revisited

After discussing the most viable alternatives to and criticisms of cybertext theory, it is time to revisit it, in order to shape it for the purposes to which it will be put in the chapters that follow. With that in mind, we'll examine the typology of textual communication from four different but interplaying angles: its general presuppositions, the selection of literary works used for its construction (following the principle of empirically observable differences), the results concerning the differences between paper and digital texts, and the derivation and definitions of the typology's basic variables and values.

2.5.1 General presuppositions

In general, Aarseth's typology of textual communication seems to presuppose the existence of an autonomous and functionally unified and stabile text (in terms of its one media position), and also a single reader or user (or at least readers and users that are or whose actions are independent from one another). This is not extraordinary, as these are features that traditionally belong to literature as we know it and they are usually not contested even in its more experimental forms. The possibility of users affecting one another's reading capabilities or possibilities explicitly emerges in *Cybertext* only in the context of *Noresbo* (an artist's book) that can be folded in several different ways during the reading process, the resulting final fold then affecting and determining the beginning position and possibilities of the next reader or reading.

These omissions or limitations have no direct bearing on the validity of the cybertext typology. Although different parts and phases of dynamic cybertexts could easily have different media positions (in Judd Morrissey's *The Jew's Daughter* some passages and "pages" are transient while the rest of the text remains intransient), that would not challenge the validity of the basic variables. Similarly, if two or several mutually dependent texts were programmed to affect one another (in which case a feedback loop would exist between them), even that wouldn't challenge the validity of the general map of 576 media positions. Each individual text as well as any hypothetical cluster of them could still be described by the values of the seven variables. The case would be the same also with different users applying different user functions simultaneously to affect each other's positions and possible ways of reading and "using" the text, as these positions and possibilities could still be described by the variable of user function. By the same token, one could argue that if ergodic challenges are coming not only from the text but from other users as well, the resulting differences in user positions[11] should be important enough to be included in the typology of textual communication. Although Aarseth discusses MUDs, the differences between single- and multi-user situations did not find its way into the typology of textual communication, but this omission can easily be remedied by adding the parameter of user position to the typology.

Since the emergence of ludology it has been easier to see that at least two of the four "genres" Aarseth discusses in *Cybertext*, text adventures and MUDs, could equally well be discussed in ludological terms. This has some bearing on the notion of traversal, as in games (unlike in hypertext fiction and text generators) that activity is rule based and goal oriented. Some consequences of this duality will be discussed later in the context of user functions.

Another complication emerges from the kind of texts that are not supposed to be traversed in their entirety but only consulted, such as *I Ching* and other ritual texts (as well as dictionaries and encyclopedias). This difference points to certain cultural and contextual differences between fictional and non-fictional literature (or between textual machines and decision-making machines)[12] that Aarseth does not discuss, and it has also some bearing on what is to be considered non-trivial work required from the user. One could argue that by following a very trivial procedure, one always gains access to an appropriate piece of *I Ching*; i.e. that there is no resistance or challenge included in this process. This leads to discerning two types of ergodicity, challenging and unchallenging (or strategic and non-strategic), which will also be discussed later.

2.5.2 *The texts*

To construct his typology, Aarseth (1997, 65–7) selected a diverse set of texts to be compared. These included books with and without signifiers forking out on the page, two game books, a loose-sheet novel, an artist's book, two textual adventure games, MUDs, hypertext fictions, and conversation programs, a prose and a sentence generator, and a linear electronic text projected by a LED sign. This selection doesn't include holographic or complex kinetic texts in which signs not only follow one another but are more dynamically kinetic. By necessity, the selection doesn't include such later novelties as locative texts that apply GPS (see Gendolla and Schäfer 2010), or are presentable only in CAVE environments, not to mention Eduardo Kac's (2003) biopoetry.

As a result, the complex challenges many kinetic, three-dimensional and holographic texts present to perception such as several simultaneous appearances and disappearances, morphing, kinetic signifiers with variable trajectories in 3D spaces, multiple and possibly kinetic textual layers superimposed on top of one another and blocking one another from the user's view, and binocular reading (in which different images are presented to each eye) are not discussed, as, in principle, the way the scriptons behave when they are presented doesn't matter. It is here that the key concepts of second-order digital literature (Strehovec 2001; 2003) and holopoetry (Kac 1996) could be used to further develop and nuance cybertext theory and to test its claim of universality and the limits of its explanatory power.

Such considerations will necessarily involve both the variable of dynamics and also the distinction between textons and scriptons. One of the main implications of texts with mobile and kinetic scriptons for Aarseth's typology is the possibility that the changing patterns of scriptons may affect the content of scriptons while the number of scriptons remains the same. Or to put it differently, the change in the content of scriptons may result both from changes in the number of scriptons and also from the changes in the position and behavior of scriptons on the presentation surface, space or area (that will henceforth be called the scripton space) while they are being presented (on this, see also Ikonen 2003).

While the distinction between textons and scriptons is clear and valid, the challenges to the user's perception of – in fact, to his ability to perceive – scriptons are much higher in temporally dynamic kinetic and holographic works than in the texts in Aarseth's selection. There may be considerable losses as the user (due to temporal limitations, visual complexity, or multiple simultaneities) may be able to perceive only a fraction of each set of scriptons presented to him, and from those perceived at least some may have to be immediately ignored in the interpretation because of temporal pressure and the user's resulting haste. Although cybertext theory doesn't conflate scriptons with the signs that the reader actually reads, the gap between these two varies considerably.[13] In this respect, printed books (including artists' books) and so-called classic hypertext fiction belong to the perceptually less challenging end of the spectrum while transient, kinetic, and three-dimensional poetry, both ergodic and non-ergodic, occupy the other and perhaps non-trivial end.

For this reason it could be useful to draft a cybertextual process leading from the strings of signs as they are in the text (textons) to the strings of signs as they are presented to the user (scriptons) to the strings of signs as perceived by the user to the strings of signs interpreted by the user and finally to the strings of signs processed (or used) by the user. The last stage concerns the next (trivial, tactical or strategic) move the user makes after interpreting the scriptons at hand.

The texts that take place in CAVEs (such as Wardrip-Fruin's *Screen*), apply GPS (such as *34 North, 118 West* by Knowlton, Spellman, and Hight), or are otherwise localized and consumable in a specific physical environment (such as Balpe's *Fictions d'Issy*), underline the importance of spatiality, movement, and locality in ways that differ considerably from the texts Aarseth's model was deduced and constructed from (with the possible exception of Holzer's *I'm Awake at the Place where Women Die*). In addition, these texts require non-trivial work that utilizes skills of movement and positioning similar to those used in physical games and athletic sports, far more physical and physically demanding than mere clicking. To account for these demands and activities, additional variables could be appropriated from Aarseth's later game typologies (Aarseth, Smedstad, and Sunnanå 2003; Elverdam and Aarseth 2007) that include such potentially promising categories for physical and virtual space as perspective (either vagrant or omnipresent), topography (either geometrical or topological), and positioning (absolute or relative; proximity based or location based or both).

Other kinds of perceptual challenge are not related to the complex patterns scriptons make on the scripton space, but to the user's understanding of how the text behaves and how it can be operated. For example, in this respect, Moulthrop's web fiction *Hegirascope* (1995), a text with static scriptons, provides a hypothetically challenging example regarding the importance of the user's perception. We can imagine three kinds of user for it: the first will read the description of the work, take it to be reliable, and will eventually learn to adapt their reading strategy to the 30-second intervals the text allows for choosing the next link to follow. In contrast to these "ideal users," we can envision both very slow and very fast users who never once cross the boundary that (temporarily) shifts the control from the user to the system: the former believe they are reading a relatively slow textual movie they can't affect at all, and the latter believe that they are navigating an ordinary web hypertext. In terms of cybertext theory, *Hegirascope* is then almost a double act: its two operating modes (active and passive) have two different media positions (the one is transient and interpretative and the other intransient and explorative).

As the links are not hidden in *Hegirascope*, and its instructive-descriptive paratext is there to be read, not to mention that its temporal interval is relatively challenging to most if not all users, it is likely that users will experience both sides of *Hegirascope*. Still, one could ask what would happen without these indicators[14] that are in principle reversible design decisions (already once revised by Moulthrop). Seen from the perspective of perceptual challenges, *Hegirascope* is therefore a pioneering work, not only in its novel use of reading time turned into a struggle between man and machine, but also in that it undermines the notion of functional unity of the text – an assumption implicitly shared by most theorists and practitioners in both codex and hypertext traditions.

The perceptual and positional challenges discussed earlier could be integrated in the typology of textual communication by adding to it a new variable, the user position, to account for texts that require the user to be in a specific location, to move in order to be able to access and realize the text, combine physical and virtual spaces in non-trivial ways, or make users at least partly dependent on one another in creating and consuming the text. The user position is determined in relation to other users, physical location, and bodily movement, each including demands that books, diskettes, CDs and web fictions don't usually present. The user position will consist of the following three variables:

1 *Autonomy*. If the user's possibilities to use and realize the text are completely independent of other users (either previous or simultaneous ones or both) his position is independent; if not it is dependent. *TinyMud* and *Norisbo*

(Strand 1992), included in Aarseth's selection, exemplify the latter position and *Moby Dick* (also in Aarseth's selection) the former.

2   *Mobility.* Some texts such as *Fictions d'Issy* (Balpe 2005) and *Astray in Deimos*[15] (Kac 1992) require bodily movement from the user as a necessary condition for their realization, while many others do not. Thus there are two basic positions: stationary and non-stationary.

3   *Positioning.* This variable describes whether the user's possibilities to use and access the text require him to be in a specific physical location (localized text) or not (non-localized text). Some texts require the user to be in a specific location (such as a CAVE or Central Park) to access and realize the text while others do not (you can read most literary texts everywhere). Some locative texts may require the user to be somewhere at a specific time – a development that could warrant adding a separate subcategory for access time.

2.5.3 *Paper texts and digital texts*

According to Aarseth's analysis (1997, 70–1), the versatility and divergence of paper texts are almost as great as those of digital texts, but a closer examination of his examples seems to contradict this, if we accept the common sense assumption that digital texts are in principle capable of occupying every media position (576) in the typology of textual communication. If we go thoroughly through Aarseth's selection of texts variable by variable and value by value instead of focusing on their combinations, we find three values for which there are no printed examples. First, the variable of transience is the only category within which there's no variation among print examples. They are all intransient. Second, although there are differences in user functions, none of Aarseth's printed examples has textonic user function. Finally, there's no print example of textonically dynamic texts. Seen in this light printed texts can occupy only 144 (2x2x2x1x2x3x3) positions of the available 576, a mere 25%.

Even if we could imagine a textonically dynamic printed text (say, *Cent Mille Milliards de Poèmes* with an added instruction that gives the reader the right to rip off one page a year thus slowly reducing the number of textons), such texts don't seem to exist. Similarly, one could easily imagine a printed text with the textonic user function if the permanently added text wouldn't have to be shared with the other users – we can always scribble whatever we like into the margins and other empty spaces of any text. However, allowing this possibility would banalize the distinctions among different user functions. Transient paper texts don't seem to exist (and imagining them is very difficult)[16] which brings us to the preliminary conclusion that they don't exist. That assumption alone reduces the versatility of paper texts to only 50% of the positions digital texts can occupy.

While Aarseth's analysis and claims based on his selection of texts are correct, the perspective presented here based on the potential of paper and digital texts to occupy the 576 media positions is also correct.[17] As this difference doesn't undermine the validity of Aarseth's typology as such, we'll continue discussing this difference in Chapter 4 while paying attention to behaviors not found in paper texts (especially transience).

However, there's still one complication to be sorted out before addressing cybertext typology variable by variable: the derivation and selection of variables that Aarseth doesn't explicitly discuss.[18] Nevertheless, something can be inferred. Determinability takes into account the long tradition of using randomness in literature, personal perspective possibly derives from roleplaying games and *Eliza* and links from hypertext theory and conditional links from Eastgate's StorySpace software, transience is needed to take into account kinetic texts on video and film, while user functions add to the traditional positions of writers (textonic) and readers (interpretative) two intermediary ones from Joyce (1995) slightly modified: the explorative and configurative ones. Dynamics implies the changes and variations vaguely attributed to digital texts in common parlance; it also characterizes one crucial aspect of MUDs and interactive fiction. Likewise the difference between controlled and random access is inherent in many common digital practices, and everyone familiar with hypertext fictions, text adventures and game books has experienced controlled access in a literary context. Seen in this light, the seven dimensions have their possible roots in the medial and generic variety of literary history.

This implicit derivation of cybertextual parameters has certain consequences regarding the by and large "false" opposition between paper and digital texts. With other kind of parameter and value, the result could be different. For example, if controlled access were further divided on the basis of its implementation, it would become evident that it is trivially easy to subvert controlled access suggested by instructions of how to read or use a printed text, whereas if programmed such constraints on access would certainly be much harder to ignore and subvert, perhaps leading to the distinction between effectively implemented and merely suggested controlled access.

2.5.4 *The old and new variables*

In Aarseth's typology, the category of dynamics is based on changes in the number and content of scriptons and textons. In principle, we could ask whether there are other qualifiers that could make a difference such as movement, position, or permanence. As movement and positioning were discussed earlier, we turn now to permanence.[19]

Printed signifiers are practically permanent: although they may eventually become unreadable and deteriorate, the words and letters remain the same and they do not morph into other words and letters. Also, their positions in relation to each other on the page where they are printed will usually remain the same, with notable exceptions such as Raymond Queneau instructing readers to cut the pages of his *Cent Mille Milliards de Poèmes* horizontally to allow billions of possible combinations of lines from different pages. Still, in Queneau's case the lines to be recombined remain always on the same page although that doesn't significantly affect the book's use as its presentation space is not a page but a combination of slips from several pages. Also, not one letter or word has vanished from Queneau's poetry book or been added to it after its publication; in other words, the number of words in the book remains the same (discounting potential accidents with scissors).

Compared with all that stability, only some digital signifiers are permanent, while others are temporary. Thus to begin with, there are both permanent strings of signs (with unlimited duration) and temporary strings of signs (with limited duration). This division is easy to introduce both in the category of dynamics, as it is related to the number of scriptons and textons, and in the category of transience, as the coexistence of permanent and temporary scriptons would somewhat blur the distinction between transient and intransient texts (if not only the appearance but also the disappearance of scriptons is triggered by the mere passing of time). In principle, as the number of textons and scriptons in a self-destructive text could be reduced to zero at some point, so also the range of variation in the number of textons and scriptons could be made to count.

Determinability is probably the most complicated parameter of cybertext typology: "This variable concerns the stability of the traversal function; a text is determinate if the adjacent scriptons of every scripton are always the same; if not, the text is indeterminate" (Aarseth 1997, 63). This stability is limited to the visible output ("adjacent scriptons") and the changes in stability don't include the possibility that a text has not one but several media positions (either successively or simultaneously), as already noted in our previous discussions of general presuppositions and *Hegirascope*. As traversal function is determined by seven variables, its stability becomes a metadimension, as there could be fluctuation between values in the other six dimensions. In such a case, the text's behavior in any given dimension changes at least once (for example, dynamic text suddenly becoming static, etc.). Therefore, the stability of the traversal function should be separated from the possible random functions at lower levels of textual behavior. It is not unthinkable either that the user's ergodic activity could affect the text's media position.

Aarseth illustrates the difference between determinate and indeterminate texts using the following example: "In some adventure games, the same response to a given situation will always produce the same result. In other games, random functions (such as the use of dice) make the result unpredictable" (Aarseth 1997, 63). This example explicitly ties determinability to repetition, randomness and predictability. While the distinction is or should be clear from the writer's and the programmer's point of view, the case is much more difficult for the user–observer to verify. First of all, the user doesn't always know whether two situations are exactly the same. What seems to be a random or at least different reaction to the same action may equally well be a carefully calculated consequence of some minor difference between two situations that has escaped the user. Second, the user may not know whether he acted precisely the same way in two situations that perhaps were identical. Third, the system may vary its response in cycles, but without knowing this from the start or without learning it through his experience (and patience) the user may interpret the system's response to be random when it is not (its experienced unpredictability resulting only from the user's limited experience and imperfect knowledge). To complicate matters even further, certain kinds of random response could become predictable. Fourth, the system may have been designed to avoid the types and patterns of repetition the user is likely to seek and recognize.

The definition of transient texts begs the question of other possible effects triggered by "the mere passing of time." Although the theme of passing time later surfaces in the discussion of internal structure (Aarseth 1997, 104) it is not developed any further in *Cybertext*. As already noted, the mere passing of time could also make the strings of signs disappear (or become unavailable) for good (as in *Agrippa*). In such a case, scriptons and textons have a limited duration and are therefore temporary and not permanent. This kind of textual behavior could be seen as a special case of textual dynamics (the number of scriptons reduced permanently to zero) and therefore it will be included in the revised typology later as a subcategory of dynamics.

In the selection of texts Aarseth used in the construction of the typology of textual communication, there are five texts that are transient: *Agrippa*, *Book Unbound*, Holzer's installation, and two MUDs. In addition to them, Aarseth discusses *Hegirascope*, another transient text. If we compare these six transient texts, we can deduce three subcategories from their temporal behavior. Unlike the others, *Agrippa* happens only once (per copy). Holzer's installation is looped: it keeps repeating its short messages, while the others are not looped. In *Book Unbound*, the user controls the interval between any two transient appearances of scriptons, while, in the others, he doesn't. Thus we'd have the following new subcategories of transient texts: the number of presentations of scriptons (limited/unlimited); loops (y/n); interval control[20] (by the user or by the textual machine).

The category of perspective contains no subdivisions. Possible additions could include the number (one or several) of personal perspectives (either in the text or available to the user or both) as well as the static or dynamic nature of the user's character. There's also no reason to assume that character is the only entity or position through which the user can assume and exercise his strategic responsibilities. More importantly, the definition of personal perspective, "if the text requires the user to play a strategic role as a character in the world described by the text" (Aarseth 1997, 63), creates a combinatory problem because the user's strategic role implies the necessity of making strategic choices related to his traversal of the text, which, in turn, implies there are several possible paths through the text. Thus these choices are necessarily ergodic and therefore personal perspective implies and requires the presence of one or several ergodic user functions. This reduces the number of media positions by 72 (3x2x2x2x3) to 504.

Access has two possible values: it is either random or controlled. This variable seems to have two underlying criteria forged into one: availability at any given time, and access to all scriptons. Certain digital texts with random access may otherwise make it impossible for the user to reach all scriptons "available all the time" in time, as the time given to the user may be severely limited. By way of contrast, books cannot conceal their textons and scriptons although they may instruct readers to do so. Based on these two examples we'd have two additional distinctions: between complete and incomplete access to the whole text (both textons and scriptons) and between temporarily limited and unlimited access.

There already exist several more nuanced categorizations of links than Aarseth's (cf. Gunder 2004) that we will resort to if necessary, but adding them to cybertext typology would add little to its explanatory and descriptive power.

The relations among the four user functions are not discussed by Aarseth except by stating that the interpretative one is always present. Thus in *Cybertext*, the interplay, relative weight, and possible mutual dependence, interdependence, servitude, or dominance of the user functions is left somewhat in the dark. These open questions are also related to the user's objectives: in addition to traversal, there are other possibilities (or subtypes of traversal) such as consulting (a ritual or other non-fictional text as already mentioned earlier), testing or sampling (for example, getting the feel of a text generator and its output to decide the degree of one's further involvement), completing (a puzzle), winning (a game) or collective playful improvisation (as in many MUDs). To account for this diversity another variable or at least a subcategory of the user function is needed. It could be called *user objective*.

This, in turn, leads to the question concerning games and the already mentioned split between MUDs and text adventures, on the one hand, and hypertext fiction and text generators, on the other hand: in short, that the former should be considered games and therefore products and practices that foreground dominantly ergodic practices (and thus "higher" user functions than the explorative). This difference doesn't show in Aarseth's classification of the selected texts; hypertext fictions and text adventures share the same user function, the explorative. The classification of text adventure games as explorative seems to contradict Aarseth's definition, as well as being counterintuitive (as it ignores the user's goal- and completion-driven activity and sees it as equal to navigating a hypertext).

Aarseth's (1997, 64) definition of configurative user function stipulates that "scriptons are in part chosen or created by the user." In text adventure games, the user's commands and directives (Montfort 2005, 28) become scriptons in the resulting log, and therefore we'll routinely classify text adventure games' user function as configurative.

Games also raise a question concerning the dominant user function. In this study, we'll assume that the fundamental interests of readers and users of literature are primarily interpretative, whether or not they are required to do ergodic work to satisfy their interests. In short, and if we agree that the rule-based manipulative activity central to games could be called configurative, we can state that literature is a dominantly interpretative practice, unlike games that are dominantly configurative or manipulatable practices. To generalize: in art, we might have to configure in order to be able to interpret, whereas in games, we have to interpret in order to be able to configure, and proceed from the beginning to the winning or some other situation (Eskelinen 2001a). This distinction has at least one important consequence for the rest of this book. In order to gain a more comprehensive understanding of literature and literary poetics, we need to cybertextualize these fields, but to better understand ergodics we need to study games (and it is only after this last move that we can have a more comprehensive view of ergodic literature).

The four user functions are by necessity very broad categories.

Not only do text adventures and hypertext fictions share the explorative user function in Aarseth's typology, but also texts that are much easier to navigate like *Calligrammes* and *Hopscotch*. These almost trivially explorative texts could be grouped under another user function. Koskimaa (2000) has suggested a suitable name for it: the s*elective user function*. However, the same qualitative difference is inherent in the configurative user function as well: combining new poems from Queneau's *Cent Mille Milliards de Poèmes* is trivially easy whereas configuring and completing a text adventure is not. By the same token, Queneau's poetry generator is configurative by Aarseth's clear definition, and one could argue that the polarity between challenging and unchallenging ergodic acts is also to be felt and observed in every category of the user function. Still, the problem is that ergodic literature is usefully described and defined as literature in which "non-trivial effort is required to allow the reader to traverse the text" (Aarseth 1997, 1). In this respect, reading *Calligrammes*, folding new sonnets from Queneau, and deciding between two options of reading *Hopscotch* (or more likely the order in which these two possibilities are performed) are almost on par with visiting a footnote and returning back to the main text.

Also the question of how independent the ergodic side or layer of a text could possibly be from its other possible layers is mostly left unanswered in *Cybertext* except in the discussion of the descriptive, narrative, and ergodic layers in Joyce's *Afternoon* (Aarseth 1997, 92–5), modelled after Genette's (1982a) insights into the relations between narrative and description. We'll return to these problems and relations in later chapters.

The precise nature of the feedback loop or differences between several possible types of loop are not discussed in *Cybertext* (for example, self-destructive works could utilize only positive feedback), and neither are the differences between the effects or consequences the user knowingly chooses and the ones he merely causes without knowing it. It is relatively easy to design and program a text (Eskelinen 2012; Eskelinen and Koskimaa 2001) that analyzes its reader's (temporal) behavior and changes its content, structure, and behavior accordingly while the reader is moving freely in the text making interpretations and enjoying random access. In such situations, readers don't necessarily make any explicit non-trivial choices although the way they read will affect the text: there's a feedback loop but the reader–user doesn't use it intentionally and may not even be aware of its existence. Still, in most cases, this conflict could be described and solved as a simple mistake the user makes (not realizing the text's configurative user function), but in some (so far hypothetical) cases this may raise a genuine question concerning the limits of the observable differences the typology of textual communication is partly based on.

We may also ask how many basic types of feedback loop there are, between which parties these loops operate, and what kind of information about users is gathered, analyzed and used in them. Schematically, we can distinguish between intratextual loops within the text between its scripton clusters (i.e. its visible parts or phases), extratextual loops between two or several texts, multiuser loops between two or several users, and the standard one between user and text as theorized in cybertext theory. Not every ergodic work has all of these. Given the plurality of digital networks, the emergence of RFID technologies and ubiquitous digital environments, and the prospects of every little thing, particle and sensor around us having its own IP address, we should perhaps pay more attention to the qualitative differences between text machines and environments that profile and respond to their users based on more intimate, personal, and embodied user data than what can be gathered by analyzing the traditional user activities of clicking, typing and selecting (one could imagine many kinds of cybertextual apartheid based on the system's interpretation and measurements of the user's body and bodily states from gender to weight, height and pulse). We'll come back to these and other ergodic nuances in later chapters that try to shed some light on ergodic texts as mosaics of feedback loops.

All in all, Aarseth's typology of textual communication is not overly detailed, although it is much more nuanced than its theoretical alternatives. Although each of its seven variables could be divided further, the pragmatic limitations could very soon become a pressing issue. Having said that, such limitations are always more or less arbitrary and context dependent; a similarly constructed game typology by Aarseth, Smedstad, and Sunnanå (2003) contains more than 220000 positions (each indicating a functional game genre) and the later revision of that model by Elverdam and Aarseth (2007) includes even more.

To sum up our discussion and revisions so far, Table 2.1

shows the variables in Aarseth's typology supplemented by several secondary variables (marked by +) and the two additional variables of user position and user objective (marked by *).

Table 2.1 Primary and secondary cybertextual variables

Variable	Possible value
Dynamics	static, intratextonically dynamic, textonically dynamic
+position of scriptons	static, dynamic
+permanence of scriptons	permanent, temporary
+permanence of textons	permanent, temporary
Determinability	determinate, indeterminate
+media positions	one, several
Transience	transient, intransient
+ number of presentations	limited (*Agrippa*), unlimited (*The Dreamlife of Letters*)
+ loops	y/n
+ interval control	by the user (*Book Unbound*) or the textual machine
Perspective	personal, impersonal
+ number of personal perspectives	one, several
+ character	static, dynamic
Access (to scriptons)	random, controlled
+ access to all textons	y/n
+ temporarily limited	y/n

Variable	Possible value
Links	explicit, conditional, none
User function	interpretative, explorative, configurative, textonic
+ additional feedback loops	none, extratextual, intratextual, multi-user
User position*	
+ autonomy	independent, dependent
+ mobility required	y/n (non-stationary/stationary)
+ positioning	localized, non-localized
User objective*	traversal, consultation, sampling, completion, winning, improvization

Cybertext theory is not reducible to the typology of textual communication, even though that typology is crucial, because it gives us a superb comparative tool for integrating theories of ergodic and non-ergodic literature through the neglected aspect of the medium and media behavior. There are many other heuristic openings, definitions, suggestions, and conceptualizations both in *Cybertext* and in Aarseth's other writings on literature, media, and games. In the chapters to come, many of these will be used to initiate, complicate, and conclude the dialogue with literary theories based on incomplete analyses of media behavior.

CHAPTER 3

Cybertextuality and transtextuality

3.1 Introduction

The multiplication of media positions and literary media, discussed in Chapter 2, implies many changes and challenges for traditional theories of inter- and transtextuality developed in the context of print literature. This chapter will first revisit some traditional theories of inter- and transtextuality to discern an inventory of different relations to be focused on. Next it will look at certain novel types of relation existing between (and within) digital and ergodic texts and try to theorize them from a cybertextual perspective. It will conclude by putting the results of this theorizing into contact with the traditional theories by expanding and negotiating their basic premises.

This chapter has three empirical points of departure. First, ever since the emergence of the internet, texts are no longer necessarily materially separated from one another and readers can move seamlessly between texts and chunks of texts that are mutually linked. Such movements are an obvious part of our everyday digital practice, but even this type of relation (or should we say connection) is not recognized by traditional theories of inter- and transtextuality.

Second, traditional theories of intertextuality are fundamentally theories of textual relations that can only be interpreted (and not acted on in any other way). Competent readers are expected to recognize the co-presence of texts within one another, or the way one text is modeled after another, but beyond recognition and interpretation (in the broad sense of producing meaning, significance, and *jouissance*) they can do nothing with the relations they have either found or fabricated. In contrast, ergodic literature (especially text generators and textual instruments) often allows its users to affect, manipulate, and sometimes even create these relations.

Third, from the cybertextual perspective, as shown in Table 3.1, traditionally theorized and recognized relations between texts can be seen to exist only on the level of scriptons[1] to be recognized, compared and interpreted:

Table 3.1 Traditional inter- and hypertextuality from the cybertextual perspective

Text 1	<interpretation and recognition of>	Text 2
textons	—	textons
traversal functions	—	traversal functions
scriptons	<imitation, transformation, co-presence>	scriptons

This three-part model both modifies many already recognized relations between and among texts, and is capable of introducing new ones. The focus on traversal functions opens the possibility of behavioral imitations and transformations both between and within media positions. Differences and similarities between texts at the level of their textons create a set of indirect relations that are much harder to observe than the relations between scriptons and media positions, although they can't be separated from the last two. In order to see all this more clearly, certain classic theories of inter- and transtextuality need to be revisited and revised.

3.2 From intertextuality to transtextuality

Intertextuality is a contested concept, but there are only a few prominent theorists to take into account. There's no need to repeat here the well-known intellectual history of the term from Bakhtin to Kristeva and poststructuralism. The most important pragmatic choice to be made is between broad and narrow definitions.

One of the classic formulations of Kristeva (1980, 36) states that a text is "a permutation of texts, an intertextuality in the space of a given text" and within it "several utterances, taken from other texts, intersect and neutralize one another." In this way (similar to Bakhtin), individual texts are inseparable from the larger cultural and social text from which they are constructed. In Kristeva's reformulation of Bakhtin's pet terms of dialogue and ambivalence, the dynamic word's horizontal axis (sender/addressee) and vertical axis (text/context) coincide within the textual space resulting in intertextuality: "Any text is constructed a mosaic of quotations; any text is the absorption and transformation of another" (Kristeva 1980, 66).

Concepts usually come with consequences, and Roland Barthes' commonsense notion of anonymous intertextuality explains one of them. According to Barthes, texts are woven:

> [E]ntirely with citations, references, echoes, cultural languages (what language is not?), antecedent or contemporary, which cut across it through and through in a vast stereophony … [T]o try to find the "sources", the "influences" of a work, is to fall in with the myth of filiation; the citations which go to make up a text are anonymous, untraceable, and yet *already read*: they are quotations without inverted commas. (Barthes 1977, 160)

From this point of view, intertextuality is a normal and inescapable condition of all literature and textuality, just as it was to Bakhtin and Kristeva, and as long as the point is not generally accepted, it is probably worth making and repeating.

When the concept of intertextuality is accepted, as it is has been for decades now within literary studies, the question becomes what to do with this hopelessly broad concept. Even if one begins with and accepts the broad notion of intertextuality, one could be tempted to take one step further (or perhaps backwards to literary scholarship) and ask whether there are any differences in these processes of construction, quotation, absorption and transformation, and whether it matters if texts quote one another explicitly or hide their relationship so that it can be found only by readers competent enough, imitate each other as parodies and pastiches or through other generic and stylistic templates, or can or cannot be enjoyed and understood without knowing their implicit references and models, and so on.

At this point, the choice is between two forms or ways of specification: interpretation and poetics. The supposedly boundless field of intertextuality (easily expandable to intermediality) allows more or less innocent readers carving out intertextual connections to back up their situated interpretations of choice, ultimately turning and taming an initially radical theoretical break into the interpretative business as usual. However, we are taking a different direction, towards poetics, towards a more nuanced and pragmatic understanding of the types of relation texts may have with one another, and more precisely towards changes in these relations due to changes in the mechanics of textual machines: in other words, we'll move from works to machines.

Genette's theory of transtextuality (Genette 1992; 1997a; 1997b) provides a detailed overview of several important relations instead of using only one broad umbrella term, intertextuality, for all of them. To Genette (1997a, 1), the subject of poetics is not the text considered in its singularity, but transtextuality defined as "all that sets the text in a relationship, whether obvious or concealed, with other texts."

Genette (1997a, 1) finds five types of transtextual relationship: intertextuality, architextuality, paratextuality, metatextuality, and hypertextuality.[2] Architextuality is a purely taxonomic relation consisting of "the entire set of general or transcendent categories – types of discourse, modes of enunciation, literary genres –from which emerges each singular text" (ibid.). The questions of modes and genres in relation to cybertextuality are discussed in Chapter 5 to explore how the status of ergodic texts (and textonomical genres)[3] can be clarified and situated in terms of discourse modes and text types.

Paratexts are heterogeneous elements that lie on the threshold of the text (such as titles and prefaces) and help to direct and guide the reception of a text by its readers (Genette 1997a, 3). They carry a pragmatic dimension, bearing and conditioning the text's "impact upon readers," and are thus interesting to us precisely because changes in textual behavior are bound to affect these pragmatic threshold texts as well. Genette (1997b, 4–5) divides paratexts into epitexts (private and public outside texts that help readers interpret the text) and peritexts (the features literally framing the text). Instructions and users' manuals are the obvious contribution of digital and ergodic texts to the already recognized variety of paratexts, and the more complicated the strategies the user has to employ in order to traverse the text, the more important they become. The peritextual prefaces to the first (1963) and second (1965) editions of Cortazar's *Rayuela* include slightly different instructions for the reader – it is only in the latter that the reader is invited to select between one of the two paths through the text (Heise 1997, 81), making the text explicitly ergodic (see also Genette 1997b, 218). It could be interesting to see whether one could make similar changes by simply giving new ergodic reading instructions to non-ergodic literary works, although that kind of transformation may be best discussed in terms of hypo- and hyper-textuality. Also any additional information provided by epitexts about possibly hidden or inaccessible dimensions of the textual machine may have a higher status or relevance to the user than a more typical epitext potentially guiding his interpretations.

Metatextuality is "the relationship most often labelled commentary" (Genette 1997a, 4). There are at least four types of new challenge ergodic and digital texts may present to metatextual practices. First, in addition to the usual interpretative skills, the critic needs ergodic skills to use the textual system in an appropriate and successful way, and should perhaps both explain and evaluate his strategy and its effects on his interpretations. Second, the potentially continuous and never ending variation and supplementation may well exceed any humanly possible attention span, making the critic's observations and conclusions necessarily provisional. Third, in certain encounters with indeterminate cybertexts, commentaries may turn out to be commentaries on one's own singular experience of ephemeral constellations of signs never to be repeated again or to be seen by any other user, as ergodic works may be very sensitive to the way they are used. Finally, metatextuality partly overlaps with the genre of essay and may therefore spawn more creative commentaries than typical scholarship. A superb example of ergodic and digital metatextuality is Talan Memmott's *From Lexia to Periplexia* (2000), which, according to its descriptive peritext, expresses certain ideas only in and by its behavior.

According to Genette's (1997a, 1) restricted definition, intertextuality is "a relationship of co-presence between two texts or among several texts," including the practices of quotation, allusion, and plagiarism. The original definition of hypertextuality (Genette 1997a, 5) is more complicated and provisional: "Any relationship uniting a text B (which I shall call the *hypertext*) to an earlier text A (the *hypotext*), upon which it is grafted in a manner that is not commentary." Later Genette revised this rather negative definition as follows: "A hypertext is a text that derives from another by a formal and/or thematic process of transformation" (Genette 2005, 10).

Genette (1997a, 28) further divides hypertextuality into imitations and transformations that can be playful, satirical and serious. Of these six subtypes, parodies (playful transformations), travesties (satirical transformations), pastiches (playful imitations) and caricatures (satirical imitations) are minor genres in their own right, but also of lesser interest to us than serious imitations (labeled "forgeries" by Genette) and serious transformations (called transpositions). In Genette, forgeries are mostly (allographic)[4] continuations, but for some reason continuations in a different medium are not included. Serious transformation is the most important of all hypertextual practices to Genette and is further divided into formal and thematic transformations based on how much they affect the meaning of the text. The formal ones do it only or mostly by accident and the thematic ones deliberately as part of their purpose (Genette 1997a, 214). The former include such self-explanatory practices as translation, versification and prosification, quantitative transformations (such as concision and amplification among others), and both intermodal and intramodal transformations (taking place between and within dramatic and narrative modes). Thematic transformations are practices that affect the spatiotemporal world of fiction or the course, motivation, or evaluation of the action within it.

To Genette (1997a, 2–3), the difference between inter- and hypertextuality is also one of scale: the former is more local and optional, taking place in semantic-semiotic microstructures "at the level of a sentence, a fragment, or a short, generally poetic, text," while the latter takes place between "works considered as structural wholes." In his actual study of hypertextuality, Genette concentrates mostly on what he calls "the sunnier side of hypertextuality: that in which the shift from hypotext to hypertext is both massive (an entire work B deriving from an entire work A) and more or less officially stated" (Genette 1997a, 9). This leaves open the darker side with more hidden and less massive relations between hypotexts and hypertexts – in short, the mesolevel between intertextual microlevel and hypertextual macrolevel, within which the relation between the text and its reader is less openly contractual and pertaining to a conscious and organized pragmatics.

The five types of transtextuality are most of all mutually connected and sometimes overlapping aspects of all textuality, and only secondarily potential categories of texts (Genette 1997a, 9). For our purposes, they provide a detailed framework of relations and practices against and within which cybertextual relations and possible novelties can be compared and theorized.

3.3 Cybertextuality meets transtextuality: ten examples

3.3.1 *10:01*

Lance Olsen's novel *10:01* (Olsen 2005) exists both as an ordinary print novel and a web fiction (by the author and Tim Guthrie). Through the web fiction's visual interface, the user can access the thoughts of any character without having to visit them in the order they are presented in the book, although that too can be done by following the timeline. The web fiction contains the print novel's signifiers and keeps them and their initial order intact in every segment (i.e. each character's thoughts are identical in both versions), but adds extra functions not available to the reader of the print novel. There are accompanying audio tracks that can be turned on and off, images popping up, and possibilities to show and hide the text (which sometimes helps navigation). *10:01* also has external links to the web, to dynamic content (in blogs, for example). These outside texts form a kind of threshold between *10:01* and the rest of the web (accessed through the links in these threshold texts) without being paratexts in the traditional sense.

As trivial as it is, this kind of external linking to the intertexts (not available in the standalone hypertexts of the StorySpace and HyperCard variety)[5] changes the notion of traditional intertextuality, because the content of the textual co-presence doesn't have to stay the same and the user has to do ergodic work. In short, we have at least two new distinctions: between static and dynamic and interpretative and ergodic forms of intertextuality. As we shall see, the varieties of dynamic and ergodic intertextuality go far beyond external linking to routinely dynamic (updated) intertexts.

In Genette's hypertextual terms, the relation between the print and web versions of *10:01* could come close to formal and quantitative transformation, although it has very little to do with extension, expansion or amplification, i.e. the subtypes Genette (1997a, 254–68) recognizes. The links to the material outside the original composition would suggest some kind of amplification (a combination of thematic extension and stylistic expansion), but as these links mostly offer only explanatory background information, the criteria may not be met in this case. By the same token, the web fiction *10:01* obviously imitates the print novel that preceded it simply by reproducing its strings of signs and thus its whole content. Still, the web fiction is neither a pastiche nor a caricature of the book and it isn't its sequel or continuation either. Perhaps the relation between print and web versions should be classified as behavioral transformation, as the media positions are clearly different. As the web version adds audio and images to the basic text of the print version, the transformation is multimedial too, but as these two types of media addition service the text (instead of undermining, contradicting or essentially supplementing it) and don't draw much attention to themselves, they are not interesting to us in this context, especially as multimedia is hardly a digital novelty.

3.3.2 Regime Change

Usually inter- and hypertextual relations are not directly announced and made explicit in the text; it is mostly left to the reader to discover and apply the relevant relationships. In many ergodic works, this situation is reversed. In *Regime Change* (Wardrip-Fruin et al. 2004a), the user is presented with two texts that are named (a newspaper article on Saddam's fall in Iraq and the well-known report of the Warren Commission). Only the newspaper article forms the invariable part of the process (and hence serves as a hypotext to be transformed) and with each new generation it is modified by a series of quotes from the report of the Warren Commission. The logic of these text replacements is based on three-grams and four-grams (Wardrip-Fruin 2009, 387). Although text generation sessions always have the same initial hypotext (the newspaper article) the generative process could continue without a determinate point of ending as generated texts could in turn serve as hypotexts for subsequent generations so that the main part of the actual n-gram play usually takes place between these different generations of generations. Therefore the main task is not to recognize the connections between the two explicitly named texts but to mix them in interesting ways. Of course, both texts are already part of their own intertextual and generic networks, but these relations are not foregrounded in *Regime Change*. From the outset, the most obvious connection between two texts is thematic: political violence. The two texts to be mixed are also non-fictional, which adds more emphasis and incentive to thematic readings and interpretations, which perhaps provides simpler criteria (and a slightly lower threshold too) for success. In *Regime Change*, inter- and hypertextuality are both configurative and dynamic; the results of playing obviously vary resulting in different hypertexts quoting the intertext and transforming the hypotext differently every time.

3.3.3 *The Impermanence Agent*

Some digital texts such as *The Impermanence Agent* (Wardrip-Fruin et al. 1998–2002) open up another dimension not theorized in the context of printed literature. *The Impermanence Agent* can react to, appropriate, and use texts that were not available or didn't exist at the time of its publication. One could say that this is exactly what machines generally do as they are designed to deal also with future objects and processes. The point is not the orientation towards future texts as such, but the nature of this relationship, i.e. that the earlier text will be the active party quoting and incorporating the later ones for its own purposes and by its own idiosyncratic rules. This operational novelty is based on the specific type of textonic dynamics of *The Impermanence Agent*: its ability to supplement itself using outside texts.

In the beginning of a process that lasts approximately one week, the user reads the original story of Nana. During the process, this fixed text will be gradually replaced so that in the end only the structure of the story remains while its content has completely changed. The replacement is based on the material (texts and images) drawn from the user's browsing, but the precise logic of this replacement works in ways that are likely to escape the user even if the user is aware of the general operational logic of the Agent.[6] Browsing is necessary for the user's progress and the text's gradual replacement, but to view this progress the user needs to employ a peripheral mode of attention (Wardrip-Fruin et al. 2002, 9): nothing happens to the Agent's text if the reader doesn't browse between his readings. The rhythm between reading and browsing is also left to the user: there are no paratexts suggesting how to fine-tune one's peripheral mode of attention, i.e. how often to take a look at the results.

With this work, two relations are of interest: not only the relation between Wardrip-Fruin's original story and the texts the user browses with or without giving it much thought, but also the relation between the user and the Agent. The user is free to visit the sites he wants or needs, but it is the Agent who decides what is important in them and how they will affect and be interwoven with the original text. Ironically then, it is the human user who does the lower level (semi-intellectual) work serving the Agent's decisions, and not the other way around. The Agent is neither a narrator nor an author, although it has powers that are almost equal to what those two other types of textual entity usually possess. In essence, the Agent is an inter- and hypertextual operator deciding how the material the user visited will be quoted and how it will transform and replace Wardrip-Fruin's original hypotext.[7]

The end results (final texts) of *The Impermanence Agent* are personalized according to the individual preferences and practices (as interpreted by the Agent) of each user. One can imagine two opposing poles of its readership: ignorant readers making no exceptions to their normal browsing routines while the Agent is on their case and experimental readers changing their browsing habits in order to tie the Agent to specific textual fields, modes, and genres or even individual texts, thus maximizing their intertextual and hypertextual power that will still be compromised by the Agent's preferences.

3.3.4 *Book Unbound*

Somewhat similarly, the user can exercise selective intertextual power leading to personalized outcomes in *Book Unbound* (Cayley 1995a), although there the user is bound to stay within the limits of the Book's output, but as the process is potentially endless the cumulative effect of certain consistent choices is also greater. Obviously, there is no reason why the user should especially focus on hunting for recognizable instances of intertextuality and feeding them back to the system, but this kind of emergent (or negotiable) long-term relationship is still possible, and this possibility as such already goes against the grain of print-bound theories of transtextuality. The seed texts of *Book Unbound* are hidden from the user and they can't be traced and identified on the basis of the text's output (dispersed as the seed texts are with the user's selections and the rules of the system), but still these hidden texts have an impact as they are also modified in the process. In other words, we know there have to be co-presences, imitations and transformations between the seed texts and the outputs of *Book Unbound*, but we just don't and will not know what they are.[8]

3.3.5 *The Speaking Clock*

In the hypothetical "Reuters version" of *The Speaking Clock* (Cayley 2001) the field of future intertextuality is also left radically open for the future texts, but the reader would not grasp (and would not have time to grasp) the specific relationship of the rapidly changing surface text of the Clock with the news feed it is derived and mutated from. Here the hypothetical text's idiosyncratic rules work also as a barrier turning the intertextual feed invisible and inaccessible, a mere hidden source authors commonly use, unless, of course, the Reuters' text were made visible to the reader as well.

3.3.6 Eliza

Dialogue programs like *Eliza* (Weizenbaum 1966) don't understand or recognize intertextual and hypertextual relations. The user could talk back to *Eliza* using well-known quotations and allusions only, or model his inputs after famous dialogues, but that wouldn't create noticeable differences in *Eliza*'s output. This doesn't prevent the user from playing such language games to see whether and how *Eliza* imitates and transforms intertextually or hypertextually charged snippets of text. We could call this type of inter- and hypertextuality projective – we are free to introduce snippets of any existing text, published either before or after *Eliza*'s birth date in the mid–1960s, in the dialogue with *Eliza* to see how it transforms and reacts to them. As *Eliza* usually answers or comments by asking questions, questions and short formulaic or dialogic texts (such as proverbs, Oulipian perverbs or scenes from well-known plays) could be the ideal form of the user's projective inter- and hypertextual input.

3.3.7 Hegirascope

The main difference between the two successive versions of Moulthrop's *Hegirascope* lies in the temporal window of opportunity given to the user to choose the next link: in *Hegirascope 1* it was 18 seconds and in *Hegirascope 2* it is 30 seconds. This is a case of purely behavioral transformation, the significance of which is evident to anyone who ever had the chance to try both versions: in the latter, there's more time to think and the rhythm of reading and navigation becomes more relaxed. As this behavioral transformation doesn't change the text's media position, it could be called an intrapositional behavioral transformation – or judged by its effects, a perceptual transformation. In comparison to print theories of transtextuality, the two *Hegirascopes* have another remarkable relation between them: the second one completely erased and replaced the first one.

3.3.8 *The Golden Lion*

The Golden Lion (Cayley 1994) has two non-anonymous (i.e. explicitly named) seed texts, *Essay on the Golden Lion* by Fazang (643–712) and Cayley's short original poem *Han-Shan in Indra's Net*. Through a mesostic[9] process, the letters of a poem change one by one to the words of the essay (within the limits set by certain procedures of collocation) in a split screen presentation. The letters of the poem are shown in bold face within the words of the essay so it is easy or easier to follow the process. Here we can witness an intermodal[10] transformation process between poetry and essay, on the one hand, and the dynamic co-presence of Cayley's seed text within Fazang's essay within *The Golden Lion*, on the other. *The Golden Lion* shows intertextuality as a dynamic process in a way that broadens the possibilities for intertextual co-presence in two ways. First, transformations take place on the level of letters, words and syntagms (accepted collocations) that determine each other in programmable ways. Second, *The Golden Lion* both intertextually quotes and hypertextually transforms Fazang's essay in ways that distort its original syntax (and meaning) to a varying degree on the level of textual presentation (scriptons) while it quotes it (the whole hypotext) in full only on the level of textons (hidden from the user who can of course try to consult the original text by other means). There are many other lessons to be learned from Cayley's ingenuity, but for our current purposes these four are enough: the distinction between textonic and scriptonic inter- and hypertextuality, the scale or operating level of transformations and quotes extended to include letters (still visibly able to be combined into words), the full presence of the hypotext on the textonic level of its hypertext, and the difference between static and dynamic mesostics.

3.3.9 *riverIsland*

In John Cayley's *riverIsland* (2008), fully visible source texts (hypotexts) change into fully visible target texts (hypertexts) through transliteral morphing.[11] Here we have intertextuality and hypertextuality as fully visible and reversible two-way processes instead of one fixed and permanent state of co-presence, imitation, and transformation. The two interchangeable ends of this process (every text in *riverIsland* functions both as a source text and a target text) consist of 16 horizontal texts (Cayley's poetic adaptations of 16 poems from the 20 quatrains of Wang Wei's *Wang River Sequence*) and 16 vertical texts (different translations of one of the quatrains).[12] Horizontal and vertical texts operated by the reader morph to each other letter by letter choosing the quickest and least resistant way through the alphabet, which means that the longest transformative chain consists of 14 intermediary letters as separate steps in the process. If we take into account only the source and target texts we have 512 (2x16x16) different hypertextual processes the user can launch and observe.

Moreover, the phases of the process wherein the target text is not yet fully arrived and the source text not completely disappeared give us a series of perceptible stages with their own intertextual specifications as letter by letter also the co-presences between the two chosen texts change and it is only in the beginning and the end of the process when there's no dynamic co-presence between the two.

3.3.10 *The Dreamlife of Letters*

The Dreamlife of Letters (Stefans 2000) paratextually announces its otherwise untraceable and unrecognizable hypotext and intertext (a short text by Rachel Blau Du Blessis). Stefans took every word from Du Blessis' text and arranged and then presented the words in alphabetical order. This procedure isn't specific to digital media, as it can be applied and its result presented in any media, but still this procedure raises the question of the limits of inter- and hypertextuality in general. As lists of words don't bear any trace of their original (or any other) syntax, they completely sever traceable relations to their possible inter- and hypotexts. Such a move also undermines the usefulness of the notions of co-presence, imitation and transformation. If such relations were to take place only on the level of individual words it would be questionable to say that one text is modeled after another or imitates or quotes it in any relevant way. However, Stefans doesn't merely alphabetize the words of Du Blessis but adds visible behavior to them; the whole point of *The Dreamlife of the Letters* is in the movements of these words, their constituent letters, and their varying sizes, shapes, positions and colors. In this way, *The Dreamlife of Letters* foregrounds its architextual relationship to visual, concrete and kinetic poetry, which overrides any need to dwell on its backgrounded inter- and hypotextuality except as a theoretical exercise we are about to conclude.

3.4 Conclusion

Contemporary theories of inter- and transtextuality (within literary studies) are based on print practices. As printed signifiers are permanent, any relation between them, be it co-presence, commentary, imitation or transformation, is also permanent (although interpretations of the relations may vary). That does not have to be the case in digital media, where we have a field of (potentially) dynamic inter- and transtextuality instead of the old static one. Print texts are also inescapably intransient, and thus incapable of letting the users witness the real-time processes of textual transformations and replacements – for example from preexisting source texts to preexisting target texts (and vice versa) as in *riverIsland*.[13]

As print texts are also closed volumes, they can only quote, allude to, comment, imitate and transform prior texts. However, as we have seen, dynamic textual machines connected to the continuously expanding and routinely updated resources of the internet such as *The Impermanence Agent* can or could do all this also to the texts published after their own publication date. To a lesser degree, this is also true with every text that accepts significant[14] configurative textual input from the reader, such as *Eliza* (1966). Based on these observations we seem to have two major fields of transtextuality: open and closed, the former actively oriented not only to the past but to the future texts as well. At the present moment most texts and textual relationships take place in the closed field and therefore we cannot proceed much further here in exploring the open field.

Second, in addition to doubling the transtextual field, we can and should be more careful to specify at which level the relationships (and comparisons) between texts take place. In addition to the level of scriptons, the relationships may also take place between textons and between the kinds of behavior the compared texts exhibit. Purely behavioral transformations could be called textonomical, as unlike Genette's thematic and formal transformations they don't necessarily affect the text's semantic meaning or its usual formal qualities (such as form, mode, or length). Needless to say, the interplay of behavioral, formal and thematic transformations and the ways they possibly mirror each other opens another new dimension to be studied.

Textonomical transformations could be divided into intrapositional and interpositional transformations, and the latter could be divided into one-dimensional and multidimensional interpositional transformations (depending on how many cybertextual variables are affected). Typical examples of multidimensional interpositional changes would include *253* by Geoff Ryman, a web fiction that later become a book (with changes in links and user function), and the already discussed *10:01* (with changes involving dynamics, links and user function). *Hegirascope 2* is an intrapositional behavioral transformation of *Hegirascope 1* (changes affecting only the specifics of its transience). The basic types of interpositional textonomical transformation are shown in Table 3.2.[15]

Table 3.2 Interpositional textonomical transformations within seven cybertextual dimensions

Dimensions	Types of change
Dynamics	Static dynamics > Intratextonic dynamics
	Static dynamics > Textonic dynamics
	Intratextonic dynamics > Static dynamics
	Intratextonic dynamics > Textonic dynamics
	Textonic dynamics > Intratextonic dynamics
	Textonic dynamics > Static dynamics
Determinability	Determinate > Indeterminate
	Indeterminate > Determinate
Transience	Transient > Intransient
	Intransient > Transient

Dimensions	Types of change
Perspective	Personal > Impersonal Impersonal > Personal
Access	Random > Controlled Controlled > Random
Links	No links > Explicit links No links > Conditional links Explicit links > No links Explicit links > Conditional links Conditional links > Explicit links Conditional links > No links
User function	Interpretative > Explorative Interpretative > Configurative Interpretative > Textonic Explorative > Interpretative Explorative > Configurative Explorative > Textonic Configurative > Interpretative Configurative > Explorative Configurative > Textonic Textonic > Interpretative Textonic > Explorative Textonic > Configurative

Media positions are based on how the traversal function generates or reveals scriptons from textons, and while this is valid as a general, macrolevel model, the relations between textons and scriptons need to be studied on meso- and microlevels as well. This is necessary especially if we wish to clarify the relationship between source and target texts that is foregrounded in poetry and text generators. This relationship should not be confused with any of the five transtextual relations discussed earlier. Schematically, the relations between source and target texts can be broken into several sub-dimensions:

1   *Type of the procedure or operation.* An almost readymade list of Oulipian operations and objects (Bénabou 1998, 44–5) could be imported just to show that procedurality is

not specific to digital media, although the difference is that in print literature the source texts to be transformed usually exist in separate volumes from the target texts.[16] Within e-poetry we could compare the use of n-grams in Cayley's texts or compare those texts to Durand and Wardip-Fruin's use of n-grams in *News Reader* and *Regime Change* (see Wardrip-Fruin 2007, 236–42).

2 *Linguistic level of operation.* Letters as in *riverIsland*, syntagms as in *Book Unbound* etc.

3 Visibility. The transformation process is either visible as in *riverIsland* or invisible as in *Book Unbound*.

4 *Reversibility.* The process (or processes) is either irreversible as in Bootz's unique reading poems (see Bootz 2007 for details) or reversible as in *riverIsland*.

5 *Teleology.* The transformation process is either finite (*riverIsland*) or infinite (*The Speaking Clock*).

6 *Ergodics.* This dimension is the same as Aarseth's user function.

7 *Access to the source text.* It is either complete (*riverIsland*) or not (*Book Unbound*).

8 *Number of source texts.* Either one as in *The Impermanence Agent* or several as in *Book Unbound*.

9 *Number of target texts.* Either one as in unique-reading poems or several as in *riverIsland*.

10 *Uniqueness.* Target texts are personalized as in *Book Unbound* and unique-reading poems or impersonal as in *riverIsland*. Source texts become personalized through the Word for Weirdos option in *Arteroids* whereas without it they are impersonal.

Needless to say, these possible relations don't necessarily say anything about archi-, inter- and hypertextual relations between and within source and target texts or between them and other texts. Therefore we could ask which set of relations is foregrounded. In *riverIsland*, there is no fascination in recognizing Wang's quatrains and their translations, as they are openly there to be transformed back into each other. In that sense, *riverIsland* fully quotes its hypo- and intertexts. The transformation processes and not their static initial and final states are the interest focus in *riverIsland*. Similarly, in *The Speaking Clock*, the reader most definitely will not have time to contemplate occasional or accidental textual co-presences.

Textonic transtextual relationships between texts are the hardest ones to study and theorize, as textons (if they don't happen to be identical to scriptons) are often concealed from the user and inaccessible to him, and if these seed texts include prior texts used as either hypotexts or intertexts or both the user may not be given explicit information about their existence and identity. Still, as textons (strings of signs as they exist in the text) belong to the ontological core of the text, they do matter and so do relationships between and among the textons. A hypothetical variation of *Book Unbound* could be used as an example of what kinds of practice are now possible. If the opening sequences of *Book Unbound* were programmed such that each copy began differently, each copy (of *Book Unbound*) could then also have been titled differently to indicate that they were entirely different texts. Given that the original textons of each copy were identical, and that use will permanently change and diversify them, this core similarity could have been concealed and copies taken for completely different texts.

Within traditional scriptonic transtextuality, major relationships can be static or dynamic, transient or intransient, and either interpretative or ergodic. To conclude this chapter, we'll revisit inter- and hypertextuality in more detail as within these relationships the changes are more visible and perhaps more important than within the other three types of transtextuality.[17] On many occasions, hypertextuality and intertextuality are tightly interwoven: hypotexts are often transformed by quotes from other texts. That's why we discuss inter- and hypertextuality together in the three dimensions mentioned (dynamics, transience, and ergodics).

3.4.1 Dynamic (scriptonic) inter- and hypertextuality

Static co-presence is the norm in the otherwise conflicting theories of intertextuality, while there are many almost unexplored ways for dynamic co-presence inherent in digital media. Dynamic intertextuality can take place in three relationships:

1 The text's relation to its intertextual network (all the texts it either quotes or alludes to). Dynamic texts can incorporate quotations and allusions from new intertexts. This is what happens in *The Impermanence Agent*, which can quote whatever new site the user may visit and in the process of replacement some older references may vanish.

2 The relation between the text and its particular intertext. If the relation is static, then the intertext is always present exactly the same way in the text. If it is dynamic, then the intertext's co-presence undergoes changes. This is what happens to the quotes from the report of the Warren Commission in *Regime Change*. In principle, dynamic intertextual co-presence between a text and its intertext could undergo both quantitative changes (the area cohabited by the intertext may expand to the point of erasing and taking over the whole text or diminish to the point of vanishing entirely, i.e. the intertext may be quoted or alluded to more or less frequently and extensively) and qualitative changes if the original quotes are replaced by other quotes from the same intertext.

3 The presence and status of a particular quote or an allusion within the text may change. Overt intertextuality (quotes) may turn into covert (allusions) and vice versa. Also the position of a quote or an allusion in the text's composition may change and be either determinate (if the quote's or allusion's adjacent scriptons are always the same) or indeterminate (if they are not).

Dynamic hypertextuality manifests first of all in the number of hypo- and hypertexts. Traditionally (as the relationship is between "structural wholes"), the ratio is often 1:1, one hypotext for each individual hypertext. Of course, there's no upper limit to how many separate hypertexts could be and have been constructed from one hypotext or how many smaller hypotextual "structural wholes" can be fused into one hypertext. Here the point is that several hypertexts and hypotexts can exist and transform to each other within the same text machine.[18] For example, *riverIsland* contains 32 hypotexts and 32 hypertexts and 512 possible processes between them (and if each morphing stage in each of these processes would count as a hypo- or hypertext or both for other stages in these processes, the number of these textual entities could perhaps both make and close the case for dynamic hypertextuality).

3.4.2 Transient inter- and hypertextuality

Here, the novelty lies in the way inter- and hypertextual processes are presented to the user. Traditionally hypotexts and hypertexts usually exist as separate volumes, although not necessarily, as sometimes a hypertext may well contain an allographic ad hoc or even an implicit hypotext it varies (Genette 1997a, 52), but they are certainly theorized as if this kind of relation were a norm. In other words, we have one static hypotext (as a permanent beginning situation so to speak) and its one static hypertext (one final outcome). Contrary to that doxa, the co-presences between any two chosen texts (i.e. a source text and a target text) in *riverIsland* change morph by morph, existing only as transient parts of the transformation process. Or, to put it differently, the relation between two text objects is shown as a transformative process. In *The Golden Lion*, Fazang's hypotext changes less frantically, one screen after another, in a one-way process. *riverIsland*'s two-way processes present another presentational variety by turning hypotexts and hypertexts into reversible positions, giving the 32 individual parts of the text a double status as both hypo- and hypertexts.

3.4.3 Ergodic inter- and hypertextuality

Ergodic inter- and hypertextuality can be either explorative or configurative. In the explorative case, the text is directly connected (linked) to its entire intertext or hypotext that can be explored. The connections can be determined by the links in the text (as in the web version of *10:01*) or by the user's browsing activity (as in *The Impermanence Agent*). Explorative forms are not particularly interesting, as it is easy to let the user have complete or limited access to the intertexts and hypotexts to be used, imitated, and transformed simply by including them in the text in their entirety.

Configurative inter- and hypertextuality can be further divided into impersonal, variable, and personal forms. Impersonal inter- and hypertextuality present the same texts and processes to every user. Regardless of which process the user happens to trigger while playing with the texts and the audiovisual streams of *riverIsland*, there are no personalized differences or outcomes in them. Variable relations take place in *Regime Change* where they are bound by the given intertext (the report of the Warren Commission) and the given hypotext (the newspaper article) that are the only available source texts (to which the user can't add anything). *Eliza* offers possibilities for unbounded personal relations, as the user's input is not limited by any pre-given text. Following the logic of the cybertextual user functions, one could conceptualize textonic forms of inter- and hypertextuality exemplified by *The Impermanence Agent*[19] and *Book Unbound* that give the user the chance to feed a recognized quote back to the pool of seed texts or to limit the field harvested for quotes.

Finally, and as we have seen, dynamic transtextual relationships are also related to and intertwined with the text's dynamic intratextuality. Varieties of expression inherent in digital cybertexts have introduced a dynamic field of intra- or autotextuality, as texts could, in principle at least, consist of several more or less autonomous parts and phases quoting, imitating and transforming one another and changing their relations to each other. Under such conditions, everything that has so far been theorized to take place only between and among texts could also happen within texts.

CHAPTER 4

The textual whole

4.1 Introduction

If we run a typical book through the typology of textual communication, it will have the following values: static dynamics, determinate determinability, intransient time, random access, impersonal perspective, no links and interpretative user function.[1] These values also determine traditional notions of the textual whole that can be applied and taken for granted in most cases of print literature. In practice, this means (among other things and effects) that we as book readers both expect and know that it will be possible to both read and reread the whole text within which the signifiers will remain the same (and do not change over time) at any time we want for as long as and as many times as we want.

However, there is a widening variety of texts that undermine these and many other expectations, conventions and commonsense assumptions. What is the textual whole (or the literary work) if it can appropriate and mix texts not yet published, cannot be read in its entirety, if only a few of its signifiers can or will be shared by all its readers, or if there's no clear termination point to its metamorphosis and reading process? Moreover, many digital and ergodic texts set conditions and constraints on their readers and users ranging from temporal limitations to personal and personalized perspectives. This affects the relationship between text and reading in ways to which we should pay more attention.

Traditional reception studies will not help us, as they are limited to the problems and conceptualizations of the reader's interpretative activity in the context of non-ergodic print literature.[2]

Of course, the concept of the textual whole has not vanished from the scene. Minimally, the title may be enough to guarantee the identity and the "wholeness" of any text, even if different readers are presented with mostly or completely different sets of scriptons. This kind of textual entity could be said to have a machinic identity, as cybertexts are machines for producing variety of expression (Aarseth 1997, 3). Between traditional textual wholes, giving every reader complete access to their static and invariable textons and scriptons, and textual machines denying that to the extreme, there are several types of textual entity that demand varieties of strategy and rules of engagement from their users that have not yet been sufficiently examined.

Early on in *Cybertext*, Aarseth states the core of his project and perspective: "The differences in teleological orientation – the different ways in which the reader is invited to 'complete' a text – and the text's various self-manipulating devices are what the concept of cybertext is about" (Aarseth 1997, 20).

The varieties in the organization of the text are bound to affect "both the reader's strategic approach and the text's perceived teleology" (ibid.). In what follows, we'll mostly deal with these two interconnected sides (self-manipulation and completion) separately without trying to force them into any preliminary conceptual synthesis.

4.2 The whole text: conventions and expectations

Conventionally, the notion of the textual whole includes at least the following five presuppositions, conventions and expectations: readers can easily read the whole text, as the only efforts and challenges associated with this conventional "goal" are of an interpretative nature; readers should read the whole text in order to be able to fully comprehend and interpret it; the point at which the whole text is read marks also the termination point of reading; it is always possible to reread exactly the same text as its signifiers don't change between (or during) readings; and, finally, that the way the text is read doesn't affect its material strings of signs. These expectations form a cluster: under "normal" textual conditions (i.e. the consumption of books) they appear together and can, in principle, be deduced or inferred from one another.

In what follows, however, we'll have to separate these conventional threads; in the expanded field of cybertextuality and ergodic literature, they are no longer necessarily clustered together. To take just a few examples, even if the reader were to have no difficulty in reading the whole text, it may be or become unnecessary or unwise to do so (as in game books and *I Ching*). Even if the reader has read the whole text the conventional way (say from the first page to the last), the text may have to be read in a different order, in which case the last page doesn't necessarily signal the termination point of reading (as it doesn't in *Cent Mille Milliards de Poèmes*). Even if the reader has successfully completed every aforementioned task, the next time he approaches the text it may be materially different (as in Jean-Pierre Balpe's generative hypertexts), and in some cases it may become illegible based on the effects of its reading. Eugenio Tisselli's "degenerative" (2005) is a web page "where each time it was visited, one character from the page is destroyed ... leading to a gradual degeneration of both its structure and content" (Tisselli 2010, 7).

At the very least, the assumed literary whole or totality can be described in interplaying perceptual, behavioral, structural, temporal, spatial, and causal terms.[3] Perceptually, printed texts give the reader all the time he needs to decipher and contemplate possible presentational complexities. Pages of concrete poetry and prose (for example in Raymond Federman's novels) may take some time to be fully perceived or should we say adequately scanned and studied, but, in principle, everything that is presented on any page can be perceived as nothing is (or could be) permanently hidden from the view. Encrypted texts may be said to constitute an exception to this condition, but they too become (or should become) fully and easily readable with the right "key"; moreover, this dimension is more about private and secret communication than literature. The split between interface and storage media in digital media divides the textual whole into two layers, compared to the only one fully visible layer of print literature that can't permanently[4] hide its strings of signs (textons and scriptons) from the reader.

It is not only the textons that may escape the user's perception in digital media, but in many cases also the detailed mechanics of the traversal function. With books the user is responsible for executing the operations needed for producing or realizing different sequences of signs, but if and when this work is performed by the textual machine and its algorithms, the way the text behaves and presents its scriptons becomes at least potentially much harder to understand, verify and control. The user may, of course, develop a certain feel for the textual machine, and may even learn to master it to some degree (much like an instrument), but there still may be elements, principles, consequences of choices and unpredictable future alterations that will remain completely outside his grasp and perception.[5] This boils down to the difference between machinic instructions and instructed humans.

Structurally speaking, the prevalent convention related to the textual whole is that the text maintains its structure both in presentation and between presentations. The book and its pages will remain the same; every printed signifier maintains its identity and doesn't move or morph into something else, and it is only our interpretations of them that may and usually do differ from one reading to the next. Obviously, this rule doesn't apply to digital media in the same way it does to paper and print. The text may change while it is being read and because it is being read in ways that have programmed consequences for the text's organization and content. To put it in another way, books (unlike some cybertexts) do not read their readers.

Spatially, the book is a volume taking up a precise physical space and an entity that is distributed in copies. In strict contrast, web fictions exist on a server as virtual entities not distributed (and shared) in copies, and are as such open to unannounced revisions by the author at any time. In other words, the author retains complete control of (or at least the power to intervene in) the text's form, content, behavior and existence after its publication (Aarseth 1997, 81). Moreover, as locative texts and textual installations show, scriptons have already moved beyond the page and screen (or at least the more familiar screens of our PCs and mobile phones) and are now more or less readable from any more or less complex surface. By the same token, we have been surrounded by textual surfaces in our physical environment since well before the advent of computers. Still, it is important to reclaim public spaces for literature and to resist the pervasive advertising litterism all around us.

Temporally, the common sense assumption is that the text doesn't self-destruct, although it may, of course, be destroyed in other ways and, if not restored or reprinted, may deteriorate over time. In other words, literary works, and especially those reproduced in print, are conventionally meant to be permanent (unlike, say, avant-garde textual performances that could, in principle, be saved only by recording technologies). Compared to this convention of permanence, digital and ergodic literature contains many examples of temporary texts and textual machines and environments. After its shutdown in 1990, the original *TinyMud* now reappears only once a year for a day;[6] in other words, it is only periodically available and at some point may cease to be so altogether. The most interesting thing here is not permanence or transience as such, but the combination of temporary and permanent elements in a single work. This implies a new type of aesthetic and (literary-poetic) decision to be made by the author or whomever it may concern. Similarly, another major temporal assumption is that the visible (scriptonic) text, its parts, and their mutual relations do not change and evolve over time. Contrary to this, a programmed and networked text can be divided into any number of semi-autonomous and dynamic segments, each of which has its own rules and conditions for its temporal development and interplay with the other segments.[7]

Causally, textual wholes are supposed to be autonomous and not affect one another's behavior and be also materially separate from one another (if not bound in the same volume). However, digital text machines can be programmed to affect the behavior and content of other text machines and linked so that the user can seamlessly move from one to another. To get a fuller view of these and other changes we have to take a closer look at the dimensions of cybertextual self-manipulation.

4.3 Cybertextual self-manipulation and traditional wholes

The seven original variables of cybertext theory will serve to illustrate the ways in which the traditional textual whole may vanish or disappear from the reader's grasp if not also from his aspirations or work ethics.

4.3.1 Dynamics

The traditional concept of the textual whole is tied to the constant number and material content[8] of signifiers, i.e. static dynamics: it is not well suited to deal with potentially endless variations of scripton and supplementation of textons. The only print examples in Aarseth's selections of texts (Aarseth 1997, 65–7) that don't have static dynamics are two game books (*Money Spider* and *Falcon*) with intratextonic dynamics. Here, the shift away from static dynamics is not very radical, as every texton and scripton could still be read should the user so wish, and in that way the alternatives to the textual output remain visible and immediately accessible. The books' game structure simply allows certain fragments to be skipped, as they don't belong to the correct or successful path to victory or completion. So in these two cases the user doesn't have to read the whole text, as the readily available parts of it happen to have different use value (which is similar to the way we use non-fictional texts from user's manuals to dictionaries). This replacement of the textual whole to be read in full with the game or puzzle structure to be completed (and often ignored after that) is also the conventional norm in digital text adventure games, which unlike their print counterparts are able to hide their strings of signs from the user.

With textonic dynamics, the challenges to the traditional notions of the textual whole become even more complicated. In principle, the source of supplements, changes and additions can be either the user himself (as in *Book Unbound*), other users (as in many MUDs), or the text can supplement itself from outside sources as in *The Impermanence Agent*[9] or John Cayley's idea (Cayley 2001, 99) of using a Reuters newsfeed to provide real-time material for one of his *Speaking Clocks*. As textons are strings of signs as they are in the text they also constitute the core components of textual ontology, and if textons can be added to (or removed from) the text or changed after its publication, we have entered a new kind of textual ontology (especially as these alterations have nothing to do with the tasks of philology, such as new editions that don't physically erase previous ones). In textonically dynamic texts, the basic units of textual variation also become dynamic, and to complicate matters textons become (and may cease to be) parts of the text at different times, which gives them different durations as textons. In principle, these self-supplementing texts open up the possibility that they could also appropriate texts that are published in the future, which makes them radically open compared to the texts that will remain closed entities after their publication.[10]

4.3.2 Determinability

Indeterminability is associated with randomness or chance, but that's only one side of it, and perhaps not the most interesting one. As noted in Chapter 2, in Aarseth's model, determinability is about the stability of the traversal function. In practical terms, indeterminability means that regardless of whether the user reacts or acts the same way in the same situation, the system itself does not respond the way it did the last time. At one possible extreme of indeterminability, there are neither same situations nor same responses available, as everything happens only once. This kind of indeterminability would not only complicate but deny the process and possibility of rereading the same text. Here too, the traditional wisdom related to the textual whole does not get us very far, as it is bound to the notions of endless repeatability controlled by the user and guaranteed by the copious permanence of print. One could say that such permanence has now become only a special case of repetition (i.e. unlimited repetition).[11]

4.3.3 Transience

Transient texts don't usually allow the reader to control the time and the rhythm of reading. Texts may be available for limited periods of time, sometimes only once, as is or was the case with William Gibson's *Agrippa*, or more precisely with its non-hacked copies. They may also set other kinds of condition for their temporal availability, behavior, reception and use. Here we are dealing with cycles of appearances, disappearances and potential reappearances in the context where the text, and not the reader, controls the presentation; i.e. we are not only reading textual objects but textual processes as well (or textual objects through textual processes). In the course of these presentations, we may have to prioritize our fleeting perceptions and try to decide what to read and see, if and when it is impossible to read and see it all. According to Janez Strehovec (2001,104), in the context of digital web poetry, this easily leads to foregrounding kinetic and visual affects, effects and constellations at the expense of the usual syntactic and semantic complexities.

Even more importantly, the text may now become a cluster of appearances, disappearances and reappearances in a process that doesn't have to have a termination point (*Book Unbound*), and which may also exceed the limitations of the human attention span (*The Speaking Clock* working around the clock guaranteeing we'll miss substantial portions of its output). Texts may also at times become illegible and be only occasionally meaningful to human observers (as in John Cayley's recent ambient texts such as *Overboard*). Generally speaking, transient texts open up the dimension of the presentation process that doesn't have to be as conventional and uncomplicated as the processes of dramatic and filmic presentations and performances.

In further theorizing the appearances (and disappearances) of scriptons and cybertextual presentations in general, it is important to notice that there are many other conventional temporal parameters besides the parameter of order that has dominated the discussion so far. While the order of the textual presentation may be linear or non-linear,[12] its duration and speed may be either variable or invariable, repetitions either possible or impossible, teleology finite or infinite, and it may or may not present two or more dynamic events at the same time,[13] as shown in Table 4.1. It is also possible that its speed may be too fast[14] or that there may be mandatory pauses in the presentation.

Table 4.1 Examples of the six main temporal variables of transient textual presentation

Temporal variables and values	Examples
Duration	
variable	*The Impermanence Agent*
invariable	*The Dreamlife of Letters*

Temporal variables and values	Examples
Speed	
variable	*Cruising*
invariable	*The Dreamlife of Letters*
too fast	*The Speaking Clock*
mandatory pauses	*The Impermanence Agent*
Repetition	
possible	*The Dreamlife of Letters*
impossible	*Agrippa*
Order	
linear	*The Dreamlife of Letters*
non-linear	*Hegirascope*
Simultaneity	
simultaneous	*riverIsland*
non-simultaneous	*Hegirascope*
Teleology	
finite	*The Impermanence Agent*
infinite	*Book Unbound; The Speaking Clock*

4.3.4 Access

If we don't have random and complete access to every part of the text, our potential mastery (readerly omnipresence) is once again denied by constraining our traditional right to traverse and skip the text any way we please. Controlled access includes the possibility that some parts of the text will remain hidden and out of reach despite the best efforts of the reader. Moreover, the distinction between textons and scriptons implies that the textual whole is divided in two. In some cases, the user can access textons as well: as already noted they can't be hidden from him in print, and, in other cases, as in classic hypertext fiction, textons and scriptons happen to be identical: every string of signs that is in the text can be read exactly as it is.

In addition, depending on the digital conditions, the quantitative ratio of hidden to visible parts or phases of the text may escape the reader. In *Reagan Library* (Moulthrop 1999), the reader is occasionally given information about the percentage of the text he has so far read. This numerical value is randomly generated and thus false, but the way this falsity can or is supposed to be figured out is more complicated. Even if the announced percentage sometimes decreases despite the fact that the reader has definitely read more, that doesn't necessarily prove a thing, as, in principle, it would be possible that the text has expanded much faster than the reader has been able to read.

4.3.5 Links

Links have the potential to complicate the relation between parts and wholes, allowing and opening several paths through the text, but, in practice, that potential should not be overestimated, because the average hypertext fiction shares many stabilizing qualities with its print predecessors, from static dynamics and determinability to intransient time and impersonal perspective. Generative hyper-texts (Balpe 2007) are more challenging in this respect, because their link–node structure is different from one reading session (or generation) to the next.

4.3.6 Personal perspective

Here, the reader is forced to assume strategic responsibility and then face the consequences of her actions. This is a very game-like feature, but it is also possible that the required strategic choices have to be made in the absence of explicit rules, goals and manipulative procedures in a more relaxed roleplaying environment. Compared to the traditional textual whole, the user's need for strategy in order to traverse the text constitutes a substantial novelty to be further theorized. In "Nonlinearity and Literary Theory," Aarseth (1994, 80) distinguishes between the figures of forking (in printed texts), jumping (in hypertexts), permutation, computation and polygenesis. Each of these will have as its necessary counterparts different series of reading, using and completing strategies.

4.3.7 User functions and the user position

Whereas the explorative user function brings in the rhetorics of choice, navigation, and labyrinth – and forced repetition (enjoyable or not), the configurative and textonic user functions clearly foreground the user's own extranoematic activity by giving him the chance or necessity of affecting the text and therefore approaching it as a playground, an obstacle, and more or less malleable raw material to build on. The continuum of the user functions also entails a continuum of the possibilities for self-expression within its higher user functions, to the degree that the texts also include personal perspective and/or such additional discourse levels as negotiation, quasi-events, and construction.[15] Interactive fiction requires that the user gives commands, which counts as a form of self-expression, although it is severely constrained by the limited variety of accepted commands. MUDs are much more flexible in this respect when they open communication channels between humans and let users construct dynamic entities (characters, rooms and objects) capable of triggering genuinely unpredictable communicative and self-expressive events.

The dependent user position brings in social conventions and norms, thus offering yet another set of organizational principles to supplement or replace the perhaps ineffective, insufficient or inapplicable literary and textual conventions. One could also imagine texts that would be absolutely unable to be read because of the excessive demands they set for the user's position, location and movement, but at this point the existence of such texts is pure speculation, although they would just continue the long (and somewhat longwinded) tradition of the aesthetics of frustration.

4.4 Variations and conventions

If we translate the aforementioned shifts in media position in terms of variation, we'll have the following types to address: variations in the output (IDT), textual constitution (TDT), situations and responses (indeterminability), textual processes and their control (transience), inaccessibility and invisibility (access), strategy and roleplay (personal perspective), paths, parts, and wholes (links and explorative user function), and temporary and permanent textual construction (configurative and textonic user functions).

The notions and conventions of reading and completing the text need to be adjusted to better suit this cybertextual or machinic variety. First of all, reading the whole text is the strongest literary convention, but as was implicit in the earlier discussion, it can now mean at least four slightly different things: reading every texton and scripton, reading every texton, reading every scripton, and taking every given path through the text (i.e. exhausting the variety of paths).

The first situation is the most common; almost any print novel gives the reader an easy access to its textons and scriptons and classic hypertext fictions (*Afternoon*; *Patchwork Girl*; *Victory Garden*) cannot ultimately hide them from a sufficiently persistent reader. The second situation happens with texts like *Cent Mille Milliards de Poèmes*; its overwhelming number of scriptons (in this case, texton combinations) can't be consumed by any reader, but instead its 140 textons can be read in almost no time. The third situation takes place, for example, in our dealings with *Eliza*; we read and respond to whatever scriptons are presented to us without knowing (or caring) what the textons and language-generating operations "beyond the surface" actually are. Finally, if there aren't too many paths through the text, we can take them all one by one as in *Hopscotch* or forking texts in pattern[16] and visual poetry.

From the user's point of view, there's a crucial difference in the difficulty between different ways of reading the whole text. To read every texton and scripton in a non-ergodic novel, every texton in *Cent Mille Milliards de Poèmes*, and every presented scripton in Eliza,[17] or to take the two specified paths in *Hopscotch*, the reader–user doesn't need to have a strategy, as it is trivially easy to accomplish those tasks. Not so with hypertext fiction that requires a strategy and in any case makes it much more difficult for the user to read every static node.[18]

In his conclusion to *Cybertext*, Aarseth (1997, 180–2) distinguishes between anamorphic (solvable enigmas) and metamorphic (the texts of change and unpredictability) works of art that are different from novels (in which Aarseth on this occasion included *Afternoon*-type hypertexts). Based on this, we have four basic types of process: regular reading in which it is trivially easy to read the whole text; hypertext reading in which reading it all is usually possible but requires non-trivial work; solving the enigma posed by an anamorphic text which also requires non-trivial work that is compensated by the decreasing need to re-engage and reread the text again; and, finally, finding ways to adapt one's strategies to a dynamic and unpredictable metamorphic text that has no final state or point of resolution.[19]

To Aarseth (1997, 181), *Afternoon* is not anamorphic as there's "no clear, final state of resolution (or ending) in which all is revealed." On the one hand, this makes sense as *Afternoon* is not a solvable enigma like textual adventure games, but, on the other hand, one could argue that a clear and final state of resolution occurs whenever we have read the whole text, in the sense of the sum total of every individual node – if that is possible (and it clearly was in the early – and mid–1990s hypertext fictions). At this point, the reader is in the same position as he is on the last page of any complex novel: he has read it all.

In short, while the need for strategy and the impossibility of exhausting every path through the text separate hypertext fictions from most novels, they both give the user the chance to read every texton and scripton. From this perspective, hypertext fiction just complicates the reading process without rendering impossible the conventional goal of reading it all.[20] This complication or enstrangement (Sklovski) is also a strong indicator for hypertext fiction's inclusion in the traditions of experimental and avant-garde literature.

In a bigger picture, however, both interactive fiction and hypertext fiction and poetry are variant complications of the usual rhetoric of the reader's preordered progression (and occasional digest). The user navigates, gets lost and gets it right by either clicking links or typing commands, cannot take every possible path through the text or produce every possible event, but regardless of this lack of exhaustion the end is sooner or later at hand for the competent user capable of being helped by textual or paratextual cues and clues. The difference is that interactive fiction flirts with game conventions and marries them with literary conventions by adding the discourse level of negotiation and shaping it as a challenge. In this context, game conventions help domesticate the potentially endless variation by providing a goal for the process and relieving the reader–user–player from having to aesthetically contemplate every textual output. Instead, it is the use value of the inescapable variations and effectiveness towards the given goal of completing the puzzle that matter. This difference between "high" experimental and "low" game aesthetics in handling the user's progression goes a long way to explain the intense tribalism on both sides of the digital fiction divide and the resulting generic stagnation.

This leaves us with the metamorphic texts that seem to pose the greatest challenge to contemporary literary theory. Much like avant-garde literature, most of these texts can't be conveniently mapped onto existing textual and literary conventions, and in the lack of such acknowledged conventions the ways these texts behave and are consumed become theoretically enigmatic. The usual game conventions wouldn't seem to fit either as there's no point of resolution or winning, but luckily there are other applicable conventions.

In Aarseth's selection, there are at least seven texts that could be labeled as metamorphic: *The Unending Addventure*, *TinyMUD*, *Eliza*, *Cent Mille Milliards de Poèmes*, *Book Unbound*, *Racter*, and *Tale-Spin*. Queneau's poetry book is the most trivial of these: the user can almost effortlessly keep on producing poems one after another, at his own pace and in as many sessions as he likes, until he grows bored with the quality of the outcome or gets the general idea (that could be called a conceptual epiphany) or is already familiar with the centuries' long tradition of *ars combinatoria*. Inherent in this monotony, there is, however, a much more important qualitative structure at play: as individual poems are complete in themselves, they are, at least in principle, aesthetically rewarding independently of one another and the hypothesized yet unattainable whole. In other words, the metamorphic process is divided into small potentially rewarding steps or phases, rekindling one's love for fragments.

In this respect, the two story generators (*Racter* and *Tale-Spin*) work in much the same way, although the process of configuring them is more complicated than mere cutting and bending pages. In these texts, the output presents one complete and simple story at a time, after which it is time to configure the system again and let it produce another story. Even if this process of producing short stories and poems could, in principle, go on forever, it too is divided into clearcut phases and outcomes that are or could be potentially rewarding enough often enough. In short, in these simpler types of metamorphosis literary convention can be applied to each individual outcome (within a potentially endless series). The *Unending Addventure* isn't any more complicated, as it can be conceptualized according to both literary conventions (serialized story) and game conventions (its information for beginners describes it as a game).

Instead of literary and game conventions, *Eliza* and *TinyMUD* are more clearly organized around conventions of social communication such as dialog, polylog, improvisation and self-expression. The user may want to save *Eliza/Doctor*'s face or to trick it out of its pretended role as a Rogerian psychotherapist in the dialogue that can always be started anew, but the question and answer format keeps the process both familiar and well in balance. More than anything, this is based on *Eliza*'s non-human limitations, as the rhythm of its failures to make enough sense guarantees that individual sessions with it will not continue endlessly: it is usually better to start again than to continue failed communication for too long. So once again there are almost natural points of resolution and termination on a microlevel.

This is even clearer within *TinyMUD*, which is (or was) regulated both by the usual social conventions and their familiar and flexible rhythms, on the one hand, and the processes of autotelic textual construction of characters, objects, and rooms, on the other hand. Under such circumstances, it matters little that the user–player–writer–socializer cannot read everything, as the textual-social world is constructed and organized around other kinds of human activity, experience, encounter and expectation that will make the multiple metamorphic processes more familiar and meaningful (including missing or missed information).

After our short inventory[21] of literary conventions (reading the whole text or a series of self-contained fragments), game and puzzle conventions (completion; winning), social conventions (dialog; polylog; collective improvisation) and possibilities of self-expression channeling, domesticating, familiarizing and motivating variation, we are still left with *Book Unbound*.

However, *Book Unbound*, although it is a metamorphic text, is far from being strenuously difficult. It gives the user the chance to set his own goals for the process, but as he is not in full control of the cumulative process these goals are necessarily fuzzy (and not clearcut) and may well be or become impossible to achieve. Nevertheless, there still remains the process of slow and partial personalization that is both intentional (the segments the user chooses to feed back into the system as parts of the seed text presumably reflect his tastes and preferences) and unintentional (the user is not fully aware of the patterns of his choices and their effects) leading the user slowly towards realizing the consequences of his choices. Besides these long-term goals and processes, *Book Unbound* gives its user the opportunity to save the parts of the output he likes. This way the process goes from one satisfactory variation (or sequence) to another through less successful variations that still play their part in the process. This kind of cumulative filtering, selection and collecting could be seen to form a series of rewarding subgoals in the absence of an overall goal or point of resolution and compensating quite adequately for that absence. Finally, the whole process is turn based, and thus the user is not time pressed in making his choices (of what to feed back to the system as its additional textons) and can take a more meditative attitude towards the whole hologographic process of giving and giving back.

It seems then that the metamorphic texts we discussed are not completely disconnected from the applicable conventional frames and goals, short- and long-term rewards, and user objectives that make the metamorphic process meaningful, although in ways that may sometimes defy current literary theories.

Regarding conventions, the main dividing line seems to be situated between the discourse levels of events and progression, on the one hand, and the discourse levels of construction and quasi-events, on the other hand. The texts organized by the former put focus on some kind of pre-given goal, closure, end, or accessible totality. The texts organized more on the latter provide room for the rhythms and often self-asserted goals of the user's self-expression and its manifold manifestations as playing, improvisation, seduction, competition, collaboration and community building (etc.). The discourse level of negotiation can serve both ends of the scale. For our purposes in this chapter it is sufficient to see the resulting difference between the meta-conventions of reading and literary-ergodic self-expression (that can, of course, be combined, mixed and remixed like everything else in this study).

4.5 Attitudes

As always there are or may be simpler ways out. If one is having a typical single-user experience without the guidance of sufficiently strong literary, media, game or social conventions and can't read it all, then so what? In principle, one could be happy and content with one's partial reading. In hypertext theory, Jim Rosenberg (1996) proposed a concept of session as a new unit of reception and attention (i.e. reading and navigating until one's current interests are satisfied – or, presumably, thoroughly frustrated) to account for the difficulties in traversing the text and variations in the reading order the hypertext reader is or was supposed to struggle with. Despite that commonsense effort, the paradigm of reading it all (while complaining about it) still reigns, probably because well-informed readers (at least) know that it is possible to read every single unchanging node of *Afternoon*, *Patchwork Girl*, and *Victory Garden*. The case is a bit different in the later works of Stuart Moulthrop, especially in *Reagan Library* and *Pax*. The paratextual introduction to the latter tries to convince the reader–user of the impossibility of reading and experiencing it all (Moulthrop 2003b), which could also be read as both permission and instruction.

The shadow of the textual whole may still be hard to shake, but it is also ultimately dependent on what the user is personally seeking. Conventions and cognitive strategies are only one part of those preferences. More than two decades before Rosenberg, Roland Barthes drafted four pleasurable ways[22] in which readers could combine their reading neurosis with the hallucinated form of the text (the form we could claim is now an inevitable result from the invisible, inaccessible and hidden layers of digital, ergodic and potentially metamorphic texts):

> The fetishist would be matched with the divided-up text, the singling out of quotations, formulae, turns of phrase, with the pleasure of the word. The obsessive would experience the voluptuous release of the letter, of secondary, disconnected languages; of metalanguages ... A paranoiac would consume or produce complicated texts, stories developed like arguments, constructions posited like games, like secret constraints. As for the hysteric ... he would be the one who takes the text for ready money, who joins in the bottomless, truthless comedy of language, who is no longer the subject of any critical scrutiny and throws himself across the text (which is quite different from projecting himself into it). (Barthes 1975, 63)

CHAPTER 5

The enigma of the ergodic

5.1 Introduction

In *Cybertext*, Aarseth discusses the relations between ergodics, narrative and description using *Afternoon* as an example (1997, 94–5), and later discusses the relations and differences between narrative and ergodic discourses in the context of adventure games (ibid., 111–14, 124–7). In the former instance, the discussion is modeled after Genette's (1982a) insights in "The Frontiers of Narrative", based on which the ergodic is seen as a discourse level alongside narrative and description. The differentiation of these three levels results in a limited combinatory game (Aarseth 1997, 95): a game (football serving as an example) has only one level, the ergodic; a video game (*Pac-Man*, for example) has two, ergodics (the forced succession of events) and description (the screen icons); narratives have two (narrative and description); encyclopedias and user's manuals also two (ergodics and description); and *Afternoon* three (ergodics, narrative, description). These examples suggest that ergodics can coexist with the other types of discourse level, but exist on its own only outside literature and representational games. The questions of textual service and dominance are more complicated: in *Pac-Man*, the ergodic level dominates, whereas in *Afternoon*, the narrative and ergodic sides seem to be in conflict (or in other words balance) with one another, which means, among other things, that *Afternoon* cannot be taken to be a merely or dominantly narrative text.

In the latter instance, Aarseth distinguishes and theorizes several seminal differences in the communication structures of narrative and ergodic discourse.[1] These are most importantly related to the number of discourse levels: narratives have one (events and progression combined), hypertexts two (events and progression as two separate layers), and adventure games and other determinate[2] cybertexts three (events, negotiation and progression). In Aarseth's discussion of MUDs (1997, 157), two more discourse levels are added: quasi-events and construction. In the context of the cybertext typology, Aarseth (1997, 65) calls media positions genre positions, and in a later paper (1999) he talks about a variety of ergodic modes that include computer games and poetry generators among many others.

Based on these suggestions and references, this chapter considers how the ergodic or ergodics should be conceptualized or, more to the point, what kind of literature ergodic literature is. Is it a text type (or a series of text types) that cannot be subsumed under argument, description and narrative, or a newly recognized mode (or a series of modes) alongside dramatic, narrative and other modes, or a genre system of its own, or something more complicated than these three fuzzy and contested but traditional conceptual categories address and presuppose? We already know that the ergodic side can coexist and be combined with traditional text types (argument, description and narrative), but how to properly theorize these relationships is another matter.[3]

There are additional questions as well. Although Aarseth's focus is on ergodic literature, the typology of textual communication contains six variables that can equally well describe both ergodic and non-ergodic texts, as the distinction between the latter is based only on one variable: the user function. Should we say, for example, that indeterminate or transient texts form a text type or a cybertextual genre of their own? Should Simon Biggs' *The Great Wall of China* (2000), which randomizes sentences from Kafka's well-known story of the same title, be classified as a narrative or a random text because randomness is arguably its most important textual feature (although it literalizes the main themes in Kafka's story)? Do digital textual movies (such as John Cayley's *windsound*) form a genre or do they belong to the transmedial genre of kinetic poetry along with video and film poetry?

Before going more deeply into these ergodic and cybertextual subthemes, it is important to state that, in this study, the questions raised about text types, discourse types, discourse modes, genres and macro-genres (the definitions of which vary and overlap from theorist to theorist) are not based on or directed towards any worn-out ideas of purity. Instead, the goal is to see more clearly the interplay between recognizable textual types, modes and organizations on different levels in a situation in which the text's behavioral repertoire has considerably expanded from what was recognized by print-oriented theories of literature. It is equally important to avoid assuming that ergodic phenomena form a homogenous field that can be reduced to one mode, genre, meta-genre, discourse type or text type. The range of ergodic phenomena is not limited to literature and arts,[4] dominantly ergodic works are often games, and practices and influences continuously migrate from one field to another. Therefore this chapter moves into two directions, cybertextually expanding (and reorganizing) the field of architextuality, and specifying the ergodic variety within it.[5]

After these clarifications, we'll first see what happens when we try to situate ergodic literature on the map based on Genette's insights on architextuality, modes and genres, Monika Fludernik's (1996; 2000) theories of macro-genres, genres and discourse types, and Seymour Chatman's (1990) ideas of textual service and dominance between major text types. The choice of these scholars is eclectic, but it also covers the most important concepts in use whenever the questions of "kind" are and have to be asked beginning with genre, mode and text type. The choice also reflects the cultural hegemony of narratives: Genette, Chatman, and Fludernik are prominent narratologists[6] and the interests of the last two in text types are motivated by their attempts to define and delimit narrative by comparing it to other text types.[7]

5.2 Genette, genres, and modes

To Genette, architextuality is the most abstract and implicit type of transtextuality, a purely taxonomic relation between singular texts and general categories such as "types of discourse, modes of enunciation, literary genres" (Genette 1997a, 1). Genette admits that this relationship is implicit and open to historical fluctuations, but that doesn't reduce its significance, because generic perception significantly guides and determines the readers' expectations. Architextuality is not reduced to the generic,[8] although Genette devotes most of *The Architext* to clearing up the confusion between genres and modes that has haunted western poetics for centuries and later (2005, 11) summarizes architextuality as "relations between texts and the genres to which one assigns them more or less legitimately."

To Genette (1992, 64), modes are modes or basic stances of enunciation – a linguistic category – not to be confused with genres that are "properly literary categories." Their relation is not one of simple inclusion, as genres cut across modes and individual works cut across genres and "modes and themes, intersecting, jointly include and determine genres" (ibid., 73). Genette ends up adding formal constants (in prose/in verse) to his tabular model of the generic system that now has three parameters (thematic, formal and modal) defining genres. Also the number of modes increases to include a non-representational mode or modes for direct expression (such as poetry and essay) that were already discussed in "The Frontiers of Narrative" (Genette 1982a, 137–8).

As the possible ergodic level of a text cannot be (properly) theorized by any linguistic criteria (syntactical, semantic or pragmatic) – what would be a prototypical ergodic sentence?[9] – ergodic texts cannot constitute a mode or modes using Genette's criteria. The ergodic is a category of user action[10] (be it work or play or anything in between) and not of language use. However, by going into the Platonic roots of this idea we could reach a considerably different "modal" criteria based on, according to Genette's interpretation, situations of enunciation (Genette 1992, 12) that are broader than the purely linguistic criterion because they are also used to separate drama from narrative. From a cybertextual perspective, the media positions define and determine at least one aspect of any situation of enunciation (cf. whether it is ergodic or interpretative) and that could serve as a point of contact and combination.

Still, the question is more complex. Genette's discourse on the architext is for the most part a treatise on the history of western poetics beginning with Plato and Aristotle and especially the latter's division between two modes of representing or imitating action: the dramatic and the narrative. The whole sad and unimpressive history of this project until the latter half of the 20th century seems to boil down to various attempts at adding Aristotle's most obvious omission, lyrical poetry, to the generic and modal system. The second possible point of contact between cybertext theory and the origins of western poetics would be the worn-out concept of imitation of action. As both determinate and indeterminate cyber-texts have close ties to simulation (Aarseth 1994, 79), what would happen if simulation as a dynamic form of representation is added on top of this poorly managed poetics project?

In principle, we'd then have dynamic representations of events and existents (simulations), direct and static representations of events and existents (drama), and indirect and static representa-tions of events and existents (narrative). From this perspective, the field of ergodic literature is immediately split into simulative and non-simulative modes roughly corresponding to the difference between dynamic and static ergodic texts, the latter (and with it hypertext fiction) obviously more easily connectible to the existing generic and modal systems and taxonomies in literary studies. Still, the obvious problem with this kind of theoretization is its reliance on the outdated ideas linking genres to imitation and representation.

Genre is a hopelessly contested and historically fluctuating concept within which multiple theoretical and practical interests are in a permanently unresolved conflict,[11] but, as luck would have it, our interests in genre can be reduced to two questions. First, to inquire whether the cybertext typology and ergodic literature can be connected with genre at all, as this question has to be asked anyway – or to put it in another way, the rising prominence of ergodic literature and its inner heterogeneity neces-sarily activates taxonomic, architextual and generic dimensions and aspirations and will continue to do so until the relationship between non-ergodic and ergodic literature becomes less unclear and problematic. Second, as generic, parageneric, and metageneric categories will, in any case, divide the literary field in all directions (Genette 2005, 8), it is not a priori impossible that similar kinds of criterion could also be used and applied to classify and divide the field of ergodic literature with more precision than that offered by the three very broad categories of explorative, configurative, and textonic user function.[12]

To begin with, Aarseth's typology of textual communication is a typology of textual machines and textual behavior. As any text can be situated within it based on how its medium functions, the typology describes a constant and almost transhistorical field of options (although its openness leaves room for future developments in this expanding field). It could be integrated as a fourth "constant" or parameter within Genette's genre system, which would then specify genres using four criteria, modal, thematic, formal and behavioral. The relative weight of these criteria varies from text to text and as always there'll be enough room for well-grounded disagreement. Thus the questions Aarseth (1997, 84) asked: "In what sense can a hypertext be a narrative? Is hypertext a literary genre or a literary technique?" could be answered (or left unanswered) in two conflicting ways by emphasizing either the modal (such as narrative) or the behavioral (ergodic) criteria. *Afternoon* would be either a hypernovel (belonging to a narrative genre of novel and to its relatively new subgenre) or a hypertext fiction (as a type of ergodic discourse).

Of course, the number of genre defining criteria could be increased even more by adding audience-related pragmatic categories to the more traditional syntactic and semantic ones as suggested by film theorist Rick Altman (1999). Whatever the number of such criteria, the force and weight of each will necessarily vary from text to text, reader to reader, context to context and period to period, which calls for other kinds of research, and one may well end up asking as Genette did whether the genre system is necessary at all. The answer depends very much on what one hopes it will be used to achieve.

From a more pragmatic point of view (within which the concept of genre has a certain unavoidable use value despite the insurmountable difficulties in defining it) genres are categories of conventions and expectations forming a kind of pragmatic rule of thumb vocabulary shared by authors and readers, or producers and consumers, facilitating their communication. In this sense, the genre system or systems definitely exist and are always already in use, as neither consumers nor producers can escape traditions and prior experiences (this includes many avant-garde and experimental works too, because frequently used labels such as surrealist, lettrist or Oulipian evoke different aesthetic, stylistic and "generic" expectations). From this perspective, it is clear that ergodic literature is not a genre, but already contains many genres, each with a different set of expectations and conventions – especially in digital media.

As we saw in Chapter 4, these conventions and expectations are not necessarily only literary but are also related to puzzles, games, roleplaying, collective improvisation, social interaction, and self-expression. Already for these reasons tentative ergodic genres such as dialogue programs, text adventures, MUDs, text generators and textual instruments differ both from one another and from the always already contested system of more or less firmly defined literary genres. This is not to say that the two don't share any features with each other – just that, for instance, reading fantasy literature and roleplaying in a fantasy environment organized as a MUD come with different sets of conventions, expectations and, most of all, requirements, although there are semantic and thematic similarities between the two texts.

More importantly, the genre-related analysis of non-ergodic texts is limited to heterogeneous and both synchronically and diachronically varying criteria of inclusion and exclusion; by definition ergodic questions, such as those concerning the homogeneous and non-negotiable requirements the text places on its users, the heterogeneity of skills, and either successful or failing strategies, do not even arise. Ergodic and cybertextual requirements should not be confused with conventions guiding and aiding interpretation, although both direct and influence the user's expectations.

To sum up, cybertextual specifications (the media positions and discourse levels) could be added as a new type of constant to more traditional parameters defining genre, especially if genres are seen from the consumption side of readers' and users' activities, as textual behavior certainly affects and directs expectations and creates its own conventions. Ergodic texts add non-negotiable requirements to the necessarily variable, more or less fuzzy, and to some degree hypothetical and exchangeable conventions and expectations and thus have genre characteristics that are empirically verifiable to a much higher degree than is the case with genres of non-ergodic literature. As long as modes are linguistically defined the ergodic, whatever it is, is not a mode or a series of them. If modes are seen as modes of representation the situation is different, as some ergodic texts display modes of simulation. Moreover, the ergodic is a category of user action to be taken into account alongside other types of action, giving us a new modal trinity of (re)presented action, imitated action, and user action, or, to avoid the representational fallacy, a duality of action presentations and user action, or to make room for poetry, there finally remains a duality of literary presentations and user action.

5.3 Fludernik: macro-genres, genres, and discourse types

Monika Fludernik (1996) tries to solve the problem of text types and genres using a three-level construction of meta-genres, genres, and discourse types (called discourse modes in Fludernik 2000). To her (1996, 356–8) meta-genres are related to basic forms and needs of human communication: phatic communication (conversation), rhetorical suasion (argument), practical orientation (instruction), and the narrative reworking of experience (narrative). In a later article, Fludernik (2000) considers adding one meta- or macro-genre,[13] the reflective, to these four to account for and include metalinguistically oriented poetry. In her model, discourse types such as argument, description and narrative (in the sense of event reports) are not classes of texts like meta-genres but parts or segments of specific texts that can be flexibly combined with one another. Between these microlevel combinations and meta-genres Fludernik situates text types that are equal to historically fluctuating genres.

The most obvious weakness in Fludernik's theory is that its four or five meta-genres are based on "naturally" occurring discourses. In all too familiar logocentric fashion, they correspond to "discourse functions observed in oral language" (Fludernik 2000), and literature, which is Fludernik's main concern, is first reduced to communication and then to clearcut prototypes drawn from oral communication. Fludernik's broad pragmatic and somewhat ideal[14] categories seem to a priori exclude and ignore possible meta-genres and discourse functions that occur only in written language and perhaps only in networked and programmable literary media. Even on this reduced level Fludernik's model runs into trouble with (non-narrative) poetry that she admits she doesn't know how to situate in the model (1996, 358). Also, in her model the overlaps between conversation and narrative are left without convincing answer.[15] Play, roleplay, ritual, riddles, and other verbal entertainment, among other social and communicative practices with pronounced verbal aspects, are not included in her basic communicative categories either, with the result of further reducing the scope of communication and discourse functions. Fludernik's meta-genres are related to non-mediated communication between humans, not to communication between humans and text machines or mediated communication between humans in programmed and programmable textual environments, which form the proper realm of cybertextuality and ergodic literature.[16]

Theoretically, the rationale for constructing the level of macro-genres is similar to that for Genette's modes: to find a set of relatively constant variables that could regulate and organize the multifaceted and chaotic field of genres and make it more manageable from a scholarly point of view. If we try to combine and compare Fludernik's four or five communicative categories and discourse functions with Aarseth's typology of textual communi-cation, we can make at least three kinds of preliminary observation.

First, the latter typology is oriented towards textual commu-nication that is not necessarily limited to literature (however we wish to define it), and which thus also provides a field or a level more constant than the one of genres, and a model not grounded in the limitations of oral communication. Second, most examples given of the meta-genres take place within a very limited number of non-ergodic media positions. Fludernik's model of text types, like most other models, separates interplaying linguistic surface struc-tures and local text types from the constructed set of global ones somehow controlling and reducing the plurality of the former. In light of possible ergodic genres such as MUDs, this reduction seems to be rather pointless as there is no valid way to unify their social, aesthetic, ludic and simulated aspects under any one overarching text type or macro-genre; instead, they should be seen as a new mode of communication (see also Aarseth 2006, 856). In short, the existing theories of text type can very well handle linear texts, but not textual machines producing a variety of expression and multiuser textual environments that are not distributed in copies but realized in communities and communicative acts between human participants.

Third, we can obviously find narrative, instructive, argumentative, "communicative," and reflective elements in ergodic texts, but there they are both organized and accompanied by elements that the theories of macro-genres and text types don't address and recognize. Instructions will illustrate the point. Should machinic instructions be included in Fludernik's model as well in order to situate programmed texts within it? If they are included, then (machinic) instructions are the only dominant text type in digital literature (as the texts couldn't exist and function without it) or perhaps they should form yet another reductive level of meta-meta-genre(s).

To conclude, if there's a need to construct a theoretical level beyond genres and generic expectations, on the one hand, and the interplay of text types or discourse types in empirical texts, on the other, then instead of postulating ideal types derived from oral communication, a more solid and also empirically verifiable level could be borrowed from the cybertextual typology of textual communication. Based on this, another three-tiered model could be constructed with levels of textual communication (specified by cybertext theory), genres, and surface level discourse modes (to be specified by linguistics). The obvious benefit is that this model contains only one fuzzy and disorganized level (of genres) instead of two (Fludernik's genres and macro-genres).

5.4 Chatman and text types, services and functions

In his groundbreaking approach to narrative and other text types, Seymour Chatman (1990, 6–73) separates surface representation from underlying structures and introduces the idea of textual service. Chatman's three text types argument, description and narrative routinely serve one another: "Narrators of novels routinely digress to describe or argue, describers to narrate and argue, and arguers to narrate or describe" (Chatman 1990, 10). The surface forms of argument, description and narrative serve functions specified by the text's underlying structure: for example, in Robbe-Grillet's *La Jalousie* the narrative function is actualized by mainly descriptive sentences (Chatman 1990, 21). As such the differences between Narratives, Arguments, and Description[17] are clear:

> "But unlike Narrative chrono-logic, Argumentative logic is not temporal. And unlike Description, Argument rests not on contiguity, but on some stronger, usually more abstract ground such as that of consequentiality." (Chatman 1990, 10)

Clear as this model is, there are at least five potential problems within it. First, how do we know or decide what overall function the surface forms serve, as their purposes cannot be decided by linguistic criteria. Chatman's answer (1990, 21) is based on overall sense and rewards: "We understand it as subservient to Narrative when the text makes more overall sense and rewards us more richly as a narrative than as a description." This is vague: in mainstream cases the question doesn't arise and when it does, say in the context of the French New Novel, then there seems to be an irreducible difference of opinion concerning the function and status of narrative and description. Contrariwise, the rewards and overall sense depend much on generic and other expectations and conventions, reducing the number of necessary levels to two: local surface sentences defined by linguistics, and global structures and purposes defined by pragmatically oriented literary studies. Ergodic literature is then, in principle, easy to situate in this model, as the purposes served don't have to be linguistically definable text types.

In MUDs, roleplaying, questing and textual construction (of objects and characters) are at the center of textual action and dominate possible narrative, argumentative and descriptive passages and exchanges. Similarly, even if single-player text adventures are overwhelmed by descriptions, the latter do not serve descriptive purposes there but instead support the completion of the quest, i.e. the ergodic ends and designs of the global text. In hypertext fiction, the service/function/surface triangle is harder to decide but in ergodic print texts, the mild ergodic features seem to serve narrative (as in *Hopscotch*) and lyric poetry (in *Calligrammes* and *Cent Mille Milliards de Poèmes*). In short, in addition to Chatman's three major text types to be served (i.e. that exist on the level of the overall design of empirical texts) there exist several ergodic purposes as well. Many of these can be almost directly derived from the four additional communicative levels (progression, negotiation, quasi-event and construction) cybertext theory introduces: puzzles, games, dialogue, roleplay, improvisation and construction that all inseparably connect the types of text to the types or modes of user activity.

Second, is service the only possible relation between text types? In many more or less experimental cases, it is equally commonplace or "natural" to think that the text types are either in balance (i.e. they are all equal and neither dominant nor subservient)[18] or else sabotage and undermine one another or perhaps exist as autonomous compartments within the same text.

Third, as theories of text types are closely related to the definition of narrative (at least in Chatman and Fludernik), we could ask if it is sufficient to compare narrative to the other classic text types. From the ergodic and cybertextual perspective the core of the problem is that if narrative is compared only to these other (two or three)[19] text types it easily receives a monopoly over temporal representation of events. As we'll see later, this kind of sloppy reasoning and culturally and historically limited contextualization excludes games, simulations, ergodic arts and ergodic literature from the relevant comparison, although the last have several ways to represent time and temporal relationships[20] including the famous double chronologic of narratives. As an example, if the whole lifespan of our solar system were dynamically represented in a 15- to 30-minute simulation, we'd have the different durations of the simulation and the simulated to compare.

Fourth, if we focus on the microlevel forms that serve greater purposes (Argument, Description or Narrative), we can probably find many more surface forms than the three mirroring forms Chatman's model includes (argument, description and narrative and only them again): lists, puns, crossword puzzles, riddles,[21] recipes (Harry Matthews' *Country Cooking*), and questionnaires to begin with, not to mention instances of lyric (i.e. non-narrative) poetry. Many ergodic and non-ergodic texts display operational or broken code on their surface, which is another obvious addition to the plurality of surface forms. By the same token, the two level heuristics will function regardless of the number of the new text types included in either the serving or served side – or both. Finally, there are limitations to how far these services can go. It is impossible to construct a narrative text by using only argumentative and descriptive sentences because of the latter's atemporal nature; there can't be global narratives without at least one narrative sentence with a temporal junction.[22]

5.5 The enigma of the ergodic

If the vocabulary of genres, modes, and text types were applied to organize the field of cybertextuality and to ergodic literature we'd easily end up outside the existing conceptual maps. In *Cybertext*, four to seven ergodic genres were discussed and situated into a larger typology: hypertext fiction, adventure games, story generators and MUDs, a list to which one could add language generators (such as *Book Unbound*), conversation/dialogue programs (such as *Eliza* and *Racter*), and presumably also hypertext poetry (such as Jim Rosenberg's *Intergrams*) that is only mentioned in *Cybertext*. Holopoetry, biopoetry, locative texts and CAVE works are also suitable generic candidates. The syntax of the ergodic genres is described as non-tropic figures[23] in "Nonlinearity and Literary Theory" (Aarseth 1994, 80): forking, jumping/linking, permutation, computation and polygenesis.[24] If genres are defined by syntactic, semantic[25] and pragmatic criteria, this list could serve as a preliminary catalogue of the syntactical modes of the ergodic organization of texts.

As cybertextuality is closely connected to the themes of communication and control, these two dimensions that underlie the typology of textual communication without being explicitly introduced into it as variables deserve another look. The most important aspect of control is the control of the traversal function. In ergodic print texts, the user performs all the operations, but in digital ergodic texts, the user's operative role is specified, limited and shared by the algorithms of the text machine.

In some ergodic texts such as MUDs, users communicate and roleplay with each other within a simulated textual world. Simulated worlds, objects, and characters also exist in single-user interactive fiction. The role of the communication with other human users and simulated entities thus forms another useful variable with enough explanatory power to make a clear difference between the aforementioned genres and print and hypertext literature. Ergodic texts either include communication between human users as a necessary part of their realization or they don't. If they don't, the user communicates with either simulated or non-simulated entities as a necessary part of the realization of the ergodic text. This dimension could be further specified by studying the five discourse levels (events, progression, negotiation, quasi-events, and construction) in more detail.

Ergodic texts also differ considerably from one another in the relations between textons and scriptons. In some cases, they are identical, while in other cases, the difference between them is both crucial and impenetrable to the common user. In print texts, the user has full access to textons as they can't be concealed from him. These fully transparent texts are then texts with perfect information and the less transparent texts that deny full access to textons are texts with imperfect information.

Finally, ergodic texts have also several modes of material existence: they can exist as multiple objects (books, CDs, diskettes), single objects (web fictions), ephemeral performances (such as Dadaist acts at Cabaret Voltaire provoking observers to participate in the action) and ephemeral communities (like MUDs). In this respect, both texts and text machines (such as *Eliza*) usually outlive more ephemeral textual environments (such as *TinyMUD* that lasted less than a year).

Taken together these modes of organization, control, communication, information, and existence determine the ergodic syntax of both real and possible ergodic genres that share their other syntactic, semantic, and thematic determinants with already existing literary, ludic and film (and other audiovisual) genres. The pragmatic determinants of ergodic genres are divided into conventions and expectations shaped by one or several user objectives and discourse levels, on the one hand, and non-negotiable requirements,on the other hand. The requirements are both idiosyncratic (i.e. text specific) and generic. Cybertext typology offers at least four broad categories of requirements: explorative, configurative and textonic user functions and personal perspective and even more if user positions are taken into account.

Probably the easiest way to apply the typology of textual communication in the grey taxonomic matters of genre division in the broader cybertextual perspective (including all media positions, not just the ergodic ones) is to see whether any value of the parameters that is different from the prototypical print parameters assumes an overwhelmingly dominant role in a group of empirical texts. The closest candidates for new text types or genre (in addition to those already described or mentioned in *Cybertext*) would then be globally random (indeterminate) texts in which randomness mostly serves itself, textual movies (a transient non-ergodic genre)   and perhaps site-specific textual installations that demand kinetic and bodily creativity from their cyber users. Alternatively, one could see whether there are texts that build on the tension between print parameters and their alternatives – for example ergodic transient-intransient texts mixing temporary and permanent elements.

There is no obvious way to end the kind of taxonomic survey begun in this chapter. We have found several possible ways of integrating the fields of ergodic and non-ergodic literature, on the one hand, and dividing the field of ergodic literature, on the other, without necessarily preferring any one solution.

The field of ergodic literature as discussed by Aarseth is extremely heterogeneous, but as we saw in our discussion of conventions and textual wholes, the field gravitates towards two or three sets of basic conventions: literary, social and gaming. As the social aspects are most of all related to roleplaying and self-expression, we could divide the field of ergodic textuality roughly in two (mirroring our findings in the previous chapter): literary texts and machines for self-expression. The former half mostly includes hypertext fiction and poetry (and ergodic poetry in general) and poetry[26] and story generators with a few possible exceptions and borderline cases such as *Book Unbound*. In addition to dialogue programs and textual instruments,[27] the latter half includes interactive fiction and MUDs that became research objects for ludology and (digital) game studies, both of which were established after the publication of *Cybertext*.

After this division of scholarly labor between literary and game studies, the hypothetical field of ergodic studies would become necessarily cross-disciplinary, and within it the perspectives of ludology and game studies will add much needed conceptual tools that are necessary and indispensable in more in-depth comparisons between three kinds of practice: dominantly ergodic (games), ergodic, and non-ergodic. In what follows, we begin with non-ergodic narrative practices, discuss them in relation to the ergodic, then move to games and finally try to synthesize our findings from these three areas in flux in terms of mode-centred transmedial ecologies.

CHAPTER 6

Towards cybertextual narratology

6.1 Introduction: the amalgam of narratologies

This part of the book (Chapters 6 to 11) focuses on narrative texts and narrative poetics. Its goal is to produce a medium-independent cybertextual literary narratology that is able to account for the expansion and multiplication of narrative possibilities and practices, especially in networked and programmable media, relative to the possibilities and practices that both classical and postclassical narratologies recognize and are able to recognize due to their more or less understandable[1] orientation towards print literature. In short, these narratologies are mainly based on narrative texts and the narrative possibilities inherent in texts that are static, determinate, intransient, and have random access, impersonal perspective, no links and interpretative user function.

This limitation offers us two broad directions of expansion, ergodic and non-ergodic, without preferring one to the other or assuming that only "interactive" narratives matter or constitute a novelty. Moreover, a dynamic and transient text supplementing and varying its expression and controlling the temporal logic of its presentation and accessibility is challenging with or without the user's ergodic activity and personal perspective (with which it can easily be combined). Non-ergodic expansions are less controversial and theoretically more legitimate, as with them we do not need to take into account the possible clash between ergodic and narrative layers that will be discussed in Chapters 11 and 12. Thus in Chapters 8 to 10, the non-ergodic expansions have the upper hand.

As we saw in the previous chapter, ergodic literature is not easily situated within the current variety of text types and literary modes. In that it resembles another relatively well-known group of texts: the status of so-called anti- or non-narratives is also unclear, as they don't seem to belong to any recognized text type except narrative, but are for various reasons excluded even from the advanced late 20th century narratologies. Hence anti-narrative has almost become and could certainly be seen as a text type in its own right: a categorical and convenient wastepaper basket for texts that are too experimental to fit nicely within any established system of text types.[2]

These texts share the shady status of experimental literature with texts at the more literary end of ergodic literature, ergodic poetry and hypertext fiction. This is not much of a problem for ergodic poetry; poetry seems to be accepted as poetry regardless of its medium or difficulty, and categories such as anti-poetry seem to be unnecessary. The case of potential digital "anti-narratives" such as hypertext fiction is considerably different. These texts definitely contain narrative layers, but they also seem to contain certain other elements[3] that clash with the many familiar and already recognized and adequately theorized narrative features. Much like postmodernist fiction, therefore, hypertext fiction is potentially narrative but actually outside serious narratological pursuits. Until recently hypertexts were only rarely discussed by competent narratologists, and, as a result hypertext fiction's theoretical contribution to various narratologies has so far been almost non-existent.[4]

This situation poses a problem for us. Without first integrating postmodernist, Oulipian and other experimental narratives into the narratological framework, to be later modified by cybertext theory and empirical counterexamples, we can't reliably study the interplay between ergodic and narrative layers and compare games and narratives. We can't even compare print narratives with literary narratives (i.e. literary narratives in any medium) with necessary precision. Hence a more inclusive literary narratology (also with respect to other actual and possible narratologies such as film narratology) should be constructed. This is easier said than done, and several difficult choices have to be made.

As narrative is a contested concept, we need to pay attention to several competing definitions of it, and especially to their possible shortcomings in the face of games and simulations that are also capable of representing events in sequence (which is probably the most common determining feature of narrative). Narratologies also abound; the comparatively unified field of classical narratology of the 1960s and 1970s has given way to a variety of postclassical narratologies to choose from and combine. Third, the spread of narratology or narratologies from literary to film studies and then after the so-called narrative and cognitive turns to a multitude of other fields and disciplines in the human and social sciences needs to be recognized, especially as a later chapter will discuss the role of narrative, narrativity and narratologies in the emerging field of game studies. At the core of this expansion are questions concerning narrative transmediality. In the rest of this chapter, we'll steer a course through or past these fundamental choices and adapt the necessarily eclectic choices to the main points of departure of this study.

6.2 Points of departure

As the general focus of this study is on poetics (as a sum of possibilities) and not on interpretation, cognitive theories (and speculations) in regard to the top-down interpretative frames that readers use to narrativize texts are only of secondary interest to us. In short, we are more interested in narrative texts than in the narrativity that many postclassical cognitive narratologies foreground (cf. Fludernik 1996; Herman 2002; Ryan 1991). Also, the state and scope of postclassical narratologies matter, as they too tend to exclude experimental and postmodernist narratives from consideration[5] (with the notable exception of Fludernik 1996, discussed later). The cognitively hypothesized "model" readers of postclassical narratology do not (and apparently would not know how to) read experimental narrative literature, at least while the top-down cognitive parameters and principles (such as frames, scripts and preference rules) to be applied are derived only from real-world events, situations and communications that experimental written narratives very rarely respect. Due to our orientation towards poetics, we cannot exclude experimental literary narratives from consideration regardless of their medium; by doing so we would run the risk of losing sight of the already existing narrative possibilities and practices and of misplacing the claims of novelty that the expansion of literary narratology from one (or very few) to several media positions is likely to cause.

Quite simply then, both modernist and postmodernist print narratives (including the experimental ones hard to classify one way or the other) are taken to form the core cultural heritage of print narrative, and any narratology that cannot address both of them falls automatically under suspicion. Luckily for us, classical and postclassical narratologies are equally guilty in this respect;[6] hence we have no other choice but to be eclectic and pragmatic in our choices and combinations of narratologies. This is not as complicated as it may seem, because classical and postclassical narratologies are not mutually exclusive: the latter are partly engaged in scrutinizing the concepts and theoretical premises of the former and developing and modifying them. Moreover, from our point of view they both lack something precisely because they have limited themselves to print literature. As one major consequence, the flexible ways of manipulating time in digital media have not informed theories of events, actions and time in either type of narratology. The same is true with the novelties and complexities in the transmission and communication of textual (including narrative) information.

The choices of narratology we'll make are ultimately based on empirically observable textual behaviors that run counter to what the existing theories presume and thus undermine their descriptive and explanatory power. These examples provide the starting points for Chapters 8, 9 and 10, which present the essentials of cybertextual narratology. As postmodernist, Oulipian and other experimental narrative fictions are not properly included in the narratological theories discussed in this chapter, the next chapter will discuss them separately in the double context of cybertext theory and the amalgam of definitions, narratologies, and transmedialities constructed in the remainder of this chapter.

6.3 Definitions and positions

In order to situate our discourse more precisely within the field of competing narratologies, we'll use the questions and alternatives presented in the entry called "Narrative" in *Routledge Encyclopedia of Narrative Theory* (2005) as a device for our conceptual navigation. This entry, written by Marie-Laure Ryan, presents six current problems of narrative and narrativity (we'll come back to the validity of this concept and its relation to narrative).

(1) "Does narrative vary according to culture and historical period, or do the fundamental conditions of narrativity constitute cognitive universals?" (Ryan 2005, 345): Here we choose the former option, for the lack of well-defined claims in favor of the latter[7] despite massive cognitive speculation on the subject. The options are not mutually exclusive though; narrative form can be understood to be both universal (or transcultural in the sense that narratives are to some degree translatable from one culture to another), at least in its simplest or most basic forms and necessarily varying and developing according to its changing contexts, cultures, theories, traditions and aesthetic inventions, which also explains Ryan's observation that theories of narrative evolved rather slowly (although this claim can already be undermined by Aristotle's *Poetics*).

(2) "Does narrative presuppose a verbal act of *narration by an anthropomorphic creature called a *narrator, or can a story be told without the mediation of a narratorial consciousness? Gerald Prince ... defines narrative as the representation of real or fictive events by one or more narrators to one or more *narratees. The opposite position is represented by the film scholar David Bordwell, who argues that film narration does not require a narratorial figure ... Some scholars have attempted to reconcile the narrator-based definition with the possibility of non-verbal narration by analyzing drama and movie as presupposing the utterance of a narratorial

figure, even when the film or the play does not make use of *voice-over narration (Chatman 1990)" (Ryan 2005, 346): We'll assume a modified anthropomorphic position (the necessity of narrators and narratees) and hence accept Prince's definition of literary narrative because they are better than the alternative. Bordwell's definition (1985, 83) disregards the narrator–narratee axis for obvious reasons and is far too broad: "A narrative is a chain of events in cause-effect relationship occurring in time and space. A narrative is thus what we usually mean by term 'story'." This definition conflates narratives with chains of events, and grants narratives an almost absolute monopoly for representing events; a film showing sunrise and sunset would constitute a narrative. Simulations and performance art (usually taken to be non-narrative) also present chains of events in cause–effect relationship occurring in time and space. Bordwell's definition also equates narratives with stories which further trivializes matters. As there are no specific narrative contents (Genette 1988, 16) we have to disregard Bordwell's point of view.

Ryan's two options seem also to be less than accurately summarized, as both the assumption of narrators being anthropomorphic (Chatman's film narrator is not anthropomorphic) and the idea of a narratorial consciousness don't have to enter the scene at all. More seriously, Ryan's trick question confuses narratives and stories (the content or the signified of narratives). The latter can be either narrated or presented on stage or film – a view advocated by both Genette's (1988, 16) insistence of situating narrative's specificity in its mode and Chatman's (1990, 113) distinction between tellers and showers of stories. Moreover, Chatman's and Genette's views support the idea that the transmedial entity is not narrative but story – a decisive point to which we'll return.

(3) "Can the feature of narrativity be isolated as a layer or dimension of meaning, or is it a global effect toward which every element of the text makes a contribution? The first position makes it legitimate to divide the text into narrative parts that move the plot forward and non-narrative parts where time stands still, such as digressions, philosophical considerations, or the moral of a *fable ... But this analysis runs into difficulties in the case of descriptions: while extensive *descriptions can be skipped without causing the reader to lose track of the plot, *characters, and settings could not be identified without descriptive statements ... If

the purpose of narrative is to evoke not just a sequence of events but the worlds in which these events take place ... then descriptions cannot be excluded from the narrative layer, and the distinction between narrative and non-narrative elements is blurred" (Ryan 2005, 346).

It is hard to deny that texts are both thematically and formally heterogeneous. As we saw in the previous chapter, many narra-tologists see narratives, commentaries, and descriptions working together in the text. To them, the possible blurs between non-narrative and narrative segments or layers isn't much of an issue, as overall designations such as "narrative" are pragmatic and refer both to generic conventions and the relations between text types. That is, if the other text types seem to serve narrative and the narrative segments dominate, then the text is of narrative type. The standard two-level model of text types (separating surface or local instances from the overall design) settles the issue as far as it can be settled. Should we choose to follow Chatman (1990), it is easy to distinguish between narrative, argumentative and descriptive passages on the local level and on the global level the aesthetic teleology is up to interpretation, but only between three major positions (argument, description, narrative) and not among a multitude of unique teleologies as Ryan suggests.

If we are talking about the meaning and interpretation of the text, then necessarily everything that is in the text (be it commen-taries, arguments, descriptions or narrative sequences) contributes to it. It also seems questionable to assume that the purpose of narrative is also to evoke the worlds in which the events take place, for at least two reasons. First, some narratives do this and others don't, which makes it a question of degree and a contingent condition for the narrative. Second, assumptions of purpose raise serious methodological questions, if the supposed purpose is taken to be more than just a projective interpretation varying from reader to reader, audience to audience and period to period.

(4) "Is narrativity a matter of form or a matter of content? The proponents of narrativity as form ... radicalize the ideas of Hayden White, who argues that a given sequence of historical events can be represented either as an unstructured list (*annals), as a *chronicle obeying certain principles of unity but lacking a comprehensive explanatory principle, or as a fully formed plot (= narrative), in which events are organized according to a global teleology. But if

historical events can be made into stories as well as into something else ..., doesn't narrative require specific types of raw materials?" (Ryan 2005, 346).

Here, too, Ryan chooses to ignore Genette's well-known argument (1988, 16) for formal and modal narratology – that there are no specific narrative contents. Second, she seems to see a problem in turning one substance into more than just one form, as if the same events can't be turned into games, drama, lists, and simulations of many kinds – which happens every day. Therefore it is unclear what the actual problem is.

(5) "Should a definition of narrative give equal status to all works of literary fiction, or should it regard certain types of postmodern novels (and films) as marginal? ... [D]oes an avant-garde text that refers to characters, settings, and events, but refuses to organize these contents into a determinate story expand the meaning of narrative, making it historically variable, or does it simply demonstrate the separability of the concepts of 'literature', 'narrative', and 'fiction'?" (Ryan 2005, 346).

The problem with the latter assumption is its equation of narrative and narrativity with mainstream modernism (at best) without giving any reason why the historical development of narrative should have stopped there. Narrative theory almost always lags decades behind narrative practices, as the 50- to 60-year distance between Proust and Genette already shows. As the prime examples of postmodernist novel were published less than 60 years ago, it may still be too early to tell. In any case, Ryan's "deter-minate story" as a criterion runs the risk of reducing narrativity to the level of simple fairy tales and more generally to the standards of 19th-century fiction. In order both to resist stagnation and incorporate the wildly inventive 20th-century narrative fiction, we have to choose the option of expansion (and equality). Moreover, within the field of literary studies it is quite unproblematic to separate literature, fiction and narrative from each other – or for the very least to understand they are not synonymous. One may also ask why and to what possible (ideological, research and cultural) end certain types of postmodern novel and film should be marginalized (as this day such exclusive tendencies and hierarchies should be considered suspicious to say the least), especially if narra-tology is supposed to be applicable to every actual and possible narrative. As our focus is on narrative poetics and not on narrative interpretation, indeterminate stories don't pose any problems, in contrast to Ryan, who had to exclude postmodernism from her model (Ryan 1991, 1) because it can't be captured by her story-oriented possible worlds approach.

(6) "Does narrative require both discourse and story, signifier and signified, or can it exist as free floating representation, independently of any textual realization? Is the phrase 'untold story' ... an oxymoron or can the mind hold a narrative without words, as when we memorize the plot of a novel?" (Ryan 2005, 346).

This seems to be another trick question or even worse, a misunderstanding. If we wish to study narratives, then we need to be able to separate these levels at least schematically. Contrariwise, if we wish to speculate on possible and potential stories that are not yet or ever inscribed into anything, then we can ignore the consequences of inscription (such as the inevitable division into signifiers and signifieds) altogether, at least until some as yet unforeseeable breakthrough in neural sciences gives us direct access to human thought processes and memory. The example of memorizing is also rather trivial: if we memorize the plot of a novel, then that memory is necessarily based on the printed signifiers of the novel, which have to be included or taken into account in the study of that very memorization.

To sum up the most important elements of our narratological position: we accept Prince's definition of narrative as the representation of real or fictive events by one or more narrators to one or more narratees, take narratology to be a formal and modal enterprise oriented towards narrative texts and not stories (that are seen as always already varying interpretations), and we do not intend to marginalize postmodernist and other complex narratives, but to accommodate them in our model in progress. We also preliminarily situate transmediality on the level of stories, and thus fictional films may present stories but not narrate them (without resorting to voiceover narration or character's speech acts).[8] With the pressing issues of definition and transmediality solved, at least for our present purposes, it is time to take a closer look at the combination of classical and postclassical narratologies we'll modify in the following chapters.

We'll begin with Genette and proceed to two major postclassical narrative scholars: Monika Fludernik and David Herman. As already noted, classical and postclassical narratologies are not seen as mutually exclusive, as their relation is mostly seen along the lines drafted by Herman (1999 and 2002). According to him, postclassical narratologies test the possibilities and limits of classical models and if necessary enrich them, "thereby coming to terms with aspects of narrative discourse that eluded or even undermined previous narratological research" (Herman 1999, 3).

6.4 Narratologies: classical and postclassical

6.4.1 Genette

Genette's narratology is taken as a point of departure for several reasons. It contains many concepts that have not been abandoned in postclassical narratology but only fine-tuned or further developed there. This is especially true with Genette's conceptualization of narrative time and its useful and compatible later additions and modifications by Bordwell (1985) for film narratology and Herman (2002) and Margolin (1999) for literary narratives.

Also, Genette's three-layered model of narrative (narration/narrative/story) is able to foreground narrating and its relation to both narrative and story, unlike the more usual binary models (*fabula/sjuzet*; discourse/story; discourse/possible worlds; discourse/storyworld).[9] In this model, both narrating and story are constructed on the basis of narrative text, and thus we have two directions for the reader's interpretative activities instead of only one (story). This in turn will be useful in integrating postmodernist narratives into the narratological frame in progress, as many postmodernist narratives seem to organize themselves along the narrating–narrative axis instead of fulfilling the usual narrative to story conventions (by foregrounding varying focalizations and temporal distortions).

Finally, the fundamental differences in basic theoretical orientation between Genette and such postclassical narratologists as Fludernik, Herman, Jahn and Ryan present a genuine choice to be made. In comparing classical and postclassical narratologies, Herman (1999, 11) formulates a question that according to him has become central to recent work in narrative analysis: "How do narrative designs both shape and get shaped by the process of interpretation?" Using Hemingway's short story as an example Herman continues: "In particular, how do Hemingway's techniques acquire meaning from their situatedness in contexts of interpretation?" (ibid.).

Herman's example is far from innocent, as Hemingway's oeuvre is already canonized mainstream narrative fiction that uses narrative techniques familiar to most readers and already competently theorized by classical narratology. The case is different with more novel techniques; if these are not studied and the studies not disseminated among the reading population, the techniques will be unrecognized by theorists and common readers alike – and if cognitive narratologists like Herman continue to shy away from technically more complex experimental narratives, the vicious circle is complete and the exclusion of challenging narrative texts with techniques to be discovered will become permanent. Second, if the focus shifts from narrative texts to narrative meaning, not even genre fiction provides techniques that wouldn't always already contribute to clashing and varying constructions of meaning according to every contextual parameter already unearthed by cultural studies. In short, if we trace meanings, narrative techniques and texts take a second seat – at best.

Classical formal and modal narratology and postclassical narrative analysis seem to be two different things and orientations, although Herman tries to reconcile them:

> [M]y point, rather, is that no description is devoid of interpretation ... The search for form and form alone is quixotic at best; at worst it entails a covert projection of time-bound interests, assumptions, and values onto narratives that are then argued to be a product of the very interests, assumptions and values that are read into them. (Herman 1999, 12)

However, exactly the same could be said about the search for meaning based on the plethora of unverified[10] cognitive hypotheses.

Even more importantly, one could ask how quixotic Genette's project actually was, as his conceptual machinery is still in (partly modified) use within Herman's own project and in many other postclassical narratologies. The values of Genette's basic parameters (order, speed, frequency, distance, focalization, time of the narrating, level, and person) are usually easy to verify in the narrative text, which grants them considerable explanatory and descriptive power. It is usually easy to decide whether a narrative text is homo- or heterodiegetic or whether or not it contains analepsis. Genette's model also allows most of these parameters to be undermined and become relatively useless (as is the case with Robbe-Grillet's achronies). If one is not too concerned with a full reconstruction of temporal order, or against the contamination of narrator's and character's discourses in certain cases of free indirect style, there's little to cause serious disputes. This is also acknowledged by Herman:

> [O]ne cannot read a homodiegetic narrative as a story told by a person not involved, in some ways, in the events being recounted. Nor does Hemingway's use of past-tense narration permit readers to interpret the actions of his characters as hypothetical forays into a future. (Herman 1999, 13)

In other words, Genette's categories have considerable explanatory and descriptive power that should not be abandoned. They constitute a conceptual level as pre-interpretative as possible and thus maximize the possible points of agreement, in contrast to any quixotic approach to the irreducible varieties of narrative meaning. Furthermore, Genette's framework is considerably less speculative than any top-down interpretative frame that supposedly organizes the reader's interpretative process and makes it meaningful. The latter may well help in figuring out readers' encounters with fairytales and mainstream realism, but a few pages into *Compact*, *Finnegans Wake*, or *Gravity's Rainbow*, the reader doesn't benefit much from such projections.

As we are not interested in meanings and interpretations, but in poetics and possibilities, Genette's formal and modal narratology is a good enough starting point for us, although it understandably isn't good enough for postclassical narratologies and narratologists. Genette's formal and modal project could have been continued by using postmodernist, digital, interactive, and ergodic narratives to modify and expand it, but for various reasons this didn't happen. As we try to make it happen, the challenge is big enough without adding any contextualizing or interpretative aspirations on top.

The tension and historical fluctuation between classical and postclassical narratological approaches should perhaps be situated within a broader perspective in the aporetic dialectics of text and reader and text and context. As classical formal narratology had pretty much exhausted itself (and its database of books) by the late 1980s, the shift of focus to reading, meaning, and interpretation was a fresh path out of stagnation. However, the digital and cybertextual expansion of form cannot be observed, analyzed and theorized by following postclassical context-oriented preferences, as we must first account for the necessary formal changes and expansions to see what kind of challenges these new works present to readers and users. Needless to say, the present approach does not exclude the latter, and once the novel narrative forms are better recognized than they currently are, another shift towards context will be more than likely.

6.4.2 Fludernik

Fludernik's natural narratology (1996) is based on two questionable premises. Narrativity is tied to experientiality and derived from oral literature and more generally from the real-world constraints of expression and communication. Narrativization is based on Culler's idea of naturalization (Culler 1975, 134–60), but the problem is that, for Fludernik, there seems to be only one form and one interpretative frame of naturalization, narrativization, which hence becomes a projective form of interpretation that can override every feature of the actual texts.[11] The premise that narratives are not necessarily oriented towards events evolving in temporal sequences, but rooted in experientiality instead, leads to curious contradictions that are unacceptable to us: lyric poetry becomes a problem for Fludernik's project (1996, 304–10) as it too can be narrativized and (more implicitly) because lyric poetry can equally well be tied to experientiality (is there anything that could not?).

What is worse, Fludernik builds too much on cognitive speculation; the process of narrativization is mostly based on analytically inaccessible levels of unspecified and speculative cognitive and cultural parameters that are called Mimesis I–III in Fludernik's less than elegant theoretical parlance. Mimesis I consists of parameters of real-life experience (Fludernik 1996, 43), whatever they are, Mimesis II (Fludernik 1996, 43–4) contains four explanatory[12] schemas of access to the story, telling, viewing, experiencing and acting, and Mimesis III (Fludernik 1996, 44) contain cognitive parameters from "well-known naturally occurring story-telling situations." Mimesis IV is "exclusively concerned with narrative parameters" (Fludernik 1996, 46). On that level, "narrativization is that process of naturalization that enables readers to recognize as narrative those kinds of text that appear to be non-narrative according to either the natural parameters of levels I and II or the cultural parameters of level III" (Fludernik 1996, 46). Only the topmost or final layer of Mimesis IV contains the more sophisticated and accessible parameters, a great many of which are or need to be borrowed from classical narratology, to properly describe and explain the narrativization processes and the other layers are "only indirectly responsible for narrativization" (Fludernik 1996, 46).

One may well ask what the theoretical benefits of the model are, especially as the inclusion of experimental and postmodernist texts narrativized by Fludernik in Chapter 7 of *Towards a Natural Narratology* (1996, 269–310) would have been easier to naturalize by and within classical narratology and its orientation towards narrative as temporally ordered and organized events and actions told by narrators to narratees. For the latter approach and definition, competing discourses, minimal stories and destructions of grammatical and syntactic structures wouldn't pose major problems, as they do for Fludernik's project that must from time to time to resort to reading experimental texts against the grain to accomplish the goal of narrativization. However, as Fludernik's examples and interpretations are usually better than her theoretical framework, we'll return to them in the next chapter. Also, Fludernik's critical comments on some of Genette's concepts will be discussed in Chapters 8–10.

6.4.3 Herman

As a contrast to the forced inclusions of Fludernik, curious exclusions haunt David Herman's otherwise path breaking *Story Logic. Problems and Possibilities of Narrative* (2002): the literary examples it takes are mainly modernist or pre-modernist and the French new novel and postmodernism are barely mentioned. A typical example of theoretical dismissal is Herman's table 5 (Herman 2002, 65), representing by genre the scale of "preferred degrees of action specification in stories," running from the fully open to the fully specified through intermittent stages that are predominantly open, moderately open, moderately specified, or predominantly specified.

It is worth quoting Herman's description of the two extremes of his scale construction. First, the fully open action specification:

> Nonnarrative [texts have no identifiable agents/actions, some experimental or avant-garde literary narratives – e.g., Djuna Barnes's *Nightwood*, James Joyce's *Finnegans Wake* – trace the boundary between fully predominantly open action specifications, their narrative logic based on a countering or even undermining of prototypical expectations about narrative itself]. (Herman 2002, 65)

In the predominantly open category, Herman's examples include the two novels already mentioned, described as highly allusive and elusive, and "narratives told by people with learning disabilities or brain disorders" (ibid.). After that we already have moderately open action specifications exemplified by such genres as detective fiction, mysteries, and ghost stories. In short, Herman's theory has nothing useful or applicable to say about narrative texts that have or consist of action specifications that are more open than those in detective fiction.

The situation doesn't look much better at the other end of the spectrum. This is what Herman has to say about fully specified action specification:

> Nonnarrative [texts are descriptively oversaturated, violating preference rules associated with tellability or reportability; i.e., that which makes states, events, or actions worthy of recounting; some experimental or avant-garde literary narratives- e.g. the novels of Robbe-Grillet and other instances of the Nouveau Roman – trace the boundary between fully and predominantly specified action representations, their narrative logic based on a countering or even undermining of prototypical expectations about narrative itself]. (Herman 2002, 65)

Based on this double exclusion that rules out complex narrative texts, the supposed narrative logic of which is too far removed from prototypical expectations about narrative, Herman is left with the moderately open examples (detective fiction etc.) just mentioned, "allegories, insinuated or elliptical stories, mildly mythopoetic novels such as *The Awakening* and 'novels of ideas'" (the moderately specified variety) and "news reports, realist fictions, fictionalized histories, nonfiction novels, science fiction, biographies and autobiographies, popular romance novels" (Herman 2002, 65) Although stories usually combine prototypical expectations and sequences with exceptional and untypical ones, both modernist experiments and the *nouveau roman* are excluded, their logic left unspecified, and the theories of preference rules and tellability tested only by and applied only to simplistic narratives.

At best, this perhaps explains a little better what we already know about simple mainstream narratives, and is capable of adding a certain taxonomic rigor to the scene of classical narratology, but, at worst, it is turning literary theory into a mere sub-branch of literary history and signaling a complete withdrawal from contemporary challenges. Instead of trying to delineate preference rules and tellability criteria also for the *nouveau roman*, Oulipian novels, modernist and postmodernist experiments, not to mention various forms of ergodic literature, it labels such texts as sabotages that counter and undermine prototypical expectations about the narrative, and does all this without even trying to contextualize the emergence and maintenance of these expectations – as if they were universally valid, globally shared, immune to change and differences in readers' taste, skill, education, reading history and aesthetic preference, not to mention cognitive capability.

Based on this broader spectrum of narratives, it is possible to claim that notions such as tellability, narrativity and minimal departure are implicitly value-ridden concepts that are biased toward simpler stories and not objective but deeply context bound. Herman (2002, 86) defines narrativity as a "measure of how readily a story can be processed as story." A few pages later the scale is constructed based on script-activating cues:

> Both too many and too few script-activating cues diminish narrativity. Further, narrative genres are distinguished by different ratios of stereotypic to non-stereotypic actions and events. An avant-garde work by Robbe-Grillet or Joyce's *Finnegans Wake* can be said to prefer a lower ratio of stereotypic to

non-stereotypic behaviors and occurrences – and thus to *display less narrativity* – than a news report, a classical epic, or a novel by Dickens. (Herman 2002, 91)

This is based on an unsubstantiated assumption that all processors (e.g. readers) prefer the same exact ratio of non-stereotypical to stereotypical as a maximum point of narrativity. While it may be true that the general reading population in the USA and elsewhere can't handle deviations from Dickens and news reports without feeling a loss of narrativity, it may not be plausible to believe that the communities of literary scholars would react in the same way.[13] The latter group are likely to have a richer set of processing capabilities than the former, and the more these scholars are focusing their intellectual efforts in processing difficult or "avant-garde" narratives, the more likely they are to learn even more complex ways of processing stories; quite possibly they are not even looking for the same simple cues to construct sequences or know enough to focus more on macro designs than to expect that they will be able to easily or quickly finalize the story construction process on a local level. Thus we either have to modify the concept of narrativity, complement it with more sophisticated concepts, or recognize considerable differences in the cognitive capabilities of readers – however uncomfortable that would be.

Regarding the narrative fiction of Robbe-Grillet, what we have in the first place is a continuous act of narration. Based on the narrative text, multiple stories can be constructed (very much at the reader's own peril), which are conflicting, overlapping, undermining and varying with one another. In short, some narratives can be more easily segmented into action sequences bearing some resemblance to readers' everyday scripts, and other narratives support this segmentation less easily if at all. In the triangle of narration, narrative and story there's no reason to always begin with and be looking for the segmentation that is only found in simple stories such as fairytales or generic fiction. Readers who are content in recognizing the text they are reading as a narrative (and not as a list, recipe, or plan – to use Herman's non-narrative examples), and do so by recognizing the existence and persistence of certain global criteria (Herman's macro design patterns), don't necessarily need to (immediately) find simple action sequences on the level of narrative micro designs, but are able (and have learned how) to keep their horizon of narrative expectations more open. If the models of narrativity would allow both bottom-up (paying more attention on micro designs and shorter time spans allowed for the story construction or saturation process) and top-down (paying more attention on macro designs and longer time spans allowed for the story construction or saturation process) processing of narrative texts, then Herman's model becomes even more questionable, as it is fundamentally about limiting the complexity of constructed stories.

If modernist narratives are designed to cause epistemological problems for the reader and postmodernist narratives are designed to create ontological problems, as Brian McHale has suggested (McHale 1987; 1992), then Herman's idea of narrativity prefers narrative transparency to these basic points of departure for the best part of 20th-century narrative fiction. By the same token, readers who are familiar with these points of departure and the narrative means used to implement them have no reason to expect that epistemological and ontological problems will be solved or closed on the level of local action sequences: these readers must have patience to cling on the frame of epistemological and ontological problems or gaps and learn to cherish many kinds of insecurity and indeterminacy within many possible action sequences in many cases until they reach the last page. Similarly, the readers familiar with Oulipian practices are able to look for constraints and specific types of textual organization (both on local and global levels) that interact with narrative organizations and complicate both the interpretation and the construction of action sequences.

To sum up, there are several frames of narrative telling the reader what to expect and giving him one or several scripts for reading, constructing and interpreting the story or stories the narrative text contains or gives rise to. We could draft a preliminary list of these principal narrative frames including 19th-century realism, 19th-century symbolism, psychological novel, canonized modernism, modernist experiments, the French new novel, Oulipian narratives (Calvino; Perec), standard postmodernism, postmodernist experiments,[14] ergodic print narratives (*Pale Fire*; *Rauyela*), hypertext fiction, interactive fiction, story generators, and narratively oriented textual instruments not to mention the narratives of the classic avant-garde. Compared to this list, what Fludernik, Herman, and Ryan suggest with their definitions and conceptualizations of narrativity,[15] tellability,[16] the principle of minimal departure from reality,[17] and story logic is no more than a one-frame model.

In practice, both classical narratology and cognitive postclassical narratology can satisfactorily or approximately explain only the first four movements.[18] They cannot account for narrative practices of the next six beyond describing them in negative terms (such as sabotage, anti-narrative etc.). Therefore, in what follows, we cannot take these limitations as our point of departure in constructing cybertext narratology, although we will take into account Herman's useful conceptual additions such as polychronic narration (to be discussed in Chapter 8) and hypothetical focalization (to be discussed in Chapter 9).

CHAPTER 7

Towards an expanded narratology

7.1 Introduction

In the previous chapter, we chose Genette's formal narratology and Prince's definition of narrative over their post-classical alternatives as points of departure in the project of expanding formal narratology. This short and intermissive chapter scrutinizes and when needed modifies these choices from three different angles, before moving on to apply cybertextual perspectives to more specific narratological matters in the next three chapters. The point is to see whether postmodernist and Oulipian narratives can be integrated into the chosen narratological framework within which they haven't been explicitly discussed.

Of the three angles of scrutiny, the first is provided by Monika Fludernik's attempt to include postmodernist narratives in her narratological framework. The second revisits Brian McHale's heuristic studies on postmodernism, and especially the distinction between epistemological and ontological dominants (of modernism and postmodernism respectively). The third and final angle of scrutiny involves a look at the conceptual heritage of the OuLiPo. Once again, however, we begin with Genette.

7.2 Genette

In Genette's narratological project, it is clear that narratological categories and distinctions can be undermined, transgressed or sabotaged, but as long as narratorial acts and activities can be recognized the text doesn't lose its narrative status that is ultimately based on mode (i.e. that it is narrated discourse). As Genette's narratology is strictly formal, it is not concerned with thematic problems, including the varying degrees of sense narratives may or may not make according to readers' interpretative schemes, skills, and expectations.

Genette's narratology allows various transgressions of its categories and distinctions, as demonstrated by his conceptual quintet of achrony, syllepsis, paralepsis, paralipsis, and metalepsis. These concepts usefully indicate a more broad-minded and pragmatic take on narratives and narrativity than most cognitive and postclassical narrative scholars are able to offer. In practice, this simply means acknowledging that narrated events cannot always be situated as earlier or later relative to one another (achrony); that they can be grouped according to dimensions other than the usually dominant temporal dimension of order (syllepsis); that adopted focalization patterns can be transgressed by providing either more or less information than the chosen type of focalization would normally allow (paralepsis and paralipsis); and that narrative levels need not always be separate and clearly distinguishable one from the other (metalepsis). This basic point of departure is easily expandable to other narratological parameters,[1] and it is also in synch with the development of narrative literature in the last 50 years or so: no longer are constructing and maintaining transparent and non-contradictory fictional worlds the unquestionable norm or rule. The problem is that most postclassical narratologists want to maintain that norm or even require it from literary works as a condition for their acceptance as narratives. While classical narratology is clearly compatible with modernism, postclassical narratology seems to be remarkably at odds with postmodernism.

7.3 Fludernik's postmodernism

In *Natural Narratology*, Fludernik (1996, 269–310) tries to incorporate postmodernist narrative fiction into her model. It is a move that separates her from many other postclassical narratologists, who usually ignore postmodernist fiction (Herman 2002) or exclude it not only from consideration but also from narrative literature (Ryan 1991, 1). Several weaknesses in Fludernik's theoretical premises and constructions were discussed in the previous chapter; here we only examine the four different types of postmodernist narrative she analyzes in order to see whether they are able to be integrated into the framework of formal narratology without Fludernik's presuppositions and narrativizing strategies.

In Fludernik's first group of postmodernist texts, despite violations of commonplace plot structures and plot consistency (such as conflicting story lines and ambiguities of reference to characters and narratees), readers are able construct a more or less unified storytelling frame; in Fludernik's words (1996, 278) they transform "the 'story' into the depiction of the reflectional activities of the protagonist, the fictional I." In other words, activities of narration and narrator(s) are foregrounded at the expense of narrating a unified and non-contradictory succession of events (story). In Genette's terms, this could be described as a shift from story construction to the construction of the narrating (or narrative instances). In Fludernik's second group of texts, such a frame can no longer "be forced on a text" (Fludernik 1996, 278) and "the novel threatens to disintegrate into a congeries of unrelated discourses whose juxtaposition at best betrays the shaping hand of an arranger behind the scenes who is responsible for the montage" (ibid.). She doesn't explain why a novel cannot or should not contain several unrelated narrative discourses – or in what way their unrelatedness threatens their status as narrative.

One could also ask why this kind of juxtaposition is such a problem, especially as the most radical subgroup of these kinds of subversion in Fludernik's opinion includes Donald Barthelme's short story *You Are as Brave as Vincent van Gogh*, which according to her (1996, 285) "refuses to be narrativized on the grounds of a consistent locus of enunciation or at least of a consistent presentation of setting." It is not clear why readers would always want to find a consistent setting or locus of enunciation. And do they really (assuming that they are capable of learning from their possibly frustrating experiences)? Second, and even more importantly, Prince's definition of narrative seems once again to have significantly more explanatory and narrativizing power than Fludernik's insistence on experientiality: as long as there are events and signs of narratorial activity, the narrative condition is satisfied regardless of any interpretative problems that more or less seasoned readers may occasionally face. Therefore Prince's definition is inclusive enough for Fludernik's first two groups of postmodernist texts, with the possible exception of her last example, Otto F. Walter's *Die ersten Unruhen. Ein Konzept* (1972), which juxtaposes different kinds of discourse – but, as we saw in Chapter 5, other discourse and text types may serve narrative purposes and vice versa. Chatman's idea of textual service is able to solve the problems in Fludernik's third category, which consists of supposedly narrative texts primarily composed of non-narrative building blocks (for instance, questionnaires).

Finally, Fludernik's fourth category includes linguistic experiments by Beckett, Joyce, and Stein that cause problems for her model. These texts don't pose a unitary frame of reference and rely more on ambiguous and multivalent references or "dismantle language in an effort to lay bare its operations and workings" (Fludernik 1996, 294). In the case of *Finnegans Wake* language "goes beyond the realistic level of sentence meaning aligned with a realistic story-frame, and the text does this by the multiple superimposition of contexts that add a metaphorical richness to the original base structure, allowing it to blossom (semantically speaking) in several directions at once" (Fludernik 1996, 295). Problems of meaning aside, there are events and acts of narration in *Finnegans Wake*, and thus the classification of the text as narrative shouldn't be a problem in Prince's terms. Beckett's "Ping" also manages to make Fludernik's unnecessary presuppositions and conditions of acceptance visible as it, according to Fludernik's exaggerated[2] interpretation:

> reduces the linguistic function even further to the point where no definite personhood can be assigned to the producer of the text, no human being is necessarily designated as the topic of the discourse, and no even minimally verisimilar or utopian

(dystopian) environment is evoked from language. (Fludernik 1996, 303)

Stein's more experimental passages of text and her play with broken syntax may well resemble lyrical poetry[3] or generative prose more than they resemble narrative (or more likely be a combination of all these three options), but, by way of contrast, the category of narrative nevertheless includes even poor and uninteresting narratives as well as narratives that don't make much sense when approached with narrow-minded expectations. Overall, Fludernik's problems with postmodernist texts stem from the shortcomings in her orientation towards experientiality, unifying interpretation, and interpretative frames. As we saw, the traditional formal orientation towards events and narrative instances can easily accommodate at least as many of her examples as her questionable strategy of narrativization, which leads to situations where texts are read "against the grain" (Fludernik 1996, 288), a sign of inadequate scholarship. It is difficult to understand why it is so difficult for Fludernik to read prose without narrativizing it, and what precisely the actual benefits of narrativizing are.

7.4 McHale: epistemology and ontology

Brian McHale (1987) divides his descriptive poetics of postmodernism into four sections: worlds, words, constructions, and groundings. The first, worlds, is of no interest to formal narratology: heterogenic and anachronous zones and multiple fictional worlds don't necessarily challenge narratological concepts and categories, as the zones are ultimately related to the content of the fictional world or worlds projected in and by the text.

McHale's (1987, 133–175) section on words discusses complications introduced by language and style into the construction of fictional worlds from the text continuum. The differences between literal and metaphorical or figural tend to be blurred to create more or less irresolvable ontological tensions in postmodernist fiction, which is also haunted by the possibilities of allegory (the missing of the literal frame to be hesitatingly supplied by the reader). The world or worlds may also be or seem to be generated from certain rules applied to language – a move that necessarily foregrounds ontological problems (while creating correlating epistemological problems as well) and denies any readymade assumptions of narrative representation or narrative as representation. Still, while drawing the reader's attention to the text continuum, and even given the presence of grammatical ambiguities created by words freed from their usual syntactical constraints, postmodernist texts still project a world "however partial and incoherent" (McHale 1987, 151). Or, to put it in another way: unlike their modernist predecessors, postmodernist texts do not project unified ontological planes (McHale 1987, 234).

McHale's two chapters (1987, 97–130) on constructions discuss devices that both construct and erase events and existents, and create various confusions regarding narrative levels (Chinese box worlds, infinite regress, strange loops etc.). From a narratological perspective, the last practices don't necessarily create serious challenges, as there's no reason to presuppose the hierarchy between narrative levels should always be maintained, as discussed already. Genette's concept of metalepsis (1980, 234–237) already allows such transgressions. The usefulness of being able to distinguish extra-, intra- and metadiegetic levels hasn't been diminished, as these levels are usually introduced before being sabotaged, and much of the effect is dependent on the assumption of separate and hierarchically organized levels. In this respect, McHale's inventory adds several new metaleptic devices and strategies to Genette's discourse on narrative levels without altering its basic premises. Erased and self-erasing events and existents and their contradictory combinations form a somewhat bigger challenge for two reasons. First, they constitute a certain novelty or innovation (of ontological flickering) that was not theorized in classical narratology; second, their existence complicates the construction processes of both story and narrating from narrative text.

In addition to constructing flickering ontologies by first presenting and then erasing events and existents, and by collapsing, stacking and short-circuiting narrative levels, utilizing multiple and incompatible discourses, using opaque styles, and hovering between literal and figural frames of reference, postmodernist practices create similar effects also by playing with the materiality and spatiality of the book and their relation to constructed fictional worlds as well as with the author's or the author function's degrees of presence and absence in the text. Many but not all practices that play with the materiality of the book produce familiar ergodic effects, including horizontally and vertically split pages and other multiplications of the reading order among many others.

Narratologically speaking, postmodernist fiction (in McHale's construction) complicates, undermines, and sabotages the construction[4] of non-contradictory stories[5] from narrative text, and also puts more weight on the relation between narrative and narrating. McHale (1987, 39) contrasts modernist perspectivism with postmodernist construction, and it is on that level that the main theoretical challenges can be most fruitfully formulated. Genette's (1980, 161–162) category of mood (consisting of focalization and distance) concerns the qualitative and quantitative sides of the regulation of narrative information, its channels (focalization) and amount (distance). Focalization is ultimately based on differences in "the capacities of knowledge of one or another participant in the story" (Genette 1980, 162). This clearly foregrounds epistemological concerns, whereas McHale consistently contrasts the epistemo-logical dominant of modernism (stressing perception, knowledge and reliability) and the ontological dominant of postmodernism (stressing fictionality, modes of being, and the nature and plurality of worlds)[6] – in short, differences in the capacities of fictional construction of one or another participant in the narrative.

One way of integrating McHale's ontological emphasis into Genette's more epistemologically oriented narratology is to divide the latter's basic categories of tense, mood and voice into epistemo-logical and ontological aspects, but that would be too impractical for our purposes, given that our aim is not to postmodernize narratology but to cybertextualize it. Another alternative could be adding construction as a fourth major category in Genette's model, but that solution would run into difficulties as tense, mood and voice are inherently involved in constructing both story and narrating from their "traces" in narrative text.[7] However, it is clear that Genette's model emphasizes story construction more than the relation between narrating and narrative. Hence the category of voice is perhaps underdeveloped in Genette, and therefore, in Chapter 10, we'll try to incorporate McHale's ontological emphasis in order to strike a better balance between two major types of narrative instance: those who represent or report and those who make things up as they go (see also Genette 1988, 15).

7.5 The OuLiPo: objects and operations

According to Jacques Roubaud (1998, 40), Oulipian literature is neither postmodern nor modern but "traditional literature true to tradition." One way to test this statement (and assess its irony) would be to see whether traditional theories of literature could be applied to Oulipian literature. From a narratological perspective that seems to be the case: the novels of Perec and Calvino don't significantly defy narratological categories, or do not do so to a higher degree than many other novels loosely and sometimes unjustly labeled as postmodern or postmodernist. In Calvino's Oulipian novels (*If on a Winter's Night a Traveller* and *The Castle of Crossed Destinies*) Ulla Musarra (1986 and 1987) found many strategies for the multiplication of narrative instances, but these were easily explainable with Genettean vocabulary, especially metalepsis. Musarra's findings also fit well within a wider variety of metaleptic examples in McHale's *Postmodernist Fiction* (1987, 112–130).

One reason for this kind of traditionalism is to be found in the nature and the area of application of the Oulipian constraints and procedures. They are "rules" for literary production only, and the end results of that production should satisfy the prevailing literary aesthetics. In other words, the experimentation and the challenges of the chosen and invented constraints occur and are negotiated in the process of writing; without paratextual information they are not necessarily detectable in its published result. The area of application of the constraints could in principle be expanded to the way the resulting text functions (in cybertextual terms) and to its reception and use. That doesn't yet seem to have been attempted despite the fact that some Oulipian works are ergodic (cf. Queneau 1962; 1998; Roubaud 1967). There are other limitations in Oulipian practices as well: most Oulipian publications are books, and the group's early interest in computers, which led to the establishment of the ALAMO group as early as 1981, didn't get much further than what could be called computer-assisted literature, using the computer as a tool and not as a medium (Burgaud 2002; Mathews and Brotchie 1998, 46; 1998, 130–131), with the notable exceptions of Jean-Pierre Balpe's generative, hypertextual, and locative works.

For these reasons, Oulipian practices don't challenge formal narratology except potentially. It is possible that in a narrative text certain detectable constraints might become so dominant that they could sabotage its functioning as narrative, but so far actual examples of such texts don't seem to exist. Oulipian systematizations (Bénabou 1998; Mathews and Brotchie 1998, 213–214; 1998, 227–228), and especially their basic distinction between objects and operations, could prove valuable in the cybertextual framework (including cybertextual narratology) and in the field of digital and ergodic literature – if applied to dynamic literary works and their reception. This short intermission concludes with three hypothetical examples; we'll return to the first at the end of our narratological investigation in Chapter 10.

If Oulipian operations (displacement, substitution, addition, subtraction, division, multiplication, deduction, contraction and intrication) were applied to narratologically specifiable objects, such as narrators and narrative levels, in textonically or intratextonically dynamic texts, we could envision narratives in which both the number and the mutual relations of narrative levels and narrators vary from one phase to another. Second, user functions, personal perspective, controlled access and in principle each major parameter of cybertext typology could be conceptualized as constraints of reception and use – at least if applied in a challenging way. Third, and to return to literary production, if a cybertext generates several successive versions of itself, the differences among these versions or phases could be analyzed in terms of Oulipian operations and linguistic and semantic objects (divided into textons and scriptons). Generally speaking, seeing literary machines as combinations of objects and operations could be useful in rethinking literary wholes, and in specifying system time, which is one of the topics in the next chapter.

CHAPTER 8

Tense

8.1 Introduction

This chapter views narrative time from four different angles. We begin by discussing the basic assumptions underlying Genette's conceptualization of tense. As a result of this investigation we will add two other types of time to Genette's pseudo-time: true time and real time. Second, to accompany the categories of narrative time and story time we deduce additional categories from two simple empirical counterexamples: system time and reading time. After these introductory moves we scrutinize category by category Genette's well-known conceptualization of narrative time, to which relatively little has been added since its completion in the early 1970s. In this we take into account David Herman's (2002) polychrony, and also when appropriate integrate categories and distinctions from David Bordwell's film narratology, because digital literary narratives can utilize both screen time and simultaneity by emulating or simulating appropriate filmic conventions such as split screens and exact running times. Finally we'll take a closer look at reading time and system time.

8.2 Basic types of time

In Genette's narratology, the category of tense operates at the level of connections between story and narrative (Genette 1980,

32). The time of written narrative is different from the times of oral storytelling and cinematic narration, as its duration cannot be measured and verified exactly; thus Genette (1980, 34) calls it pseudo-time, "false time standing in for a true time." Moreover, this time is necessarily entwined with space and measured as space:

> The temporality of written narrative is to some extent conditional or instrumental; produced in time, like everything else, written narrative exists in space and as space, and the time needed for *crossing* or *traversing* it, like a road or a field. The narrative text ... has no other temporality than what it borrows, metonymically from its own reading. (Genette 1980, 34)

This kind of narrative pseudo-time affects at least two of Genette's three temporal categories (1980, 35): order ("connections between the temporal *order* of succession of the events in the story and the pseudo-temporal order of their arrangement in the narrative") and duration ("connections between the variable *duration* of these events or story sections and the pseudo-duration of [in fact, length of text] of their telling in the narrative"). The case with frequency is slightly different as this category is about "relations between the repetitive capacities of the story and those of narrative" (Genette 1980, 34). There doesn't seem to be pseudo-repetition quite in the same sense as in the two other categories, as in print narratives the relation between repetitive capacities can be as easily verified as in oral narratives that unfold in true time. However, repetition is inherently inexact (i.e. cases of exact ad verbatim repetition are rare as they tend to go against strong literary conventions emphasizing variation) and in that sense repetition definitely is only pseudo-repetition.

The medium-dependent constraints of Genette's discourse are relatively easy to see here, and as written digital narratives can borrow or simulate filmic conventions (among many others), our cybertextual narratology should not limit itself to pseudo-time, but take into account measurable and verifiable true time as well. David Bordwell's film narratology (1985) includes the concept of screen duration to account for the duration of the film, and thus there are not two but three registers of time at play in his theory of narrative temporality: screen time, narrative time and story time – the last two derived from Genette.[1] However, we shouldn't limit our discourse to merely combining the temporal aspects of film and

literary narratologies, as they don't exhaust the variety of temporalities that are found in digital media.

First, both in film and in oral narratives, the duration of presentation usually equals the time of reception (hearing or viewing),
and although there are exceptions to this (the audience could
be physically prevented from seeing or hearing the whole show)
they do not occur under normal conditions of distribution and
presentation; therefore there has been no need to theorize such
exceptions. In cybertextual terms, the difference boils down to
textonic and intratextonic dynamics and controlled access that can
be effectively implemented in digital media.

As we saw in earlier chapters, textonically and intratextonically
dynamic texts like *Agrippa* (Gibson 1992) or *The Impermanence
Agent* (Wardip-Fruin et al. 1998–2002) are capable of reducing the
number of their original textons and scriptons to zero within a limited
period of time. *Agrippa* can be presented and read only once (per
copy); as the text is transient and has verifiable duration the reader
must adjust his reading speed to the speed and duration of presentation and can no longer take all the time he may need to read the
text. Other kinds of transient text establish less severe and more local
temporal limitations for their reading – in *Hegirascope* (Moulthrop
1995) it is 30 seconds per node per visit while the whole text and
each and every node can be visited as many times as one likes. To
understand and theorize the temporality of such texts, we must add
two new temporal registers to the classic two: system time to account
for the varying degrees of the text's permanence (the appearances,
disappearances, and possible reappearances of the text and its parts
and phases), and reading time for the text's potentially limited and
controlled temporal availability and accessibility to the reader.[2]

As such, system time and reading time apply to any kind, type,
mode and genre of textual presentation in digital media; they are
not intrinsically related or limited only to narrative and narrative
use. Still, system time and reading time cannot be excluded from
cybertext narratology, as one may assume that in narrative texts
they serve narrative purposes or, to put it differently, we'll limit our
discussion to the narratologically relevant uses and arrangements
of system and reading times and their entwinement and interplay
with narrative and story times. Following Bordwell we could say
that system time and reading time belong to the stylistic system of
digital texts.

If system time and reading time were to be applied to print narratives, they would usually have both unlimited system time and unlimited reading time, because they are supposed to be permanent and there are no temporal limitations set to their reading (they can be read as many times, as often and as fast or slowly one wants). The always possible[3] but mostly hypothetical exceptions to this could include specific instructions or threats to the reader ("burn this book in 2010"; "God will punish you if you read this book twice" etc.) and material solutions that turn books into self-destructive artifacts (vanishing ink,[4] pages deteriorating in a month etc.). System time and reading time are also static in printed works, as their settings do not change.

Second, the duration of a modern[5] film remains exactly the same from one screening to another (disregarding technical errors and variant versions or cuts). In any kind of programmable media, duration and other temporal aspects are potentially variable, whether they are to be measured in pseudo-time (as space) or true time. If new scriptons are added to a narrative text or old ones removed from it these operations may well affect the settings of order, duration and frequency: new events could be added and have to be situated into the order of events in the story, scenes may become summaries and ellipsis filled, and some events may be recounted again. Thus the relation between story time and narrative time can be either variable or invariable, and not merely invariable as it is taken to be in equally print-oriented classical and postclassical literary narratologies.

To make some of these points and basic differences clearer, it is useful to compare *Moby Dick*, *Agrippa*, *Reagan Library* and *Hegirascope* (in Table 8.1) in four temporal registers.

Moby Dick exemplifies what is taken for granted (for a good reason) in print narratology: there are no temporal limitations applicable to the book's existence and reading. As already noted, *Hegirascope* limits reading time at the level of nodes that can be revisited without limitations. *Agrippa* happens only once; hence its system and reading times are limited. In these three texts, the relation between narrative time and story time, measured either in pseudo-time or true time, is invariable because the scriptons to be read remain the same (nothing is added to or removed from them). In this respect, *Reagan Library* exemplifies a crucial difference: the length of its nodes expands until the maximum length is reached, usually after three or four revisits,

Table 8.1 Four registers of time in *Moby Dick*, *Hegirascope*,
Agrippa and *Reagan Library*

	Moby Dick	Hegirascope	Agrippa	Reagan Library
system time	unlimited	unlimited	limited	unlimited
reading time	unlimited	limited (locally)	limited (globally)	unlimited
narrative time: story time	invariable	invariable	invariable	variable

which means that the relation between narrative and story time is
variable[6] until the maximum or full length is reached, after which the
relation remains or seems to remain invariable.

System time, reading time and the relation between narrative
time and story time can be further divided into ergodic and
non-ergodic times, depending on whether it is possible for the
reader to affect or manipulate those times. If such possibilities are
not available, then the temporal settings are non-ergodic, and if
such possibilities are available, then the narrative text's temporal
settings are ergodic. Narrative texts may, of course, have both
ergodic and non-ergodic settings (for instance for different aspects
of time or different parts of text), and there's no reason to believe
that either of them will always be more powerful and important.

Finally, in addition to pseudo-time and true time, there's a
third type of time that may have narrative uses and consequences:
the real-time textual communication among users within the
text as an essential part of its consumption and construction.
This multiuser aspect as executed in networked and programmable media is more typical of games than literature, but as
Aarseth's discourse on MUDs and adventure games (Aarseth
1997, Chapters 5 and 7) shows there are many possible discourse
levels that may contribute to and constitute textual events and
actions: construction, quasi-events, negotiation, progression and
events. Discussion of real time and discourse levels is postponed
until Chapters 10 and 11, which center on narrative situations
and their alterations and alternatives.

All these limitations complicating reading and rereading may seem to run counter to our cultural conventions and therefore to be an exercise in futility. Still, if one of the main attractions of narratives is the challenge to construct and reconstruct a set of temporal relations on one level from various explicit and implicit cues and hints embedded in another temporal level, and if temporality is of primary importance to narrative and human existence as many scholars argue, then why not add more temporal levels and nuances to that challenge?[7] As reading time and system time remain provisional theoretical constructions that are at the present moment useful to apply only to very few narrative texts, we'll first discuss more common temporal registers and aspects of time in narratology.

8.3 Order and simultaneity

8.3.1 From achrony to polychrony and beyond

David Herman (2002) adds several useful subcategories to the treatment of order in classical literary narratology with its well-known anachronies and achronies (Genette 1980, 35–84). The general term anachrony "designates all forms of discordance between the two temporal orders of story and narrative" (Genette 1980, 40). These include analepsis or "flashbacks" and prolepsis or "flashforwards" and their specifications. Achronic events cannot be placed "at all in relation to the events surrounding them", as:

> [T]o be unplaceable they need only be attached not to some other event (which would require the narrative to define them as being earlier or later), but to the (atemporal) commentarial discourse that accompanies them. (Genette 1980, 83)

Such events without temporal reference are temporally autonomous and express, among other things, "the narrative's capacity to disengage from all dependence ... on the chronological sequence of the story it tells" (Genette 1980, 84).

Herman's revision is based on a certain contradiction or oversight in Genette's treatment of achrony. As Herman argues:

[T]emporal indefiniteness should not be conflated with timelessness or achrony: not knowing the exact temporal position of several events occurring within a larger narrative sequence does not make those events achronic. (Herman 2002, 219)

Furthermore, the achronic and the temporally indefinite ("the only partially temporally ordered") should be distinguished from the temporally multiple "where the narration anchors events in multiple temporal frameworks and thereby promotes competing ways of sequencing those events" (Herman 2002, 219). Herman proposes the term polychrony for these partial and multiple orderings of events[8] and distinguishes between modes of narration that code "the temporal position of events through partial or multiple ordering" and modes of narration that code "the temporal position of events as inherently inexact" (Herman 2002, 213). In the latter case, "events themselves are coded as irreducibly temporally multiple" (ibid.). It seems then that we have two types of multiple ordering, one playing more with the mutual relations of events and the other more with ambiguous temporal qualities of individual events.

Thus in addition to Genette's strictly timeless or "temporally autonomous" achronies, there are fuzzy polychronies within which temporally determinate (with the values of earlier and later) and indeterminate events combine in ways that result in partially and multiply ordered chains of events. However, Herman's conceptual contribution is not incompatible with Genette's theory, as it only adds new "end results" to the comparison between the order of events in the narrative discourse and in the story. These last events can be fully ordered, partially ordered, multiple ordered – or not ordered at all as is the case with syllepsis (Genette 1980, 85; Prince 1987, 95), which organizes events and situations by a non-chronological principle (spatial, thematic or other).

As helpful as this is, it is only one part of the story. Genette and Herman share a severe limitation as they both presuppose there's only one order in which the events are narrated (i.e. printed) in the narrative. As we know this is not the always the case in print literature, as certain experimental novels (cf. Cortazar 1966; Johnson 2007; Saporta 1962) made clear years before Genette's *Figures III* (1972) and decades before Herman's *Story Logic* (which was also predated by the emergence of non-linear hypertext fiction).

If this relatively "recent" multiplication of presentation orders in narrative print fiction is to be taken into account, then at least three different types of presentation order can be readily observed in print narratives: fully linear (narratives with only one presentation order – the traditional arrangement), randomly non-linear[9] (narratives consisting of events or segments that can be presented in any order such as Saporta 1962), and non-randomly non-linear (narratives with several presentation orders such as Cortazar 1966 and Johnson 2007).

It is only through combining these two sides that a more comprehensive understanding of order becomes possible. Regardless of the type of the presentation order, the order of the events in the story can have different degrees of constructibility: they can be fully ordered, partially ordered, multiply ordered, or remain completely achronic (or temporally random in the sense that every possible order of narrated sequences evokes the same "feel" of achrony and the need to find another organizing principle than order to understand the grouping or groupings of events). If these possibilities are combined we have 12 different types of order as shown in Table 8.2 (within which Proust refers to *Remembrance of Things Past*, which serves as Genette's prime example in *Narrative Discourse*, and Robbe-Grillet to *Topologie d'une Cité Fantôme*).

Table 8.2 Twelve types of order

Story/constructed order	fully ordered	partially ordered	multiply ordered	achronic
Narrative/presented order				
linear		Proust	Robbe-Grillet	
non-linear	The Unfortunates	Afternoon	Hopscotch	
randomly non-linear		Composition No. 1		

8.3.2 Hypertext theory and the problem
of multiple presentation orders

Using these 12 types of order, we can now shed light on the conceptual challenges and theoretical difficulties caused by hypertext fiction. In their discussion of the relative novelties of hypertext fiction, many commentators and scholars have overstressed the importance of order, while other temporal aspects have been either overlooked or misinterpreted. Still, the focus on order is to some degree understandable, as in most hypertext fiction order is the only temporal and sometimes also the only narratological aspect the arrangement of which is markedly different from what is theorized in literary narratology (i.e. in the paradigm we just saw to exclude print exceptions from Saporta to Johnson). As long as neither content nor number of signifiers of the node changes (and they don't in classic hypertext fiction), there are no changes in duration (ultimately measured as the length of the text) or frequency. A scene is still a scene, a summary a summary, and we can still count how many times the famous car accident happens and is recounted in the classic hypertext fiction *Afternoon* (Joyce 1990); consequently, it may seem that we are left only with the aspect of order to theorize.

Against the background of the 12 types of order, the ongoing confusion and hype around supposed changes and complications in one single temporal aspect of narrative seem both unwarranted and surprising. Early hypertext theory's (Bolter 1991, Douglas 1994; Landow 1992) often exposed[10] theoretical weaknesses explain the early problems in theorizing hypertext fiction from the perspective of narrative theory, but surprisingly some of the initial confusion continues even in the 21st century, as these two quotes from Marie-Laure Ryan illustrate:

> What for instance will I do if in the course of my reading I encounter a segment that describes the death of a character, and later on a segment that describes his actions when alive? Should I opt for a supernatural interpretation, according to which the character was resurrected? (Ryan 2001b)
>
> In classical hypertext, the network is usually too densely connected for the author to control the reader's path over significant stretches. Randomness sets in after one or two transitions.

> But randomness is incompatible with the logical structure of
> narrative. Since it would be impossible for the author to foresee
> a coherent narrative development for each path of navigation,
> the order of discovery of the lexia cannot be regarded as consti-
> tutive of narrative sequence. (Ryan 2001b)

We can only conclude that by Ryan's supposedly "logical" criteria
even flashbacks are too complicated to be compatible with her
conception of narrative coherence. Moreover, hypertext sequences
are usually not totally random (very rarely if ever nodes are linked
to every other node in a fully rhizomatic fashion), and the wide
variety of possible presentation orders (of static chunks of text)
would be less of a challenge to readers familiar with narrative and
anti-narrative experiments and postmodernist tricks of mid- and
late 20th century fiction.

First, the obvious point is to try to reconstruct the succession
of events in the story, regardless of how these events are arranged
in the narrative. Although hypertext fiction doesn't present its
signifiers in any one fixed order and there are several presentation orders, the attempt is not necessarily futile. Second, the
reconstruction process can be more or less difficult, and it can be
undermined by achroric and temporally indeterminate sequences.
Hypertext readers familiar with Robbe-Grillet and Saporta are not
likely to expect that they can always fully piece together the chronological order of the story events either in print or in hypertext
fiction. Third, order is not always the dominant temporal aspect
of narrative. Events and situations can also be arranged in
non-chronological principles, as Genette's (1980, 85) concept of
syllepsis makes clear. In Robbe-Grillet's case, trying to figure out
the narrative logic of repetitions and variations is much more
important and rewarding than any vain attempt at establishing
the "true" order of events in the story; attempts or constructions
of the latter type are often explicitly mocked in Robbe-Grillet's
novels. Finally, most scholars who have written about *Afternoon,*
from Aarseth (1997) and Douglas (1994) to Gunder (1999) and
Walker (1999), have managed to piece together a story, perhaps
not fully, but only partially or multiply ordered – definitely not
random.

Regarding order, the usual primary distinction made in narratologically oriented hypertext theory[11] has been drawn between the

multiple potential orders of reading the hypertext nodes and the actual one or ones chosen by the reader. The profusion of proposed terms (such as Liestol's 1994 story as stored, story as discoursed, discourse as stored, and discourse as discoursed or Gunder's 1999 omnidiscourse and actual discourse and omnistory and actual story) need not concern us here, as the point is not to rename that distinction (between the whole text and its partial readings) yet again.

The main problem with this distinction is related to its use value in the narratological framework. Narratology in general and Genette's narratology (which both Gunder and Liestol apply) in particular are both concerned only with omnidiscourse and omnistory; actual stories and actual discourses would matter only if it were impossible to read every bit of the omnidiscourse and construct or reconstitute the omnistory from it (to the degree that it is possible). In the examples Liestol and Gunder use (cf. *Afternoon*), it is definitely possible albeit difficult to read the whole omnidiscourse as a basis for more or less successful constructions of the omnistory.

Within the general framework of 12 types of order, the analepsis and prolepsis Genette theorizes lose much of their use value in the reconstitution process, as these are tied to the supposed one and only order of presentation in the narrative text. If there are multiple orders, then the relevance of the aforementioned concepts is severely limited to the order of events within individual readings and actual discourses.[12] This doesn't exclude the possibility that there may also be sequences of two or several events that are always presented in the same order regardless of the way the text is explored (the reader knows there has been a car accident in *Afternoon* before learning what possibly caused it etc.). We could say that in the latter case the analepsis and prolepsis are absolute (taking place in every actual discourse or not being contradicted in any actual discourse) and in other cases that they are only relative (taking place in one or several but not in all presentation orders).

8.3.3 Beyond hypertext fiction

Textual instruments (Wardrip-Fruin 2003; 2007; Wardrip-Fruin et al 1998–2002) challenge the theories of order even further than multiple presentation orders do. One of the most basic assumptions in print narratology is related to the idea of a closed textual whole, but as we saw in previous chapters, digital texts can in principle supplement themselves. Such supplements could affect the order of the events in the narrative text by adding, altering and erasing events from it, as is the case with *The Impermanence Agent*.[13] Therefore it is useful to distinguish between narratives with open order from those with closed order (or orders).

In addition, generative literature may further complicate theories of narrative time in all its basic aspects. Jean-Pierre Balpe introduces the concepts of alepsis and translepsis to explain narrative temporality of generative texts in which "none of these texts will ever be presented to the reader for a second time and no reader will ever have the same set of texts" (Balpe 2007, 310). However, Balpe's alepsis (Balpe 2007, 313), "a text not situated in a relation of time to the previous one", is similar to Genette's achrony and syllepsis and to Herman's polychrony. Translepsis (Balpe 2007, 313), "an infinitely moving hypothesis of diegesis", describes a situation in which diegesis is and remains a hypothesis, as there's no end to the generative process and the order never closes. In contrast to the open but ultimately finite order of *The Impermanence Agent*, which both begins and ends with one order (although the latter is dependent on the user's idiosyncratic browsing habits), we can call the order that Balpe's concepts designate an infinite order. The extremes of this type of order are somewhat balanced by the reader's likely focus on what Balpe calls microfictions, individual generations, within which the diegetic axis still has some use value and order can be constructed in the way and to the degree it is constructed in the otherwise more typical narrative texts that Genette and Herman's theories addressed and presupposed.

8.3.4 Succession and simultaneity

Despite ingenious manipulations of the written space in experimental narratives such as Raymond Federman's novels, simultaneous presentation in print narratives is at best pseudo-simultaneity, as strong reading conventions (from left to right and top to bottom in the west) dictate the order in which the text is supposed to be and will be read or at least the corner from which the reader should begin to traverse the page. Vertically, horizontally or otherwise split pages don't behave like split screens in film, as the unchanging and immobile text is already there in an equally unchanging and immobile arrangement and nothing moves on the page, disappears from it or suddenly appears on it.

Unlike in literary narratology, in film narratology simultaneity is a real option. According to Bordwell's (1985, 77) commonsense conceptualization, both simultaneous (story) events and successive (story) events can be presented either simultaneously or successively. Using digital media or any other media with dynamic presentation surfaces, narrative literature can utilize these basic presentational possibilities, most easily achieved by adopting split-screen conventions within which two or several segments of text could appear, disappear and reappear simultaneously (at exactly the same time), and thus expand narratological possibilities from a print heritage that only includes successive presentation.

Simultaneous appearances need not take place only in the reader's field of vision. It is possible that several parts of text might be synchronized together so that additional text appears in them (or they go through other kinds of change) at exactly the same time regardless of what part the reader is reading at that moment. In a bigger picture, this is just one possible consequence of textonically or intratextonically dynamic texts consisting of dynamic parts that can be timed to alter themselves (Eskelinen and Koskimaa 2001).

8.4 Frequency

Frequency was the novelty Genette introduced to the theoretization of narrative time. Frequency concerns the repetitive capacities of the text (Genette 1980, 35). To put it simply, an event can happen only once or several times and it can be told only once or several times. Before asking what will happen when narrative frequency becomes programmable, we will first limit our discussion to Genette's theoretization that has been accepted and incorporated into other formal narratologies (such as those of Chatman, Prince, and Bordwell) without major revisions.

To Genette, frequency is less an exact category than a heuristic mental construction. It is more about resemblance than about absolute identity between parts of the text (Genette 1980, 113). It is hard to imagine this could be otherwise, as the logic and conventions of fictional literature seem to work against exact repetition. Based on the two dichotomies just examined (of events and statements) there are four basic possibilities that Genette (1980, 114–116) reduces to three because in two cases the relation of frequency between narrative and story are the same. These three basic categories are the following: singulative narrative (narrating once what happened once and narrating n times what happened n times), repeating narrative (narrating n times what happened once), and iterative narrative (narrating one time what happened n times). Genette also refers to the fourth (or fifth) possibility that what happens n times is recounted m times (m not being equal to n or one). Rimmon-Kenan (1983, 137) calls this option *irregular frequency*.

The indicators of frequency can be as easily undermined and erased as those of order. It could be only partially possible to count with certainty how many times certain events occurred and how many times they were narrated, and there may be multiple possible and mutually contradictory frameworks in which to situate the events and their recounting. Ulrika Heise (1997, 113–146) has detected some of these devices in her reading of Robbe-Grillet's *Topologie d'une Cité Fantôme*. To sum up some of her findings, events may resemble one another so closely that it is impossible to know whether they constitute a case of singulative or repeating narrative, and if similar events take place in two or several storylines (separated perhaps by centuries in the fictional world) the impossibility of situating the event within only one of these storylines necessarily affects the reconstitution of the narrative's repetitive capacities. Following and mirroring Herman and Margolin's approach to order, such fuzzy cases of frequency could be termed indeterminate, and here too we can distinguish between recounting that is indeterminate because we can relate the recounted event to several storylines and recounting that is indeterminate because we can't decide whether it constitutes a case of singulative or repeating narrative. The latter could be called possible repetition and the former multiple repetition; one doesn't need look any further than Robbe-Grillet to find a wealth of examples of both.

The reader's experience of repetition is, of course, dependent on the order in which the text is being read, and when there's only one printed order without suggestions to read otherwise than in that order, this dependency is easily verifiable. Thus in hypertext fiction with explorative user function and controlled access also the question of frequency becomes more complicated than that which is generally recognized in print narratology. This has given rise to confusion in certain instances where the inevitable effects of the mandatory choices of the reader have been mistaken for the actual organization of the text.

In hypertext theory, Gunnar Liestol confused different aspects of narrative temporality with one another, and in the case of frequency he also misunderstood Genette's iterative narration by claiming that "summary nodes and overviews are also iterative" (Liestol 1994, 95). As Anna Gunder (2004, 98) rightly remarks, this contradicts Genette's definition, as summaries and overviews don't have anything to do with how many times the events happened in the story (and moreover, summaries are much more likely to constitute instances of repeating narration).

Jill Walker (1999) proposed that in hypertext fiction that forces the reader to read or at least visit many parts of the text more than once, the number of these visits should also be taken narratologically into account. While it is trivially true that the reader of a hypertext can or may have to read many nodes more than once during his sessions with it, the difficulty is that the number of these revisits can be neither predicted nor (usually) verified. The number of visits also varies in different readings or sessions with the text, from one reader to the next, and according to the readers' goals (reading the whole text, just sampling or rereading it), interests, ergodic skills, and strategies. While it is probably possible to prove that at least certain "key" nodes have to be read at least a certain number of times if one intends to read the whole text, the theoretical and empirical value of such knowledge is doubtful, both because it would be based on an almost impossible and statistically insignificant case of "ideal reading", and because rereading occurs in linear and non-linear texts alike. Even more importantly, rereading has no effect on narrative order (there are still the same multiple presentation orders to explore, and if there are conditional links new connections will usually open because certain nodes are visited and not because they are revisited, although this is a reversible design convention), speed (nodes still contain and constitute scenes and summaries etc.) and frequency except when there's a programmed connection and correlation between the number of visits and the content of nodes, as in *Reagan Library*. This kind of repetition with further narrative consequences calls for more profound theoretical modifications of narrative frequency, understood as the text's repetitive capacity.

Reagan Library rewards the persistent reader by adding more text to the revisited nodes. These nodes usually reach their full length and final content only in the fourth reading (there are exceptions to this). This practice creates a series of successive versions or phases of the text while making visible a new way of designing narrative fictions. Users are not merely navigating and choosing paths in a static labyrinth where each and every part and node forever stays the same, but also reacting to the system that reacts back by changing the content and length of its parts (and doing so several times). In other words, *Reagan Library* goes through several states from its initial state to its final and permanent state.

This has interesting consequences for the category of frequency, which should perhaps be divided in two different relations from now on. The first relation is situated between the textonic and scriptonic layers, and it determines which parts of the text are permanent and which parts are temporary (that is, repeated only for a limited number of times). The second and more traditional relation lies between scriptons and the events they narrate. In *Reagan Library*, the first three versions of the node are not repeated as they appear only once, after which they are replaced by the next version, and it is only the last version which behaves like the traditional permanent text.[14]

The fact that *Reagan Library* contains temporary parts (although only within its nodes; i.e. the number of its nodes remains the same all the time) has several interesting consequences besides its connection to (and disconnection from) narrative theory. One of these is the status of transitory phases; in *Reagan Library*, they are usually reduced versions of the final one and extended versions of the previous versions, which to some degree balances the possible effects of enstrangement (as this way nothing really vanishes from the text); in other words, rereading reduces "noise" in narrative information. A bit paradoxically we can then say that from the traditional perspective on narrative frequency, Moulthrop's fiction multiplies repetition by four.[15]

8.5 Duration and speed

In printed written narratives, duration is the most problematic aspect of time. The comparison between the duration of a narrative and the story it tells is more difficult than comparing order or frequency "for the data of order, or of frequency, can be transposed from the temporal plane of the story to the spatial plane of the narrative" (Genette 1980, 86). In fact, "no one can measure the duration of a narrative" (ibid.). In principle, the duration of readings and recitations of narrative texts are measurable, although they vary with the circumstances (Genette 1988, 33), but in the pseudo-temporality of print narratives duration is "difficult, if not impossible, to measure: it is not equivalent to the (variable) time to read or write a narrative nor is it the same as the time the given narration is said to have taken" (Prince 1987, 24).

Given these impossibilities and difficulties, in print narratology, narrative speed or tempo is taken to be more relevant than duration, and in retrospect Genette (1988, 34) thought he should have "entitled the chapter [in *Narrative Discourse*] not *Duration* but *Speed*." Genette's solution (1988, 34) to the dilemma is to measure speed as "the relationship between the duration of the story and the length of the narrative." Speed has two aspects, external (the average time covered per page that is possible to measure only if the temporal limits of the story are indicated) and internal, which is more important as it concerns "variations of tempo" (Genette 1988, 35).

Genette's system includes four basic speeds (scene, summary, ellipsis, pause),[16] to which Chatman (1978) added stretch, the symmetrical fifth option to mirror summary. These different speeds give narratives their rhythm, but they are just conventional approximations relative to one another. The fivefold scale of speed is based on the convention according to which dialogue realizes "the equality of time between narrative and story" (Genette 1980, 94) – without being able to indicate the speed of pronunciation or the possible dead spaces in the conversation. Narratives with steady speed are rare, and it is the shifts between two or more speeds that really matter as they give narrative its rhythm. This rhythm is necessarily dependent on the order of presentation, and if there are multiple presentation orders then the available rhythms usually multiply as well.

The media-dependent aspects of these theorizations were to some degree already revealed earlier. Rhythmic variations resulting from non-linearity (in Aarseth's sense) can take place both in digital and printed narratives, although these variations are not theorized in print narratology. The notable addition written digital narratives are capable of introducing into literary narratology is measurable and verifiable duration (i.e. duration in true time). As that kind of duration is already theorized in film narratology, it might be useful to see how it functions there before modifying literary narratology by adding verifiable true-time duration to it.

Bordwell conceptualizes what he calls screen duration by adding it as a third level to the *fabula* and *syuzhet* duration (Bordwell 1985, 82–84). In this model, there's either equivalence ("fabula duration equals syuzhet duration equals screen duration") or non-equivalence, where *fabula* duration is either reduced or expanded. In the former case, there are two options (Bordwell 1985, 83): ellipsis ("fabula duration is greater than syuzhet duration, which is itself equal to screen duration") and compression ("fabula duration equals syuzhet duration, both of which are greater than screen duration"). In the former case (ellipsis), there's a discontinuity is the *syuzhet* while in the latter there isn't. Likewise, if *fabula* duration is expanded, the two options of insertion and dilation arise (Bordwell 1985, 84). In the former case, "fabula duration is less than syuzhet duration, which is itself equal to screen duration" (Bordwell 1985, 84) – and thus there's also a discontinuity in the *syuzhet*. In dilation, "fabula duration equals syuzhet duration, both of which are less than screen duration" (ibid.) – leading to no discontinuity in the *syuzhet*.

If one tries to adapt this theory to literary narratology, screen duration and *fabula* (i.e. story) duration are easier to handle than *syuzhet* duration, because the latter will bring us back to pseudo-time. Transient narrative text that scrolls on the screen at its own pace for a given and verifiable time has screen duration similar to film, story duration similar to both film and print narratives (being more or less inferable from the narrative), and narrative duration similar to print narratives as written narratives necessarily take up and appear as space. In other words, if screen time is to be added to literary narratology, there are at least two ways of doing it. Either duration will be split into two sub-aspects and measured both in time and as space, or narrative duration will be equal to the length of the text and screen duration equal to the "running time" of the narrative text. The choice between these two options is not especially important as in both cases the different types of measurement are easy to distinguish from each other – for example a story covering two years (story duration) is narrated in 10 000 words (narrative duration/ narrative duration in pseudo-time) and scrolls on the screen or is available for 30 minutes (screen duration/ narrative duration in true time). The more important thing is not to confuse these times with reading time, even though it may sometimes be equal to screen duration.

This simple scheme could be complicated by including written narrative texts that include or are accompanied by audio files narrating certain parts of the story.[17] These instances of oral narration necessarily have a verifiable temporal duration, in which case duration could be measured both in true time and in pseudo-time within the same work. The following comparison (Table 8.3) between applicable durations in literary narratives in different media and mixed media combinations will perhaps clarify the issue of duration.

Table 8.3 Types of duration in literary narratives

	Pseudo-time duration	True time duration
Printed narrative	yes	no
Oral narrative/audio files	no	yes
Printed narrative with audio files	yes	yes
Hypertext fiction	yes	no
Hypertext fiction with audio files	yes	yes
Kinetic digital narrative text	yes	yes

The key distinction between kinetic[18] digital narrative texts and printed or hypertext narratives that include audio files, is that, in the former, the duration of every part of the text is measured both in pseudo-time and true time, whereas, in the latter, written parts are measured in pseudo-time and audio parts in true time.

As the limits of story time are often not indicated, the relationship between narrative duration (measured as space) and screen duration is the relation that could be easily verified as words per appropriate time unit. Should this temporally verifiable and measurable presentation speed (words per second – another novelty in literary narratology) vary, then perhaps the need arises to study its accelerations and decelerations as well. Contrariwise, such comparisons and measurements seem almost irrelevant: they would tell very little about the narrative in question, because they are totally disconnected from the story time and story construction that give Genette's temporal comparisons (between narrative time and story time) their qualitative importance. Perhaps the only qualitatively important aspect of presentation speed is its relation to the reader's capacities of perception and cognition. If the text moves too quickly, then parts of it will be inevitably missed, at least until the next presentation (if any). This kind of arrangement may, of course, serve a wide variety of aesthetic purposes.

Compared to these complexities, the case of classic hypertext fiction is much simpler. Despite appearances and some claims to the contrary, classic hypertext fiction doesn't call for major revisions of the concepts of duration and speed as they are theorized in print narratology. Liestol makes a categorical mistake by claiming that in hypertext fiction the reader "is in principle free to manipulate a scene, compress or decompress it. The reader can shrink a scene into a summary or an ellipsis" (Liestol 1994, 95). It remains a mystery how the reader is able to do that, as in hypertext fiction that Liestol discusses the reader cannot change or erase the text but only explore it.

Liestol seems to believe that by choosing his own path through the text the reader somehow manages to create ellipsis (by not reading some nodes) or summaries (by choosing shorter paths),[19] as he states that "the act of reading is at the same time the act of choosing and deciding between the various kinds of duration" (Liestol 1994, 95). However, such choices have nothing to do with Genette's definitions that Liestol pretends to apply, instead they are more like those caused by tmesis: if the reader leaves some parts unread there's less for him to read to be sure, but that has no effect on the organization of the narrative text and its duration:

there still are exactly the same amount of unaltered strings of signs that narrate specific story events regardless of what the reader chooses to read or not to read. As noted before, the rhythm caused by differences in speed (in pseudo-time) may differ based on the variety of chosen paths, but that doesn't change any single ellipsis, pause, scene, summary, or stretch one bit.

Although in digital media narrative texts can have measurable temporal duration, it is far from being a novelty as such, as the same can be said of texts that have appeared on film (from experimental films to ordinary subtexts and title sequences), video, or electronic billboards. Various verifiable true-time speeds and durations have been executed in countless projects from video and kinetic poetry to textual movies in digital (multi)media. Somewhat curiously (as narrative and time are closely linked in many general theories of human cognition), narrative applications of these possibilities are still difficult to find beyond *Hegirascope* and *Agrippa*.

Hegirascope offers another complication for our theoretization of duration. The individual nodes of *Hegirascope* have screen duration (30 seconds), but *Hegirascope* as a whole doesn't, and even the "local" screen duration of 30 seconds can be routinely bypassed by any reader who chooses a link elsewhere within that period of time. This indicates first of all that we should distinguish between two levels of true time duration: the level of whole texts and parts (or phases) of text.[20] This distinction is utterly trivial except when only the latter have temporally verifiable duration: if we try to determine the duration of *Hegirascope* as a whole the results will vary, as in principle the slide show could continue forever and will stop only when stopped by the reader. Second, the 30-second interval constitutes verifiable presentation speed (30 seconds per node) that is varying (as nodes are of different length). This speed is also a minimum speed, as the user doesn't have to wait that long to move on with and within the presentation.

8.6 Reading time

Cybertext theory and cybertextual parameters can shed some light on the possible settings of reading and system times. Textonically dynamic texts, where both the number and content of textons change, indicate that different strings of signs have different durations, as the text contains both older and newer parts and possibly temporary and permanent parts too (and in some cases only temporary ones).

Moreover, some dynamic texts open themselves to potentially endless supplements from the outside. Indeterminate texts undermine the stability of the text's functioning and also the reader's possibilities to reread the text as it once was. Texts with controlled access may challenge the practice and convention of reading the whole text, as in principle such a "goal" could be made impossible to reach. Transient texts set their own pace and thus partly dictate the ways in which they could be read. They are also capable of introducing several and severe temporal constraints on reading. The duration of reading or the number of allowed revisits could easily be limited, and in principle nothing prevents texts from stretching their necessary reading period over several decades or even lifetimes. Access could be periodically allowed and denied, in which case texts would have specific opening and closing hours and seasons. Textonic and configurative user functions may give the user a chance to alter and affect temporal settings. Texts could also be programmed to collect information about the temporal behavior of the reader and to modify the content and number of their textons and scriptons accordingly (Eskelinen and Koskimaa 2001).

In contrast to these and other possibilities, reading time is not only unverifiable (and conceptually useless) in print fiction, but there are also no effective[21] temporal limitations set to reading. Although the difficulty of the text, the reader's prior knowledge of themes and genres, material circumstances of reading and countless other factors have an obvious impact on reading, one can still read as slowly or as fast as one possibly can, take breaks as often as one wants, and reread the book as many times as and whenever one likes. As digital texts can be programmed to react to the way they are being read and to set conditions[22] on the reader and the reading process, a new dimension of constrained[23] reading and programmed time has opened up. If we wish to stay within traditional aspects of time, specific constraints could apply to the speed (how fast or slow the text must be read), duration (how long it is possible to read the text) and frequency of reading (how many times it is possible to read the text).[24]

First, the duration of reading may be limited. In essence, this means that the length of the text doesn't have to have any reasonable relationship to the time given to the readers for reading it (say, *War and Peace* in 60 minutes). This may lead to necessarily incomplete readings that under usual circumstances are not culturally accepted practices in the context of reading "serious" fictional literature. In applying such limitations, the most important qualitative difference is between literary works that give the reader enough time to read the whole text and those that don't. Although this factor to a certain degree depends on the individual skills of readers, there are limits to human skills in this respect, and certain extreme limitations of duration will be far too severe for anyone to be able to read the whole text. The object of limitations may also vary as limitations may apply only to rereading or first reading or they may concern the total time the reader is allowed to read the text (in one or several sessions).

In principle, the verifiable temporal limitations of duration may concern the whole text or only some or all of its parts. *Hegirascope* allows the reader to read its nodes in 30 seconds or under before intervening in the reading process. Still, there are no limitations to the total duration the reader can spend reading the whole text, and neither are there any limitations to the total duration one can spend with each node, as rereading is not constrained in *Hegirascope* either. Thus the 30-second limitation only slightly complicates reading *Hegirascope,* as eventually every node could be read in its entirety during one or multiple visits.

The concept of reading time and especially its aspect of duration becomes more meaningful and relevant if the duration of reading is not equal to the duration of textual presentation in true time. As we already saw, Bordwell's film narratology can omit the concept of viewing time, as that usually coincides with screen duration and in principle there are no limitations to the number of times a film can be watched. To narrative texts that have duration only in pseudo-time (print literature and most hypertext fictions), limitations of reading time (in measurable and verifiable true time) constitute a conceptual novelty.

Second, the possible speed of reading may be limited or constrained. Parts of the text may move or be replaced by other parts at a certain speed that may exceed the reader's reading speed, be slower than it or more or less equal to it.[25] At one extreme, the presentation of the text may completely stop for a certain duration of time, as in *The Impermanence Agent* where the reader has to pause to browse something else in order to make any progress in his reading. This discontinuity in textual presentation constitutes a mandatory pause, and comes close to the usual practices of serialized stories in newspapers and on television. There's no theoretical upper limit for such pauses or intervals between new installments: waiting periods between parts and phases and the duration of the whole process of textual presentation could last over one's lifetime.[26] Texts may also set minimum speeds for their reading and once again *Hegirascope*'s 30-second limitation serves as a prime example.

Third, reading may have its own frequencies as well. It may not be possible to reread the text at all or as it was before. Such restrictions may apply to the whole text or to only some parts of it. *Reagan Library* changes the content of a node when it is being revisited, and thus one may say that it is not possible to read certain parts of the text as they were in the first time (or place). Still, as many of these changes in *Reagan Library* are only additions, the text previously read is usually still there to be read as a part of an updated node. Just as with *Hegirascope* and its limitations of reading duration and speed, the constraints of frequency in *Reagan Library* take place only on the micro level of the text: there are no limitations to the number of times *Reagan Library* (as a whole) can be visited.[27] If each part of the text had a limited reading frequency and some of these limitations were different from each other, then the text would gradually (and not at once) become inaccessible to the reader (the more you read the less you have so to speak) – another new temporal arrangement that could support many interesting narrative purposes and strategies.

Non-ergodic limitations of the duration, speed and frequency of reading simply shift the control of these aspects from the user to the machine, likening the reading situation to the conditions of film viewing and unique performances. Ergodic limitations give the reader the chance to affect the settings of reading speed, duration and frequency (or at least one of these aspects) for better or worse (readers could be rewarded by giving them more time or punished by reducing their time with the text – or vice versa). The effect of the reader on the text's settings of reading time could be either a matter of explicit choice or a more implicit one resulting from his actions in ways that he may be only vaguely (or not at all) aware of. In principle, there are three major types of setting of reading time: given (i.e. beyond the reader's influence), chosen, and caused.

If we sum up the dimension of reading time and its two levels (local and global) and three aspects, frequency (the number of times the work can be visited), duration (the allowed duration of reading), and speed (the possible limitations of the reading speed such as mandatory pauses or required minimum speeds) as shown in Table 8.4, we'll end up with 64 (4x4x4) basic ways of constraining reading time, only one of which, the one containing no restrictions whatsoever, is compatible with classical narratology. *Reagan Library* occupies two positions in the table because it rewards the persistent reader by adding more text to its nodes in the first three revisits. In our terminology, its frequency on the local level is limited during these revisits and unlimited after the text no longer changes.

Table 8.4 Reading time

Level	Local		Global	
Aspect	unlimited	limited	unlimited	limited
Frequency	*Reagan Library*	*Reagan Library*		*Agrippa*
Duration		*Hegirascope*		*Agrippa*
Speed		*The Impermanence Agent*		*Agrippa*

8.7 System time

Earlier in this chapter we proposed the concept of system time to account for the varying degrees of permanence of the text and its parts and phases. Like reading time, system time has several aspects. Fundamentally, it is about what is permanent and what is temporary in the text. Temporariness implies that something changes, and in order to understand change we should come to terms at least with what changes, how it changes, and why it changes. To some degree the usual aspects of time, especially repetition (frequency), duration, and speed also have explanatory power in this context.

Books and printed texts are permanent until they deteriorate or are in other ways destroyed to the point that they cannot be read any longer. Their normal process of deterioration occurs over a time span longer than human lifespan, and as that process is not controllable (except in rare cases of vanishing ink and other non-standard material) it is also devoid of any aesthetic interest to us. Moreover, whatever the material condition of a printed text, its signifiers don't change to other signifiers: a letter A may gradually become invisible but until it is invisible it will remain an A. Only a combination of standard and vanishing inks could create a text in which different parts of that text will have different durations – or to put it more precisely there would be only two different sectors in the text: the permanent one and the disappearing one. Even in such a case, the process (of disappearing) would be irreversible, whereas digital texts can go through several temporary states, the changes of these states can be either reversible or irreversible, and the changes can affect every aspect of every signifier (i.e. a letter A may not only change its size, shape and color, but it may also become another letter or sign again and again).

As with reading time, also with system time do the interesting effects take place between the two main extremes: the standard permanence of books (i.e. unlimited duration) and the equally standard temporariness of a unique (one time only) performance (i.e. limited duration). Only when some parts are permanent and others temporary does system time really matter, as it presents a new type of aesthetic challenge to both writers and readers. In theorizing the combination of temporary and permanent parts, we need to take into account the partition of the text in ways that don't exist in literary and film narratologies (as to begin with we need to know what changes and what doesn't).

In theorizing partition (the what of textual change) and processes (the how of textual change), the Oulipian distinction between objects and operations could be helpful if it were applied to the behavior of texts and not only to the process of their creative production. In Benabou's (1998) systematization, objects are linguistic (from a letter to a paragraph and beyond) and semantic (such as events and characters), and operations include multiplication, division, addition and substitution among other options.[28]

In discussing narrative temporalities, the most interesting semantic objects are events, and if one or several of the operations listed earlier were applied to events in order to move the text from one phase to another, the consequences for the aspects of order, duration, speed, frequency and simultaneity would be enormous. Also the type of textual change matters, as changes can be either reversible or irreversible, the combination of which leads into complex patterns.

Luckily at this point, there seems to be no need to theorize these patterns in the context of narrative theory, as it is very difficult to find narrative texts to illustrate these possibilities. The same lack of necessity applies also to theorizing the reasons for textual changes (the why of textual change) beyond the already mentioned triangle of given, caused, and chosen consequences. We'll therefore close this chapter by quickly schematizing the basic dimensions of system time.

System time is either static or dynamic (i.e. its settings either change or they don't). It can be further divided into the aspects of duration, frequency (the number of changes the text undergoes during its limited or unlimited lifespan) and speed (the speed of changes).[29] As inferred already, books have unlimited duration (they are supposed to be permanent), unlimited frequency (their printed text doesn't change but will stay the same), and no speed (as there's no change there's no speed of change either).

The situation with digital and ergodic texts is more complex, because the different degrees of permanence could equally well apply to the possibly dynamic parts and phases of the text and not just to the text as a whole. The division of texts into parts (existing simultaneously) and phases (existing successively) also include the possibility that each part and phase could have its own temporal specifications in system time, and here the more exciting theoretical possibilities begin to emerge. In other words, there could be permanent texts in which some parts are temporary and others permanent, and temporary texts in which different parts have different specifications of temporariness (i.e. they don't vanish at the same time etc.).

The main difficulty in this theoretization is that on the local level of parts and phases the values of system time may become easily confused and conflated with the values of narrative time, at least in the category of duration. For example, if a node scrolls by in 30 seconds, its screen duration is 30 seconds, and it may well seem that the system duration of that node will be 30 seconds as well. However, the system duration of a node (or any other result of the text's division into parts and phases) will be 30 seconds only if that node also vanishes after 30 seconds – in other words, system time measures the degrees of permanence so the duration of the node's existence could in this case be anything from 30 seconds to infinity.

Finally, it is also important to see the difference between system time and reading time, as their settings don't have to be the same either, although reading time definitely depends on system time. If the text's duration (its lifespan) is two hours, its reading time can be equal to or less than that; if the text presents itself only twice it can be read once or twice; and if a web fiction will self-destruct or become inaccessible after 100 readings or readers it is very unlikely that one reader could read it 100 times. Even if the text is permanent (i.e. having an unlimited duration), there may be limitations to the duration and number of times it can be read by any one reader. In short, it is only when there's a difference between reading time and system time that the latter becomes theoretically important. That time is not yet here, so it is time to conclude this segment by using a hypothetical literary example in comparing the main aspects of system time and reading time. The hypothetical text in Table 8.5 is a web fiction that will be online for 12 months (system duration), during which it will change once a month (system speed), with 12 times (system frequency, i.e. the number of changes) in all. During

Table 8.5 Hypothetical example of the mutual irreducibility of system time and reading time

	Duration	Frequency	Speed
System time	one year	12	one phase/month
Reading time	24 hours	2	5 minutes/node

these 12 months the reader can access it twice (reading frequency) for a total time of 24 hours (reading duration). The reader will have to read or to be stuck with each node for at least five minutes after which he can proceed to the next node (reading speed).

8.8 Conclusion

In this chapter, we discussed certain fundamental additions to the theoretization of time in literary narratology. As there are at least three kinds of presentation order (one; multiple; multiple and random), as well as different degrees of story construction (full; partial; multiple; random/achronic), there are now 12 basic types of order instead of Herman's three or four (that only concern the degrees of story construction) and Genette's three (that we can call fully constructible, mostly constructible à la Proust, and thoroughly sabotaged à la Robbe-Grillet). Orders can also be open (as in text machines that supplement themselves with other texts), not only closed (i.e. permanent either because of the limitations of print or design decisions that don't allow aforementioned supplements). These orders may be affected by the reader, in which case they are ergodic, or they may not, in which case they are non-ergodic. Finally, in non-linear texts that don't present their scriptons in one fixed order, anachronies (analepsis and prolepsis) are either relative or absolute.

Successive presentation ceases to be the only option for narrative presentation. By adopting cinematic conventions, literary narratives in digital media can achieve true simultaneity in presentation, as two or several strings of signs can now appear on the screen and disappear from it at exactly the same time. In contrast to cinematic conventions, however, there may be two types of simultaneity taking place within and outside the reader's field of vision (for example, several hypertext nodes could go through irreversible changes simultaneously).

Because of multiple presentation orders (that for some reason were not theorized in print narratologies) the tempo or the narrative speed also becomes more varied (relative to the reader's choices of navigation). More importantly, in digital media literary narratives can have duration that is measured not only in and as space but also in exactly verifiable true time that can be either ergodic or non-ergodic. This true time can take place either on a local level (of parts and phases of text) or globally – or both. As a consequence, and just as in film narratology, there are three types of duration in our expanded literary narratology: screen duration (measured in minutes and seconds), narrative duration (measured as word and letters), and story duration. Thus there are also two new relations to be studied: between screen duration and story duration and between screen duration and narrative duration. As the latter is more easily verifiable and relates directly to the two sides of narrative presentation, it is the more important one. It constitutes a new kind of narrative speed measured as words per second, and it has obvious consequences for the readers' ability to perceive, access, and interpret any narrative: texts may simply be too fast even for the fastest readers. The aspect of frequency also becomes more complicated than it is in print narratology, as the text's repetitive capacities include also the possible repetition of scriptons and textons. These become or could become relevant categories in generative hypertexts such as Balpe's *Fictions* (2004) in which narrative statements (as scriptons) belong either to one, several or every generation.

In addition to these changes in the five traditional aspects of narrative time, the chapter added two additional registers of time, reading time and system time, to the traditional pair of narrative time and story time (the relation of which may now be either variable or invariable). Although these two new registers are not narrative ones as such, but can be applied to any other mode or genre of literature, they can have narrative impact, as they can be used for narrative purposes. Reading time and system time are also implicitly present in print narratives, although there they are usually unlimited and static (except in certain experimental and hypothetical cases where the reader is instructed to limit his reading time or the material conditions undermine the print text's assumed permanence).

Reading time can be either unlimited as it is in print fiction (as long as readers ignore possible instructions trying to persuade them otherwise) or limited in terms of duration (how long the narrative text can be read), speed (at what maximum or minimum speed it allows itself to be read) or frequency (the number of times it can read). These three types of limitation are all the more effective if they appear together, and if the reader can to some degree affect their settings (i.e. be rewarded or punished by the changes in temporal settings).

As reading time is dependent upon system time (if the text only appears once for a couple minutes the possible limitations of reading time are severely constrained by that limitation), it is best to theorize the two together. System time is needed to conceptualize the varying degrees of the text's permanence, including the appearances, disappearances and possible reappearances of its parts and phases. It specifies what is permanent and what is temporary, as in digital media permanence has become just a special case of repetition. If some or all parts or phases of a text are temporary, we need to address the aspects of textual change: what changes, how it changes and why it changes. The first of these aspects concerns the partition of texts into any number of parts and phases each with its own specifications of repetition, duration and speed. The second aspect concerns reversible and irreversible (or linear or cyclic) changes, and the third concerns what triggers the change (the system or the user). Finally, system time was schematically divided into the aspects of duration, frequency and speed to theorize the lifespan of the text, the number of changes it goes through during that lifespan, and the speed of these changes.

CHAPTER 9

Mood

9.1 Introduction

To Genette (1980, 162), the category of mood concerns the regulation of narrative information. Distance is the quantitative modulation ("how much?") of narrative information, and perspective (different types of focalization in Genette) the qualitative one ("by what channel?") (Genette 1988, 43). Distance has to do with the fullness of detail and the more or less direct way of delivering that detail to the reader; in practice, the latter part mostly concerns the representation or (re)production of characters' speech. Focalization is not about who narrates, but about who perceives or where the perceptual focus of the narrative is situated. It is a delivery channel for narrative information, and its functioning as a narrative device is ultimately based on uneven distribution of knowledge: narrative information is regulated "according to the capacities of knowledge of one or another participant in the story (a character or group of characters)" (Genette 1980, 161–162).

Since Genette (1980, 162) describes perspective and distance as "the two chief modalities" of regulating narrative information, we could well ask whether there are others. From the cybertextual perspective, it is obvious that the media position of a narrative may considerably affect its possibilities to regulate narrative (and other) information. Regulating narrative information in a text with random access is potentially very different from regulating it with controlled access; in addition, the other cybertextual parameters can affect the way in which narrative information is regulated and transmitted, as we'll later see in this chapter. From the cybertextual perspective, it is necessary to distinguish between narrative information as it is in the text (henceforth called textonic narrative information) and narrative information as it is presented to the reader/user (henceforth called scriptonic narrative information), as these don't have to be identical. The same distinction is equally applicable to characters and narrators.

In digital and ergodic fiction, narrative information is already regulated in ways unknown both to Genette and to the print tradition as a whole. In *Reagan Library* (Moulthrop 1999), the way in which text is navigated affects the release and available amount of narrative information. The regulation is tied to revisiting nodes that increases coherence by offering more information to the user.[1] Revisiting primarily affects the amount of available information in *Reagan Library*, but once again this is just a design decision; this novel regulatory device could serve many other information altering and regulating purposes as well. It is important to notice that although these new ways of regulating narrative and other information may strongly affect both distance and focalization, they don't render the latter categories useless, but only complicate and complement them: it still makes sense to ask and figure out how *Reagan Library* is focalized. This is for the most part because Genette's category of mood operates at the level of connections between narrative and story (Genette 1980, 34) and determines the relations between the narrator's and the character's discourses, whereas cybertextual regulative devices operate primarily between user and text (while also being capable of affecting the relations between narrative and story and the relations of narrators to characters).

Cybertextual mechanisms and devices can be used for many purposes other than for regulating narrative information (they are not narrative devices as such), but, in this chapter, we are focusing on their narrative use. In principle, there are four kinds of addition and modification to choose from. First, the functioning of the literary medium may alter and expand the way distance and focalization can be used in the narrative text. Second and third, both non-ergodic and ergodic media positions may affect the reader's traditional print-based omniscience in relation to narrative information and regulate its flow from text to reader and user in novel ways. Finally, there may be changes in the channel, in the sense that neither the dynamic nor the AI-based simulated characters necessarily behave in the same way in which their print cousins do.

Thus, in what follows, we are less concerned with various alternatives and additions to Genette's influential model of perspective or criticisms of it (although some of these are briefly discussed), as the theoretical and conceptual reformulations of focalization are equally tied to the materiality of books that cannot effectively hide their scriptons from the reader. The major alternatives (or some of them)[2] to Genette's conceptualization are only important to the degree they reveal dimensions and devices of regulating narrative information not included in Genette's original model. Once again we begin our narratological and cybertextual excursion by taking a closer look at Genette's formulations of distance and focalization, and postpone theorizing the majority of cybertextual novelties until a little later.

9.2 Distance

The category of distance has its roots in Plato and Aristotle, and the long tradition of contrasting mimesis and diegesis resurfacing as a contrast between showing and telling in early discussions of point of view. Genette shifts the terrain from imitation and representation to information for reasons worth quoting (as the idea of narrative as representation is still far too prevalent in many discussions and theoretizations of narrative in digital media):

> [T]here is no imitation in narrative because narrative, like everything (or almost everything) in literature, is an act of language ... therefore, there can be no more imitation in narrative in particular than there is in language in general. Like every verbal act, a narrative can only *inform* – that is, transmit meanings. Narrative doesn't "represent" a (real or fictive) story, it *recounts* it – that is, it signifies it by means of language – except for the already verbal elements of it (dialogues, monologues). (Genette 1988, 42–43)

This leads Genette to theorizing the narratives of events and words.[3] In the former, distance is mainly based on two interrelated factors:[4] the degree of detail (i.e. how detailed or developed a narrative is) and the degrees of absence and presence of the narrator (Genette 1980, 166). The degree of detail necessarily affects the speed of narrative and the degree to which the narrating instance is present is necessarily related to the narrative voice. In Genette's (1980, 166) words: "Mood here is simply a product of features that do not belong to it in its own right" (Genette 1988, 46).

Distance in the narrative of words[5] concerns "the degree of literalness in the reproduction of speeches", which Genette (1980, 171–172) originally divides into three groups that are, in the order of increasing literalness, narrativized, transposed, and reported speech.[6] Finally, Genette (1988, 62) combines this gradation with Dolezel's (1973, 4) division of narrative text into the narrator's discourse and character's discourse.

From the cybertextual perspective, it is evident that in textonically and intratextonically dynamic texts the relations between the narrator's and the character's discourse, as well as those between the narrative of words and the narrative of events, may undergo several changes. In extreme cases, one or several of these discourses may end up being erased and its contents transformed to another kind of discourse. For example, the reader may be left with only the character's discourse and dialogue while everything else disappears, or vice versa leaving the reader with more or less accurate and vivid memories of the characters' speeches. Should we then say that there's also a user's discourse consisting of memorized speech and/or memorized discourses?

In some ergodic texts, the user's discourse is more concrete, and we may have to ask at least two additional questions. How do we situate the possible user's discourse in this scheme? And if there is a separate user's discourse, is it also an indication that the text in question is not a narrative?

In principle, the user could take the place and the role of a narrator or a character. In *Eliza/Doctor*, there are two discourses, the character's and the user's, or to put it differently, a dialogue between two characters and thus only a discourse of the two characters. *Eliza/Doctor* is by no means a narrator, as it mainly asks questions, but as part of his role playing the user–patient is free to narrate, describe and comment in any combination he may find appropriate. Aarseth's category of personal perspective (the user playing a strategic role as a character in the world described by the text) is both relevant and slightly problematic here, as the roleplaying aspect doesn't have to be connected only to a character but could, in principle, be extended to other existents as well (narrators and narratees to begin with).

The user's discourse (when it is of narrative nature) is preliminarily situated within Genette's and Dolezel's grid in Table 9.1.

Table 9.1 User's discourse in ergodic narrative discourse divided by object and mode

Mode	User's discourse (UD)	Narrator's discourse (ND)	Character's discourse (CD)
Object			
Events	Situated narrative	Primary narrative	Secondary narrative
Words	Narrated, transposed and reported speech	Narrated speech and transposed speech	Transposed speech and reported speech

In this model, the user has all the states of character's speech at his disposal (including the zero degree of distance), and the fact that his narrative discourse is situated means that it functions either as an addition to the already existing discourses of narrators and characters or replaces some or all of the latter. Obviously, if the user doesn't roleplay a narrator, but merely a character, there's only dialogue and no narrative distance.

There are seven possible combinations of these three main types of discourse: texts with only the user's discourse (of multiple users presumably), the narrator's discourse, or the character's discourse, and texts with two discourses (ND+CD; UD+ND; UD+CD) or with all three discourses (UD+ND+CD). Still, the classification of each individual text as narrative depends on the strength of its narrative side compared to other text and discourse types. This is also a question concerning the differences in communication structure between narrative and ergodic discourses, one of the main topics in Chapter 11.

9.3 Focalization

Genette divides focalization into three types: zero (or nonfo-calized), internal, and external. The first one roughly[7] corresponds to the traditional omniscient narrator that "knows more than the character, or more exactly says more than any of the characters knows" (Genette 1980, 189). In the internal focalization that is typical of modernism, "the narrator says only what a given character knows" (ibid.). There are three subtypes of internal focalization: fixed (using only one focalizing character), variable (using several), and multiple (in which the same event is evoked from the perspective of several focalizing characters). In external focalization, "the narrator says less than the character knows" (ibid.), which is typical of "objective" and "behaviorist" narra-tives. This tripartition is simply a pragmatic typology clearing the confusion between mood (who perceives?) and voice (who narrates?)[8] in earlier classifications, as well as merely a reformu-lation and systematization of standard ideas, as Genette (1988, 65) later put it. Genette's (1980, 195) more original contribution lies in the conceptual pair of paralipsis and paralepsis transgressing the chosen type of focalization by giving away either more or less information than its logic would allow. These two combined with the three (or five) focalization types form a flexible scale of restricting and selecting narrative information.

From the pragmatic and functional point of view, the goal of filtering narrated events through or without a character's or characters' perceptions and consciousness is to provoke imaginary alternatives to them in the reader's process of story construction (in Genette's model both mood and tense operate between narrative text and story). In external focalization, these imaginary alter-natives include reader's speculations and inferences concerning characters' thoughts and emotions that they (and the narrator or narrators) don't have access to. These alternatives are strictly imaginary, as they don't explicitly exist anywhere in the text, but they are meaningful constructions and hypothesis within the reader's interpretative frame. In zero focalization, the imaginary alternatives have to do with various ways of assessing and evaluating the narrator's narration: its reliability, relevance, and possible exclusions. Within the three types of internal focalization, imaginary constructions consist of the hypothesized viewpoints of the characters through which events are not focalized (in fixed and variable focalization). To some degree, the same applies to multiple focalizations, which first of all require comparisons to be made among the explicitly presented focalizations.

Genette's three types of focalization contain several underlying dichotomies complicating his model (see also Jahn 1999, 95): the narrator's unlimited versus limited access to information (corresponding to the difference between zero focalization, on the one hand, and external and internal focalization, on the other), presentation from within versus from without a character's mind or consciousness (corresponding to the difference between internal focalization and external focalization) and global versus situated knowledge (corresponding to the difference between zero focalization, on the one hand, and internal and external focalization, on the other).[9]

The three types of internal focalization (fixed, variable, and multiple) add yet another dimension to be accounted for: the relation of focalization to focalized events. In a pseudo-Genettean fashion the differences could be expressed as follows: one channel for all events (fixed internal focalization), several channels for several events (variable internal focalization), and several channels for one event (multiple focalization).

Genette's original distinction has been debated ever since its publication, and there's no consensus in sight regarding the problems, theories, and conceptualizations of mood and focalization, which is markedly different from the almost general acceptance of Genette's categorization of tense. After reviewing the main revisions suggested for Genette's model and clearing up a good part of the confusion surrounding them (at least those based on taking Genette's visual metaphor of seeing literally), William Nelles (1997, 79) draws the conclusion that Genette's focalization is fundamentally "a relation between the narrator's report and the character's thoughts." In short, "the narrator either has no access to them, has (and is limited to) access to them, or has (but is not limited to) access to them" (ibid.).

Ultimately then, this is just a pragmatic and operational model. One of the obvious limitations and difficulties in its application is related to the standard tricks of narrative practice: narrators don't have to identify themselves or the characters through which the events and speeches are focalized, and they don't have to explicitly mark or indicate the shifts between the types of focalization or between characters through which the narrative is focalized. The rhythm of these changes and the duration of a particular focalization also vary greatly, from a type of focalization remaining consistent throughout the entire novel or short story to several changes of focalization that may sometimes take place even within a sentence.[10]

It may seem that after Rimmon-Kenan's (1983) reorganization of Genette's triad into character focalizers (internal focalization) and narrator focalizers (zero and external focalizations),[11] Chatman's (1990) division between slants and filters[12] (of narrators and characters respectively), Bal's (1983) and later Jahn's (1996; 2005) probes further into the fields of vision and perception, Jost's (1983) distinction between focalization and ocularization to better separate between information and perception, Genette's (1988, 74) reformulation of zero focalization as a combination of variable and sometimes zero focalization and his introduction of prefocalization (1988, 78) to account for the constraints of focalization in homodiegetic narration, Fludernik's (1996) introduction of interpretative macro frames of narrativization, and Herman's (2002) shift to epistemic and modal issues with the notion of hypothetical focalization, there is nothing particularly new to be added to the already vast and only partly compatible variety of conceptualizations of focalization. However, all these conceptualizations are based on a particular kind of literary work that occupies one single media position in the cybertextual typology of textual communication: static, determinate, intransient, random access, impersonal perspective, no links, and interpretative user function. Before teasing out the implications of that limitation, we'll conclude this section by discussing Monika Fludernik reformulations and criticism of focalization (1996, 344–347) and David Herman's hypothetical focalization (HF), as these two postclassical narratologists have suggested more than just minor revisions to the theories of focalization.

9.4 Herman

In *Story Logic*, David Herman ventures beyond classical typologies of focalization by proposing hypothetical focalization (HF) that is:

[T]he formal marker of a peculiar epistemic modality, in which, to use the terminology of Frawley (1992), the *expressed world* counterfactualizes or virtualizes the *reference world* of the text ... the reference world is made up of all those propositions having the value True in the possible world mentally modeled via storyworld reconstruction.[13] (Herman 2002, 310)

This marks a shift both from narrative form and formal narratology to narrative semantics inspired by theories of possible worlds, and also from the idea of regulating narrative information to the reliability of information and the degrees of epistemic doubt regarding "the status of narrative agents (are they there or not) ... their thoughts and behavior (do they do/think/perceive that or not?) [and] their circumstances (is their world like that or not?)" (Herman 2002, 326–327).

Herman distinguishes between direct and indirect and between weak and strong types of HF. Direct HF "entails explicit mention of a counterfactual observer or witness" while indirect HF "covers those stretches of narrative discourse the interpretation of which requires that readers *infer* the focalizing activity of a merely hypothetical onlooker" (Herman 2002, 311–312). In weak HF, "the narrator merely imputes virtual acts to actual figures instead of calling on one or more virtual figures to perform an equally virtual act of focalization" (Herman 2002, 315).

The main problem here is not the use value of Herman's additions, but the way he situates them in the existing continuum of focalization types (of Genette and Rimmon-Kenan). The incompatibilities are partly based on Herman's linguistic and cognitive orientation. He seems to believe (2002, 304) that Genette's categorization is more than metaphorically derived from linguistics, which allows him to state (Herman 2002, 303) that accounting for HF "requires that we draw on ideas developed after, or at least independently of, the ensemble of linguistic and philosophical concepts on which the early narratologists by and large relied." However, if one takes seriously Genette's insistence (1980, 30–32) on his loose metaphorical use of linguistic categories and analogies, the idea of regulating narrative information cannot be reduced to varying degrees of certainty and cognitively and/or linguistically based epistemic modalities. In fact, there are three different dimensions at play or at odds with each other in Herman's (2002,

322) typology of modes of focalization: Genette's (and Stanzel's) regulation of narrative information and Herman's two additional dimensions, the identity of the observer/focalizer (explicit or to be inferred – i.e. direct or indirect), and the status of focalizer and his focalizing acts in the fictional world (actual; partly virtual i.e. weak; wholly virtual i.e. strong). The two last dimensions could equally well be attributed to Genette's three initial types of focalization (zero, internal, external), which would then have direct and indirect as well as weak and strong variants or subtypes.

From the cybertextual perspective, it is important not to lose Genette's original focus on the regulation of information, as it has strong ties to media positions and media-specific ways of regulating information, both narrative and non-narrative. In short, the shift to epistemic modalities within fiction doesn't recognize the possibility that the reader's or the user's role in positioning himself relative to narrative information and its regulations will change according to the mechanics and conventions of the text and the textual medium.

9.5 Fludernik

Fludernik (1996, 346) ends up with a simplification of previous models of focalization. She is willing to preserve only two sets of distinctions from them: the difference between an external and internal viewpoint and the degrees of access to internality. In this sense, there's nothing positively new in her proposal except her insistence on the primary importance of the macro-frames of her natural narratology (the problems of which were discussed in Chapter 6):

> If it is unclear whether there is a story or a fictional situation and what precisely the discourse is meant to signify, parameters such as access to internality (whose internality?) or focalization on objects (who is there to observe what?) evaporate as applicable terminology. It is only when one has determined on a macro-frame (the text is an interior monologue, the text represents the jealous husband's observations) that one can then proceed to discuss *how* the details of this are handled in the discourse. (Fludernik 1996, 346)

However, this process cuts both ways, as the construction of a macro-frame may become dependent on the way in which focalizations are interpreted – and, in many cases, it may be easier to figure out whether focalization is external or internal (in Genette's terms) than to find out convincing answers to Fludernik's who, what, and whose, let alone to decide what the discourse is meant to signify.[14]

From the cybertextual perspective there is at least one important affinity between Fludernik and Genette's approaches to focalization: the role of the reader. Fludernik (1996, 344) states: "The person who 'sees' is the reader, but *à travers* the linguistic medium, and not in terms of *visual perception*." This is to a high degree compatible with Genette's idea of focalization as:

> [A] restriction of "field" … a selection of narrative information with respect to what was traditionally called *omniscience*. In pure fiction that term is, literally, absurd (the author has nothing to "know", since he invents everything), and we would be better off replacing it with *completeness of information* – which, when supplied to the reader, makes him "omniscient". (Genette 1988, 74)

It is exactly this latter omniscience, the completeness of information, which is at stake in cybertextual regulations of information, including narrative information.

9.6 Cybertextual regulations of information

The reader's complete and random access to the whole text could be said to be the standard operational practice in print narratives. Under this convention, the regulations of the information that are relevant to the construction of story belong only to the fictional communication between various fictional existents (narrators, narratees and characters) or between the whole text or its implied author (depending on one's theoretical preferences) and the positions of these fictional existents relative to it (as for example in unreliable narration). When the reader doesn't necessarily have random, complete and temporally unlimited access to every part of the text, the questions of access and information regulation necessarily grow more complicated. In the history of written narratives, this constitutes a turning point, as the possibilities of controlling narrative information expand to regulating and restricting the reader's access to narrative text and the static or dynamic information it contains.

From the cybertextual perspective the regulation of narrative information takes place on at least three different levels:[15]

1 between textons and scriptons
2 between narrative text and reader/user
3 between narrative text and story (as in Genette).

By applying the main cybertextual parameters, we can preliminarily locate several changes in the regulation of information. In textonically and intratextonically dynamic texts, the amount and content of information changes as the number and content of scriptons and textons change. Indeterminate texts do not deliver the same information[16] in the same situation every time because of random elements, and, as we saw in the previous chapter, transient texts may set complex or too difficult temporal conditions for their reception, forcing the reader to necessarily miss some information. Texts with controlled access and conditional links may deny or at least seriously delay the reader's access to relevant information; personal perspective necessarily filters information and does even more so if there are several personal perspectives to choose from or to be constructed, as is the case with multiuser environments; and finally, configurative and textonic user functions require the user to make permanent or temporary changes to the text and/ or its functioning, sometimes including changes in the ways its information is to be delivered. Needless to say, none of these possibilities is available for literary narratives in its most common media position of static dynamics, determinate determination, intransient time, impersonal perspective, random access, no links and interpretative user function.

In theorizing the cybertextual regulation of narrative information, we can mirror traditional theories of focalization because of the major affinities in their historical point of departure: the hegemony of the omniscient narrator of pre-modern literary narratives and the omniscient[17] reader of pre-digital literary narratives who has complete, random and temporally unlimited (cf. endlessly repeatable) access to narrative text. It is critically important to see the difference between real filtering, selection and restriction of existing information between reader–user and text versus the pretended (or should we say fictional) regulation of information with which the traditional and print-based theories of mood are concerned. Regardless of the way in which a print narrative is focalized, its one pattern of focalization is all there is: there is only the "filtered" information to begin with, or to put it differently, the fictionally filtered information is equal to the complete information available. The alternatives to chosen focalizations and distances in a printed narrative are merely hypothetical (as stimulating as they are to the reader's interpretative appetite), whereas in the cyber-textual situation the information in the text is not necessarily the same as the information given or accessible to the user.

If we wish to model cybertextual regulation of information after Genette's original model, we would maintain a simple distinction between omniscient readers and users, and situated readers and users with a more or less limited access to information. If we ask the same quantitative and qualitative questions as Genette, "how much?" and "by what channel?", we can cybertextualize the category of mood, and expand both distance and perspective from the relations between fictional narrators and characters to the relations between narrative texts and readers or users.

If the relation between user and text is theorized in terms of access to narrative information, we can use the distinctions already made in discussing the cybertextual parameter of access. In Chapter 2, we made two additions to Aarseth's basic distinction between random and controlled access: the first between complete and incomplete access to the whole text (to both textons and scriptons)[18] and the second between temporally limited and unlimited access.[19] The basic distinctions relevant to the position of the user are shown in Table 9.2.

As can be seen, texts that combine random and incomplete access seem to be non-existent. This is hardly surprising, as these two features are associated with codex conventions, on the one hand (random access), and experimental digital conventions or possibilities, on the other (incomplete access). *Semtext* (Eskelinen 1990) is a novel in which certain segments have expiring dates after which they are not supposed to be read.[20] *Agrippa* is once again

Table 9.2 User's cybertextual distance to the text in terms of access

ACCESS	Temporally unlimited		Temporally limited	
	Complete	Incomplete	Complete	Incomplete
Random	*Finnegans Wake*		*Semtext*	
Controlled	*Afternoon*	*Addventure*	*Agrippa*	*Agrippa*

occupying the most atypical positions and confirming Aarseth's (1997, 67) conclusion that its behavior is very different from that of other texts.[21] Although hypertext fictions such as *Afternoon* reward persistent users by granting them complete access, downgrading *Afternoon's* accessibility rate from 100 to 99% (for example by programming its last five unread nodes to self-destruct the moment when the rest has been read) would create a staggering number of more distant *Afternoons*.

9.7 Changes in the channel

The difference between textons and scriptons opens up the possibility of textonic characters and scriptonic characters, or more precisely the understanding that a character has two sides, textonic and scriptonic: the former describes how it is in the text and the latter how it is presented to the reader or the user. Characters in print fiction are ultimately strings of signs or, to put it differently, the material basis of their fictional existence is based on printed strings of signs. Thus characters are permanently positioned (they appear on some pages and are absent from others),[22] they have certain explicitly given characteristics (Chatman's traits and moods) that remain the same (i.e. are described the same way) in every reading, and if these traits and moods are attached to an identifiable and explicitly named character then that identity will also remain the same reading after reading. All these limitations could be lifted in both ergodic and non-ergodic digital narratives, and consequently we need to come to terms with both static and dynamic characters capable of altering their position in the text, their identity and their characteristics either dependently or independently from the reader's actions.

Characters in traditional literary fiction and non-fiction are also non-communicative, in the sense that we only read about them, but they don't concretely talk or write back to us,[23] and we obviously can't discuss or otherwise communicate with them but only interpret them. However, there are certain digital entities also called characters with whom we can exchange verbal messages. These AI-based entities have existed ever since *Eliza*, and they now populate both multi- and single-player digital games. In short, and without reducing the capabilities of these programmed entities to narrative purposes, it is clear that the number and behavior of possible regulators of and channels for narrative (and other) information has recently multiplied. We could call the kind of characters known to narratology (both literary and film narratologies) objects (as that is what they are to readers and spectators), and this latter subset of game characters subjects because of their autonomous behavior (however limited). Finally, some of these characters are to be controlled by the user while others are not (being either NPCs or adversaries). These simple differences in the behavior (static or dynamic), communication (one way or two way) and control (by the user or the text) of a character give us eight possible combinations, but only three of these can be traditionally (characters in print narratives), hypothetically (the dynamic cybertextual characters), or occasionally (*Eliza* – depending on the nature of the user's input) connected to narrative discourse. Simple NPCs can and often do deliver information about the game's back story, but games are not narrative discourses, as we shall soon see.

CHAPTER 10

Voice

10.1 Introduction

Genette's category of voice concerns the relationship of narrating to both narrative and story. Narrating is to be inferred and constructed from the traces it has left in the narrative text, and in that sense it is at the same level as story. In retrospect, and after postmodernism, one could argue that Genette spends much more time and space on the construction of story (through tense and mood) than on the construction of narrating or narrative instances, and thus his model may be slightly underdeveloped in the latter dimension. Narrating is "the generating instance of narrative discourse" (Genette 1980, 213) and Genette (1980, 215) divides it into three basic but simultaneously interplaying categories: time of the narrating, narrative level, and person (i.e. relations between the narrator and the story he tells). Interestingly, these three categories don't fully account for Genette's open list (1980, 215) of the web of connections among the narrating act: "its protagonists, its spatio-temporal determinations, its relationship to the other narrating situations involved in the same narrative, etc."

Genette also briefly compared the relations among narrating, narrative and story in fiction and non-fiction and in oral narratives to correct what to him is the greatest defect in his tripartite model: "its order of presentation, which corresponds to no real or fictive genesis" (Genette 1988, 14). In a nonfictional narrative, the actual order is story (the completed events), narrating (the narrative act), and narrative (the product of that act, "potentially or virtually capable of surviving it in a form of a written text, a recording, or a human memory") (ibid.). It is only this remanence that "justifies our regarding narrative as posterior to the narrating" (ibid.). The obvious alternative to this is the situation in which narrative is wholly simultaneous with narrating, as, for example, in some cases of oral narrative. In such a case, the distinction between narrative and narrating is less one of time than of aspect: "*narrative* designates the spoken discourse (syntactic and semantic aspects in Morris' terms) and *narrating* the situation *within* which it is uttered (pragmatic aspect)" (Genette 1988, 14–15).

In fiction, the true order begins with narrating, "the narrative act initiating (inventing) *both* the story and its narrative" (Genette 1988, 14–15). Moreover, in fiction "the real narrative situation is pretended to – and this pretense, or simulation (which is perhaps the best translation of the Greek *mimésis*), is precisely what defines the work of fiction" (Genette 1988, 15). Finally, the question "how does the author know that?" doesn't carry the same weight in fiction as in non-fiction, because in fiction authors have the license of making up, although in the canonical system of fiction "an author is not supposed to be making up, but reporting" (Genette 1988, 15).

This short summary of Genette's position in regard to narrating gives us several pairs of narrative meta-situations:[1] real and fictional, temporally simultaneous and successive, and oriented either to reporting or to inventing. These are important to us for at least two reasons. As printed narratives are permanent records, it is clear that they are end products that cannot be simultaneous with their act of writing – a limitation that can be lifted in digital and other media that could show the process of writing in real time. It is also possible that a published text will later be supplemented by additional texts,[2] and it may be in the reader's best interests to witness the "transmission" of the additional text when it occurs.

Second, most narratologies, including Genette's but to a lesser degree than the postclassical narratologies of Fludernik, Herman, and Ryan, either explicitly or implicitly prefer narratives oriented towards reporting or a pretense of reporting to those focused on inventing and making up. Among other things, this leads them to pay more attention to story construction than to the construction of the narrating instances and their potentially very complex machinery of inventing, generating, and making up, including the acts of erasing and undermining the reality status of the narrated events and existents. It is here that McHale's (1987, 39) distinction between perspective and construction becomes most relevant, but from the cybertextual perspective, there's even more at stake.

In *Cybertext*, Aarseth finds, describes, and theorizes fundamental differences between ergodic and narrative discourses. These differences specifically concern their communicative structures, and therefore we also need to situate narrating, the narrative acts and their ingredients in a larger communicative scheme. Even without the challenge of dominantly ergodic discourses, it is evident that many of the presuppositions concerning the chain of narrative communication from the real author to the real reader, however it is theorized, have to be revised in order to support any narrative theory focusing on or including digital media. When both authors and readers can add more text and programming to a published work of literature, and assume and play roles within it and with other users, and when every event, existent and narratological category has its textonic and scriptonic aspects, the communicative boundaries and limitations of the printed text have been thoroughly transgressed, even if many of these transgressions are or may not be narrative or even in the service of narrative purposes. In such a situation, the standard models of narrative communication (from Chatman 1978 to Jahn 2005) can only serve as points of departure and comparison.

In the rest of this chapter, we'll re-examine Genette's subcategories of narrative voice from the cybertextual perspective, and then propose a few new subcategories. The next chapter compares narrative and ergodic discourses. The differences between them will lead us to the realm of game studies and the poorly understood and analyzed debate between ludologists and narrativists.

10.2 Traditional categories revisited

10.2.1 Person

Genette's category of person concerns the relation between the narrator and the story he tells. The commonsensical basic distinction to be made is that between the homodiegetic narrator that is present as a character in the story he tells and the heterodiegetic narrator absent from the story he tells (Genette 1980, 244–245). In *Narrative Discourse*, Genette sees the boundary between these two positions as absolute and impassable, but later (Genette 1988, 103–105) he revises his position towards varying degrees of narratorial absence and presence in the story. The change is based on certain "mixed and ambiguous borderline situations" constituted by narrators that are more like contemporary chroniclers "always on the verge of participation, or at least of a presence in the action that is in effect of the presence of a witness" (Genette 1988, 104).

In intratextonically and textonically dynamic texts (where the number and content of scriptons and/or textons changes), it becomes possible for narrators to move between these two positions as the signs explicitly stating or merely implying the narrator's degree of presence in the story can be erased, supplemented, replaced and altered. In some cases, this can lead to the situation where what was once a narrator becomes a mere character (or vice versa), with nothing in the text indicating that he occupied a narratorial position in some past version, phase, or generation of the narrative text. Similar movement between positions could include and involve different types of narratee as well – a former narrator could thus continue to be present or absent in the story only as its narratee.

These possibilities indicate that we should reserve a new category of bidiegetic narrator for narrators that either reversibly or irreversibly shift their position between homodiegetic and heterodiegetic positions. We should also distinguish between static and dynamic homo- and heterodiegetic narrators – the dynamic ones being those whose degree of presence in the story changes (dynamic homodiegetic narrators could become more or less central characters in the story they tell for example) – and conceptualize part-time or temporary narrators that cease to be narrators after a while (and become mere characters or narratees instead – or simply vanish from the narrative) in addition to permanent narrators. An important question is whether all new digital entities will seamlessly fit within the traditional narratological types of narrators, characters and narratees – and even if they do, how should the obviously necessary extensions to their behavioral repertoire be theorized?

10.2.2 Narrative levels

Genette (1980, 228) distinguishes narrative levels based on the common sense principle according to which *"any event a narrative recounts is at a diegetic level immediately higher than the level at which the narrating act producing this narrative is placed."* Thus we have extra-, intra- and metadiegetic levels and narrators to begin with. Regardless of the names given to the levels,[3] they are recognized by all major narratologies and narratologists, as what is at stake here is the systematization of the traditional notion and practice of embedding.

Although narrative levels are theoretically positioned in a hierarchy, such hierarchies can easily be transgressed.[4] Genette's general term for these transgressive practices is metalepsis (1980, 234), more elegantly defined by Gerald Prince (1987, 50) as "the intrusion into one diegesis (*diégèse*) of a being from another diegesis." Metalepsis has been further classified by William Nelles (1997, 152–155), who makes three distinctions that are of interest to us. The first distinction concerns the direction of metalepsis to either "inward" (moving towards intra- or metadiegetic levels) or "outward" (moving towards the extradiegetic level). The former type is called intrametalepsis and the latter extrametalepsis. The second distinction is about possible[5] temporal shifts involved in a metalepsis, with narrators or characters involved in a metalepsis going either back or forward in time. The former constitutes analeptic and the latter proleptic metalepsis. Third, Nelles distinguishes between verbal (or epistemic) and modal (or ontological) metalepsis. In the latter case, there's a "physical movement to a different world" whereas in the former there is not, but the characters or narrators display knowledge of the other world or diegesis. As clear as all this is, the limitations of the print medium affect metalepsis too: the outward movement cannot lead to the existent's complete disappearance from the narrative text (the existent cannot erase its traces in the text) and also the range of metalepsis is limited from the start, as the number of narrative levels will stay the same in printed narratives – or at least in those known to literary narratology.[6]

Within print fiction, one of the main problems related to narrative levels lingers around Gerald Prince's assumption (1981, 35) that it is always possible to determine the first narrator who introduces the other narrators, and from that finding to eventually deduce which is the first narrative (that is also extradiegetic by definition) framing or embedding the others. All one needs in order to subvert this assumption is to write a narrative with at least two "first narrators." This could be achieved if there are two different points of beginning for the reader, which can be indicated in an explicit paratext (such as the one in *Hopscotch*), by using slightly unusual material solutions to produce a book with two front covers (requiring the reader to choose which is the front cover and which the back cover and hence determining the point of departure for reading), or by employing two languages with different reading conventions (for example by mixing English and Arabic, as the former is read from left to right and the latter from right to left).[7] Even without actual examples, these hypothetical examples that would be easy to actualize undermine Prince's assumption by demonstrating that it is predicated on mainstream binding practices and monolingual conventions.

Another issue that can be raised with Prince's claim is the possibility of heterarchic or multi-centred narratives. The former term was proposed by Aarseth (1997, 89) for fictions such as *Afternoon* that seem to subvert hierarchical structures and "where the reader is denied access to any dominant hierarchical structure and therefore caught in a heterarchy" (ibid.). Aarseth's comment is not directly related to the arrangement of narrative levels, but his term is descriptive enough to be applied to them too. Thus in a heterarchic narrative the levels can be arranged into two or several equally valid hierarchies of levels or, to put it differently, the levels mutually embed each other in the absence of any one master narrative framing the others.

In printed texts, both hierarchic and heterarchic arrangement of narrative levels are possible, but in light of the multiplicity of cyber-textual media positions the issue of narrative levels becomes more complex. Levels may vanish, collapse, expand or fuse together reversibly or irreversibly, more levels could be generated, and the reader may not have access to all levels the relations among which may also change from one reading or one point in the reading to the next. Once again, all this may happen without ergodic user functions as an effect of the mere passing of time, the reader only interpreting the results and perhaps deciding whether or not to have another session with the text.

With ergodic texts that have either configurative or textonic user function, such complications multiply, as then it is possible for the user's own explicit decisions to trigger changes in narrative levels: in their content, number, and mutual relations to begin with. Independently of ergodic user functions, it should be clear that the concept of narrative level could and perhaps should have several new attributes and variables attached to it. One important consequence is that narrators are not necessarily tied to their original position on the narrative levels (whether or not these narrators also take part in metalepsis is another matter) but could in principle change their position within a level and also increase or decrease the number of levels on which they appear. Therefore we have to distinguish between the distribution and mutual relation of narrative levels in the text, on the one hand, and the distribution and positioning of narrators within these narrative levels, on the other.

Schematically then, we can distinguish several parameters within the previously homogenous concept of the narrative level: the number of levels in the narrative text (textonic levels),[8] the number of levels presented to the reader/user (scriptonic levels),[9] the distribution of the narrators within the narrative levels, the position of the narrator(s) on a level, and the mutual relations of levels as presented in Table 10.1.

Table 10.1 Main dimensions of narrative levels in non-ergodic cybertexts

Parameter	Possible values
Number of textonic levels (t)	invariable, variable, unlimited
Number of scriptonic levels (s)	t = s; t > s
Mutual relations of scriptonic levels	hierarchic, heterarchic
Mutual relations of scriptonic levels (II)	static, dynamic
Distribution of narrators (within levels)	static, dynamic
Positions of narrators (on a level)	static, dynamic

10.2.3 The times of the narrating, transmission, and reception

There is still more to be said about time, as classical narratology recognizes yet another dimension of time in narratives: time of the narration locating the story in time with respect to the narrating act. Narrators can recount events after they happen (subsequent narration), before they happen (prior narration), while they happen (simultaneous narration), or between the moments of action (interpolated narration) (Genette 1980, 217).

In textonically and intratextonically dynamic cybertexts, these four types can change into one another, which gives us 12 (4x3) types of basic[10] temporal shifts that can have very powerful disorienting effects for those too determined to establish stable temporal distances between acts of narration and narrated events.

Genette used Todorov's article *Les Catégories du récit littéraire* (1966) as a basis for his own conceptual construction of narrative time (Genette 1980, 29). Todorov's model also included the times of the reading[11] (or perception) and writing (or narrative enunciation). Genette reasoned that those two dimensions didn't matter much to his studies of narrative time and the category of tense, principally because he reserved those considerations to be situated within another order of problems within his tripartite system: the relationships between narrative and narrating (Genette 1980, 29). As such, Genette's fourfold scale was originally just common sense, but, by the same token, the systems within which the acts of narration take place have changed and with them also the communicative resources and contexts of narration.

In print fiction, writing and reading occur as separate stages in a clear chronological continuum from writing to printing to publishing to distributing and finally to reading a text. As discussed in the introduction, in digital narratives the two layers or stages of the narrative process (narration and narrative) can now occur both successively (narration predating narrative) and simultaneously within a single text, and therefore we have to take into account the additional temporalities of narrative transmission and narrative reception.

It may be helpful to see these kinds of hypothetical narrative text as combinations of a stable product (such as a book) and several processes or transmissions that supplement and modify that product. In these situations, it could be important for the user to be able to participate in the communication process at the right time, or at least witness the textual transmission when it occurs, in order to receive it at all.

By loosely following Genette (1988, 14–15), we can discern three elementary types of fictional narrative meta-situation.[12] In the successive narrative meta-situation the narrative text is finite and not to be supplemented by any additional acts of narration. In simultaneous narrative meta-situations, the narrative text is simultaneous with its narration. In hybrid narrative meta-situations, the narrative text consists of a prior text and a series of supplementary "live" acts of narration that may or may not become permanent parts of the "updated" narrative text.

Generally speaking, theorizing the temporal determinations of the narrating instance in the realm of cybertextuality opens the door to many other theoretical considerations in addition to the times of the narrating, reception, and transmission, as in principle every position described and discussed by Genette within the triangle of person, level, and the time of the narrating can be either permanent or temporary to begin with. Therefore certain new categories and determinations could be introduced into the category of voice, as we shall see in section 10.4. The category of voice could also be supplemented in terms of modality in order to better balance the orientations towards reporting and inventing (or constructing).

10.3 New determinations: from tense and aspect to modality

Uri Margolin (1999) proposed a model of narrative to correct the paradigmatic emphasis in classical narratology on the states, events and actions that are past, factive, and completed. Margolin's model is based on the tense-aspect-modality (TAM) approach that has its origins in general linguistics (Margolin 1999, 145). In Margolin's application of that model, every narrative proposition consists of a nucleus (the actions, events, or states described) and three viewer–relative operators attached to it. The operators are temporal ("the temporal placement of the event or state relative to the NOW of the viewing act as earlier, contemporary or later"), aspectual (the event's temporal contour: completed or in progress), and modal ("the speaker's modal attitude toward his/her claims about it") (Margolin 1999, 145).

As useful as some parts of Margolin's model are, he seems to exaggerate its explanatory power, its capability of "bringing a sense of order and unity, an inner logic to a wide range of phenomena, many of which could not be accounted for by the tools of classical narratology" (Margolin 1999, 164). Actually, only one-third of the TAM model is new to classical narratology. Margolin's operator of tense corresponds to the distinctions among subsequent, simultaneous, and prior narrating in Genette's narratology, and Margolin's aspectual difference between completed events and events in progress is already recognized in Genette's interpolated narration (Genette 1980, 217). In short, Margolin's suggestions only add modality to classical narratology, while ignoring many important aspects of the latter (tense; mood; person; narrative level), albeit acknowledging that all reporting is "undertaken from a specific viewing position, narrative perspective, subjectivity, or experiencing mind" (Margolin 1999, 145). As two-thirds of the TAM model is already included in one category of Genette's narratology (time of the narrating), and its third dimension (modality) is related to the "reporting act" (Margolin 1999, 145), it is clear that Margolin's model is only about the narrative voice and not about narratology as a whole, except perhaps on the metatheoretical level of its basic premises.[13]

In principle, Margolin's operator of modality could be added to classical narratology as a "new"[14] subcategory of voice in addition to person, narrative level, and the time of the narrating. Margolin (1999, 144; 1999, 154–159) usefully specifies several modalities such as actual, nonactual, indeterminate, counterfactual, hypothetical, doxastic, optative and deontic.[15] The problem is, however, the use value of modality. The speaker's modal attitude towards the propositional content of the utterance is a mere surface phenomenon, and it is only from the larger fictional context that the reader may be able to infer or decide whether narrators or characters "really" believed and knew what they said they believed and knew and what strategic and rhetorical purposes the propositions served in their discourse. Margolin relies on the explanatory power of surface grammatical features in this respect (seeing them as "indispensable clues" and "practically the only means of access") while acknowledging that there's no 1:1 mapping between them and "the underlying semantic, cognitive, or pragmatic factors" (Margolin 1999, 146). However, there are no grammatical indicators for unreliable narration, intertextual references, genre conventions, or fallible perceptions of characters (etc.) that form indispensable parts of the overarching textual framework within which the narrative propositions and modal attitudes are expressed.

As our focus is formal and not semantic, the questionable use value of Margolin's indispensable clues is not much of an issue. Far more promising than the sentence level modalities, is Margolin's (1999, 144) idea of "reality status", although in his discourse it seems to be identical to the microlevel modalities. If the reality status were to be observed in the macrolevel of the narrative voice instead, we could distinguish among the possibly different reality status of narrators, narratees, and narrating acts – and not only that but also the reality status of what the acts of narration construct, make up, and invent (contradictory or non-contradictory fictional worlds and chains of events to begin with). This variety of modalities could also become relevant in specifying the reality status of events and existents in postmodernist narrative fiction that does not project unified ontological planes (McHale 1987, 234), and within which the tension between narrative and narrating may be more important than the relations between narrative and story, because the narrators' activity is focused more on inventing than on reporting events. In short, instead of focusing on the knowledge, ignorance, hypothesis, beliefs, wishes, and orders expressed by narrators, we could use the variety of modalities to specify the range of the narrators' activity in inventing events and existents and its end results (either unified or conflicting ontological planes or to put it differently modally compatible or incompatible narrative levels).

These postmodernist observations and practices point to certain omissions in Genette's narratology. Although his tripartite model includes multiple connections between story and both narrative and narrating, there is one traditional story component missing from the scene: the setting. It is taken for granted, which indicates that the model is biased towards representation at the expense of invention. The category of tense is about sequences of events and actions, mood about the narrators' use of characters in delivering narrative information, and voice about narrators and their relations to characters, events and other narrators. The relation of narrators to the setting they either invent or report to be there is not discussed, quite probably because the narrative world of modernism is ontologically stable and unified.

McHale's postmodernist poetics offer at least five different ways of world breaking: driving a wedge between multiple worlds (by setting them in conflict with each other within a set of non-hierarchical relations), into a world (by first creating and then erasing the same events and existents), between language and world (by the ambiguity between literal and allegorical or metaphorical meanings and frames), between author function and world, and between medium and world. The cybertextual machinery offers plenty of new ways to accomplish the last trick, may add authorial metalepsis to the second last, turn both sides of any ambiguity into temporally alternating and varying surface expressions, and change the content, number and mutual relations of events, existents and worlds. Still, to combine McHale and Genette, one could add a new subcategory to voice, in order to take into account one or several non-unified ontological planes constructed by one or several narrators (jointly or separately).

This digression aside, cybertext theory gives us several additional reasons to scrutinize both the activity and the properties of narrators.

10.4 Narrators and narrative communication

In fictional print narratives, narrators are textual constructs, neither living human beings that they are in oral narration, nor programmable entities they may become in digital media. As these constructions are ultimately based on the material strings of signs, we made a fundamental distinction between textonic and scriptonic entities in Chapter 9. As this book never tires of repeating, these strings of signs can undergo radical changes in textonically and intratextonically dynamic texts. If the number and content of scriptons and textons change in the narrative text, then the chances are that the properties of narrators and narratees will change as well.

As we saw earlier in this chapter, dynamic narrators could change both their position on a level and the number of levels they exist on, as well as alter the degree of their presence in the story and the temporal distance between their acts of narration and the events they narrate. However, these parameters constitute only one, although very important aspect or property of the narrator; let's call it his/her/its position. It is helpful to take a quick look at two other aspects: the narrator's identity and his/her/its basic qualities or attributes.

There is no consensus about the most important attributes of narrators, but in order to illustrate my point Meir Sternberg's (1978) three categories of knowledgeability, self-consciousness and communicativeness will be sufficient. Although the readers' interpretations of these qualities in any given narrative may vary the qualities still go a long way towards describing the narrator. Although the narrator may remain anonymous and give away very little information about himself (as many extradiegetic and hetero-diegetic narrators do), we still project an identity for him because the information (implicit and explicit, minimal or abundant) given about him and his defining qualities as a narrator remain the same, reading after reading, given that the scriptons related to them do not change.

In print fiction, these three dimensions (the narrator's position, identity and attributes) are necessarily glued together and static, but that no longer needs to be the case. They can be dynamic, separated from one another, and freely recombined. Narrators may change their position, identity, attributes, or all of these. Hypothetically speaking, in narrative practice these new combi-natory possibilities could lead to narrators exchanging their pasts, competing with each other for the key positions (in terms of time, space and credibility) inside the fiction they invent, and maybe as a result of these transformations or for other reasons, changing both the number and the identity of the possible narrators in the subsequent phases of the narrative text. Cybertextual constellations may also require the expenditure of additional or even excessive amounts of effort to determine whether a narrator is unreliable or not, because usually (in all cases where that is not apparent) that can be decided only after the whole text is read.

However, there are even more aspects to these new dynamic entities. Cybertext theory enables us to add two more dimensions to this already complicated scene: the relation between textonic and scriptonic narrators and the cybertextual qualities of narrators. Schematically, we can posit at minimum the following types of cybertextual narrator as a contrast to their traditional counterparts that are static, determinate, impersonal and permanent:

1 dynamic narrators capable of changing their qualities, identity, and position in the text

2 indeterminate narrators not telling the same story every time

3 personal narrators present only for some but not all readers/users

4 temporary or part-time narrators that belong to and are present in the narrative text only for a limited period of time.

The dimension of permanent and temporary narrators leads us to the relations between textonic and scriptonic narrators, the number of which doesn't have to be the same. If we make a further distinction between the maximum and minimum number of scriptonic narrators, we can draft a simple rotational scheme for narrators. The number of textonic narrators tells us how many narrators there are in the text, and the numbers of scriptonic narrators tell how many of these are presented (available) to the reader at any given point in time. The maximum number of scriptonic narrators may but doesn't have to be equal to the number of textonic narrators. In narrative practice, these differences could be actualized in a narrative system that has a certain pool of narrators from which only some but not all narrators are distributed and positioned in the narrative text presented to the reader for a given period of time, after which there'll be another selection and distribution of narrators, and so on.

It is time to put at least a temporary stop to producing theoretically grounded hypotheses without empirical examples. Still, all the possibilities drafted and discussed in this section fit well also within the standard notions of narrative communication and its basic premises: the roles of its participants (including the interpretative, non-ergodic role of the reader), the impenetrable threshold between intra- and extratextual communication, and the unidirectional and hierarchical nature of the process.

The standard models of narrative communication from Chatman (1978) to Jahn (2005) are unanimous in excluding the extratextual communication between real authors and real readers from the intratextual communication between narrators, narratees, and characters. The differences and disputes around the necessity of the concepts of implied author[16] and implied reader or among different types of audience do not need to concern us here, as it is precisely the difference between extratextual and intratextual communication that programmable and networked digital media is more than capable of undermining.

The canonical models of narrative communication are also unidirectional and hierarchical. The real (and implied) readers are there only to receive and interpret what the real (and implied) authors choose to communicate, and the information always flows only from the latter to the former through narrators, character and narratees. Bi- or multidirectional communications do not constitute foreseeable options.

Fictional transgressions aside, the levels of communication are also sealed from each other. According to Jahn (2005), communicative contact is possible on the extratextual level of non-fictional communication between author and reader; on the intratextual level of fictional mediation and discourse between narrators and addressees; and on the intratextual level of action between characters. To these three, we can already add at least the following ergodic complications, which foreshadow the fundamental differences between narrative and ergodic discourses that will be the main topic of the next chapter: extratextual users (including the author or authors) roleplaying as intratextual characters and/or narrators; ergodic communication between text and user through one or several ergodic user functions (extratextual users in some cases creating and affecting intratextual levels); and ergodic communication between users.

10.5 Narrative and other situations

Genette's formal and modal narratology, which has served as our point of departure in the last three chapters, is a relatively simple system of eight freely combinable parameters (order, speed, frequency, distance, focalization, time of narration, person, level). We have expanded and modified it in several ways, but there are still a few things that have to be settled before moving on. While we have frequently tried to see what happens when the individual parameters and values in Genette's narratology and in our cybertextual additions to it are dynamic and not static, we have not discussed this on the level of the whole system. In short, the question is what would happen if the combination of both static and dynamic parameters and categories were set in dynamic and dependent relations to one another. In such a case, the values of tense would start affecting the values of voice (etc.), either as a result of the user's ergodic efforts or the mere passing of time (perhaps relative to the user's current point of traversal or some random elements setting the variables in motion). If in this way, the narrative text becomes a combination of mutually dependent dynamic parts (events, existents and their narratologically specified relations), should we say its operational logic is simulative?

If the answer to this question is positive (or even if it is not), we can then add two hypothetical novelties to the continuum, from non-ergodic and mildly ergodic (such as *Hopscotch*) print narratives to their two well-known ergodic contenders, hypertext fiction and interactive fiction,[17] as shown in Table 10.2, which takes into account the cybertextual parameters of dynamics and user function, the material medium (print/digital), and whether the "genre" is based on simulation.

Table 10.2 Continuum from static narratives to interactive fiction

I static, non-ergodic and non-simulative print narrative
II static, ergodic and non-simulative print narrative
III static, ergodic and non-simulative hypertext narrative
IV dynamic, non-ergodic and simulative digital narrative (as explained earlier)
V dynamic, ergodic and simulative digital narrative (as explained earlier)
VI dynamic, ergodic and simulative interactive fiction

The point of this intellectual effort is not only to point to the next chapter, which discusses the differences between ergodic and narrative discourses based on Aarseth's reading of text adventures, but also to show that narrative can be made dynamic and even simulative without adding ergodic ingredients and to remind ourselves once again that the mere existence of ergodic layers (or narrative layers for that matter) is not necessarily an indication of the text's status as ergodic (or narrative). The difference between our two hypothetical examples of dynamic and simulative digital narratives and interactive fiction is that the former are not text-accepting and text-generating systems. They are neither transgressing the traditional models of narrative communication (i.e. the boundary between and the internal logic of intra- and extratextual levels remain intact) nor introducing new types of existent. But as these hypothetical narratives do not exist, it is finally time to shift the terrain from narratives to ergodics and games.

CHAPTER 11

Ergodic and narrative discourses

11.1 Introduction

This "interval" chapter concludes the narratological section and prepares for our move into the ludological section. It discusses three closely related issues: the potential transmediality of stories and narratives (already briefly summarized in Chapter 6), the properties of the narrator (what it is and what it does or is supposed to do), and finally narrative as communication, given the differences and similarities between ergodic and narrative discourses theorized by Aarseth.

11.2 Transmediality[1]

Throughout the chapters on narrative and narratology, we have used Gerald Prince's classic definition of narrative as:

[T]he recounting (as product and process, object and act, structure and structuration) of one or more real or fictitious events communicated by one, two or several (more or less overt) narrators to one, two or several (more or less overt) narratees. (Prince 1987, 58)

As we have seen, narrators can be human beings as in oral narration, textual constructs as in written fiction, or programmable entities as in some digital fictions (as Prince's definition is not anthropocentric, we don't need to worry about the gender and other possibly simulated qualities of programmable entities). By limiting the narrator's activity to recounting, Prince's definition works effectively against the transmediality of narrative, assuming that the latter is taken to mean its expansion to drama and film and not the widening variety of media readily available for oral and written narratives. The exclusion of drama is explicitly stated by Prince: "Moreover, a dramatic performance representing (many fascinating) events does not constitute narrative either, since these events, rather than being recounted, occur directly on stage" (Prince 1987, 58).

The same restriction applies to cinema, although films may sometimes use voice over narration and characters may occasionally mention or recount events that are not presented audiovisually (Bordwell 1985, 79). It is clear that similar practices can be used on stage as well. Hence, both stage drama and film occasionally, but only occasionally, share the narrative qualities of written and oral narratives. However, the main transmedial component here is not narrative, but story (i.e. actions, events, characters, and settings) that may be narrated, performed on stage, or presented by many other means than by cinematic or dramatic devices.

For some reason, transmediality on the level of stories is not good enough for some narratologists. Then the obvious way to achieve the goal of their transmedial narratology is to remove the recounting condition (and with it narrators and narratees) from the definition of narrative. In some cases, the reasons for trying to construct transmedial narratology without narrators and narratees seem to be purely ideological.[2] For example, Marie-Laure Ryan (2006, 4–6) lists two positions hostile to the transmediality of narratives, but doesn't refute their claims except by vaguely referring to trends in recent narratology and by confusing terms and concepts when arguing against the position insisting on the unique expressive resources of each medium: "This position ignores the productivity of transmedial borrowing in narratology: for instance, theme comes from music, perspective from painting, and camera-eye narration from cinema" (Ryan 2006, 6). However, it doesn't matter much where the terms originated, as they are conceptualized differently in each field.

An alternative way of trying to achieve the same goal is not to let go of the concept of narrator but, on the contrary, to stretch it as far as it goes and at least well beyond an entity that merely recounts events. This is what Seymour Chatman (1990) has to offer.

11.3 Narrators and presenters

In *Coming to Terms* (1990), Seymour Chatman revises some of his earlier beliefs about narratives (especially about the contradictory existence of his non-narrated narratives), and discusses literary and cinematic narrators in the context of his theory of text types. In this discussion, Chatman once again takes up the notions of mimesis and diegesis and argues for a broader view of narratives that could include both "told" and "shown" or performed stories. Without actually solving the dilemma, Chatman (1990, 113) introduces the narrator both in the broad sense called a "presenter" (that could be either teller or "show"-er) and the narrator in the narrow sense (i.e. the traditional teller figure).

To Chatman, the distinction between diegesis and mimesis is of lesser consequence than the one between narrative and other text types, and therefore to him "any text that presents a story – a sequence of events performed or experienced by a character – is first of all a narrative" (Chatman 1990, 117). However, this move destroys the distinction between story and narrative, by reducing the latter to the former. In Genette's terms, narrative and narrating do not count as criteria; only story does. Plays, novels, and films may share "the common features of a chrono-logic of events, a set of characters, and a setting" (Chatman 1990, 117), but as Chatman recognizes this only makes them stories – not narratives – given that one wants to maintain the basic distinction between story and discourse.

Another problem in this idea is that "narration" equals any kind of presentation or representation of events. This becomes evident when Chatman (1990, 124–138) tries to draft a cinematic narrator to overcome difficulties in Bordwell's film narratology, which replaces narrators with a strange subject called narration. In the end, Chatman's cinematic narrator becomes "the composite of a large and complex variety of communicating devices" (Chatman

1990, 134) consisting of the variables of noise, voice, music, editing, and cinematography among many others. Once this composite equals the whole media-specific presentational capacity of film it becomes both theoretically and pragmatically problematic if not untenable.[3]

Chatman's reduction of the criteria for narrative transmediality to story and its basic components (a sequence of events, character(s), and a setting) comes close to granting narratives a poorly justified monopoly for representing events, as performances and happenings (which are usually taken to be non-narrative) also include sequences of events, as do scientific simulations and both non-representational and representational games.[4] It would be as hard to classify all these later modes and genres as narratives as it would be to classify them as descriptions or arguments – a dilemma that seems to point to serious limitations in the analytical and descriptive power of Chatman's all important text types.

As Chatman's attempt to turn recounting narrators into overall presenters failed, the transmediality of stories is good enough for us, in addition to being an everyday practice in the entertainment industry, and we haven't found analytically or pragmatically valid reasons to equate narratives, stories and events,[5] we are firmly back where we started and ready to discuss the differences between narrative discourses (within which narrators recount events) and ergodic discourses.

11.4 Ergodic and narrative discourses

Aarseth's theory of ergodic discourse is most fully developed in the chapter in *Cybertext* devoted to textual adventure games (Aarseth 1995, 108–143). In these games, instead of story and discourse, Aarseth finds intrigue and discourse. The difference is articulated on the basis of Chatman's (1978, 42) concept of the event dimension, which consists of events (actions and happenings) and existents (characters and settings) fixed in a linear sequence. Aarseth (1995, 127) contrasts this with a multidimensional event space that "unfolds through the negotiation of this space by text and user." This unfolding produces a kind of log, "a recording of series of experienced events" (ibid.). Thus "instead of the story/ plot-constituted narrative, we get the intrigue-oriented ergodic log, or, to adopt Genette's and Chatman's term, ergodic *discourse*" (ibid.).

The concept of intrigue ("a scheme which depends for its success on the ignorance or gullibility of the person or persons against whom it is directed") is borrowed from drama theory, with the difference that, unlike dramatic intrigue, ergodic intrigue takes place on extrafictional level, and is directed against the user "who must figure out for herself what is going on" (Aarseth 1995, 125) There must be more than one explicit outcome; the degree of successfulness depends on the player.

Finally, Aarseth compares the discourses of narratives, hypertext fiction and adventure games in terms of discourse planes:[6]

> In a narrative, the discourse consists of the event plane, where the narration of events takes place, and also what we shall call the progression plane, which is the unfolding of the events as they are received by an implied reader. Here, these two planes are identical, as the reader's progression follows the event line. In an exploratory ergodic text such as a hypertext, the progression plane is divorced from the event plane, since the reader must explore actively and non-trivially to make sense of the event plane. In adventure games, the relation between events and progression is defined by a third plane of discourse: a negotiation plane, where the intriguee confronts the intrigue to achieve a desirable unfolding of events. (Aarseth 1995, 139)

Negotiations in an adventure game take place between the implied user and what Aarseth (1995, 127) calls the game's "voice," "the simulated correspondent that relates events to the implied user." Aarseth (ibid.) admits that "in a linguistic sense" this entity is a narrator, but, contrariwise, it is not "functionally identical to the various types of narrators that we observe in narrative fiction." This is because "the ergodic voice is both more (a negotiator) and less (a mechanical construct in a real sense) than the teller of a tale" (ibid.).

It is not clear, however, what the term mechanical construct means here. Later in the same chapter, Aarseth clarifies his position on this as follows:

To sum up, what I refer to as voice seems not to be identifiable as a singular speaker but, rather, as a composite, mechanical chorus coming from both inside and outside of the intrigue envelope. To classify this group as a narrator seems to be inappropriate because the most narrating of the voices is also the least dynamic one, and also because they do not fit together as one whole person, nor as several individuals. Instead, we might perhaps see them for what they are, an imperfect simulacrum representing the intrigant, and speaking with several tongues. Another reason is that the relationship between this chorus and the intrigant does not match that of a narrator and an implied author. (Aarseth 1995, 133–134)

This is problematic for several reasons. Genette's logical critique of the concept of the implied author (quoted in the previous chapter) can be applied to the intrigant as well: everything presented to the user is attributable either to the author/programmer or fictively to the voice that is the only entity the user communicates with – there's no need to postulate additional ghosts in the machine. Also, it is linguistically clear that the voice both narrates and describes; to quote one of Aarseth's examples: "Sergeant Duffy walks up as quietly as a mouse. He takes the cup from you. 'I'll return soon with the results', he says, and leaves as silently as he entered" (Aarseth 1995, 132). Moreover, there is no reason to assume that the narrator should always be one whole person or several persons; it can very well be a composite such as the collective we-narrator in *62: A Model Kit* (Cortazar 1994).

It seems then that Aarseth's argument rests on the negotiating function of the voice. Following Chatman's idea of textual service (discussed in Chapter 5), we could argue that description and narration are at the service of the voice's negotiating function, and thus the ergodic voice is a negotiator and not a narrator. The user has to explore the adventure game's event space, and the only way to do that is to negotiate with the voice that both helps the user in solving the mystery by providing information and complicates it by being his opponent and ally at the same time. The user's position here is very different from the triplet of narratee/implied reader/reader of literary narratives – not only because his position is ergodic – but also because the ergodic levels are organized as a puzzle or a game the solving or winning of which is the explicit goal. This explicit goal forms the challenge that the voice's discontinuous narrations and descriptions serve by both distracting the user and giving him the information he needs to solve the puzzle (or to put it differently, the user's occasional position as the voice's narratee serves the construction of his position as an intriguee in the intrigue or a player in the game).[7] Moreover, as the ergodic voice's speech acts (descriptions, narration, suggestions[8] etc.) are prompted by the user's commands and questions that drive his exploration and possible progression in the event space, we could argue that the content of those speech acts and the text types found in them are embedded in the ergodic discourse to serve as cues and clues for solving the mystery.[9]

Our partial disagreement with Aarseth's use of narratology and the decapitation of implied creator and intrigant from his model as unnecessary theoretical constructs don't affect the outcome of Aarseth's reasoning: the difference between ergodic and narrative discourses and adventure games positing "an alternative structure for articulating events and existents" (Aarseth 1995, 142). More importantly, the differences between the two discourses or discourse types need to be rearticulated. Aarseth does this by positing from three to five discourse levels in the context of determinate (cf. adventure games) and indeterminate (cf. MUDs) cybertexts, and by analytically separating three kinds of representation (narration, description and ergodics) from each other while discussing hypertext fiction (Aarseth 1997, 94–95).[10]

Following Genette (1982), Aarseth treats description only as a subservient aspect of narration and not as an independent text type on par with narration and other text types. Therefore we can assume that in his model description and narration both contribute to and constitute the one and only discourse level of narratives. So far so good, but the one narrative level and the one to four additional ergodic levels beg the question of dominance. This topic is briefly touched on in a later paper (Aarseth 1999) in the context of games between the levels of ergodics (that doesn't always dominate) and description. The conflict between narration and ergodics is also taken up in the non-game[11] context of *Afternoon* where it is left unresolved: *Afternoon* is situated as "a limit text between ergodics and narration" (Aarseth 1997, 95).

It is clear that narrative texts can contain ergodic features and vice versa, and that the relationship between the narrative and the ergodic is not dichotomic but dialectic. (Aarseth 1997, 5; Aarseth

1999) It is also clear that the difference between dominantly narrative and dominantly ergodic works doesn't correspond to the difference between interpretative and ergodic user functions, regardless of the fact that both communicative models (such as Chatman's or Genette's discussed earlier) and constructive models (such as Bordwell 1985) of narrative limit the role of the real reader and audience to interpretation only. In Aarseth's typology (1997, 69), *Hopscotch* is an ergodic text because it has the explorative user function. If we ask whether *Hopscotch* is a dominantly ergodic text the answer has to be negative. *Hopscotch* requires a simple choice to be made between reading two narrative versions and thus it is clearly a dominantly narrative text. Likewise, if we were to construct a text that instead of poetic lines offers simple narrative sentences to be combined in the manner of Queneau's *Cent Mille Milliards de Poèmes*, the result would be a dominantly narrative text of one hundred million million short stories.

To return to existing examples, hypertext fictions that separate the two discourse levels of events and progression from one another to a much more complicated degree than *Hopscotch* don't change the situation. Linguistically speaking we find signs of narrators, narratees, and characters (and the narrated events), the mutual communication of which doesn't violate the relations already theorized in classical narratology. There are no other kinds of existent in the text, and the user's efforts are limited to locating and piecing together one narrative node after another. There are no entities or existents to be negotiated with and no goals, scores, rules or opponents to organize the user's ergodic activity and to turn the ergodic text into a puzzle to be solved or a game to be won or completed. It would then seem that the discourse level of negotiation is a far better indicator of the text's ergodic dominant than its user function in itself, as obviously also a text with the textonic user function may be devoid of the discourse level of negotiation and oriented towards constructing a narrative (for example by processing narrative strings of signs the way *Book Unbound* did for "poetry"). Similarly the discourse levels of quasi-event (and more generally communication between several users) and construction especially when appearing together do not indicate narrative dominance.

After expanding literary narratology to suit the plurality of media positions in the last five chapters we have finally reached at least a preliminary limit to the expansion. It is based not on the existence of one or several user functions in the text, as all these can, in principle at least, be converted to serve the dominant narrative purposes. Obviously this doesn't mean that this could be done in any text that includes a narrative discourse level, but simply that the mere existence of an ergodic user function doesn't necessarily make the text dominantly ergodic. That depends on how the user functions are arranged in the text and what purposes they serve. If these purposes are limited to traditional text types or to literary modes and genres,[12] the result is always the same: ergodic features play a supporting and subservient role (similar to the role Genette gave to description).

From the perspective of cybertext narratology, this could be taken to mean that the expansion of literary narratology could include not only the non-ergodic media positions but also the ergodic positions. However, in that greater expansion, one should take into account that if the ergodic discourse levels are arranged to constitute a game or a puzzle or a roleplaying world, then the latter could hold their own and place the text's narrative aspects (if there are any) in a subservient position. In short, then, the main dividing line is to be situated between narratives and games as cultural modes of communication and expression. Within ergodic literature, the dividing line seems to lie between the levels of progression and negotiation and not between the ergodic user functions.

If, as in hypertext fiction, there are only the levels of progression and narrated events, the ergodic arrangement doesn't change the text's status, as the user's (main) purpose is to piece together a narrative (there's nothing else to achieve) – but if the user has to negotiate his progress with other human or simulated entities (that are then by definition engaged in other activities than narrating) and if the process of progression and exploration through negotiation has a goal, then we have left the domain of narrative behind and entered games and gameworlds.[13] This is also the direction we'll be moving in subsequent chapters.

If we take one final look at cybertext narratology, we can add two more observations to it. First, its domain is extended to ergodic texts without the levels of negotiation and quasi-events. Second, this extension wouldn't add much to our discussion in the five previous chapters, as the dynamic and temporal effects we conceptualized can be achieved both without (as system events) and with the user's ergodic activity.[14]

CHAPTER 12

Ludology and the exhaustion of narratology

12.1 Introduction

This chapter marks the transition from literary studies and narratology to game studies and ludology. Subsequent chapters will (re)construct what I call the first generation paradigm of ludology and game ontology, which will then be reflected back on literary, ergodic, and media studies in the final chapters. However, as a prolegomenon to the fully ludological chapters, it is helpful to revisit the founding debate of digital game studies: the exchanges between ludologists, narratologists, and narrativists. In these exchanges, the ludologists (cf. Eskelinen, Frasca, Järvinen, and Juul) and game ontologists (Aarseth) exposed and analyzed the limits and shortcomings of the narrativist paradigm, challenged its hegemony, and focused their own research on formal and experiential features more native and central to digital games than the stories that such games occasionally contain: rules, gameplay, simulation, player structures, fiction, transmediality, game genres, game space, player experiences and emotions, and the gaming situation (just to name a few).[1] Consequently, it became painfully obvious that digital games constituted an autonomous and interdisciplinary research area or field that could not be subsumed within other similarly autonomous and interdisciplinary fields such as literary, film, media or cultural studies, not to mention narratology. This realization in turn speeded up the emergence of the necessary institutional structures (peer-reviewed journals, conferences, organizations, academic chairs and departments etc.) that now support an international community of game researchers (or should we say postclassical ludologists?) and a multitude of approaches and research programs.[2]

The debate was also important to narratology and narrative theory, as it pointed out the limits beyond which the descriptive, explanatory and analytical power of narratology quickly become exhausted. Our interest in this debate is both narratological and ludological, and strongly related to the limitations of both narratology and narrative.[3] In subsequent chapters, the emphasis will be fully ludological as we leave the debate behind, but in this chapter ludology is mainly used to demarcate the limits of narratology and narrativism, the ideology that sees stories and narratives everywhere.[4]

The debate also merits revisiting because its nature and many positions within it are not yet well understood, despite recent attempts to partially summarize them. Many recent brief summaries situate scholars in inaccurately constructed positions, either without quoting them at all or without quoting their core arguments. Frasca's early summary of the debate (Frasca 2003b) is an exception, but because of the paper's limited length and its ironic statements about the debate not having taken place, Frasca's points were not well received let alone understood (for typical misunder-standings, see Pearce 2005; Ryan 2006). Obviously, the debate took place, but one of its major paradoxes was that the narratological basis for some of the points the ludologists made were not discussed until long after the publication of Frasca's paper (cf. Ryan 2006).

An even more alarming flaw in the debate was that the criticism hurled against ludology and ludologists was for the most part non- or even un-academic (a sign of its ideological and institu-tional motivations): in contrast to the ludologists, the opponents of ludology didn't often bother to define the contested concepts (game, narrative, and story to begin with) around which the debate revolved. Since we play according to academic rules, non-academ-ically constructed arguments can be left out of the discussion (that should never be reduced to guesswork) – except when they illuminate certain often repeated, ungrounded, and unfounded assumptions about games, stories and narratives.

The first problem in presenting a usable history of the debate involves establishing its precise temporal limits. In some ways, it started in 1997 with the publication of Aarseth's *Cybertext*, which grounded many subsequent ludological positions, or in 1998 and 1999 when Gonzalo Frasca and Jesper Juul formulated their first thoughts on ludology. What was probably the most heated period in the debate began with the publication of the first issue of *Game Studies* in 2001 (www.gamestudies.org), especially the papers by Eskelinen (2001a)[5] and Juul (2001) in that issue, and extended a bit beyond the print and web publication of *First Person* (Wardrip-Fruin and Harrigan 2004), which contained several articles that had also been written in 2001. After that the debate was most evident in short, partial and more or less misleading summaries in the first wave of textbooks covering or trying to cover or introduce the full range of digital game studies (for instance, Carr et al. 2006; Mäyrä 2008; Salen and Zimmerman 2004). Ultimately, the debate ended not with a scholarly consensus, but with the discovery of a wealth of research topics to be engaged with that were more interesting and challenging than the game of defining, redefining - or not defining - narrative; with the exception of Murray and Ryan, the principals in the debate seem to have moved on.[6]

Given the research interest expressed in this introduction, I'll loosely follow the temporal trajectory of the debate or discussion, and first summarize the position of the major ludologists in regard to games and narratives. After clarifying the basic ontological position of the ludologists, I'll discuss the specific points made by the most notable advocates of narratively oriented game studies: Henry Jenkins (2004a; 2004b); Janet Murray (2004; 2005); and Marie-Laure Ryan (2001a; 2006). I'll conclude the chapter by summarizing both the major fallacies and the major point of agreements in the debate.

12.2 Ludology and game ontology: the basic position(s)

Game ontologists and ludologists (Aarseth; Eskelinen, Frasca; Juul) made an ontological argument (games are not narratives or stories) that was misread as something completely different: a claim that games could not or should not contain stories or narratives or narrativity.[7] The ontological argument of the ludologists has some minor internal variations, but usually it boils down to two inter-connected basic tenets: no narratological theory has ever addressed or explicitly included the basic elements of games that most if not all game definitions address: the rules, variable outcomes, and player activity (for useful summaries see Salen and Zimmerman 2004, 73–80 and Juul 2004b, 22–25).

The study of these and other defining features common to all games was privileged in early ludological research, and in this respect the ontological argument about games not being narratives or stories is just one conclusion out of many that could be drawn from that research. The main contextual reason for making that simple point was the dominance of the narrative paradigm among the scholars of "digital media": video and computer games were being studied as if they were interactive narratives, although no narrative theory could specify the way they were (or were not) narratives. This attitude is perhaps best exemplified by Murray (1997) in which narrativizing interpretations are applied even to abstract games such as *Tetris* (see Eskelinen 2001a for an interpre-tation of this interpretation).

Quite logically, in the very beginning of his ludological project (Frasca 1999), Gonzalo Frasca saw the role of ludology as comple-mentary to narratology: to explain and describe the core features of games that the existing narratologies could not. In his own words, the goal is "to show how basic concepts of ludology could be used along with narratology to better understand videogames." (Frasca 2003b, 94)

Likewise, in the first chapter of *Cybertext*, Aarseth stated that "to claim that there is no difference between games and narra-tives is to ignore essential qualities of both categories. And yet, as this study tries to show, the difference is not clear-cut, and there is significant overlap between the two." (Aarseth 1997, 5). In a later paper he even more explicitly argued that "the relationship between the narrative and the ergodic is dialectic, not dichotomic. Narrative structures and elements can be found in ergodic works, and narrative works may contain ergodic features, to the extent that only a single element from one mode is found in a work belonging to the other." (Aarseth 1999, 34)

The only doubt Aarseth casts upon these hybrids is upon their usefulness, as it seems that "an audience will want the work to perform as either one or the other, and their own role to be either that of player or observer." (Aarseth 1999, 35) Even that standpoint is not set in stone: "Perhaps more complex works yet to come will have solved the aesthetic problems of games trying to be narratives and narratives trying to be games, by implementing a 'model user' position in balance between the two." (Aarseth 1999, 35)

Jesper Juul argued against treating games as stories, but also stated quite clearly that computer games could contain narrative elements:

> I would like to repeat that I believe that: 1) The player can tell stories of a game session. 2) Many computer games contain narrative elements, and in many cases the player may play to see a cutscene or realize a narrative sequence. 3) Games and narratives share some structural traits. (Juul 2001)

In retrospect Juul claims that most of the debate was ultimately caused by different definitions of narrative, turning it into "a battle of loosely defined words" (Juul 2004b, 173), but I take this to be an inaccurate description; as we shall soon see, the participating ludologists defined their terms, but very few of the narrativists even attempted to define the contested concepts they used.

In my own case, I recognized the possibility of hybrids in my treatment of the temporal aspects in games and narratives in the first ludological paper I wrote (Eskelinen 2001c; reprinted as Eskelinen 2004a):

> The key concept here is the dominant. As we all know, narratives such as Stuart Moulthrop's *Hegirascope* (1995) and *Reagan Library* (1998) can utilize both user and event times for narrative purposes and games like *The Last Express* can use story and discourse times for gaming purposes (...) Despite these possible hybrids (...) (Eskelinen 2004a, 39)

In the concluding section of The Gaming Situation (Eskelinen 2001a) I wrote:

> The old and new game components, their dynamic combination and distribution, the registers, the necessary manipulation of

temporal, causal, spatial and functional relations and properties
not to mention the rules and the goals and the lack of audience
should suffice to set games and the gaming situation apart from
narrative and drama, and to annihilate for good the discussion
of games as stories, narratives or cinema. In this scenario stories
are just uninteresting ornaments or gift-wrappings to games, and
laying any emphasis on studying these kinds of marketing tools
is just a waste of time and energy. (Eskelinen 2001a)

Rune Klevjer (2002, 191–192) and far too many scholars after
him read this as a radical ludological and aesthetical argument,
according to which games should never include stories (or other
narrative elements). In order to do so, he quotes me out of context.
I don't have much to add Frasca's debunking of Klevjer's argument:

Looking through the ludologists' work there is one claim from
Markku Eskelinen from 'The Gaming Situation' which could be
interpreted as a sign of ludological radicalism. Rune Klevjer pays
particular attention to it in his 'In defense of cutscenes': 'In his
excellent article about configurative mechanisms in games, The
Gaming Situation, Markku Eskelinen rightly points out, drawing
on Espen Aarseth's well-known typology of cybertexts, that playing
a game is predominantly a configurative practice, not an interpretative one like film or literature. However, the deeply problematic
claim following from this is that stories 'are just uninteresting
ornaments or gift-wrappings to games, and laying any emphasis
on studying these kind of marketing tools is just waste of time and
energy'. This is a radical ludological argument: Everything other
than the pure game mechanics of a computer game is essentially alien
to its true aesthetic form." To start with, Klevjer's quote is incomplete and, I think, it should be read in context. Eskelinen actually
said 'In this scenario stories are just uninteresting ornaments […]'.
The scenario he was referring to is the one provided by elements
for game analysis that he previously mentioned on his text. In other
words, it seems that he was referring to what the focus of game
scholarship should be. (Frasca 2003b, 95)

The only comment I wish to add[8]: when I used the term "stories" I
was obviously referring to the definition of story I had previously
offered – a definition Klevjer doesn't challenge or discuss – and

he does not provide his own definitions of any of the contested concepts he uses.

Based on all this we can only validate the conclusion Frasca (2003b) already presented: according to all major ludologists and Aarseth, narrative and story elements may be included and embedded in games. This is perhaps the one single point on which ludologists, narratologists, and narrativists have agreed all along, although without the knowledge of the latter two parties.

However, there is more at stake in the debate than the more or less innocent misunderstanding of the clearly stated and often repeated ludological position on narratives and stories in games. The major disagreement concerns both the role of narratology in game studies and the importance and nature of narrative/story elements in computer and video games. To some degree these issues are dependent on the definitions used, and it is exactly here that we move beyond mere more or less innocent misunderstandings and misinterpretations of ludology. The problem is not that ludologists and their opponents use different definitions of games, stories and narratives. Instead the main difference is that ludologists define all the contested concepts – which are necessary for any valid comparison to be made and around which the debate raged and revolved – and their narrativist and narratological opponents or commentators do not.[9] The presence and absence of the requisite definitions in six papers by six major participants in the debate are shown in Table 12.1.

Table 12.1 Academic dimension of the debate

Definition of	game	narrative	story
Frasca 1999	yes	yes	yes
Juul 1999	yes	yes	yes
Eskelinen 2001a	yes	yes	yes
Jenkins 2004a	no	no	yes
Murray 2004	no	no	no
Ryan 2006	no	yes/no	yes

To see what precisely is at stake we'll pay close attention to arguments, definitions and models put forward by Henry Jenkins (2004a), Janet Murray (2004; 2005), and Marie-Laure Ryan (2001a; 2006) in reverse order of importance (unlike the two others Ryan ultimately tries to construct a narratology capable of including games) and the degree of academic argumentation (as can be seen from the figure above Murray's discourse is fully non-academic, Jenkins' two-thirds non-academic[10], and Ryan's only one-third non-academic[11]). The most important common factor in these three approaches is that although the main topics of their discussion are games and narratives, narratology and ludology, none of the scholars sees any need to define games – the fact that clearly shows their common narrativist bias.

12.3 From narrativist to narratological positions: Murray, Jenkins, and Ryan

12.3.1 Murray

Probably the lowest points in the discussion were reached in Murray's article in *First Person* (Murray 2004) and in her keynote at the 2005 Digra Conference (Murray 2005). Murray (2004) doesn't define any of the contested concepts, beginning with but not limited to games or stories, which are central to her argument. Instead and in a completely un-academic fashion she makes extreme statements such as the following: "Games are always stories, even abstract games such as checkers or *Tetris*, which are about winning and losing, casting the player as the opponent-battling or environment-battling hero" (Murray 2004, 2).

Murray's absolute pan-narrativism is made evident when she explains why she's drawn to discussing digital games in terms of stories and why there's so much "storytelling going on in electronic games": "the digital medium" is one "that includes still images, moving images, text, audio, three dimensional, navigable space – more of the building blocks of storytelling than any single medium has ever offered us. So gamemakers can include more of these elements in the game world" (Murray 2004, 2).

The basic cultural fact that such building blocks of expression are and can be routinely and traditionally used for a wide variety of purposes other than constructing stories seems to have completely escaped her.

In the absence of any academic framework that could justify Murray's extreme position, this blindness to diverse cultural practices and forms of expression becomes an idiosyncratic preference, although she tries to generalize it by stating that: "For me, it is always the story that comes first, because storytelling is a core human activity, one we take to every medium of expression, from oral-formulaic to the digital multimedia" (Murray 2004, 3). Obviously, almost any medium can be used for presenting stories, but that doesn't mean that every work in every medium is presenting stories. Moreover, as we saw in Chapter 2, there's no single unified digital medium,[12] but a plenitude of digital media.

Murray's position is no better grounded in the preface to her keynote (Murray 2005). Once again it is non-academic in the sense that she doesn't define the contested concepts around which the debate has revolved for several years, even though it is a debate she wants to bring to closure. Hence her keynote is a purely rhetorical plea for peace without any scholarly merit. However, as it is the only instance in which Murray explicitly addresses the ludological criticism against her (instead of merely repeating her position with no reference to game scholarship), and given that it was delivered in an allegedly highly academic context (an international conference of specialist game scholars), I'll briefly review its major flaws.

First, Murray (2005, 1) repeats the false claim that ludologists are only interested in formal features of games. As is shown by Frasca's consistent focus on the politics and rhetorics of simulation and Juul's combination of rules and fiction, among many other possible examples, this is incorrect. Second, when projecting an ideology onto the ludologists, Murray confuses the tasks of theory and analysis:

The ideology can perhaps be called game essentialism (GE), since it claims that games, unlike other cultural objects, should be interpreted only as members of their own class, and only in terms of their defining abstract formal qualities. (Murray 2005, 2)

Needless to say ludologists haven't made such claims against interpretation and Murray, as usual, does not substantiate her claim by actually quoting a ludologist. Third, Murray falsely believes that ludologists are discussing or theorizing the player's experience: "According to this [ludologist] view, games in general and computer games in particular display a unique formalism which defines them as a discreet experience" (Murray 2005, 1). Once again she doesn't quote any evidence to substantiate her claim.

Fourth, Murray (2005, 2–3) doesn't understand Aarseth's point that ludologists are trained in narratology, unlike their many opponents (including Murray), and instead of responding to it ventures into speculating about the anxiety of influence narratology has supposedly caused to ludologists (who actually use narratology to make their points). Fifth, she contradicts her own paper (Murray 2004; quoted earlier) when responding to Aarseth's statement that before games are shown to be stories in a well-argued and defined way, the burden of argument rests with narrativists by stating the following:

> To which we have to ask whose burden? Who is obliged to defend the position that games are stories? What Aarseth [and] his followers would like is a formalist argument, starting from the texts that have been most influential in European narrative studies (Eskelinen 2004a). In fact, no one has been interested in making the argument that there is no difference between games and stories or that games are merely a subset of stories. Those interested in both games and stories see game elements in stories and story elements in games: interpenetrating sibling categories, neither of which completely subsumes the other. (Murray 2005, 3)

Murray obviously doesn't feel compelled to defend her position of the previous year: "Games are always stories" (Murray 2004, 2). And, even more importantly, she again fails to define the concepts she keeps on repeating. The last sentence of the preceding quote is hard to understand: without any definitions it is impossible to know what the actual elements are. Perhaps her point is that we do not need to know as long as we are interested in both. In the absence of definitions this is just a rhetorical trick trying to make us believe that these two "sides" are equally important in games and game studies. Moreover, according to every salient definition of story, the game elements in stories can only be semantic, i.e. stories about games. By applying Murray's rhetoric we can make similarly interpenetrating pairs out of absolutely anything: those interested in both food and games see culinary elements in games and game elements in eating and so on, ad absurdum.

In addition to all these significant problems, Murray's paper contains one quite typical fallacy. She (2005, 1) claims that ludologists treat "the advent of electronic games as a new entertainment and art form" and as "an event divorced from cultural history" although, in fact, most ludologists (for instance, Eskelinen 2001a; Juul 2001), unlike most new media scholars like Murray, see electronic games as the latest newcomer in the long cultural history of games. Murray's claim is an interesting variation of what I call an *ahistorical fallacy* (the idea that games, and computer and video games in particular, do not have a cultural history): she projects her own position onto her opponents and then criticizes them on the basis of that projection.

Murray admits that ludologists have made several contributions to game study:

> First of all, as ideologists, they have energized and focused the field by insisting on the legitimacy of computer games as objects of study in their own right, rather than as "colonized" examples of film or narrative. Secondly, as proponents of a formalist methodology, parallel to the narratological approach to stories, they have already made some highly useful observations. For example, it is helpful to think of games, as Aarseth has suggested, as "configurational" structures, which require us to actively manipulate their components. Furthermore, by calling attention to the formal properties of games, they have opened up a range of productive questions about the definition of games, the form of games, the boundaries between games and other cultural forms, that can be addressed from many directions. (Murray 2005, 2)

This reads like a shortened list of the positive effects her approach was and is unable to deliver, because of its constantly non-academic and speculative nature, which has been severely criticized by not only ludologists but also narratologists (cf. Ryan 2001).

12.3.2 Jenkins

In "Game Design as Narrative Architecture," Henry Jenkins found four ways for narrativity to enter games on a local level:

> Environmental storytelling creates the preconditions for an immersive narrative experience in at least one of four ways: spatial stories can evoke pre-existing narrative associations; they can provide a staging ground where narrative events are enacted; they may embed narrative information within their mise-en-scene; or they provide resources for emergent narratives. (Jenkins 2004a, 123)

Depending on one's point of view, the first way either confuses narrative associations with useful prior knowledge, or prefers narrative associations to all the other possible intertextual and intermedial associations designers can play with (and since when associations count in a supposedly academic discussion about games and narratives – any novel mentioning chess will create game associations); the second confuses similar events in films and in games without paying any attention to effects of the change of context, medium and the user's role; the third either confuses narrative information with information in general or prefers narrative information to all the other types of information; and the fourth either confuses games with one possible use of games or prefers that one possible use to all the other possible uses.

As Jenkins doesn't define what he means by narrative, it is impossible to infer what, if anything, he means by narrative associations, events or information, or in other words what separates them from other types of associations, events and information.[13] The only terms Jenkins defines are story and plot (Jenkins 2004a, 126), and although he defines them as the Russian formalists did (the difference between *syuzhet* and *fabula* or plot and story), their definitions are at odds with the term spatial story that he frequently repeats without defining it, although he comes closest to a definition in a footnote stating that "my concept of spatial stories is strongly influenced by Michel de Certeau (1988) *The Practice of Everyday Life* and Henri LeFebvre (1991), *The Production of Space*" (Jenkins 2004a, 130). Jenkins doesn't seem to notice that his undefined concept of spatial stories[14] and the formalist concept of story are very likely at odds with each other – if one takes seriously the former's grounding in de Certeau's and Lefebvre's overtly metaphorical use of the term "story."

However, in a section titled "Spatial Stories and Environmental Storytelling," in which the undefined concept is somewhat further developed, the only source Jenkins cites is Don Carson, "who worked as a Senior Show Designer for Walt Disney Imagineering" (Jenkins 2004a, 122). Jenkins approvingly quotes Carson at length about situating "the story element into the physical space a guest walks or rides through" and the original story (unexplainably) providing "a set of rules that will guide the design and project team to a common goal" (Jenkins 2004a, 123). When Jenkins compares this with a game (*Sea Dogs*), he finds a difference, however:

> The most significant difference is that amusement park designers count on visitors keeping their hands and arms in the car at all times and thus have a greater control in shaping our total experience, whereas game designers have to develop worlds where we can touch, grab, and fling things about at will. (Jenkins 2004, 123)

Obviously, this very difference is what makes games games and not amusement park rides, but instead of learning from ludology how to understand this difference Jenkins relies on his vague analogue and proposes the four forms of "environmental storytelling" discussed earlier.

A similar flaw occurs when Jenkins claims that computer games are "undertheorized hybrids between games and narratives." The grounds for this conclusion are as follows:

> The market category of "games", in fact, covers an enormous ground, including what the traditional ludologists would classify as play, sports, simulations, and toys, as well as traditional games. Some, but certainly not all, of these products also make bids on telling stories, storytelling is part of what they are marketing and part of what consumers think they are buying when they invest in this software. (Jenkins 2004b)

Once again, Jenkins gives no reasons why or how play, sports, simulations, and toys are or could be connected to storytelling, which is yet another activity Jenkins doesn't care to define in his essay. Marketing strategies and (unverified) consumer beliefs are poor substitutes for academic reasoning, for many reasons, including the former's rhetorical licence to mislead and the likelihood that the latter may be mistaken and ignorant.

In the same context (Jenkins 2004b), Jenkins admits that "there is no question in my mind that current narrative theory would need to be significantly rethought before it can be applied to computer and videogames." For some reason, this doesn't prompt Jenkins to rethink narrative theory beyond suggesting his vague analogue between computer games and amusement park rides and his insistence that the models of narrative and narration should be broader than they are (Jenkins 2004, 121). Obviously, the need for broader models stems from the objective of including games or at least substantial aspects of games in revised narratologies or narrative theories, which is an ideological aspiration – as there's no valid reason for such expansion (ludologists ground their arguments in existing narratologies and not in speculative, hypothetical and non-existent ones). The burden of proof for the descriptive, explanatory and analytical power of such hypothetical models lies in the narrativist camp, and so far such models are as non-existent as they were when ludology began to take shape more than a decade ago (with the exception of Ryan's 2006 model that will be discussed later). Interestingly, Jenkins doesn't address the reworking of narrative theory that has already occurred within ludology, which includes a narratological side as well.

If computer and videogames are the kind of hybrid Jenkins claims (without producing evidence) that they are, the study of them necessary requires theorizing "the game side" as well, and this is also one of the tasks Jenkins doesn't undertake: his essay fails to discuss rules, variables outcomes, or player structures. In short, even if Jenkins' hybrid exists, his essay doesn't even begin to make a contribution towards theorizing and analyzing it.

These and many other contradictions and weaknesses in Jenkins' essay are to some degree explained by the orientation he later described in his response (Jenkins 2004b) in which he explicitly situates his essay outside any academic context, debate, or exchange, as the following two quotes make clear:

Eskelinen asks for a definition of terms. My essay is talking about computer and videogames as they are constituted within the current marketplace ... Eskelinen is involved in a particular kind of game – defining and defending the borders of an emerging academic discipline – and he is doing so according to some traditional rules: define terms, lay down axioms, cite core theorists, and then engage in debate around those various abstractions ... I see myself involved in a rather different exercise, attempting not to construct an academic discipline around games, but to intervene in a public debate among game designers, game critics, and game players – as well as policy makers and other media producers and consumers – about the current state and future development of an emergent and hybrid form of "interactive entertainment." (Jenkins 2004b)

> Most game designers know a great deal more about the theory of play and games than they know about narrative. Most of the game design books currently on the market tell little or nothing about character and plot. Yet, these practitioners consistently express a hunger to know more about traditional storytelling; sessions on games and narrative have been among the most highly attended at industry conferences. My essay's arguments came out of that dialogue with the game design community rather than within a more academic context. (Jenkins 2004b)

One final comment to be made here is that, although educating theoretically ignorant game designers about the market category of interactive entertainment could be a formidable task or vocation in itself, it should not and cannot be confused with making a valid scholarly argument in a theoretical and academic debate with game scholars.

12.3.3 Ryan

In her early paper on narratology in game studies, Ryan made the following concession that is similar to Jenkins's point on narratology's need to be reworked:

> [T]he inability of literary narratology to account for the experience of games does not mean that we should throw away

the concept of narrative in ludology; it rather means that we need to expand the catalogue of narrative modalities beyond the diegetic and the dramatic, by adding a phenomenological category tailor made for games. (Ryan 2001a)

The need for such narratology is left unexplained, as it has also been left by Jenkins and many other scholars who cling to the narratological or narrativist framework: the advocates of that view seem to think without being able to conceptualize it that games do tell stories and hence the narratological framework should be extended to games as well. The obvious alternative to that speculative approach is to apply existing narratological theories to the features that both ludologists and narratologists see as story or narrative elements in games: cutscenes and backstories. The paradox is that this doesn't require substantial (or any) reworking of currently existing well-established narratological theories; neither is it difficult.

In 2001 the existence of the narratology Ryan argued for was pure speculation, and this non-existence easily justified throwing away the idea that extending the concept of narrative beyond cutscenes and backstories is important to ludology. However, unlike Jenkins and Murray, Ryan later came to understand that the burden of proof rests with those making the types of claims quoted earlier, and in *Avatars of Story* (2006) she finally tries to integrate games into her preliminary construction of "interactive narratology."

To achieve this, she first borrows and renames two distinctions from Aarseth. The difference between personal and impersonal perspective becomes the difference between external and internal interactivity, and the difference between explorative and configurative user function becomes the difference between explorative and ontological interactivity (Ryan 2006, 107–120). These can be combined in four ways, and the examples Ryan uses to illustrate them include games in three cases out of four. Only her explorative–external interactivity (i.e. the combination of impersonal perspective and explorative user function) is exemplified by classic hypertext fiction (Ryan 2006, 122). Therefore it is essential to her project of interactive narratology to treat games as narratives, and to achieve that objective she tries to refute some statements the ludologists have made against that position. However, as we shall see she doesn't take up or address let alone refute the most central ludological arguments.

In the beginning of the chapter titled "Computer Games as Narratives," Ryan (2006, 181) says she will ask three questions: the theoretical one ("can games be narratives or possess narrativity?"),[15] the aesthetic and functional one ("what is the role of narrative within the game system?"), and the methodological question ("how can the concept of narrative be fruitfully invoked in game studies?"). Actually, there are four questions: the two parts of the theoretical question are two different questions, and more importantly neither matches the ontological question (are games narratives?) to which the ludologists' answer is a firm no. In short, even at the beginning of her argument, Ryan sets her stage so that the ontological focus of ludologists is not properly represented.

A little later Ryan writes: "The ludologists believe, with good reason, that what makes a game a game, and what distinguishes it from other games, is its set of rules" (Ryan 2006, 184). However, she doesn't challenge this ontological claim, try to refute it, or discuss the fact that the definitions of narrative, both the one she uses and the many she opposes, do not mention rules at all, unlike virtually all game definitions (as could be seen in the surveys of both Juul 2004b, 22–28, and Salen and Zimmerman 2004, 73–80) that take them to be defining features of games and gameness.[16] Ryan's move is revealing, as she completely dismisses the value of traditional game scholarship and existing definitions of games, and seems to believe that the whole issue can be settled by redefining narrative and narrativity such that games could be included in it.[17] Ironically, in the end, she has to admit that: "For me some games have a narrative design and others do not" (Ryan 2006, 192). Presumably, both kinds of games still have rules, variable outcomes and player activity not worthy of her attention.

After avoiding the issue of rules (that narratives do not have and all games have) and not providing even a provisional definition of game, Ryan (2006, 185) moves on to discuss "several arguments raised by the ludologists against the narrativity of games." However, contrary to what Ryan claims (and very unlike her own practice), ludologists do not confuse the basic ontological questions (what are games? are games narratives? etc.) with the question of the games' hypothetical ability to possess narrativity. In short, ludologists do not address the narrativity of games except to maintain that it is not the defining feature of games. In contrast, Ryan maintains the confusion between the two when she addresses what she calls "The 'Games and narratives are different things because they have different features' Argument" (Ryan 2006, 185). To her, that argument consists of "enumerating features of literary narrative and of film that do not occur in games" (ibid.). Once again, this is a remarkably one-sided description, as it leaves out an even more important ludological argument enumerating features of games that do not occur in literary narratives and film such as rules, variable outcome and the configurative activity of the player, but, here again, Ryan has nothing to say about the latter: we can conclude only she takes them to be insignificant to any discussion or study of games.

In the section mentioned earlier, Ryan sets out to "review some points that have been invoked by Eskelinen and Juul" (Ryan 2006, 185). There are four points she tries to refute; in this section, I address two of them.[18]

The first attempted refutation to be considered is, "even if games are built on stories this doesn't make them narratives, because the narratives involve 'the presence of narrators and narratees' (Eskelinen 2001a, 3)." First, here Ryan misunderstands the general framework for the criterion that narratives involve "the presence of narrators and narratees" derived from Prince's (1987, 58) definition of narrative. Even though some games do or may have narrators, most games do not, and thus this feature (the presence of narrators) is not more suitable for defining games than such features as rules and player activity that are defining characteristics of every game. Second, she misses that the player who is informed about the game state is not necessarily a narratee[19] in her example (*EverQuest*, where the bulletin board informs the player about what he just did).

Third, she generally objects to Prince's definition of narrative but never gives any valid grounds for her objection except to remark that Prince's definition would limit narratives mainly to literary narratives and thus ruin her project of transmedial narratology (Ryan 2006, 5). Fourth, she misses the ontological point concerning the dominant features: the occasional presence of narrators and narratees in some games doesn't turn them into narratives, because the game features dominate the "narrative" ones. Should we follow Ryan's criteria and dismiss the question of dominance and dominant features, then we could claim that novels and films are descriptions and not narratives because they contain description, or better still that *Hopscotch* is not a narrative but an instruction.

To move to the second attempted refutation, in a similar fashion Ryan (2006, 186) quotes and misunderstands my point in regard to open series of events not reducible to the notions of story and plot: "Plot-lovers often conceive stories as mere plots or closed sequences of events, in which case they should come to grips with games containing open series of events" (Eskelinen 2001a). She (ibid.) claims that "not all games have open series of events: in the type that Juul (2004b, 72–73) calls progression games, the player has to fulfil a quest by solving problems in a rigidly prescribed order," but confuses the structure of the quest with events produced by the player's activity and misses the context of my argument.

First, my comment was about coming to grips and it was ironically addressed to "plot lovers", asking them to expand their horizons beyond closed sequences of events (typical of story/plot oriented narratologies). After 10 years I still haven't seen a narratology, interactive or not, that properly addresses this extremely significant expansion in the arrangement and production of events. Ludology, by way of contrast, has no problem theorizing both open series and closed sequences of events – and their combinations. Second, I say that games contain open series of events, but I do *not* say that games consist *only* of open series of events, as there are closed series and sequences of events as well. Third, the open series of events take place whenever the player tries to fulfill the quest, because his attempts to solve it involve negotiation and retries that result in several different sequences of events until the right sequence of necessary events is found[20] and executed propelling the player forward in the quest. This partly trial-and-error-based activity (gameplay) produces different series of events that also vary from one player to the next. If the player fails and is stuck in the game, unable to progress and complete it (which happens very often), all he can do is either quit or continue producing open series of events with no definite point of ending.[21] Even if the player chooses to cheat and use a reliable walkthrough explaining what he should do and in what order, the resulting events could still differ from one attempt to the next and from one player to the next, as there are smaller events that are more or less contingent to the series of main events necessary to the player's progression (completing a task, a quest, or a level). Also the temporal qualities of the events in the sequence or the series may vary, for instance because some players are faster and better than others or apply different tactics and strategies. Needless to say these kinds of variation do not occur in narratives and stories that one can either effortlessly read from beginning to end while being engaged only in interpretive activity or explore without having to negotiate one's way to the goal.

In the end, it becomes evident that Ryan misses the whole ontological point repeated by the ludologists:

> But let's imagine that Eskelinen's and Juul's observations present no exceptions … Would it mean that games cannot suggest stories? No, it would simply mean that they do so in a partly different mode from novels, drama, and movies. (Ryan 2006, 187)

The ability to suggest stories is a very poor criterion for classifying games as narratives – if it is a criterion for anything at all, as there is almost nothing in this world and in human life that cannot suggest stories. Ludologists are not concerned with suggested stories, but theorizing games and game ontology. In short, Ryan shifts the terrain from game ontology to one possible side effect of games (their ability to suggest stories). She doesn't offer even a provisional definition of game, and doesn't address the ludologists' game definitions either.

The weakness of Ryan's counterarguments to ludology (or the parts of the ludological argumentation she dares to address) boils down to the weakness of her definition of narrative:

> Narrative is not a genre that excludes but a type of meaning that permeates a wide variety of cultural artifacts, and the ludologist claim that game and story form mutually exclusive categories betrays a lack of understanding of the nature of narrative. The fact that games may subordinate narrative to gameplay rather than making it a focus of interest can be easily accounted for by recognizing an instrumental mode of narrativity. (Ryan 2006, 197)[22]

The definition of narrative as a type of meaning is untenable for several reasons: there are no specific narrative contents as Genette observed, and we'd need an endless anti-occamian list of defining features to separate narrative meanings from other types of meaning, an enterprise likely to fail because of the ways that meanings emerge from highly context- and culture-dependent frames of interpretation that are more than likely to clash with one another. Compared to that unproductive dead end, it is considerably easier to agree on such defining formal features as the presence or absence of rules, as the majority of narrative and game scholars do and have been doing decades before Ryan's idiosyncratic construction of narrativity.

From the game studies perspective, Ryan's model is of limited or no value, as it has only one dimension, the varying degrees of narrativity, and thus games differ from each other only in the degree of narrativity they possess. Games also share this "quality" with films, novels and everything else in this world, because Ryan's criterion of narrativity hardly excludes anything: "In my own view a retrospective availability of meaning is sufficient to ascribe narrativity to games. (Ryan 2003, 334). Based on this, I would guess that aphorisms, concrete poetry, Gertrude Stein's 'a rose is a rose is a rose,'" t-shirt with logos, shopping and laundry lists and music without a libretto contain narrativity according to Ryan. Perhaps the kindest possible interpretation of Ryan's scholarly position is to situate it outside ludology and narratology, as she studies neither games nor narratives but narrativity (that is everywhere around us just as gameness or playfulness).

Not surprisingly, Ryan is not the only narrativist conflating narrative or narrativity with meaning. An even more extreme definition was presented by Michael Nitsche (2008, 42): "For our discussion of video game spaces, narrative is best understood as a form of comprehension that can be triggered and affected by the game world." Nitsche's (2008, 54–55) approach narrativizes the presentation layer: "The discourse in video games comes to life through the interactive functionality, but also on the level of the presentation. Video games still tell. There is an inherent situation of narration in playing a video game because each game includes the mediated plane." The logic of such claims is always the same: look, there are events and descriptions and characters on the screen, therefore it must be a story or a narrative – regardless of the differences in the overall communication structure (between game and player and between players), cultural genres and modes of expression (games/quests/performances/narratives etc.), the mechanisms producing these representations (the user's ergodic action; the game algorithms etc.), and the behavior and function of the presented entities in delivering information related to the rules, goals and the behavior of the game system to begin with. Usually this is backed up by shaky or absurd definitions of narrative (if there are any) – in Nitsche's case narrative as a form of comprehension. The nature of this comprehension is revealed in his comment on Aarseth's views on adventure games as quests: "Aarseth is correct in his overall claim that 'the purpose of adventure games is to enable to fulfill quests. This, not storytelling, is their dominant structure.' (2008, 368) Yet comprehension of game elements during play is where the narrative elements come to work in the discourse. Without narrative elements, a 3D video game would be in danger of disintegrating into singular unconnected splinters of momentary interaction" (Nitsche 2008, 64–65). I see more danger in scholars who lack the common cultural knowledge necessary to allow them to distinguish between game, quest, narrative and performance structures (providing connections between their constituent elements) although they may use similar elements (that all look alike to an untrained narrativist eye that can only detect and comprehend narrativized meanings and elements). But let's leave this particular monocognitive fallacy behind us for a while.

From Ryan's perspective, the main reason for using narrative concepts in game studies is "to come to terms with the imaginative dimension of computer games – a dimension that will be overlooked if we concentrate exclusively on rules, problem-solving, and competition" (Ryan 2006, 203). However, the ludologist camp (cf. Frasca 2004; Juul 2004b) has already addressed the imaginative dimension, but has discussed it in terms of fiction and simulation, not narrative. As Juul notes:

Video games project fictional worlds, and at the time of writing, this carries with it a terminological problem in that *fiction* is commonly confused with *storytelling*. This is highly misleading since storytelling is simply one of the many ways of creating a fictional world. (Juul 2004b, 109–110)

This confusion is related to what could be called a representational fallacy that conflates either narratives, stories, or both with events, actions, (re)presentations, fiction, or information (or meaning as we just saw) – or all of these, usually without bothering to offer definitions. We can find many variations of this fallacy in so many other narratively oriented video game theories (for instance in Klevjer 2002) that they would almost deserve a whole book about them.

Ryan (2006, 200) mentions Juul's point about video games projecting a fictional world, but addresses neither his point about the confusion nor the two crucial specifications Juul makes about the relation of rules and fiction. The first concerns their non-symmetrical relationship:

> [S]ince all games have rules and since rules are a distinct aspect of games, it was possible in the previous chapter to discuss rules without mentioning fiction. But it is not possible deal with fiction in games without discussing rules: the fictional world of a game is created in a variety of ways –using graphics, sound, text, advertising, by the way of the game manual, *and* by the way of rules. (Juul 2004b, 109)

Second, rules and fiction are not equally important, as the player can potentially ignore the special status of the representation of a game (i.e. its role as fiction) (Juul 2004b, 109).

As can be seen from Juul's research, in the first phase the ludologists focused on the primary and definitional features common to all games, and then moved on to connecting various secondary features to them. This kind of movement also enables the discussion of the interplay among various aspects of video and computer games, while not losing sight of the core features of games that justify the existence of game studies as a relatively autonomous discipline and field of research.

Compared to that progress the narrativist-narratologist camp (including Jenkins, Murray and Ryan) failed to expand the understanding of the core features of games (such as rules) and therefore couldn't build valid theories and models about the interplay between the primary features of games and their more contingent aspects such as game fictions, cutscenes, and backstories.

12.4 Conclusion: fallacies and agreements

As we have now seen, the narrativist-narratological discourse, regardless of its origins in media studies (Jenkins), drama studies (Murray), or literary studies (Ryan), not to mention film[23] and cultural studies,[24] has a remarkably similar set of conceptual, theoretical and methodological blind spots, problems, and short-comings. The general assumption underlying or overarching the discourse of these three prominent scholars is that games need to be studied or would benefit from being studied from the narratological or narrativist perspective. If and when pressed, the proponents of that idea admit that before one could undertake such study one would have to rewrite narratology to include so called media-specific features of games, but, with the exception of Ryan (2006), none of them tries to do this. Ludologists, by the same token, began with existing definitions of games and existing definitions of narratives and stories (and therefore with broad scholarly consensus among both narrative and game scholars) and drew the obvious conclusion that the latter's explanatory and descriptive power was close to non-existent in studying games. In short, there are no compelling reasons to believe that a revised narrative theory is what (video and computer) game studies need either in the first place or later on.

There are several important differences between Jenkins, Murray, and Ryan in their orientation towards narrative theory. Although both Jenkins and Ryan realize that narratology has to be reworked before it can be applied to games, only Ryan tries to begin that process of reworking. Murray doesn't even recognize that need in her non-academic pan-narrativism, according to which everything is always already a story. As Ryan's attempt fails in both theoretical and pragmatic terms,[25] and Jenkins contradicts himself (in the absence of the kind of narratology that according to him is needed to conceptualize the supposedly narrative side of games, he cannot claim that such a narrative side exists and continue to interpret information as narrative information or events as narrative events etc.), they are back at the beginning, that is, with existing narratologies that can easily explain the story or narrative elements in games, such as cutscenes and backstories, which both ludologist and narratologists (not to mention narrativists) take to be narrative or story elements in games. Given this consensus among game scholars, and the compatibility of ludology and formal narratologies, the scope and role of narratology in game studies remains narrow and not particularly challenging. In other words, computer and video games do not constitute a hybrid between games and stories, because cutscenes and backstories are far from being as dominant and important features in games as rules and gameplay are.

In retrospect, it may well be that the major part of the problem constituted by widespread and indiscriminate use of narratological vocabulary in game scholarship is explainable by Lev Manovich's observation that "in the world of new media the word *narrative* is often used as an all-inclusive term, to cover up the fact we have not yet developed a language to describe these new strange objects" (Manovich 2001, 228). As we shall see in coming chapters, the work of major ludologists and game ontologists has already produced a much more precise and specified vocabulary to describe and analyze the primary features of games and their interplay – or simply adapted it from the vast scholarship relating to non-digital games.

CHAPTER 13

Game ecology and the classic game model

13.1 Introduction: from definitions to ecologies

As became obvious in the previous chapter, games are not narratives or stories (although they may include, adapt and embed elements of them). We have already hinted at different game definitions and definitional and primary features of games such as rules, variable outcomes and player activity. As part of their own definitions of "game," both Juul (2004b, 22–30) and Salen and Zimmerman (2004, 73–80) compared game definitions from a number of previous authors.[1] Salen and Zimmerman (2004, 79) reached this conclusion:

> All of the authors except Costikyan include rules as a key component. Beyond this there is no clear consensus. Although 10 of the 15 elements are shared by more than one author, apart from rules and goals, there is no majority agreement on any of them. (Salen and Zimmerman 2004, 79)

One could add player effort to the consensus, as none of the authors denies games need to be played, and all of them also include or imply some aspects of play in their definitions.[2]

Because such definitions necessarily serve different purposes and reflect the different disciplinary contexts of their authors, in many cases the same or similar ideas are expressed differently. As Juul (2004b, 22) points out, "the definitions do not necessarily try to describe the same aspect of games: some concentrate on the game as such, some on the activity of playing a game." Despite these differences and difficulties the comparative effort is far from useless – especially as it can be used to separate the core features of games from more contingent ones. As Salen and Zimmerman state:

> Some elements, such as games being voluntary or inefficient, do not seem to apply to all games. Others, such as the fact that games create social groups describe the effects of games rather than games themselves. Still other elements, such as the representational or make-believe quality of games, appear in many other media and do not help to differentiate games from other kinds of designed experiences. (Salen and Zimmerman 2004, 79–80)

This is not to say that such secondary features are not or could not be important in games, but that they are just not important on the definitional level that sets games apart from many other types of cultural artefacts. The necessarily reductive (or universal) perspective is also necessary for the purpose of properly drafting a transmedial game ecology and situating the ecology of games and digital games in relation to other transmedial ecologies. In short, the consensus or majority agreement among game scholars and designers on rules, goals (or variable outcomes), and player effort as the main definitional features of games is good enough to serve as a generally accepted point of departure, which points to several interplaying areas that need to be investigated.

As the general focus of this study is on theory and poetics, this and subsequent ludologically oriented chapters primarily discuss the relations of games to other games, but here the trouble begins, as we enter a territory which, at least in scholarly terms, is mostly uncharted. For example, if we were to apply a common intertextual slogan to games and try to model our approach to games highlighting the idea that a game is a mosaic of other games, this exercise would quickly reveal what's missing both from video game theories and from actual scholarly practice not to mention methodology. In short, how should we handle the relationships, co-presences, imitations, implementations, adaptations and transformations between and among different rule systems, goals, quest structures, tasks, challenges and obstacles, player representations, resources, non-playing characters, gameworlds, game engines and platforms, and so on?

Compared to sophisticated theories of intertextuality and transtextuality in literary and film studies, we are a long way from establishing even the basics for similar inter- or transludic networks in game studies. As Aarseth, Smedstad, and Sunnanå (2003, 48) observed: "Unlike literature, film, music, painting and architecture, the systematic study of game genres have been neglected over the centuries." A systematic study of game genres is not the only piece missing from the slowly emerging field of comparative game studies, as the same could be said about the transmediality of games. While it is been recognized (for instance, in Eskelinen 2001a) it has not been "explored in any systematic way" (Juul 2004b, 42).

Methodologically, only by combining historical and ontological perspectives can we understand the transmediality of games and the web of relationships among games – and based on that knowledge, see more clearly the relationships between games and other transmedial modes of cultural expression. Because of this necessary double perspective, our discourse temporarily bifurcates in this and the next chapter, in which we'll adopt a synchronic perspective and move from universal game definitions deeper into game taxonomies and ontologies and especially into the finer details of Espen Aarseth's studies on game ontology (Aarseth, Smedstad, and Sunnanå 2003 and Elverdam and Aarseth 2007). Game ontology provides a synchronic model of games, but in order to put the differences and similarities between traditional non-digital games and digital games (video, computer and mobile games etc.) in a deeper historical perspective, we also need to have a diachronic model of games at our disposal. Therefore this chapter takes Jesper Juul's classic game model (Juul 2004b, 19–51) as its main point of departure. Juul's model will be supplemented and balanced by taking into account the most potent differences between digital and non-digital games as theorized in two game design-oriented perspectives (Crawford 1982; Salen and Zimmerman 2004). The critical combination of these perspectives may give us a glimpse of a general game ecology, and perhaps an understanding of how much hard work remains to be done within this vast area before game studies begin even to approach scholarly maturity.

13.2 Juul's classic game model

Jesper Juul's classic game model (2004b, 19---51) is first and foremost an attempt to build a universal understanding of pre-digital games. In that sense, it has two heuristic edges, the second one being its power to show how some digital games differ from the model that is supposed to have held good for the last 45 centuries (at least). This is obviously helpful in our search for the main connections and dividing lines within a general game ecology. After comparing several relatively well-established game definitions, Juul discerns their essences and reduces their differences to a system of the following six dimensions:

1 *Rules*: Games are rule based.[3]

2 *Variable, quantifiable outcome*: Games have variable, quantifiable outcomes.

3 *Value assigned to possible outcomes*: That the different potential outcomes of the game are assigned different values, some being positive, some being negative.

4 *Player effort*: That the player invests effort in order to influence the outcome (i.e. games are challenging).

5 *Player attached to outcome*: That the players are attached to the outcomes of the game in the sense that a player will be the winner and "happy" if a positive outcome happens, and loser and "unhappy" if a negative outcome happens.

6 *Negotiable consequences*: The same game [set of rules] can be played with or without real-life consequences. (Juul 2004b, 30)

In short form, Juul's definition is the following: "A game is a rule-based system with variable and quantifiable outcome, where different outcomes are assigned different values, the player exerts effort in order to influence the outcome, the player feels attached to the outcome, and the consequences of the activity are optional and negotiable" (Juul 2004b, 30).

Juul's six defining features are not all on the same level, as his definition combines element from three different registers: the game as formal system, the player and the game, and the game and the rest of the world (Juul 2004b, 30–31). The rules, the outcome and player effort clearly characterize games as formal systems. The other three criteria are less formal and as such more ambiguous and controversial. Values assigned to possible outcomes (i.e. valorization of the outcome), player effort, and player attached to outcome define the relationship of the player to the game, and negotiable consequences the relationship between the game and the rest of the world.[4]

At first negotiable consequences seem to form a necessary criterion, which helps to highlight the optional nature of real-life consequences assigned to games (Juul 2004b, 35). This criterion sprang from the pioneering studies and speculations of Caillois (1979) and Huizinga (1950) and received widespread acceptance. However, it is in fact not universal: in many ritual and some political settings, harsh real-time consequences were accepted by the players or forced upon them regardless of their personal willingness.[5] In more recent game and play scholarship, this perspective is perhaps best expressed by Brian Sutton-Smith's suggestion (1997, 218) that play "should not be defined only in terms of restricted Western values that say it is non-productive, rational, voluntary, and fun." Although Sutton-Smith talks about play and not necessarily about games and gameplay as Juul does, certain games contain inevitable and irreversible real-life consequences such as the infamous *Russian Roulette.*[6]

Frasca discusses this criterion at length and concludes that:

[G]ames are not part of an alternative reality that shields them from the so-called "real life". Their consequences are very real. However, games are a cultural form that allows players minimize these consequences to the ones that they are willing to cope with. Frequently, this works fine and the consequences remain within the expected boundaries. (Frasca 2007, 74)

The same idea is also reflected in his new game definition:

> A game is to somebody an engaging activity in which players **believe** to have active participation and where they agree on a system of rules that assigns social status to their quantified performance. The activity constrains players' immediate future to a set of **probable** scenarios, **all of which** they are willing to tolerate. (Frasca 2007, 70)[7]

At first glance, Frasca's definition seems to solve the problem, as clearly the player's willingness to tolerate every probable or foreseeable consequence plays an important role in his engagement with or attachment to the game.[8] However, Frasca's criterion of tolerance leads to other kinds of problem and borderline case: militarist madmen may turn genocide into a game, all consequences of which they are willing to tolerate.[9] At this point, we conclude that games may or may not have negotiable consequences depending on the game, the players, and the socio-cultural-historical context; therefore (unlike the three formal criteria) it doesn't serve as a universal criterion of games.[10]

Another, smaller problem with Juul's model has to do with the player's attachment to the outcome, as it runs the risk of either reducing the range of the player's personal attachments, motivations, styles, and reasons for playing into the mere outcome or preferring one type of attachment to all the others. Sometimes people play out of plain boredom or for social reasons (for instance, playing for a benefit) do not attach much or any value to the outcome of the game,[11] and it is equally common for virtuoso players to focus on displaying their brilliance or to pay more attention to the way or the style of their playing than to the outcome (sometimes to the detriment of team play). In professional team sports, the relative importance of a game varies within a season or a tournament (not every game is equally important for achievement of the team's primary goals) and hence the attachment of professional players to the outcome may vary from game to game. Here, too, our conclusion is the same as with negotiable consequences: the player's attachments vary and cannot be reduced to only one type.

Moreover, the degree and the primacy of the player's attachment to the goal also depend on the nature of goals the game has and how strictly their attainment is enforced. As Juul's later paper (Juul 2007) discusses, games like *GTA: San Andreas* give the player significant opportunity for self-expression and the use of playing styles that are or may be less effective in attaining the game's ostensible goals.

Another related problem is that the three criteria (value assigned to possible outcomes; player effort to influence the outcome; player attached to the outcome) specifying the relationship between the player and the game are all related to the outcome (Juul 2004b, 28; criticized also by Frasca 2007, 67). As Frasca notes, this leads to "a retrospective, teleological approach to games that can only identify them once they are over, without telling us much about what happens during the game itself" (Frasca 2007, 67). The difference between negative and positive values assigned to variable outcomes may also be more subjective in serious gambling (at least in light of psychological or psychoanalytical theories stressing some players' deeply seated and more or less self-destructive need to lose that again may serve other purposes as it did in Dostoevsky's case) and in MMOGs where the goals are partly socially and partly personally determined (in the absence of a single, explicit, and overarching goal signaling the winning conditions and the end of the game). Contrariwise, if the values are explicitly assigned (for instance by stating what the one and only goal is) then the common sense and conventional assumption is that reaching the goal and/ or winning the game are better than not reaching the goal and/or losing the game.

In practice, Juul's model leads to three types of phenomenon: games, not games, and borderline cases (Juul 2004b, 38). This is not necessarily a problem as long as we understand the reasons for inclusion and exclusion (as Juul also argues). Still, Juul's borderline cases merit a closer look. The three formal criteria seem to have produced three such cases: pen and paper roleplaying, games of pure chance, and chance-based gambling. Of these, Juul (2004b, 38) only comments on the first, stating that "pen and paper roleplaying games are not normal games because, with a human game master, their rules are not fixed beyond discussion." This points to an unnecessary problem caused by fixed rules; in Juul (2004b, 26) the idea is that rules should be "designed to be beyond discussion." This is hardly a necessary criterion – a game could be deliberately designed to create disputes about rules to serve certain rhetorical or educational purposes. By way of contrast, a game doesn't cease to be a game when it turns out to be poorly designed and the flow is too often interrupted by the necessity of discussing rules. Such discussion is not always a problem or a flaw because it can be pleasurable in its own right, as Juul (2004b, 64–65) also notes. The presence of a human referee or a game master responsible for deciding the outcomes of actions and interpreting the rules usually guarantees playability, and one could also argue that the game does have fixed rules in the sense that the referee or the game master has the final word and can overrule the players' interpretation of rules.

Chance-based gambling and games of pure chance obviously lack player effort, whereas skill-based gambling also constitutes a borderline case in Juul's model because it lacks negotiable consequences – a criterion that, as we have already seen, is problematic. The borderline status of skill-based gambling could easily be remedied by removing the dimension of negotiable consequences from the model. If one sees the borderline status of chance-based "games" as a problem (which I do not), the criterion of the player effort could be tweaked in the direction suggested by Frasca (2007, 52) in his game definition; i.e. that "the players believe in their active participation." The obvious problem of this new criterion is that it opens the door for the players' delusions.[12] It is also not clear whether players drawn into chance-based gambling actually believe in their active participation in the game. It may equally well be that they are desperately and entirely focused on the possible monetary payoffs of their gamble. Thus it could be more occamian to argue that chance-based gambling and "games" of pure chance are not games but types of more informal playing or risk taking.

The fifth and final borderline case in Juul's model is related to the relation of the player to the game:

> [O]pen-ended simulations like SimCity are not pure games since they have no explicit goals, i.e. no explicit value is attached to the possible outcomes of the game, but what happens in the game is still attached to the player and the player invests effort in playing the game. (Juul 2004b, 38)

This relatively new exception or borderline case doesn't affect the historical explanatory power of Juul's classic game model, but it is also unclear whether it violates Juul's third criterion ("the different potential outcomes of the game are assigned different values, some being positive, some being negative") – especially if and as long as the player is the one who assigns values to the variable outcomes of his efforts. In short, we could and perhaps should separate between given (or player-independent) and chosen (player-dependent) goals that can be either personal or social – or both.

As we have seen, the six criteria of the classic game model are not equally valid and strong. The three formal features define every game (given the modifications suggested earlier) and, historically speaking (i.e. until the fairly recent advent of open-ended roleplaying and simulation games), the valorization of the outcome serves as a criterion as well. Both the player's psychological attachment to the outcome and the degree of negotiable consequences are clearly weaker and contextually varying features and should probably be dropped from the model. Incidentally, if these two are removed from the model it then becomes more compatible with Avedon's (1971, 419–426) model of the structural elements of games. Avedon's model includes 10 main structural elements of games derived from the insights of "the mathematicians and the behaviorists" and "personnel in the field of recreation"[13] (Avedon 1971, 422).

Avedon's synthetic approach is valuable to us, as it sums up many of the main trends in formal and structural game scholarship before the raise of digital games and ludology. It contains the following features: *purpose of the game* (its aim or goal, intent, the *raison d'être*), *procedure for action* (specific operations, required courses of action, method of play), *rules governing action* (fixed principles that determine conduct and standards for behavior), *number of required participants* (stated minimum or maximum number of persons needed for action to take place), *roles of participants* (indicated functions and status – role and power function may differ for each participant or be the same), *results or payoff* (values assigned to the outcome of the action), *interaction patterns*, *abilities and skills required for action* (aspects of the three behavioral domains – cognitive, sensorimotor and affective – utilized in a given activity), *physical setting and environmental requirements* (manmade or natural facility in which action takes place and natural circumstances that are indispensable or obligatory), and *required equipment* (manmade or natural artefacts employed in the course of action) (Avedon 1971, 422–425). These elements can easily be grouped into four: players (number; roles; interaction patterns; required skills), action (rules; procedures), outcomes of the action (goals; values attached to the outcome), and optional physical objects (equipment; setting; environment) – or three if actions and outcomes are combined.

Of the 10 elements, only the first seven are based on Avedon's combination of "the work of the mathematicians and the behaviorists" (Avedon 1971, 422): the last three reflect the interests of "personnel in the field of recreation" (ibid.). Abilities and skill are obviously always present but don't work well as criteria for classification and comparison (because of their interplay and inherent vagueness). Of the last two elements (required environment and equipment), Avedon (1971, 425) notes that they may not always be present. This leaves us with the first seven. Interaction patterns and the number and roles of participants overlap with Juul's player effort that they specify, purpose of the game is compatible with Juul's variable and quantifiable outcome, results are equal to Juul's valorization of the outcome, and rules and procedures overlap with Juul's rules. Thus Avedon's synthesis strengthens the value of Juul's classic game model, or more precisely, its modified version that contains only four criteria. The interesting historical difference is related to the role of equipment: unlike many of Avedon's non-digital games, digital games cannot be played without equipment (a combination of game hardware and game software).

The real power of Juul's classic game model lies in its comparative and descriptive value in the transmedial ecology of games, as well as its ability to show exceptions to, modifications of, and developments beyond the model (including its implicit assumptions) brought about by computer games. Juul (2004b, 50–51) already lists plenty of those: games with automated rules leading to more complex rules and decreasing the necessity of the players having to know the rules from the outset; games with no final outcome and with several outcomes from the same saved session; outcomes and consequences of the player's actions and decisions that can be based on data that would not be discernible to human players or referees; games that don't describe some outcomes better than others; and the player's ability to control a large number of automated units (which would not be possible in non-digital games with non-automated units).

Before continuing the discussion of Juul's model and its contributions to establishing the bare bones of a transmedial game ecology (and the theoretical and practical consequences of that ecology), we'll take a step back and discuss the differences between digital and non-digital (or traditional) games based on the insights of game designers, to whom the relation of computer games to their predecessors and the millennia-long history of games is not the novelty it still is to far too many academic game scholars.

13.3 Crawford

Chris Crawford was taking the differences between games and computer games seriously as long ago as 1982. From his game designer's perspective, Crawford (1982, Chapter 4)[14] found six major advantages in computer games as compared to games based on other game technologies.[15] First, there's a greater responsiveness to the player's wishes. This is because "the computer is dynamic; it imposes little consistency on any element of the game." Second, the computer can serve as game referee. Third, there's an advantage in real-time play, as "the computer is so fast that it can handle the administrative matters faster than the humans can play the game." The computer is also able to provide an intelligent opponent and to limit the information given to the player in a purposeful way. And finally, "the use of telecommunications for game play makes possible game structures that are out of reach of other game technologies. It allows us to create games with huge numbers of players." These advantages were to some degree offset by several disadvantages: the poor I/O rate, single-user orientation in the hardware design and the harsh requirement of programmability.

Much of this is now common knowledge, a history that has already happened now that we see advanced single-player games and massively multiplayer online games all around us. Still, Crawford's list merits another look, to follow certain trajectories and dimensions it opened, and also because it would be short-sighted to assume these advantages have been exhausted.

In hindsight, the vast potential of Crawford's first advantage (little need for consistency) seems to be the most underdeveloped one, while having always been taken for granted by both game scholars and game designers. Crawford writes:

> If the action in a card game or board game starts to drag, the players have no choice but to plod through it or take desperate

measures. There is no reason why a computer game in similar straits could not speed up the game on demand. It could change the length of the game, or the degree of difficulty, or the rules themselves. (Crawford 1982)

However, at least some of these options are also available in card and board games – the players could diminish the number of rounds in a card game or speed up a game of chess by agreeing on stricter temporal constraints (although not in professional contests). One could also argue that if a computer game bores the player, there's equally little he could do – even less if the changes he wishes to make are beyond its parameters (including metarules, cheat codes, and game editors).

Second, there's much more to the computer's plasticity than simply catering to the player's wishes in changing the speed, length, difficulty or rules of the game, as the computer could equally well work against the player's wishes or evaluate them differently than the players themselves do. Third, as Crawford also notes it is much easier to work with and manipulate virtual as opposed to physical space: "Territories in wargames can be switched around the map of the globe more easily than we move a chair in the living room" (Crawford 1982).

Crawford's artificial referee points in the direction of greater complexity of rules and of game causality in general, and therefore implicitly to the possibility that several (over)ambitious non-digital games (such as many social simulation games),[16] which were perhaps felt to be too complex and hard to play because the players and the referees had to uphold the rules, could be more successful if that responsibility could be delegated to the computer. The type of agency upholding the rules (artificial referee/human referee/the player or players) seems then to form one possible comparative dimension among game technologies, and according to the same line of reasoning the type of opponent (artificial/human/both) forms yet another comparative criterion.

When Crawford compares computers to other game technologies in terms of real-time play he notes that "other game technologies must have pauses and procedural delays while administrative matters are dealt with" (Crawford 1982). One could argue that this is not the case with chess, as the players don't have to do anything other than think and move their pieces (it is not necessary to keep a written track of the moves). Obviously, chess is turn based, but another counterexample would be sumo wrestling: when the match begins it usually runs quickly and continuously, without administrative interventions, to the end.

The nature of hidden and purposefully limited information in computer games is much more dynamic than it could possibly be in traditional games of imperfect information. If we play card games with a standard deck, we always know the possible range of information that is not available to us, but we usually don't have that same luxury or primitiveness when trying to figure out the quantity, quality and dynamics of what we need to but don't yet know in computer games of average complexity. Contrariwise, assessing the actual advantage of computers in this respect is slightly more complex. Crawford makes his case as follows:

> Limited information forces the player to use guesswork. The nature of this guesswork can be very intriguing. For example, guessing a random number between one and ten is not a very interesting challenge, but guessing your opponent's resources based on your assessment of his actions and personality is a far more interesting exercise. When the guesswork is included in the framework of a complex and only partially known system, the challenge facing the human player takes on a decidedly real-life texture. (Crawford 1982)

The ability of computers to challenge players using complex and only partially known systems is clearly one area in which computers are superior to the other three game technologies (card games, board games and physical sports) with which Crawford compares them. Still, one could make the same claim for open-ended roleplaying games with a human game master and its powers of improvisation and storytelling (see also Aarseth 2006, 852–853). Also, the thrill of "guessing your opponent's resources based on your assessment of his actions and personality" is something which card games such as poker or bridge excel at providing, and the same observation could apply to certain contact and team sports.

Crawford's sixth advantage combines telecommunication networks, game structures "out of reach of other technologies" and huge number of players. In retrospect, Crawford's over-optimism about the number of administrative personnel that MMOGs would need is obvious:

> Until now, administrative problems have made it necessary to limit the number of players in any game. Six players is a rough upper limit for a non-refereed game; twelve players will require several referees and twenty players or more will require many referees. Obviously, games with hundreds of players will face many administrative problems. Indeed, the logistic problems of assembling all the players are themselves prohibitive. All these problems are solved by computers linked through a telecommunications network. (Crawford 1982)

Given the size of the administrative and tech teams responsible for running contemporary MMOGs on multiple servers, it appears that administrative problems didn't go away that easily.

Without denying the many novelties of the MMOGs (many of which are based on earlier games developed in text-based MUDs), one could still ask how many players actually play actively together (in current MMOGs such as *The World of Warcraft* the most complicated tasks require more than 50 players to cooperate) in comparison to two-team games such as soccer (11 players per team, 22 players sharing the field) and American football (more than 45 players per team, of whom 11 are on the field at one time) and how many of these can actually observe each other's actions in real time.[17] Given the multitude of servers supporting each MMOG, one could risk comparing these platforms to the unknown sum total of stadiums and other arenas soccer players use, create or appropriate all around the world at any given time. Obviously, the major difference is not in the size of teams but in the number of participants per playing field (if a server accommodating 100 000 or more players is compared to the 22 players of a soccer game).

Of Crawford's three disadvantages, programmability is directly connected to game design as a basic requirement missing from other game technologies, and single-player orientation,[18] a second disadvantage, has since Crawford's day been balanced by multiplayer games.[19] This leaves us with the problems of I/O: "the computer must communicate its responsiveness to the human; it does so through I/O. Most output is through graphics and sound; most input is through keyboard, joystick, and paddle" (Crawford

1982, Chapter 4). Despite dance mats, *Nintendo Wii, Microsoft Kinect*, and casual games with mimetic interfaces (Juul 2010, 18) shifting action to this side of the screen, keyboards and joysticks are still in common use. Here's Crawford's summary of the results:

> Actions that are simple and obvious with other technologies become arcane with the computer. If I give you a bat and tell you that your goal in baseball is to hit the ball, you will have few problems deciding that you should swing the bat at the ball. A computer baseball game is not so easy to figure out. Do you press H for "hit" or S for "swing" or B for "bat"? Do you press the START key or press the joystick trigger? (Crawford 1982)

The resulting counter-intuitiveness and the difference between direct and mediated actions points to inevitable differences in the bodily and physical action required from the player in sports and in computer games. As compensation for their still limited bodily input, computer games can model and display events that would be plainly impossible in sports (or at least in sports valuing the lives of their participants).

13.4 Salen and Zimmerman

Two decades after Crawford, Katie Salen and Eric Zimmerman (2004, 87–90) saw the differences between digital and non-digital games in less absolute terms. They discerned four special qualities of digital games: immediate but narrow interactivity, manipulation of information, automated complex systems, and networked communication. These features are also present in non-digital games (not in all of them, of course), but digital games usually embody them more robustly. Salen and Zimmerman's criteria are in many ways similar to Crawford's, and in principle they confirm and repeat his findings. The capability of manipulating, hiding and revealing information overlaps with one of Crawford's advantages, and digital games as automated complex systems contain much of what Crawford says about responsiveness and artificial opponents and referees. Salen and Zimmerman's fourth point, networked communication, is compatible with Crawford's last advantage.

This leaves us with immediate and narrow interactivity to focus on (although it mirrors Crawford's first disadvantage). It foregrounds easily forgotten limitations in the power of a computer to mimic other "media"[20] and provide a wide range of experiences. As Salen and Zimmerman put it:

> Compare the anemic activities of clicking, dragging and typing with the range of possible non-computer game interactions: the kinaesthetically engaging athletic, perceptual and strategic interaction of Tennis; the performative theatrical communication of Charades, the ritualized formality of a professional Go match. So although the immediate interactivity of digital games is a powerful element for designers to consider, the medium is rife with limitations. (Salen and Zimmerman 2004, 87)

If we take narrow but immediate interactivity as a point of departure, we may want to ask what other options there are. How about delayed and broad interactivity, and what about the combinations of the four basic possibilities this move opens? Even if the immediate response is deemed necessary, this doesn't exclude the question of precisely determined delayed consequences. By these I don't mean the usual cumulative long-term consequences (such as the ones resulting from the way you train your creature in *Black & White*), which are ultimately dependent on the player's strategic goals and skills (or lack of) as well as his adversaries' actions and therefore negotiable, reversible and uncertain at least to a certain degree. We could call such consequences *conditional*. In contrast to them, we are interested in the relative novelty of several irreversible, non-negotiable, hidden and delayed consequences of one and same action. While it might be possible to design a non-digital game that has such consequences, it would be very hard for a human to implement and keep track of them while keeping the game playable.

The relative difference between broad and narrow interaction could be made a bit clearer by applying Jesper Juul's (2004b, 43–44) distinction between game adaptations and game implementations.[21] Many physical games and sports can be only roughly adapted to a digital game,[22] while most if not all classic board and card games can be digitally implemented without causing significant changes in their rules and possible game states.

Salen and Zimmerman also draw out certain consequences of their four traits of digital media that are included in Crawford's exposition. They are related to the rules. In relation to information manipulation they make the following point:

> Digital games manipulate ... information in ways that non-digital games generally cannot. In a typical board game it is necessary for at least one of the players to learn the rules and understand them fully before a game begins. On the other hand, with a digital game it is possible, as designer Karen Sideman has pointed out, to learn the rules as it is being played. (Salen and Zimmerman 2004, 88)

Furthermore, automated complex systems allow the maintenance of greater complexity of rules and procedures than that which can be facilitated in a non-computerized context (Salen and Zimmerman 2004, 88). This could be interpreted as a disadvantage as well, because in practice it usually denies the players any understanding of the internal game mechanics: "Because of the automated nature of digital games, computer wargames generally leave the internal machinations out of the picture, diminishing a player's experience of the game" (Salen and Zimmerman 2004, 89).

Based on our discussion so far, there seem to be at least two adaptive barriers within the game ecology. The first barrier is the limited and narrow physicality one encounters in adapting sports to sport simulations. The second barrier manifests itself in card games such as poker: psychological manipulation (including bluffing) can't be translated into the repertoire of an artificial or a mediated human opponent to a degree that matches the intricacies of the unmediated presence of another human player. While the former barrier may gradually vanish through ubiquitous computing and all the networked sensors and tracking devices that come with it, the latter is less easily bypassed, as it is deeply rooted in the inherent problems and dead ends of AI research.

We can also, somewhat preliminarily, pick several comparative dimensions from Crawford and Salen and Zimmerman to function as building blocks of game ecology: the consistency of game elements, nature of opponents, presence of human referees, upholder of rules, degree of bodily involvement, prior knowledge of rules, rule complexity, and number of players and game tokens.

Before seeing how these could be grafted onto Juul's classic game model, we need to revisit Juul's discussion on transmediality, and also to briefly discuss the type of games not discussed by Juul, Crawford and Salen and Zimmerman: social simulation games.

13.5 Social simulation games

Social simulation games have been discussed in the context of ludology and computer games by Stewart Woods. He observes several structural differences between these games and video games related to "the role of the player, the nature of the gameworld, the structure of gameplay and the singularity of the game experience" (Woods 2004). From our perspective and needs in this chapter, these differences boil down to two dimensions.

First, misinformed players:

> This type of technique is employed in R. Garry Shirts' highly successful game, *Starpower* (1969). The game models a three-tiered social structure through a trading game executed with poker chips. Much of the impact of the experience on players depends on the deliberate misinforming of participants as to the nature and outcomes of the game. Participants believe themselves to be playing a simple trading game with the goal of obtaining the highest score. They are not told that the chips are unevenly distributed to favor one group over another, nor are they informed of the true purpose of the game – to bring about conflict and highlight power structures within society. (Woods 2004)

Given the computer's capability of hiding and limiting information and the already discussed possibility that the players learn the rules as they play, misinforming players (and also keeping track of their misinformed actions) is a design strategy well suited for computer games and easily implemented in them.

Second, unbalanced gameworlds:

> Much of the strength of *SIMSOC* (Gamson 1966), for example, can be said to lie in the ability to completely restructure the

functioning of the game through simulated political process. On occasion, participants are even invited to alter aspects of the manipulation rules during game play. The societal simulation *Starpower* (Shirts 1969) provides a clear example of this approach. One of the pivotal moments in the game comes when the participants who have been the most successful are offered an opportunity to change any or all structures within the game, highlighting the impermanent nature of hegemonic power. (Woods 2004)

As Woods notes this goes against deeply seated notions and expectations of fair play, but, by the same token, and given the existence of *SIMSOC* and *StarPower*, it is just a convention already broken.[23] Misinformed players in unbalanced gameworlds (within which both rules and goals change) illustrate the range of possibilities inherent in Crawford's first advantage (little need for the constancy of game elements), but in a non-digital environment. In this respect one of the most important design decisions is to what degree the game serves and caters to the player's wishes or, to put it differently, to what degree game designers deny the expressive powers of games in order to serve and protect players.

13.6 Theorizing transmediality and game ecology: adaptations and implementations

The notion of transmedial game ecology is based on a few simple observations. As Juul (2004b, 43) puts it: "It is quite clear there is no set of equipment or *material support* common to all games." Instead, there is a common *immaterial support*: the upholding of rules that can be performed by humans or computers.[24] The reason why games are transferable to the computer is equally simple: "The computer can uphold and *compute* the rules that would normally be upheld by humans" and "the computer has the *memory* capacity to remember the game state" (Juul 2004b, 43).

Obviously, not every game is fully transferable to computers, and therefore Juul distinguishes between implementations and adaptations using examples from other game technologies:

Card games on computers should be considered *implementa-tions* since it is possible to unambiguously map one-to-one correspondences between all the possible game states in the computer version and in the physical card game. Sports games on computers are better described as *adaptations*, since much detail is lost because the physics model of the computer program is a simplification of the real world, and in the interface because the video game players' body is not part of the game state. Adapting soccer to computers is therefore a highly selective adaptation. (Juul 2004b, 43–44)

As a result we have "an ecology of game media that support gaming, but do so differently, and of games that move between different media, sometimes with ease, sometimes with great diffi-culty" (Juul 2004b, 43).

Juul's argument contains several interesting aspects concerning the limits of adaptation, the nature of relationships (implemen-tation and adaptation) and implicitly the relations among the meta genres or greater groups of games Juul includes in his discussion (video games; board games; card games; sports).

The distance between soccer and simulated (whether digital or mechanical) soccer is great, highly selective as Juul puts it, because of the major differences in gameplay and the player's bodily involvement in the game; therefore one could argue that soccer and simulated soccer (and by extension any physical sport and its computer game simulation) are different games. Be that as it may, in principle, there should be a threshold beyond which adaptation is so thorough and changes so many core aspects of the game and gameplay that even the word adaptation doesn't adequately describe the relationship between the two games.

One could also introduce various subtypes within both adapta-tions and implementations, as the distinction between them concerns only whether it is possible to fully copy (or imitate) one game in another game medium (or technology) (Juul 2004b, 43–44). In principle, there are many other possibilities:[25] partial implemen-tation or simplification (leaving out certain game states that could be implemented),[26] amplified implementation (full implementation and additional game states),[27] and also reductive adaptation, amplified adaptation and augmented adaptation depending on whether the adaptation contains only the game states that could be faithfully mapped from the adapted game, makes qualitative changes in order to increase the relative importance of some game states existent in the hypogame,[28] or adds entirely new game states to compensate what has to be or has been left out.

Juul (2004b, 44–45) briefly discusses the transmedial relations among sports, board, card, and video games. According to Juul (2004b, 44), most board and card games are "immediately implementable in computer programs." However, the physical setting around the games "does not translate well" (ibid.), and one could perhaps add certain charms of manipulation in poker to the list of poorly or partly translatable features (despite the immense success of online poker). Theoretically speaking, there are no full implementations, as there's always something that doesn't translate well or at all. However, if we stick to the four dimensions of the revised classic game model (leaving out the player's attachment to the outcome and negotiable consequences) we could monitor translatability at the level of the four core features to which the physical setting of card and board games do not belong (i.e. the player effort does not require an invariable type of setting).

Juul (2004b, 45) mentions some poor-quality adaptations of arcade video games to board games, but doesn't discuss the possibility (or the probable impossibility) of implementing video games as card or board games or adapting video games into card games. Neither does Juul offer examples of card games implemented or adapted as board games or vice versa, quite probably because such examples would be hard to find. The barrier between these two meta-genres is likely based on their different strengths: spatial gameplay with perfect information in board games versus non-spatial gameplay and imperfect information in card games.

Juul (2004b, 45) presents one example of the rare "video games to sports adaptations": some players of paintball have adopted the rules of Counter-Strike to their game. Adaptations between sports, on the one hand, and card and board games, on the other, seem to be non-existent based on Juul's discussion although nothing prevents card and board games being at least thematically based on sports.[29] Thus we can sum up the major connections between the four meta-genres as follows: card and board games may serve as hypogames to be implemented in computer games[30] whereas sports and computer games can (realistically) be only adapted to other meta-genres. However, that's not all there is to transmediality.

Unlike game implementations that concern games as a whole,[31] game adaptations reveal the differences between game elements that move between games with ease versus those that move with difficulty or not at all.

Before shifting the perspective from the transmediality of games to the questions of game ontology in the next chapter, we'll conclude the present chapter by presenting yet another chart. In Table 13.1, several historical lines of change and variation derived from Crawford, Juul, Salen and Zimmerman, and Woods' observations are introduced into the revised classic game model and grouped under that model's four main features into dimensions along which trans- and intramedial (or more accurately trans- and intragametechnological) comparisons, adaptations, and implementations between games can be made. Implementations maintain the values of the parameter in the hypogame whereas adaptations do not and therefore the chart most of all describes the field and basic dimensions of possible game adaptations. To maintain presentational clarity the different subtypes of adaptation and implementation were not included in it. The values of each sub-dimension are given in parenthesis (except in the dimensions of rule complexity, the number of players, and the number of player controlled units). Rules include manipulation rules, ludus rules, and metarules (Frasca 2003a, 232–233).[32] Games with clearly defined successful outcomes are teleologically finite; those without them could in principle go on forever and are thus teleologically infinite (Aarseth, Smedstad, and Sunnanå 2003, 51).

With this in many ways preliminary model we leave transmedial concerns behind for a while. For now it is important to realize that games have their own transmediality that should not confused with or subsumed into other kinds of transmediality (for instance those of "narrative"[33] or poetry). This is not to say that these and other transmedialities are completely sealed off from each other and there's no interaction between and among them, or that games couldn't share elements with other kinds of artefact and practice. However, these shared elements do not include the combination of the rules, variable outcomes and gameplay that are our main concerns in the ludological chapters – and are for the most part limited to certain representational qualities of the gameworld. The relations between different transmedialities will be discussed in

Table 13.1 Field of trans- and intramedial game adaptations and implementations

RELATION DIMENSION:	adaptation	implementation
rules:		
constant during the game (y/n)		
fixed beyond dispute (y/n)		
fully explicit (y/n)		
maintenance (players; referee/game master; computer)		
required prior knowledge (y/n)		
complexity		
variable and quantifiable outcome:		
teleology (finite/infinite)		
data for determining the outcomes (discernible/not discernible to humans)		
values attached to the outcome:		
hierarchical valorization (y/n)		
player effort:		
misinformed players (y/n)		
intentionally unbalanced game world (y/n)		
networked communication (y/n)		
opponent (human/artificial/human and artificial)		
networked communication (y/n)		
degree of bodily involvement (high/low)		
number of player controlled units		
number of players and teams		

later chapters along with the limitations of the concept of transmediality, but before that we need to know more about variations of games and game elements.

The shift of focus from implementations of whole games to adaptations of central game elements also paves the way for the next chapter that takes a more detailed look at the game elements. Ecologically speaking, we are shifting the focus from a preliminary sketched general game ecology to the more specific lower level ecology of digital games and their constituents.

CHAPTER 14

Game ontology

14.1 Introduction: from game definitions to game ontology

Game ontology provides a synchronic model of games that complements the diachronic undertaking presented in the previous chapter. In that chapter, we referred to comparisons of game definitions in both Juul (2004b, 22–30) and Salen and Zimmerman (2004, 73–80) and noted an overwhelming consensus that rules, goals or variable outcomes, and play or player effort are the main definitional features of games. Based on that consensus, we'll work our way through several game taxonomies and ontologies, expand our views on the ecology of digital games,[1] and finish by discussing the finer details of Espen Aarseth's studies on game ontology (cf. Aarseth, Smedstad, and Sunnanå 2003; Elverdam and Aarseth 2007).

Although there are several game ontologies, taxonomies and classifications to choose from, most are conceptually vague or self-contradicting, too intuitively and ideologically constructed, and less nuanced than the models discussed here. There are also models optimized for the purposes of game design as opposed to academic game studies, most notably the Game Design Patterns project (Björk and Holopainen 2003; Björk et al 2003) that attempts to produce a descriptive tool for game design purposes, i.e. fundamentally to produce good games. Still, there is a connection between the two worlds of game design and academic game scholarship, as Björk and Holopainen point out in describing their approach:

The reasoning behind this design oriented approach is that we believe that a theoretical tool which is able to aid the creation of games is going to be useful also in classification and analysis and thus be able to function as a bridge between the two communities. (Björk and Holopainen 2003, 1–2)

Models that try to combine academic and design purposes (with the notable exception of that of Björk and Holopainen)[2] tend to include narrative as a key component. They typically either fail to define the term narrative or define it poorly, and are far from being narratologically sophisticated. For instance, Lindley describes his model as follows:

In the taxonomy system proposed here, some fundamental distinctions are drawn between game forms and functions based upon narrative, repetitive game play and simulation; computer games can be seen to manifest these three functional and formal aspects to differing degrees, depending upon the particular game or game genre. (Lindley 2003)

This is followed by a vague definition of narrative (which is one of the three main parameters he proposes): "We can define a narrative as an experience that is structured in time" (ibid.). It is difficult and very likely impossible to find an experience not structured in time (non-narrative performance and circus acts are experiences structured in time as well),[3] which makes Lindley's definition untenable. Lindley's discussion of the narrative parameter is further undermined by his conflation of it with the three-act structure derived from drama. Based on our detailed discussion of narrative, narratology, and the debate in previous chapters, Lindley's model is fundamentally flawed and lacks both descriptive and analytical power.

14.2 GOP

The project that comes closest to the multidimensional typology discussed here is Georgia Tech's Game Ontology Project (GOP). The Game Ontology Project's aim is "to develop a game ontology that identifies the important structural elements of games and the relationships between them, organizing them hierarchically" (Zagal et al. 2005, 2). However, the project is not entirely disconnected from game design purposes:

> The ontological approach is also distinct from genre analyses and related attempts to answer the question "what is a game?" Rather than develop definitions to distinguish between games/non-games or among different types of games, we focus on analyzing of design elements that cut across a wide range of games. Our goal is not to classify games according to their characteristics and/or mechanics, but to describe the design space of games. (Zagal et al. 2005, 2)

On the top level of the GOP ontology, there are five main elements: interface, rules, goals, entities, and entity manipulation. They are described as follows:

> The *interface* is where the player and game meet, the mapping between the embodied reactions of the player and the manipulation of game entities. It refers to both how the player interacts with the game and how the game communicates to the player. The *rules* of a game define and constrain what can or can't be done in a game; they lay down the framework, or model, within which the game shall take place. Rules regulate the development of the game and determine the basic interactions that can take place within it … *Goals* are the objectives or conditions that define success in the game. *Entities* are the objects within the game that the player manages, modifies or interacts with at some level. This definition is broader than "game tokens" since it also includes objects that are not controlled by the player. Finally, *entity manipulation* encompasses the alteration of the game made either by the player or by in-game entities. Entity manipulation thus refers to the actions or verbs that can be performed by the player and by in-game entities. (Zagal et al 2005, 4)

The discussion of these five elements is necessarily condensed and sketchy in the paper outlining the project. The section on interface separates input devices from input methods:

The presentation hardware describes the physical details of the visual, audio and haptic displays used in the game, while the presentation software describes how the games state is communicated by means of the hardware. (Zagal et al. 2005, 6)

The rules section defines two types of rule: "Gameworld rules define the virtual world where the game takes place, while gameplay rules impose rules and constraints on top of the gameworld" (Zagal et al. 2005, 7). The goals section defines only the difference between long- and short-term goals (ibid.), and the entity manipulation section defines only the problematic distinction between attributes and abilities of game entities, i.e. the properties that entity manipulation alters either permanently or temporarily[4] (Zagal et al. 2005, 8). The entity section says even less as "the entity hierarchy is currently the least developed section of our ontology" (Zagal et al. 2005, 8).

The GOP is a project in progress; in addition to the paper describing the project and briefly discussing the five top-level elements (Zagal et al. 2005), the only specific papers that have been published are those on spatial configurations (Fernández-Vara, Zagal, and Mateas 2005), temporal frames (Zagal and Mateas 2007), segmentation in the "retro" context of arcade games (Zagal, Fernández-Vara, and Mateas 2008), and on video games and learning. In what follows, we will be informed by the GOP group's achievements (especially in our discussion of game time in Chapter 16 and also in discussing spatial configurations later), but as the GOP model is still far from complete, we'll begin with an open-ended and nuanced model that is already complete and fully available for use.

14.3 Aarseth's game ontology

The detailed typology of digital games proposed by Espen Aarseth, Solveig Marie Smedstad, and Lise Sunnanå (2003) and its later revision by Aarseth and Christian Elverdam (2007) will be our main point of departure,[5] as both versions offer well-defined, detailed and so far uncontested accounts of the essential features of games, resulting in several hundreds of thousands of formally different game types. Like all models, it is necessarily reductive, but, because it allows such a staggering variety of game types, the more likely complaint would be that it is not reductive enough. Still, it gives us the necessary means to divide games into smaller features and dimensions that will be further discussed in relation to the players' manipulative actions in the next chapter focusing on the gaming situation.

The purpose of the typology is to "identify essential differences between games and then classify them in a precise and analytical way" (Elverdam and Aarseth 2007, 4). The typology consists of "dimensions that describe specific game elements" (ibid.), and like Aarseth's typology of textual communication it is open-ended, meaning that "individual dimensions can be modified, added, or rejected without compromising the integrity of the model as a whole" (ibid.). The model is also explicitly connected to the evolution of games: "the individual dimensions face a continuing refinement to raise the precision of each dimension and to reflect that games as such are evolving" (ibid.).

This comparative approach to games is an alternative to genre-based approaches that suffer from general problems of genre (already partly discussed in Chapter 5) and the underdeveloped and confusing state of genre discussion in game studies and the game industry.[6] Developers, publishers, fans, gamers and journalists have their own ideas of genre, which results in games being classified by "arbitrary, contradictory, or overlapping genres" (Elverdam and Aarseth 2007, 4).

Currently there are eight meta-categories in the open-ended model: virtual space, physical space, external time, internal time, player composition, player relation, struggle, and game state.[7] In the rest of this chapter, we first discuss them in pairs (space; time; players; struggle and game state), comparing them to pre-digital typologies of Avedon (1971) and Gump, Redl, and Sutton-Smith (1971) when appropriate. Finally, we briefly return to the problems of genre in games and generic approaches to games in light of the strengths and weaknesses of the comparative ontologies discussed in this chapter.

14.3.1 *Virtual space and physical space*

Virtual space has the following three subcategories, the first two of which overlap with similar subcategories of physical space:

Perspective describes whether the player has a complete overall view of the game space (omnipresent) or if the avatar (or game tokens) must be moved strategically (vagrant). Positioning describes whether the player can discern his or her position exactly as the game rules dictate it (absolute) or if he or she must relate to other objects to decide his or her position (relative). Environment dynamics describes whether the player is allowed to make additions or alterations to the game space (free) or if such alterations only alter the status of predetermined locations (fixed) or finally if no changes to the game space are possible (none). (Elverdam and Aarseth 2007, 7)

Two subcategories (perspective and positioning) are applicable to both physical and virtual spaces – allowing this model to follow digital games from screen space to player space and beyond (see Juul 2010, 16–20). In physical space, the category of perspective is similar to its virtual counterpart with its omnipresent and vagrant values (the latter referring to the player's and not the avatar's movement). Positioning, however, is slightly different in physical spaces, as it is based on the player's physical location, or his or her proximity to other game agents, or both (Elverdam and Aarseth 2007, 9). Environment dynamics seem to be meaningful (and existent) only in games in virtual environments, and thus environment dynamics can be used to highlight the differences between traditional games in physical spaces and digital games in virtual spaces.

In soccer, the player's perspective on the physical space of the game alters between vagrant and omnipresent, depending on the point of observation (the whole field can be best observed from its four corners) and according to the functional role differentiation of the players (the goal keeper's perspective is omnipresent more often than the other players' perspective). Games that connect changes in the player's physical position to changes in the type of his or her perspective on the virtual space could also pose a problem for the typology, but, however, the model doesn't explicitly rule out the possibility that a game could occupy more than one value within a dimension (for instance a game that alters between omnipresent and vagrant perspectives, or evolves from the former to the latter at higher levels, or rewards players by giving them a more advantageous perspective, or divides the two types of perspective among different players or teams).

The spatial dimensions of the typology are related to the relation between the player and the playground: the player's position in it and the possible ways he can perceive and alter it. However, these are not necessarily the only relevant or essential spatial aspects. The typology (of Elverdam and Aarseth) discusses neither the physical movement of the player nor the virtual movement of his avatar or game tokens except in relation to his perspective on the playing field. The dimensions of space don't include the often suggested distinction between 2D and 3D virtual spaces either. Aarseth, Smedstad, and Sunnanå see the latter distinction as "mostly historical, since the early games were mostly 2D and the modern games are usually 3D" (Aarseth, Smedstad, and Sunnanå 2003, 49). The authors also note that the dimensional distinction "does not allow for a good representation of board games that are two-dimensional in movement and three-dimensional in representation" (ibid.).[8]

However, as the historical dimension is important as such (for instance, in the presence of retro gaming) and as Elverdam and Aarseth also use historical examples such as *Chess* to illustrate their typology that is supposed to be applicable to all games, their discourse can easily be supplemented by Fernández-Vara, Zagal, and Mateas' (2005) historically oriented discussion and categorization of the basic spatial configurations in video games. They (Fernández-Vara, Zagal, and Mateas 2005, 1) define these by using three basic features: cardinality of gameplay, cardinality of gameworld and representation.

Cardinality of gameplay defines the player's ability to move around in the gameworld: the movement can be one, two, or three dimensional (Fernández-Vara, Zagal, and Mateas 2005, 2). Cardinality of gameworld describes the way in which the player can navigate the gameworld. These two interrelated cardinalities are "different from the spatial representation, which can be either in two dimensions or in three, but it does not mean that the player can move around in those same dimensions" (ibid.).[9]

In addition to these dimensionalities, the basic spatial configurations contain the dichotomy between discrete and continuous spaces that is related to the screen as the basic unit of space in videogames "since it frames the interface" (Fernández-Vara, Zagal, and Mateas 2005, 3). Thus the dichotomy considers:

how the virtual space is contained within that frame, whether
the gameworld is encompassed within a single screen, or extends
beyond its limits. In the second case, the representation must
be segmented, and the player will experience that space in a
fragmented way. This segmentation can be realized either in
a discrete or a continuous way. (Fernández-Vara, Zagal, and
Mateas 2005, 3)

The GOP group's rather limited spatial configurations model sums
up a certain historical trend in video game technology, as the
authors are well aware:

Our discussion of spatial configurations highlights how the
development of technology allows spaces increasing in size
(extending beyond the single screen) and complexity. We have
also noted how the cardinality of the gameplay space is usually
minor than that of the gameworld and its representation, e.g. a
space represented in 3D may only be navigable in two dimensions. As technology has progressed, an increasing amount of
games have achieved spatial configurations where the cardinality
of the representation is equal to that of the gameworld, and
finally to that of the gameplay. (Fernández-Vara, Zagal, and
Mateas 2005, 8)

They conclude by stating that: "Technology is not likely to bring
about new ones, since we have reached a point where the cardinality of gameplay and gameworld coincide with that of the
representation" (ibid.), which confirms Aarseth, Smedstad, and
Sunnanå's (2003, 49) claim about the historical nature of the
distinction between 2D and 3D spaces in computer games.
    Elverdam and Aarseth's categories of space do not take into
account the differences between representational and non-representational game spaces. Card and dice games do not need specific
game spaces, board games (with the exception of themed board
games) have non-representational game boards (Go) or game boards
with marginal representational residues (chess), and playgrounds
and sport arenas tend to be non-representational, whereas LARPs
have representational physical spaces and non-abstract digital
games have dynamically representational gameworlds (if the world
is more than a decorative element).

Finally, without denying the importance of spatiality in games (with the notable exception of card games), one could ask to what degree the spatial categories discussed earlier relate to gameplay as dynamic elements that the player is allowed and has to manipulate in order to reach his objective. Obviously the dimensions and their values describe features that (usually) remain invariable in the game (a vagrant perspective will remain vagrant etc.), but of the five spatial dimensions of the typology, only environmental dynamics in certain cases (free and fixed dynamics) lets the player manipulate the game space and make changes in it. The other four dimensions also frame gameplay from start to finish, but they simply describe the properties of spatial context and setting (while obviously affecting gameplay by setting invariable constraints to it). In this light, the fact that five categories out of the total 17 are devoted to space may seem slightly excessive, although the dimensions themselves are capable of making high-level distinctions among spatial organizations in games.

14.3.2 External time and internal time

External time includes the categories of teleology and representation. Teleology specifies whether "the game ends at a given time (finite) or if it in principle could go on forever (infinite)" and representation either reflects "the way time would pass in our physical world (mimetic)" or is "disjointed from reality (arbitrary)" (Elverdam and Aarseth 2007, 10).

Internal time consists of haste, synchronicity and interval control. Haste describes "whether the mere passing of real time alters the game state (present) or not (absent)," synchronicity "whether game agents can act at the same time (present) or if they take turns (absent)," and interval control "whether the players decide when the next game cycle will commence (present) or if such control is denied (absent)" (Elverdam and Aarseth 2007, 11).

The distinction between external and internal time is important because it creates a two-level model, unlike the original model (Aarseth, Smedstad, and Sunnanå 2003) that grouped them together. Although this two-level structure superficially resembles the supposedly "unique" two-level organization of narrative time, there are obvious differences both within the levels and in their relationship. We'll be discussing game time in a later chapter, where Elverdam and Aarseth's model of game time will be connected and compared to other models and theories of game time. Therefore, we'll limit our comments to only three observations here.

The distinctions in internal time among haste, synchronicity, and interval control replace the dichotomy between turn-based and real-time games in the previous model with a more detailed and accurate model, thus showing how the typology is able to react to evolution in games (Elverdam and Aarseth 2007, 5–7). This is done by adding more dimensions to the typology (i.e. at the expense of the model's economy), a gesture that could be repeated with every dimension that would also become more accurate and descriptive if one or several sub-dimensions were added.

Mimetic time provides one example, as in principle speed could be represented arbitrarily and duration mimetically (or vice versa). This seems to be the case with *FIFA 2002* that Juul discusses as a violation of game time because "the on-screen clock counts 45 minutes for each half," "in real time each half lasts four minutes, a speed up of 11.25 times," but "the normally agile David Beckham takes an amazingly slow 12 seconds *according to the clock* to run the few meters" (Juul 2004b, 134). In other words, the game's duration is somewhat mimetic (depending on how we judge the 11.25 times acceleration or condensation), but the speed of actions and events within that timeframe are arbitrary (the virtual player spending 12 seconds to move a few virtual meters). The problem could be solved by dividing the dimension of representation into two new sub-dimensions of speed and duration.

Second, despite being defined in relation to the ending in time, the dimension of teleology implicitly raises the issue of causality and temporality, as one could argue that the relationship between them needs to be clarified precisely because the player plays an elementary part in the causal network connecting game events.

Third, spatiotemporal categories take up more than half of Elverdam and Aarseth's typology (10 categories of 17), and thus it is fair to say it is spatiotemporally oriented. Compared to the best models of non-digital game studies, that orientation couldn't be more different: only one of Avedon's (1971) 10 categories, the combination of physical setting and environmental require-ments, is related to space. Spatial and temporal concerns play a similarly limited role in Gump, Redl, and Sutton-Smith's (1971) 30 dimensions: in addition to respite possibilities (to be discussed later in another context it may also fit) only two other dimensions, use of space and temporal considerations, are connected to them. The difference is only partly explainable by the different orientations of the three models (describing and comparing games as accurately as possible and avoiding the pitfalls of generic approaches in Elverdam and Aarseth; defining games by structural elements central to all games in Avedon; and describing dimensions most relevant to player behavior in Gump, Redl and Sutton-Smith). Based on these differences, one could say that the typology of Elverdam and Aarseth is oriented towards games as objects (or formal frameworks of play) and the model of Gump, Redl and Sutton-Smith towards games as processes to be played.[10]

14.3.3 *Player composition and player relation*

Player composition describes "how the players in a game are organized (single player, single team, two player, two team, multiplayer, multiteam)" (Elverdam and Aarseth 2007, 12). Player relation includes two factors: bond describes "whether the relation between players can change during play (dynamic) or not (static)" and evaluation "how the players or the outcome of the game is quantified. The individual player can be evaluated (individual), the players can be evaluated as a team (team), or they can be evaluated both as a team and as individual players (both)" (ibid.).

The typology of Gump, Redl, and Sutton-Smith (1971, 408–418) also contains at least three parameters – interdependence of players, trust dependence, and permanence of allies – that could be used to further specify the dynamic bond between players. The already noted differences of emphasis between Avedon and Gump, Redl, and Sutton-Smith, on the one hand, and Elverdam and Aarseth, on the other, are easily remedied, as the models can usefully supplement one another.

Avedon (1971, 424–425) also proposed a considerably more detailed typology of player relations, taking into account not only the required number of players but also interaction patterns[11] and the possible roles of players. The disregard for roleplaying and role-taking factors is not explicitly explained by Elverdam and Aarseth. Gump, Redl, and Sutton-Smith (1971, 411–412) discuss them in terms of function differentiation and fantasy content. These could be added to the typology in terms of presence and absence: function differentiation present (soccer), function differentiation absent (chess), fantasy content absent (soccer and chess), and fantasy content present (MMOGs).

Another subcategory is needed to separate major roleplaying genres from one another: in tabletop roleplaying games, the players have roles but their actions are described more than acted; in LARPs, the players embody and act out their roles; and in digital roleplaying games, the player's character and his actions are digitally represented and maintained.

14.3.4 *Struggle*

Struggle combines two dimensions: challenge and goals. Challenge is related to the opposition a game provides:

> It can come in the form of predefined challenges, which are exactly the same each time the game is played (identical). It can come from a predefined framework that is varied by mathematical randomness (instance). Finally, opposition can come from game agents whose actions are autonomous (agent). (Elverdam and Aarseth 2007, 13–14)

Goals "describe if the game has an exact and unchanging victory conditions (absolute) or if the goals are subjective to the unique occurrences in a specific game or the players' interpretations (relative)" (Elverdam and Aarseth 2007, 14).

The combination of three kinds of challenge and two types of goal result in six types of struggle. One may ask whether those six are all the relevant ways of describing struggle even in the context of an overarching typology that is always at risk of becoming too detailed to be useful. Struggle (or contest or conflict) is at the heart of games and could be argued to be more important than the spatiotemporal frame within which it takes place. Be that as it may, several sub-dimensions can easily be imported from other typologies if necessary.

Juul discusses the way challenges are presented in games and distinguishes between two important types: games of progression "that directly set up each consecutive challenge in a game" and games of emergence that "set up challenges indirectly" (Juul 2004b, 68). These two ways can also be combined although they exist in their pure state too (Juul 2004b, 72). Also, several dimensions in Gump, Redl, and Sutton-Smith 1971 are related to challenges and winning: competition factors,[12] pleasure–pain content of winning and losing,[13] spread of winnership,[14] penetration of game by rewards and punishments,[15] outcome clarity,[16] nature of obstacles,[17] and challenges. The last in particular merits closer inspection.

Gump, Redl, and Sutton-Smith (1971, 417–418) found eight basic types of challenge within which the purposes of actors and counter-actors mirrored one another: the race (to overtake/ to stay ahead); the chase (to catch/to outdistance); the attack (to overcome/to defend); the capture (to take/to avoid being taken); the harassment (to lure/to see through the trick); the hunt (to find/ to hide); the rescue (to be the "savior"/to be a jailer); the seduction (to tempt/to resist temptation).

While it is clear that complex contemporary computer games combine several of these types or include them as options the player can choose from, many simpler and earlier games may still be classifiable according to these simple action types, although that could bring classification attempts dangerously close to the often proposed but very vague and often overlapping game genres such as action and adventure.

Interestingly, Gump, Redl, and Sutton-Smith comment on this dimension by connecting challenges to themes and by denying the applicability of the usual readymade psychological dichotomies:

> Challenges. These are the themes of the game which put partici-
> pants in various sorts of relationships to each other. Although
> these relationships can be considered active-passive; dominant-
> subservient; etc., the psychological flavor is missed by such
> labels. These challenges usually do present two roles, however,
> which roles we might call actor and counter-actor. (Gump, Redl,
> and Sutton-Smith 1971, 417)

Seeing challenges as themes may have certain consequences for discussions of genre, as it shows the way themes can be connected to actions (and not only to representations).

14.3.5 *Game state*

The meta-dimension of game state also divides into two sub-dimensions, mutability and savability. Mutability "describes how changes in the game state affect the game agents (be they player or computer controlled)" (Elverdam and Aarseth 2007, 15). These state changes can be passing (temporal), last throughout the game (finite), or span beyond multiple game instances (infinite) (Elverdam and Aarseth 2007, 15).

In essence, mutability describes resources that are or may become available to the players. Elverdam and Aarseth do not specify the nature of these changes; i.e. whether they strengthen or weaken the player's position and possibilities in the game. In the earlier model, the described changes were seen as rewards that control player behavior (Aarseth, Smedstad, and Sunnanå 2003, 52). The typology does not contain other kinds of resource or reward (or punishment).

Savability describes whether "the game state can be saved and restored at the player's discretion (unlimited), if this is only allowed in certain circumstances (conditional), or if it is impossible to save the game state (none)" (Elverdam and Aarseth 2007, 15).

This dimension describes the player's temporal control over the course of the game and is somewhat similar in function to Gump, Redl, and Sutton-Smith's (1971, 413) dimension of respite possibilities, although the latter is considerably broader, as it includes both "safety zones or positions" and "built in rest periods." The latter authors describe and justify the category as follows: "In games where action is fact and perhaps threatening, the presence or absence of respite possibilities may be crucial" (Gump, Redl, and Sutton-Smith 1971, 413).

The obvious differences between the two models here are based on the possibilities of digital saving and restoring in the first place (although, for instance, a chess game can be replayed from any given and recorded point onwards) and, in practice also, on the practical needs of segmentation given the length of many contemporary computer games, but on the functional level the idea of resting periods between game sessions is common to both models. The earlier model's safety zones and positions have also found their way to digital games – if not every then almost every MMOG includes areas that are reserved for players socializing in between campaigns, raids and tasks.

14.4 Conclusion: beyond genre

Traditionally, genres (in literature, drama, and film) have been determined by the combination of themes and modes or more generally by syntactic and semantic features and lately also by pragmatic concerns. As we saw in Chapters 3 and 5, genres and systems of genre are both necessary and impossible; literary and cinematic fields (among other fields) need to be and are always already divided according to higher level concepts such as genres, discourse modes, or text types to name a few. As genres do not usually exist in their pure state, are easily mixed and parodied, change over time, and there is a general lack of consensus about their defining features among different interest groups (academia, industry, retailers, designers, players, and journalists), the term genre is probably best thought of as a rule of thumb device connecting the expectations of audiences and artists.

Similar confusions also reign in the realm of digital game studies, which doesn't have the benefit of strong genre-defining scholarly traditions. In practice, this means that those who still want to think in terms of genre have either to transport their conceptual points of departure from film, drama or literary studies or to foreground some game elements at the expense of others. The most obvious danger in the former situation is related to the role of representation and superficial surface similarities between films and video games. Settings and characters, especially those in transmedial franchises, necessarily create expectations about the kinds of event and situation the player will be facing in the game (if the player has seen the film or read the cartoon or the novel), but as game representations are primarily representations to be manipulated and the goal of the manipulation is either to win or complete the game – or improve one's status and position in the gameworld – these latter game-specific dimensions (crucial to the players' expectations and experiences relative to their success in the game) should be taken into account in the definitions of game genres, which brings us back to game elements and their relative importance.

Elverdam and Aarseth briefly discuss the strength of their typology also in relation to problems of genre, and come to the conclusion that the typology works well as a comparative tool, but it doesn't offer solutions to the genre problem (Elverdam and Aarseth 2007, 4). This is more than clear also in light of the typology's combinatorics. Already, without the two dimensions of physical space that may not always be present in computer games, we have 15 dimensions resulting in 746496 possible combinations, each a well-specified type of game.[18] In defining literary genres, western poetics managed relatively well with two dimensions, genre being the combination of modes and themes, and even if forms and media functioning were added to these two, the number of basic dimensions, values and resulting combinations would be much more manageable than the precision achieved in the typology of Elverdam and Aarseth. Obviously, that precision must be sacrificed if one wants to continue the discussion of game genres, but it is very hard to find compelling reasons for doing so. It may be better to leave genre to linger on as the vague umbrella term it already is in many other scholarly fields and direct scholarly efforts elsewhere.[19]

Should one try to reduce the number of genre defining criteria, Aarseth's (2004a, 47–48) dissection of games into rules, gameplay and gameworld (the last being the most accidental part) could serve as a preliminary generic grid of syntactic (rules), semantic (gameworld), and pragmatic (gameplay) features. Alternatively a tripartite grid could be constructed on the basis of action, and following Gump, Redl, and Sutton-Smith's insights connecting game themes to game challenges, as a combination of syntactic (rules), semantic (challenges) and pragmatic (player to player relations) dimensions.[20]

In such scenarios, the usefulness of old generic markers are at best limited to the visual surface of the gameworld; even if one adds Altman's (1999) pragmatic dimension of competition among user groups to the scene, generic discussion would not advance without a much better understanding of the rules and gameplay – and especially the interplay of the two. At the center of this are the modes of action and play, as the one thing the player (or the would-be player) needs to know is what the game requires from him. These are among the main topics of the next chapter.

CHAPTER 15

Rules and configurative practices

15.1 Introduction

In the previous two chapters, we drafted a general and transmedial (or transtechnological) game ecology from both diachronic and synchronic perspectives. Combined, these two perspectives form a necessary basis for comparative game studies. In this chapter and the next, we shift the focus from game ecology to the gaming situation; in short, we adopt a more player-centric perspective. From that perspective, games are configurative practices at the center of which is player effort as rule-based and goal-oriented activity.

After beginning with a brief sketch of configurative practices and the interplay of configuration and interpretation (to which we'll return from another perspective in Chapter 17), the rest of this chapter will focus on the rule-based relation between the player's actions (player effort) and game events. The primacy of rules is based on the fact that the behavior of every necessary element of the game, including its players, is controlled and constrained[1] by rules, and the player cannot go against them (except by cheating) without ceasing to play the game.[2]

In addition to rules that constrain player effort all the time, there are goals that also constrain player effort by giving it direction and motivation. Goal-dependent constraints are less absolute than rule-dependent ones because (depending on the game structure and type of goal or goals) the players can also play to a varying degree against goals, pursue objectives other than the implied or explicitly prescribed goals, not orient their actions towards the goal(s) at all, or remain largely passive and inactive in the game without major or immediate consequences or punishments. So although rules and goals belong to the same game structure and work together in constraining, directing and enabling the player's actions, their influence on player effort differs in both range and emphasis. Nevertheless, they will be discussed together, as in a broader view goals belong to the system of rules as goal rules (Frasca 2007, 118).

In what follows, we discuss player effort on three levels. In this chapter, we concentrate on the player's rule-based manipulative effort[3] mostly on micro- and mesolevels. In Chapter 16, we examine the player's activity on the macrolevel of a whole game from its initial to its final state (and its alternatives), and the temporal and causal (conditional) coordinates of that process.

15.2 Games as configurative practices

In "The Gaming Situation" (Eskelinen 2001a), I introduced the notion of configurative practice that was based on my interpretation of Aarseth's typology of textual communication. The idea was to approach games as configurative practices in which the roles of configuration and interpretation are reversed (or remarkably different) compared to two other domains: dominantly interpretative practices (such as ergodic literature and cinema) and purely interpretative practices (such as non-ergodic literature and cinema). In short: "in art we might have to configure in order to be able to interpret, whereas in games we have to interpret in order to be able to configure, and proceed from the beginning to the winning or some other situation" (Eskelinen 2001a).

In another paper (Eskelinen 2007, 199), I very briefly compared several foregrounded aspects of interpretative and configurative practices. The former are characterized by interpretation, economy of representation, conventions, meaning guaranteed by minimal coherence, reception, fiction, work and text, and spatiotemporal orientation, whereas the latter prefer action, economy of means and ends, rules, variation pacified by rules and goals, play, simulation, system and model and causal and functional orientation. The more accurate version of this didactic dichotomy would be to state that configurative practices also include the features associated with interpretative practices, although they are then organized differently because they are shaped by their configurative counterparts. However, for the purposes of this chapter the difference between these two types of practice could be simplified by once again comparing games and narratives.

As we saw in the narratological section, the relations between narrative and story, narrative to narrating, or simply between story and narrative discourse are of interpretative nature: stories and narrating instances are constructed from narrative discourse by interpreting the latter. That is not the case with the gaming situation, at the heart of which is the player's manipulative activity, and at the heart of this activity is the dynamic and rule-based relation between player actions and the resulting game events – a configurative relation.

Before moving on to rules, a few clarifications are in order, mainly because the shift from interpretation to the various forms of interplay between interpretation and configuration was often misread to mean that the role of interpretation was severely diminished or almost non-existent, when in actual practice the intrepretative process is only intensified when it is shaped by the configurative pressure.

First, although configurative (manipulative) action is the dominant form of action in games, it is not the only form, as the players usually have to explore the game space, and they may be permitted to add new constructions and surface modifications to it (such as rooms and buildings, on the one hand, and skins and other more decorative and self-expressive elements, on the other). Multiplayer games add an extra dimension to this by enabling communication and collaboration between players, in addition to often making configurative action more challenging. Needless to say, most digital games also contain purely interpretative sequences, such as cutscenes that may inform or reward the player, accentuate and pace his gameplay, or simply occupy attention during the time required for loading the next level. Schematically then, the gaming situation may combine five major kinds of activity: configurative action,[4] explorative action, constructive action, communication (between players), and interpretation.

Second, to say that the player's interpretations serve his configurative activities is not to say that these interpretations don't matter. The real difference is elsewhere. In literature, theater and film everything matters or is conventionally supposed to matter equally – if you've seen 90% of the presentation that's not enough, you have to see or read it all (or everything you can)[5] because every part of the presentation carries irreducible expressive value that is at least potentially crucial for the spectator's or reader's interpretation of the work. This is characteristic of interpretative practices in general. In contrast, in games some actions and reactions in relation to certain events and challenges will bring the player more quickly to a solution or help him reach the winning (or improved) situation sooner or more effectively than others. Therefore the player either can't or doesn't have to encounter every possible combinatory event and existent the game possibly contains or could generate as a response to the actions of the player, as these differ in their ergodic importance. We may even say that it is one of the player's primary tasks to reduce this configurative excess to a more manageable and useful player repertoire – assuming that there is excess in the first place (this concept should not be wasted on very simple games).

In short, configuration and interpretation are necessarily intertwined and work together, although the former dominates the latter almost in the exact way described by Jakobson: "The dominant may be defined as the focusing component of a work of art: it rules, determines, and transforms the remaining components. It is the dominant which guarantees the integrity of the structure" (Jakobson 1971, 107). The case is more complex though because after poststructuralism and deconstruction, we readily detect irreducible thematic and formal surplus or excess that is always already wherever we wish to look. Transposed into the realm of games, this axiom means there have to be both configurative and interpretative excesses, an inexhaustible number of combinatory configurative possibilities mentioned earlier, and interpretations not merely serving configuration and creating configurative use value (i.e. more directed towards expressive and self-expressive potential of the screen or other representations).

Interpretative excesses aside, in the configurative gameplay process (where interpretation guides configuration that feeds interpretation) it is in the player's best interests to interpret at least the following six aspects of the game:

1 his own actions and resources (possibilities for and outcomes of actions) for tactical and strategic reasons

2 his adversaries' (be they other humans or artificial entities) actions, resources, tactics and strategies

3 the actions and resources of his teammates (if any) for reasons of effective and advantageous collaboration

4 the structure of the game and its current, upcoming and known challenge(s)

5 the behavior of the simulated/dynamic objects in the gameworld (including the gameworld itself)

6 the fictional content (if there is any) of the game state representations and game events for embedded cues and clues.

Third, in addition to his prior knowledge (of the game, its supposed genre, and the other players), the player gains information about all these six aspects in digital games through the game interface – and it's only the lazy cinematic gaze that may lead scholars (such as Nitsche 2008, 54–55, already discussed in Chapter 12) to believe that this necessary presentational layer is an inherently narrative one.

To better understand this, we need to address the shift from analog to digital games and the role of representation in digital games. In non-digital card games, board games and competitive sports, the game state resides in the cards and other game pieces and objects and in the player's body (Juul 2004b, 44), but in video games the game state resides in the computer's memory. The rules of the game are also upheld by the computer (CPU) that also performs the transitions between game states. Therefore there has to be a way to communicate the game states and changes of game states to the player, which is exactly what the audio-visual-textual representational surface (TV or computer screen) does.

Consequently, what the player sees represented on the screen or hears or reads from it is there to inform him about the game state, show him the consequences of his actions, and suggest options for further action. In short, the digital game interface and the representations displayed on the screen are necessarily tied to the feedback loop between game state description (or information) and gameplay, and the primacy of these two intertwined levels should be taken into account in every hypothesis concerning the dynamic semiotic surface of digital games. Representations have or may have other functions such as presenting game fiction, but this is the primary one necessary for both abstract and representational digital games. Schematically speaking, besides the always present configurative use value (including also the game information in cutscenes), the screen representations have expressive value (just as any other audiovisual or text-based presentation from novels to films and cartoons), and self-expressive value, because at least some of the actions (and sometimes descriptions too) are owned by the player.

In short, what we have to consider in this chapter is the feedback loop between represented game states and the player's actions and reactions to those states. Representations are dynamic, changing according to the player's input and the game's algorithms. From the player's perspective the perceived changes in game state, i.e. the game events, result either from his actions, the other player's actions, or the game system's player-independent actions: they are combinatory events. In short, we can describe digital game representations as dynamic and combinatory representations of game states and player actions – and these, like any other necessary element in the game, are regulated and shaped by its rules.

 ## 15.3 Rules

In Chapter 13, we found several historical, technological and "generic" differences in the implementation and nature of rules. These were related to constancy, compatibility, fixedness, explicitness, maintenance, complexity and the player's prior knowledge. Some of these were intentionally designed to violate the usual and normative functioning of game rules best described in Salen and Zimmerman's (2004, 122–125) common sense account: the rules limit the player's action and are supposed to be explicit and unambiguous, fixed, binding, repeatable, and shared by all players.

However, the six defining features of this description are slightly different in weight. As we already saw, the degree of explicitness and fixedness may vary, and different groups of players can play the same game with different rules (that they wrongly believe to be shared by every player) at least for a while, but the processes thus instigated are still games. Likewise it is possible to create or agree on the rules of a new game, play it once, and then forget its rules, in which case the rules are not repeatable (this is somewhat typical of games that children improvise), or design a game in which the players are supposed to cheat and thus undermine and break the very idea of binding rules. Contrary to these more or less hypothetical cases, it is difficult to conceive of a game that would not limit the player's action in any way. In principle, such a game could consist only of a given goal, which the player is allowed to pursue as he sees fit using any means necessary. Such boundless allowances seem to be more typical of practices that are only metaphorically games: various military and political campaigns and criminal and business strategies ("kill Castro whatever it takes" etc.) come to mind.

In ludological research, both Aki Järvinen (2003; 2008) and Gonzalo Frasca (2001a; 2003a; 2007) have usefully specified the functioning of rules, albeit from two different perspectives that nevertheless seem compatible.

Järvinen (2003) has focused more on the realms and elements that different rule sets control and define. He distinguished five elements games may consist of: components, environment, mechanics, interface, and theme. Of these five, only components and mechanics are mandatory. The rest (environment, theme, and interface) are optional and not found in every game: card and most dice games can do without a specific game environment, digital games need an interface to give players the necessary access to game mechanics, and abstract games don't have a theme.[6] Based on this theory of elements, Järvinen describes five kinds of rule (one for each element), the first two of which are mandatory for any kind of game:

1 Rules that govern game components by stating their number, status, value, etc. Also, component functions, i.e. roles within a mechanism, are specified.

2 Rules that govern procedures' relation to other elements, i.e. define allowed mechanics and their consequences.

3 Rules that define game environment(s): the physical boundaries of components and procedures.

4 Rules that dictate how game theme is implemented.

5 Rules that define how the interface is used to enact procedures and mechanics within the game environment, complemented with rules about providing the player information about her progress. (Järvinen 2003, 77)

Later the number of elements in Järvinen's model increased from five to nine (Järvinen 2008), the additional ones being players, contexts, information – and rule sets. This could result in adding player rules (or more likely rules for player to player interaction; i.e. something like coordination rules), context rules, information rules (already suggested by Juul 2004b, 67), and last but not least rule rules (akin to Frasca's metarules), but Järvinen's approach is oriented differently in his later work as it moves more towards applied ludology, game design and game psychology (Järvinen 2008).

Frasca's (2007) new and revised typology of rules is based on his new game definition, and more precisely the combination of two of its six main criteria: games have rules and player performance is measured and evaluated. In addition to winning and losing, there are smaller gains and losses measurable according to the preference system of the game (such as, for example, socially and operationally valued experience levels in MMOGs). This type of "grading" of player performance leads Frasca to slightly revise his former typology (Frasca 2003a) of rules:

> Rules will be distributed among three main categories: model rules, grade rules and goal rules. Alternatively, these categories can also be better understood, respectively, as what the player respectively "can", "should" and "must" (or "cannot", "should not" and "must not") do according to the system. A fourth category, metarules, is also present and it remains unchanged from how I previously defined it (ibid). Metarules state what the player "could" do, not within the game but with it as an object. (Frasca 2007, 116)

More specifically model rules "define how a game or play activity is modelled – in the sense of a simulational model" and "state how the playworld works," including the behavior of both objects and possible avatars (Frasca 2007, 117). Grade rules "deal with any characteristic of a game or play activity that is measured within its system" (ibid.) and "apply to anything that creates a gain or a loss for the player as measured *from the system's perspective*" (Frasca 2007, 118). Goal rules "define the states that lead to victory and defeat – and therefore, to the closure of the game session" (ibid.). In some cases, these rules specify only winning or losing conditions but not both (ibid.). Finally, metarules define "how the player can modify the game's rule system" (ibid.).

These four categories and conceptual pairs (can/cannot; should/should not; must/must not; could/could not) define, constrain, and enable the player's action and could be further elaborated both within the framework of modal logic and theories of action.

Before beginning those elaborations, however, we could add to Frasca's four-part typology what Juul (2004b, 67) calls information rules[7] that govern the ways information about game states is given and revealed to the players (differently in games of perfect and imperfect information). The distribution and delivery of information can be clarified in terms of ludologically modified theory of exposition. Theories of exposition were developed in literary and film narratology (Bordwell 1985, 56–57; Sternberg 1978, 161–162). Exposition concerns the initial layout of necessary and relevant information in relation to the beginning situation. It may be given to the player/reader/spectator in the very beginning (preliminary) or later (delayed), and it can be given in a lump (concentrated) or in several installments (distributed). This gives us three basic options for distribution: preliminary and concentrated, delayed and concentrated, and delayed and distributed.

The first option gives the player solid ground for jumping in; there's nothing much left to learn once you understand that you should kill everything that moves in *Quake* or how to arrange *Tetris* blocks. At the other extreme, in MMOGs crucial information concerning the gameworld and the players' positions and advancement in it just keeps accumulating without a definite point of ending. In many quest games such as *Myst*, there wouldn't be much of a game without the delayed and concentrated exposition that gives the player the crucial bits of information about the sons and their father.

However, there are crucial differences in information in linear narratives (which are Sternberg's and Bordwell's research objects) and in games. In the latter, information is distributed differently (invested in formal rules for example), it is to be obtained differently (by manipulating the equipment), and it is to be used differently (in moving toward the goal). To account for these differences, the concept of exposition in game studies should additionally take into account the behavioral variety of game elements (the ways rules, goals, agents, objects, and gameworld are exposed to the player may differ from each other), the difference between unconditional and conditional delivery of information (i.e. information depending on the success or failure of the player's actions or some other condition), and also the type of information giving the player either declarative (knowing what) or procedural knowledge (knowing how).

Frasca's model rules could be divided into two groups along the lines his definition already suggests: player rules (that define how gameplay is modeled) and gameworld rules (to describe how the other elements in the simulation work independently of the player's choices and actions). This difference is the same as the distinction between gameworld rules and gameplay rules (Zagal et al. 2005) mentioned in the previous chapter. As gameplay consists of rule-based manipulation, the latter will be called manipulation rules according to Frasca's original suggestion (2003a, 231), and together with gameworld rules they define what relations and properties can be affected, how deeply, for how long, under what conditions and so on. We could further divide gameworld rules into component and environment rules, based on Järvinen's distinction, and undoubtedly we could go into greater detail within these subcategories as well.

Player rules need one more specification in multiplayer games: the rules regulating the interaction and communication among multiple players. The latter aspect (communication) is clearly part (or a subtype) of information rules, but the former is a somewhat trickier case. From the player's perspective, the actions and events in the game result from what he did, from what the other player or players did, or from what the system did. To use Järvinen's terms, these events are owned by self, by others, or by the system (Järvinen 2008, 340). In actual practice, from the individual player's perspective the last two may be difficult to separate from each other, as they are both beyond him and his actions even if they may directly respond to them, and also because all rules are upheld by the computer. In non-digital games these aspects are usually easier to distinguish one from the other: the rules of soccer describe not only what individual players can and cannot do with the ball, but also what the players can and cannot do to each other in the game (specific kinds of permitted and penalized tackles etc.). Still, it makes conceptual sense to distinguish between these three separate sources of actions and events, and for lack of better terms the rules regulating and articulating the player to player dimension could be called coordination rules.

The seven kinds of rule are presented in Table 15.1, in which they are combined with the players' epistemological, doxastic and boulomaeic attitudes, i.e. their knowledge, beliefs and wishes concerning the rules that govern and delimit their actions.[8]

Table 15.1 Rules and player attitudes

Rules/attitudes	Epistemological	Doxastic	Boulomaeic
I			
Information rules			
Game world rules			
Manipulation rules			
Coordination rules			
II			
Grade rules			
Goal rules			
III			
Metarules			

In this context, epistemological attitudes relate to the player's knowledge of the rules, and doxastic attitudes relate to his beliefs and doubts about them (for example that they are fair and shared

by every player etc.). The player's knowledge and beliefs about
different rules differ from game to game (based on his prior
knowledge and experience, assumptions about and familiarity with
the genre), as may the relations between knowledge and beliefs,
neither of which may be static. Rule structures also support certain
beliefs (that have to remain beliefs) by not giving any reason for
doubt. For example, it may be difficult or impossible to prove
and thus to know that the game is fair, but if nothing contradicts that belief, there's no reason to give up that belief. In other
words, the player doesn't necessarily know that the game (i.e. the
combination of the different types of rule) is fair, but he usually
and conventionally believes it is. In the kind of social simulation
games discussed earlier, the situation is reversed: at first, the player
doesn't know the rules are not fair, but believes that they are fair,
then begins to doubt that, and finally learns they are not fair.
Undoubtedly, many patterns between these and other positions
could be located and scrutinized, but that is not our concern here.

In the course of a typical game, the player's relative non-knowledge
of the rules is gradually replaced by knowledge, but the depth and
degree of this knowledge may vary greatly. As computer games are
capable of effectively hiding their many rules, and for pragmatic
reasons must hide some of them (the more complex and extensive
the gameworld is, the more impractically extensive the game
manual becomes); if the player is not also the designer of the game
he plays, full knowledge will most probably be an illusion. As a
rule of thumb, one could say that information, coordination, goal,
and metarules tend to be more explicit and knowable in order to
support fair play and lower the threshold of the player's entering
the game, but that does not have to be the case in every game.

However, there's more to this, as the relationships among
different rules should also be worked out. Metarules stay firmly
outside gameplay, as the game is actually played with all the other
"in-game" rules.[9] The most important distinction among them is
that both grade and goal rules evaluate the player's performance
whereas model rules (the combination of gameworld, player,
coordination and information rules)[10] do not. Therefore, we have
two major types of rule: objective model rules the player cannot
play against, and evaluative (grade and goal) rules that are less
binding in the sense that player can at least try to play against
or ignore them. This aspect creates and leaves more room for

the player's self-expression,[11] and, therefore, in addition to the player's doxastic and epistemological attitudes towards his action and action possibilities, his boulomaeic attitudes also need to be taken into account: his wants, wishes, desires and preferences that metarules may also serve, support and channel to a varying degree.

As manipulation rules separate impossible actions from possible ones (this has nothing to do with action that is unexpected, unforeseen and even destructive from the viewpoint of either game designers or other players), grade rules separate preferable from less preferable actions, and goal rules separate conditions necessary for winning from the rest, we could say that their combinations determine the mode of action for the implied player or players. To make clearer the way in which rules and especially grade and goal rules constrain the player's action by evaluating and directing the player's performance for the entire duration of the game, we'll take a closer look at five different but intertwined things: what happens if the player fails, does nothing, plays (or has or tries to play) according to his own preferences and goals, ignores explicit goals, or foregrounds certain secondary aspects (such as roles, representations, or player to player communication) because of their affordances for self-expression.

15.4 Microlevel: doing nothing and failing

The most obvious extreme of diverting one's actions from the game's explicit goals is to do nothing. Some games such as early adventure games allow this to happen without any consequences and changes in the game state (there was no haste), while many others bring themselves to closure if that state lasts for too long (the adversary wins; the non-playing player loses all his resources; the time for play is up etc.). In terms of self-expression and alternative action, this choice doesn't offer much except perhaps the pleasures of observation, assuming that there is something interesting or necessary to observe while one lasts in the game.

Contrariwise, the more interesting question concerns the minimal requirements for the player to stay in the game. In team sports such as soccer, it often seems that some players do absolutely nothing either because for long periods of time they have no need to do anything (the goalie of a superb team) or because they patiently wait for a decisive opportunity. These states (that may sometimes be hard to observe from the outside) are different from failures, i.e. the situations in which the player is not doing what he intends or is supposed to do (which could lead to immediate or delayed repercussions from the coach or the other members of the team).

Furthermore, because the game of soccer is guaranteed to last 90 minutes both teams and most players will be guaranteed the same 90 minutes of playtime provided that they are not seriously penalized and driven out. The grade rules of soccer leave lots of room and time between dispreferred penalized actions and preferred actions (scoring goals) that rarely succeed. This gives ample opportunities both for doing nothing remarkable and for playing well (about which the grade rules don't say anything) without scoring or being penalized. At the other extreme are games such as tennis in which one and same challenge (serving and returning the ball) is repeated over and over again throughout the whole game, and in which every failure to successfully return the ball counts and affects the outcome of the game. Therefore, there's very little if any room for alternative action; one could say that games like tennis represent the absolute tyranny of grade and goal rules, i.e. they control and grade the outcome of every available player action and thus narrow the range of the player's expression of his bouleomaeic attitudes.

In computer games, the player's actions (in the physical space) are translated into action representations in the virtual space,[12] and combined with the action representations of the other players and the changes intrinsic to the game system they form more or less continuous game events. In short, what we have on this microlevel is the fundamental relation between player actions (causes), action representations, and game events (effects) arranged into a feedback loop. It is important to see the differences among these three parts of the microlevel loop. Actions happen in the physical space and their representations and results are displayed on the dynamic screen.

Within this simple basic cycle it is useful to distinguish between intention-success and purpose-success (Van Dijk 1977, 174). In the first case, the intended action is performed and, in the latter, the desired end is achieved (ibid.). If this is applied to rule-constrained and goal-driven gameplay, we can make a couple of observations. In some games intention-success seems to be guaranteed; the player can play the card he intends in the card game or move the piece he intends to move in the board game without intervention or effective interference from the other players or the game system (as long as it is an action allowed by the model rules), whereas in games that allow synchronous action from the players or set other temporal constraints on the player's action they may and often will fail to do what they intended to do. If intention-success is guaranteed then the player is free to perform any allowed action or move, but in most cases a series of poor moves work against the player's chances of staying in the game for long (i.e. the duration of intention successes may be limited).

Intention successes and failures can both lead to purpose successes and failures,[13] but in terms of the game structure the most important aspect is the relation of the player's subjective purpose success and failure to the game's preference system (Frasca's grade rules) i.e. if they constitute gains or losses from the game system's perspective as well and whether or not the player is or is made aware of this (which is the matter of information rules).

Only very short games such as *WarioWare Inc.* and its one action per one mechanic challenges are easily describable in this simple model. There's only one action to perform per challenge, the player can either succeed or fail, and he is immediate informed about his intention and purpose successes and failures that fully overlap with the game's grade rules. The same relentless and inescapable cycles of action are repeated in arcade games that also explicitly and continuously announce the quantifiable results of the player's actions. There's very little if any room for alternative action that would go unpunished and thus allow the player to move into directions other than what the game structure prefers.[14]

If explicit scores present the positive side of informing the player of the degree of his objective purpose success, punishments present the negative side. Juul (2009) lists four kinds of possible punishment for the player's failure: energy punishment (loss of energy, bringing the player closer to life punishment), life punishment (loss of a *life* or "retry," bringing the player closer to game termination), game termination punishment (game over), and setback punishment (having to replay part of the game; losing abilities). The player's failures may also go unpunished, or at least the relationship between failure and punishment is less explicit and immediate. In the realm of digital games, Juul's four failures have their roots in arcade games, but equivalents to them can be located in many classic non-digital games, although the option of game termination in them usually signals the adversary's victory. Explicit and immediate punishments are very effective means of directing the player, and they also determine minimal requirements for the player to stay in the game and to some degree they also regulate how long the player can stay in the game if he continues to fail or perform dispreferred actions.

On the failure side, we then have three kinds of failure: intention failure and subjective and objective (grade rule-based) purpose failure. In respect to these, Juul's four types of punishment can be divided in two: unlike termination and setback punishments, energy and life punishments don't immediately lead to discontinuity. The game doesn't have to make its grade rules explicit or continuously inform, reward or punish the player for his success and failure, and theoretically the time span after which the player recognizes (or is allowed to recognize) objective purpose successes may equal the duration of the whole game. This moves us from the micro- to the meso-level, on which the players have to combine their actions into sequences that move them towards explicit, personal or social goals reflecting their preferences.

15.5 Mesolevel: directions and deixis

Both subjective and objective purposes on the mesolevel concern the orientation and direction of player effort beyond the recurring microlevel cycles of actions and events. In principle and depending on the game structure, the player may choose not to make this move, and instead cling on to some recurring microlevel activity that has no major consequences for the continuity and completion of the game and is as such neither preferred nor dispreferred by the game system (grade rules). Mary Flanagan (2005) documents the behavior of young players who stay clear of the goal-oriented tasks in *GTA3* and just keep driving around in the vast gameworld. In a similar fashion, one could imagine players who are more attracted to the visual pleasures of the landscape in *Myst* than to actually solving the puzzle. Still, these two examples are somewhat negative and are based on the range and depth of the grade rules, in the sense that they consist of insignificant actions neither preferred nor dispreferred (or neither rewarded nor punished) in the game and come close to non-playing or non-gaming (in the sense that they do not create alternative personal challenges). In short, they do not allow the players to win, lose, succeed or fail in an interesting way if they disregard or ignore the official goal, and neither do they offer significant opportunities for the player's self-expression in terms of playing well (showing off one's skills), virtuously (Sicart 2009) or with a distinctive style, or modding his avatar.

The case is different with games like *Civilization*, in which the grade rules are complex enough to the degree that the player can disregard the overall objective of winning and explore other, self-set scenarios and objectives; in short, the player may prefer the affordances and outcomes of the model and grade rules to the final outcome dictated by the goal rules and be an active player losing in an interesting way or accidentally even winning.

Despite its vast "counter-gaming" possibilities, *Civilization* is clearly a game that fully evaluates the player's performance. The case is different with games and software toys that remove goal rules (MMOGs) and even grade rules as well (*The Sims 2*) and thus turn the evaluation (valorization) of the player performance and its outcomes into more or mere personal or social matters. Although the infinite teleology and business model of the MMOGs capitulates and de-emphasizes the overarching goal that signals winning and the end, they prefer the player's advancement in gaining higher levels and encourage and often require cooperation, which means that there are social sanctions and punishments for those otherwise inclined, not to mention the imbalances of power that work against not working one's way up the ladder. Nevertheless, if seen in the light of the triangle of allowed non-playing, mildly sanctioned failure and opportunities for ignoring both explicit and socially enforced goals, MMOGs present a certain borderline case for game scholarship as Juul observes:

> [A]ctual playing can be a mix of social interaction, exploration, strategic planning, and aesthetic preferences on character creation. In such multiplayer games, we can in principle perform a strategic analysis for various situations such as battling monsters, but in actual play, many other considerations can intervene. (Juul 2007)

Sims 2 provides another extreme by removing grade rules, making it hard to decide whether it is a game or a software toy. It has fixed model rules, player effort and variable outcomes, which makes it a game according to our definition and a borderline case in Juul's classic game model that requires different valorization for different outcomes. Be that as it may (both perspectives have merits and one could argue that its status as a game or a toy depends on its use), in any case the lack of inbuilt evaluative rules creates a new situation and points to suggestive ergodic similarities: "a number of other rule-based activities *are* interesting without goals: Musical instruments, Lego, Tangram, playing sequences of games with goals without keeping score. These activities are popular because they allow for a range of discernibly different expressions" (Juul 2007).

In addition to the removal of goal rules (MMOGs), or both goal and grade rules (*Sims 2* and many previous simulation games), reducing the importance of the overarching explicit goal (*GTA 3*; *Civilization*), and not punishing the player for failures and inactivity, there's yet another extreme against which to measure the negotiable power of the evaluation rules. In the absence of strongly enforced grade and goal rules, roles provide a strong secondary principle full of expressive power for organizing and constraining the player's actions. In this respect, LARPs and their fully embodied roles (in contrast to digitally represented roles) provide a fertile testing ground for the most expressive and complex balance between affordances and constraints: in other words, the expressive potential of role-based action is probably the best alternative or substitute for goal orientation in the kind of games that have only model rules that are non-negotiable by definition.

What is common to both these "extremes" and most classic games is the importance of the player's activities on the mesolevel.[15] This has to do with the player's position, orientation and direction in a game and could be called game deixis. This game deixis is related to other forms and contexts of deixis, especially those that occur in performative arts. Keir Elam's category of deictic orientation (Elam 1980, 186) includes spatial, temporal, functional, activity, and person deixis. If we modify it to suit games, we'll have the following 12 dimensions at our disposal:

1   singular or plural distal orientation toward the adversary
2   plural proximal orientation toward one's teammates

3 singular proximal orientation toward the player

4 orientation toward non-player characters

5 proximal orientation toward context (here)

6 distal orientation toward elsewhere (there)

7 proximal orientation toward context time (now)

8 distal orientation toward other time (then)

9 orientation toward current activity

10 orientation toward absent activity

11 orientation toward present object

12 orientation toward absent object.

We can use these dimensions in at least four different respects. First, not all games include or activate all these orientations. There may be no "elsewhere" outside the one arena; there isn't necessarily any other time to consider other than that which goes on now ("then" only means the game's over), and there might be no NPCs or teammates to communicate with. Second, and to apply the ancient formalist keyword, usually one or a few of these dimensions dominate or even exclude the other ones at any given moment of the game. Third, the player's subjective and objective purposes and types of intention and purpose successes and failures can be more accurately described in relation to the possible combinations of these orientations. Fourth, these basic orientations can be combined with and further specified using more game-specific descriptions and distinctions, such as Elverdam and Aarseth's game typology and Juul's distinction between games of emergence and progression, which bring us to the macrolevel of whole games and their temporal and causal segmentation as products and processes, the topic of the next chapter.

CHAPTER 16

Game time

16.1 Introduction

There is no general scholarly consensus about the temporality of games, but there are no major incompatibilities either between different theories, as they seem to address slightly different aspects and dimensions of time. I will begin by examining the strengths and limitations of several models proposed so far (cf. Aarseth 1995; 1999; Aarseth, Smedstad, and Sunnanå 2003; Elverdam and Aarseth 2007; Eskelinen 2001a[1]; Juul 2001; 2004a; Wolf 2001; Zagal and Mateas 2007). These models contain several at least partly overlapping dimensions, and over time they have also seemed to become more nuanced and detailed. Aarseth's first model (Aarseth 1998/1995) contains two explicit temporal dimensions; the next one (Aarseth, Smedstad, and Sunnanå 2003) contains three; and the latest one (Elverdam and Aarseth 2007) five. Early ludological models (proposed by Eskelinen and Juul) have either two or three timeframes, while the composite model of Zagal and Mateas has four. Although it would be tempting to force the discussion to proceed by frames or dimensions, we'll proceed model by model, both for the sake of clarity and in order to avoid prematurely reducing the diversity of approaches.

16.2 Aarseth's early theories of game time

As we saw in our discussion of the multidimensional models of Avedon and Gump, Redl, and Sutton-Smith, temporal structures were not at the center of scholarly attention. In performance theory Richard Schechner (1988, 6–7) made the useful distinction between set time (the game will be over when a given time is up) and event time (the game will be over once all the necessary events are completed). From very early on game designers and game journalists have been able to distinguish between real-time and turn-based games, but more systematic studies of game time and temporal structures had to wait until the late 1990s and the early 2000s.

Aarseth's earliest game typology from 1995 included two categories of time: teleology (either finite or infinite) exactly as it is in the later typologies (Aarseth, Smedstad, and Sunnanå 2003; Elverdam and Aarseth 2007), and "time" that can be either discrete (the player controlling the speed of his progress in the game, i.e. the passing of time doesn't change the game state), or synchronous or asynchronous (in these two last cases the computer sets the pace and the time of the game events is either realistic or arbitrary) (Aarseth 1998, 85). In Aarseth's next typology, (Aarseth, Smedstad, and Sunnanå 2003), these two distinctions (finite/infinite teleology; mimetic/arbitrary representation) are supplemented with the category of pace, which merely repeats the old common sense distinction between turn-based and real-time games.

Aarseth, Smedstad, and Sunnanå also make some pertinent observations about the difficulty of theorizing time:

> Time is a hard category to describe in relation to computer games. Since games are usually dominated by space, and struc-tured spatially, the use of time varies from game to game, as well as within the same game. (Aarseth, Smedstad, and Sunnanå 2003, 50)

They use *GTA3* as an example: the game's missions are "time-based in different ways" and also different from the time for between-missions game "where the player-character can be left standing around for 'days' without consequences" (ibid.). This variety is especially problematic in the context of constructing a typology of games: "Since most time-related structures so often vary within the same game, they are almost useless for classifying games" (ibid.). Therefore the temporal categories in the typology are meant to be "general enough to be distinctive" (ibid.). We'll return to these categories later, but it is already clear that these typologies of time are only a starting point for investigations of game time.

Aarseth, Smedstad, and Sunnanå also argue that "the functions of time ... seem to be governed by the social structure of a game" (ibid.). This brings in the difference between multiplayer and single-player games: because of coordination problems, multiplayer games do not allow saving and quite probably within them "bullet time" would be perceived as unfair. Although social structures matter, they are hardly the only reason for the wide variety of temporal structures and functions (or otherwise theorizing and categorizing social structures would be sufficient to determine the functions of time).

Cybertext is another major source for Aarseth's thinking on games. In the chapter on adventure games, Aarseth (1997, 125–127) distinguishes between the three discourse planes of events, progress and negotiation. In a later paper (Aarseth 1999), they constitute ergodic time. The most important part is the level of negotiation:

> where the possible event times are tested and varied, until a sufficiently satisfying sequence is reached, or not reached. If it is reached, a third level of time has been affected: that of progression of the game from beginning to end. (Aarseth 1999, 37)

Given Juul's focus on how challenges are presented, and the resulting distinction between games of emergence and progression, it may seem that Aarseth's tripartite ergodic time is slightly biased towards the latter. However, this is not the case, as negotiation takes place "on a level outside the game's event time" (ibid.), and although the structure of the negotiation level may vary from game to game, "the user's strategy of gaining experience by varying a difficult maneuver until a useful technique is reached, is the same for every time" (ibid.). The only difference in the negotiation level mentioned by Aarseth in this context is between games that can be saved and those that "must be played repeatedly to gain the necessary experience" (ibid.). The player's capability to save the game constitutes a dimension in the two later typologies (Aarseth, Smedstad, and Sunnanå 2003 and Elverdam and Aarseth 2007), but it is not included in the meta-category of time in either.

In any case, using Aarseth's system of discourse levels, we have five kinds of time to investigate: event, progression, negotiation, communication, and construction times.

16.3 Wolf

In *The Medium of the Video Game*, Mark J.P. Wolf devoted a whole chapter to "Time in the Video Game" (Wolf 2001, 77–91). He begins with stillness and movement that according to him "give the player the experience of the time passing" (Wolf 2001, 77). Wolf situates movement at three levels: the levels of the medium, the image, and the content of the image (Wolf 2001, 78). While connecting time to motion, and claiming that "accelerating action and accelerating time can be seen as different aspects of the same experience," he takes up an example of the "zip mode" in both *Myst* (1993) and *Riven* (1997) which allows the players to jump to places seen in the distance – and interprets this both as "speeding up the player's movement, or condensing his or her travel time" (Wolf 2001, 80). Here the problem is that two distinct phenomena are confused with one another: although Wolf's interpretation of the zip mode may be correct, speeding up the player's movement is categorically different from transportation or teleporting between different locations, although their effects may sometimes overlap. Another problem is Wolf's focus is on the experience of time, which necessarily varies from player to player, rather than on the explicitly designed temporal structures of games.

After discussing stillness and movement, Wolf moves on to the patterns of their form. When the movement repeatedly returns to the same position, the player is facing "cyclical or looped time" (Wolf 2001, 80), the mastery of which is necessary to the player's timing of his action and to his advancement in the game. This is the same kind of movement Aarseth previously discussed in *Cybertext* and in "Aporia and Epiphany" (Aarseth 1999): the tripartite system of event, negotiation, and progression times, in which the middle term designates the player's search for the right actions and action sequences to overcome the aporia (i.e. the challenge) in order to make progress in the game. Wolf doesn't seem to be aware of previous theorizations, and his discourse also lacks references to theories of time and temporal structures in film studies, although Wolf constantly compares temporal experiences in video games and films.

Wolf's third group of temporal phenomena includes beginnings, endings and interludes, in short, various forms of cutscenes the player usually can't interact with. From there he moves to discuss the pace in games and distinguishes between the aforementioned interludes, "computer-controlled characters and events whose speeds can be varied by the game, and the speed of the player's own decisions, reactions, and movement through the games world" (Wolf 2001, 86). The pace may also be affected by speed settings, pauses and saves that Wolf briefly and unsystematically introduces. Finally, he discusses time pressure and finds two types of timer in games: "a stopwatch" and "an hourglass." To quote: "In the former type, the task is fixed and the amount of time taken to complete it varies, while in the latter, the amount of time is fixed and how much the player accomplishes varies" (Wolf 2001, 89). In short, Wolf is able to locate the basic difference between unlimited and limited duration (of tasks or whole games) and rediscover Schechner's event and set time.

Wolf comes close to the question of time as a varying resource in games like *Spy vs. Spy* (1984), but interprets it only as one possible combination of limited and unlimited time (Wolf 2001, 89). The chapter's concluding paragraph exemplifies the shallowness of Wolf's findings:

Whether time is used for action or for contemplation, is limited, unlimited, or some combination of both, or flows at different or even controllable rates of speed, it is often closely tied in to game play. While the same malleability of time available in film is available in video games, the video game often involves the player more in the temporal structure of the video game experience, and thus can vary greatly depending on the player. While films have a fixed length or running time, video games do not. (Wolf 2001, 90)

In general, Wolf's unsystematic discussion of time is too constrained by his focus on the experience of time and by his narrativist bias (Wolf sees video games as one form of interactive narratives), which is also oddly uninformed by any proper film or literary narratology that could make his comparisons more accurate and valid.

16.4 Play time and fictional time (Juul's game time)

In some ways, Juul's theory of game time (2001; 2004a; 2004b) seems to be a specification of the dimension of time representation in Aarseth (1998/1995), Aarseth, Smedstad, and Sunnanå (2003) and Elverdam and Aarseth (2007). Juul makes the basic distinction between play time and fictional time. The former "denotes the time span taken to play a game" (Juul 2004b, 125) and the latter "the time of the events in the gameworld" (Juul 2004b, 126). In playing the game, the player projects the former onto the latter – except in abstract games such as *Tetris* that have only play time. In Aarseth's typology, such games would have arbitrary time.

Juul focuses on games that have both types of time (play time and fictional time), while taking into account several distortions in their relationship, most notably the ones caused by cutscenes and loading times. In both cases, play time is paused and disconnected from fictional time (Juul 2004b, 130–131). Cutscenes have their own projective relationship with fictional time, and they can inform the player about the fictional time that predates the player's involvement with the fictional world; in cases like this, the cutscene works just like a movie flashback. The player's actions and play time are also paused when the game is loading new data.

Juul's third and more complex example of temporal distortions occurs when a level changes in a game with an incoherent gameworld (cf. when different levels represent ontologically different or separate gameworlds). In such a case, the level change doesn't indicate a corresponding change in the gameworld, and thus both play time and fictional time are left undefined (Juul 2004b, 132). One could argue that play time and fictional time are defined in relation to each level or separate world – and in Juul's example of *Pengo*, everything else except the cutscene signaling the change of levels makes sense. This seems to be Juul's standpoint as well: "Pengo is an incoherent world game, but each individual round is somewhat coherent" (Juul 2004b, 133). As Juul readily observes, these inconsistencies are related to the division of play time into separate rounds:

> Incoherent round-based worlds seem connected to the rounds found in sports and other pre-electronic games. The rounds make sense on the rule-level, as an activity in play time, but not in the fictional world and time. (Juul 2004b, 133)

The bigger problem here is the emphasis on and the conceptual intertwining of fictional world and time, as if game time cannot be theorized without foregrounding the fictional world and (coherent) fictional time.

Juul also discusses instances in which the player has several speed settings at his disposal. These necessarily affect the relation of play time to fictional time by allowing the player to move faster in the gameworld, which may otherwise continue to function at its own unaffected pace. This happens for instance in *Space Quest 1*, where "acid drops falling from a ceiling have a constant speed regardless of the speed settings" (Juul 2004b, 134; example derived from Rau 2001). Although this may well be an unintended design error as Juul (2004b, 134) thinks it probably is, another way to look at it would be to accept that speed settings don't necessarily affect every aspect or element of the game in the same way. Thus, gameworld speed and player speed may differ from each other and their mutual relation may become variable as well.

Another example is the already mentioned *FIFA 2002*, a soccer game where the two halves that in real life take 45 minutes each are played out in four minutes (11.25 times faster). To complicate matters further, certain individual actions or events (such as David Beckham running) in the game happen much more *slowly* than they do in real life. Juul also takes up the temporal complexity of a taxi ride in *Grand Theft Auto 3*. There two clocks are presented to the player, and Juul's commonsense interpretation is that one of them measures fictional time and the other play time, but still it is "impossible to decide how long time passed in the gameworld" (Juul 2004b, 136). Juul concludes (ibid.) that "the fictional time of the gameworld is incoherent and contradictory" and leaves the discussion at that.[2]

Based on Juul's examples we may ask whether a more nuanced temporal stratification would be in order. In *FIFA 2002*, there seem to be at least three temporalities at work instead of only two: play time as in Juul's model[3] (2x4 minutes); what could be called event time[4] connected to individual actions and events in the game (for example Beckham puppet running very slowly); and finally, 90 minutes of fictional time passing in the gameworld as a whole. If we connect them in pairs, we'd have three temporal relationships to scrutinize: play time to fictional time, play time to event time, and event time to fictional time – not just the first one.

Juul's *FIFA 2002* example and the discrepancy in it between speed and duration could also be explained away by invoking Juul's concept of game adaptation and seeing the game as a necessarily reductive simulation of real soccer. The simulation is most accurate in including two halves of equal duration (although in soccer the actual duration of the halves is rarely if ever exactly the same), less accurate in the actual length of the halves (the ratio of 11.25:1), and totally off the mark in the running speed of virtual players. This kind of layering or multi-dimensionality inevitably leads to dividing the gameworld in a variety of aspects or elements, each with its own temporal specifications not necessarily displaying the same relation between play time, event time, and fictional time. In *Civilization III* and in many simulation games, fictional time runs much more quickly than play time, but if one focuses on the event time of individual actions and events (building cities, planting crops, conducting diplomatic negotiations etc.) their relation to their real-world counterparts and to play and fictional time varies greatly.

In Juul's model, play time as such is purely duration from the initial to the final state of the game. The problem is that most computer games do not employ set time, and therefore the duration of play time becomes variable and unspecified and depends on the skills and decisions of the player. Juul is well aware of this, but discusses it only in the context of abstract games that do not present a gameworld within which fictional time passes (Juul 2004b, 126). In another context, that of turn-based non-abstract games, Juul's chief temporal axis, the relation of play time to fictional time, becomes dangerously or impractically complicated, because play time remains irreducibly unspecified in these games, at least as long as it is measured as the duration between the initial and the final states of the game. Therefore we may need other kinds of temporal model to understand how game time works in these games.[5]

Juul's concept of game time, the relation between fictional time and play time, is one of speed with seemingly only two main options. The relation is either 1:1 as in *Quake* and many other real-time action games, or what could be called *acceleration* (play time being shorter than fictional time). Parallels to narratological theories of speed are obvious, and could be extended at least to pauses (initiated by the game or the player) and stretches or decelerations (the famous "bullet time" in *Max Payne*). Furthermore, one could argue that speed is not the only temporal dimension that can or must be specified in comparisons between play time and fictional time. For example, nothing prevents the game's fictional time from being as flexible as or even more flexible than its counterpart in literature and film. Fictional time could change its direction as a response to the player's actions or the way he uses his play time or for a player independent reason as well.[6]

There's also a problem of relevance implicit in almost any theorization of time, which can be illustrated by Juul's two timeframes. In abstract games such as chess, *Tetris*, or soccer, the duration of game is not of much importance. To know that a soccer game lasted 94 minutes says nothing about the game's temporal dynamics, to know that a chess game lasted only four may tell us something about the quality of the players, and to know the exact length of a *Tetris* game is just a relatively good indication of the score. In all these cases, there's no fictional time, and we may well wonder whether there's anything more useful to know about the temporality of these classic games.

16.5 Timeframes (Zagal and Mateas 2007)

José P. Zagal and Michael Mateas build on and synthesize previous scholarly work on game time, and discuss game time in four different but interplaying frames of:

real-world time (events taking place in the physical world), gameworld time (events within the represented gameworld,

including events associated with gameplay actions), coordination time (events that coordinate the actions of players and
agents), and fictive time (applying socio-cultural labels to events,
as well as narrated event sequences). (Zagal and Mateas 2007,
516)

Of these four frames, fictive time is similar to Juul's fictional time,
while real-world time includes not only Juul's play time but is more
expansive than it, including other real-world temporalities as well:

Play time addresses the duration of a play session, but does not
account for other temporal frame interactions, such as events in
a game that depend on specific labeled times in the real world,
or on the passage of specific real world durations. (Zagal and
Mateas 2007, 518)

These include events that the player triggers that either have or
announce their real-world duration such as timed tasks (i.e. tasks
that the player has to complete within a limited time), countdowns
and subperiods (Zagal and Mateas, 518). This is slightly confusing,
as, in principle, every event can be measured in real-world duration
(although whether it is relevant to do so is another matter), and in
this respect the frame also resembles Schechner's set time (a session,
period or task ends when the time is up – although this setting
may also be open to manipulation). In any case, Zagal and Mateas
explicitly state that the events in this frame "establish a reference
temporality outside of the game" (Zagal and Mateas 2007, 518).
Zagal and Mateas see the relations between events in every
timeframe in terms of cycles and durations. "A **cycle** is a sequence
of repeating events, that is, a sequence of events in which a subset
of the world repeatedly reestablishes the same state. **Duration** is
measured by counting events in a cycle" (ibid.). Here, the problem
is between explicitly given duration and the duration in turn-based
games that is supposedly measured in moves, turns or separate
actions. For clarity's sake, these two types of duration should be
distinguished from one another; the latter could be called pseudo-
duration. Also, the concept of a cycle may have to be broken into
subdivisions, in order to make it more useful as an analytical
concept. For starters, cycles have different ranges, rhythms, and
conditions for reoccurrence, and they are necessarily connected to

the issues of replayability, irreversible actions, linearity, and time control (including interval control and haste theorized in Elverdam and Aarseth 2007).

Zagal and Mateas' useful novelty of coordination time specifies how play time is organized and segmented:

> *Coordination time* is established by the set of events that coordinate the actions of multiple players (human or AI) and possibly in-game agents. Coordination events are the markers that regulate gameplay through moments of synchronization and coordination. (Zagal and Mateas 2007, 519)

Here the examples include tick- and turn-based games and games organized in rounds. The theorization of coordination time introduces two potential points of confusion. First, coordination events may overlap with and depend on the general temporal segmentation of a game that could be addressed in the real-world frame as well, but because the frames can overlap and be embedded within one another that is not a great problem. Second, the actions of multiple players and other in-game agents have to be coordinated at all times to avoid the game becoming unplayable, and, in this respect, coordination time is pulverized all over the game; only the degree of its explicitness varies.

Finally, gameworld time is:

> established by the set of events taking place within the represented gameworld – this includes both events associated with abstract gameplay actions, as well as events associated with the virtual or simulated world (the literal gameworld) within which an abstract game may be embedded. (Zagal and Mateas 2007, 518)

Gameworld time can establish its own cycles and durations that don't have to be dependent on the cycles and durations in the real-world frame (such as its own day and night cycles that are usually far shorter than 24 hours). Gameworlds can contain several more or less mutually independent and incoherent temporal frames (for example, one per each mission) which again brings us away from general frames (that measure both play time and fictional time as a whole) to more specific frames within games. Therefore it could be useful to distinguish at least between macro- and mesolevels of temporal phenomena and their observation.[7]

Like Juul, Zagal and Mateas discuss temporal anomalies that they refer to as causing "a sense of temporality that is inconsistent, contradictory, or dissonant with our experience of real-world time" (Zagal and Mateas 2007, 521). These include temporal bubbles (mutually clashing timeframes in two or more locations where the supposedly sequential events take place), temporal warping (different actions and events having different relations to real-world temporality), non-uniform temporality (the fictive duration of a round varies), and hardware- related anomalies (Zagal and Mateas 2007, 521). These anomalies are similar to the ones we discussed earlier in the context of Juul's model. They result from different game segments or elements having different temporal specifications in one or several temporal frames or dimensions. Once again this goes to show that more attention should be paid to the mesolevel temporality of these segments (be they rounds, tasks, locations or whatever) instead of assuming a temporally unified or uniform game to be the norm. In the first phase, this could lead to the construction of a new meta-category of consistency relating to the nature of the temporal frames and their interplay.

At the end of their discussion, Zagal and Mateas (2007, 522) mention the manipulation of time allowed to the player as part of gameplay in games like *Viewtiful Joe* and *Max Payne*. Their analysis of manipulation of time doesn't go beyond naming the available options in those games (rewinding and slowing down), but suggests it may constitute another frame to be constructed in future research. The strength of Zagal and Mateas' model is in its openness (allowing additional frames if necessary) and flexibility in handling the interplay of the four frames.

16.6 Elverdam and Aarseth

As discussed in Chapter 14, game time in Elverdam and Aarseth (2007) is divided into internal and external. The latter consists of teleology and representation. The meta-category of internal time consists of three factors: haste, synchronicity, and interval control. These three dimensions replace the category of pace (real-time or turn-based action) in the previous typology (Aarseth, Smedstad, and Sunnanå 2003).[8]

As we already saw in discussing Juul and Zagal and Mateas, it is not uncommon that different events and actions in the same game have different relations to their real-world counterparts. If representation of time is studied on the level of individual events and actions in the game, the classification becomes more difficult and complex, as we'd then have to ask how mimetic the order, duration, speed, repetition and simultaneity of the actions and events are. The most probable answer would then be that events in representational games constantly fluctuate between arbitrary and mimetic positions, depending on the supposed "mimetic" accuracy of simulation (or those parts of it that are modeled after the outside world) and the skills and strategies of the players. Moreover, the definition relies on an unspecified combination of duration and speed of the events ("the way time passes on in the game"), leaving out the other possible temporal aspects, and implicitly assuming a non-contradictory or unified way of time passing in the game. All these factors slightly undermine the use value of the representation category, although there are plenty of games that can be reliably described as either realistic or arbitrary in time representation.

Teleology gives us the idea of the direction towards which the actions and events in the game tend to gravitate, and, in that respect, it is closely connected to goals, challenges and player evaluation. Teleology may have more to do with causality than with time. Teleologically finite games end when they are "won or completed" (Elverdam and Aarseth 2007, 10), but there's quite a difference between games that have a given and invariable duration after which they end (i.e. Schechner's set time), and those that end after the game is completed or won (i.e. Schechner's event time). In the former case, the game ends at a pre-given point regardless of what the players do and don't do or accomplish, but, in the latter, the ending is conditional and is dependent on the player's ability to perform all necessary (or sufficiently effective) actions. Only the former point or way of ending seems to be properly temporal.

Although teleologically infinite games can, in principle, go on forever, there are huge differences within this category, as, in principle, many arcade games could also go on forever (if the player is skillful enough), as can a chess game, especially if played by two inexperienced or stubborn players who think they can win in a situation where a draw is the most likely or even the only possible outcome. This is not the case with MMOGs, although it is unlikely that any current MMOGs will be still around in the year 3000 (which amounts to saying nothing lasts forever). Contrariwise, chess has a clear termination point stated in its rules and MMOGs do not, so regardless of how we choose to name it there's a crucial teleological and temporal difference between those two types of game.

The use value of the categories of internal time is most of all that they replace the age-old and primitive distinction between real-time and turn-based games (also criticized in Zagal and Mateas 2007) with more accurate descriptive categories. Haste connects the passing of external time to the changes in the game state, synchronicity relates to the temporal distribution of allowed player actions, and interval control to the player's control of the game time or cycles of game time. Such connections open up the possibility of regrouping categories differently, as well as building new ones, which is explicitly allowed in this open-ended theory formation.

If the parameters of internal time were centered on action, the absence of haste denotes that the players control the changes of game state (i.e. that is only their actions that change the game state and affect the progress of the game), and the presence of haste that control is shared between the players and the game system. Likewise, the presence of interval control means that player action is discontinuous, and the absence of interval control combined with the presence of synchronicity means that it is (or is allowed to be) continuous. The presence of synchronicity means that the players can act at the same time and the absence of synchronicity means that they cannot. In short then, we would have simultaneity and successiveness of action, continuity and discontinuity of action, and control of internal time (measured in changes of game state).[9] Among other things these dimensions could be used to specify Juul's play time, more precisely how the time taken to play the game is structured from the point of view of the players' action.

16.7 Conclusion

There's no obvious way to synthesize the observations, frames and models discussed here. Although pure duration (of play time) and duration-based comparisons (between play time and fictional time) do not carry us far, Juul's binary model makes sense as a point of departure because the other models do not contradict but expand it (it would take an extraordinary act of scholarship to exclude both play time and fictional time from games). Elverdam and Aarseth's category of teleology introduces two types of duration that are useful in making Juul's play time (the time taken to play the game) more detailed: finite and infinite – or to put it differently (and expanded by Schechner), temporally specified (finite in set time), conditionally specified (finite in event time), and unspecified (infinite). The coordination time of Zagal and Mateas and the three categories of Elverdam and Aarseth's internal time (haste; synchronicity; interval control) can be used (among other things) to further expand Juul's play time and make it more applicable to multiplayer games.

Furthermore, in reading Juul we added event time (connected to individual actions and events) to mediate between play time and fictional time. This type of time (previously theorized in Eskelinen 2001a and 2001c) could be combined with Elverdam and Aarseth's mimetic and arbitrary representation of time, on the one hand, and with Zagal and Mateas' gameworld and real-world time, on the other, depending on how we want to measure it – and this leads us to the first phase of our conclusion.

Most game scholars see games as systems. To David Parlett (1999, 3), formal games are systems of ends and means (consisting of specific procedural rules of how to manipulate the equipment), and to Juul (2004b, 30) games are rule-based systems with variable and quantifiable outcomes (etc.). Salen and Zimmerman (2004, 50) see games as complex wholes and state that "games are intrinsically systemic: all games can be understood as systems" – "a group of interacting, interrelated or interdependent elements forming a complex whole." This idea of system and its basic elements (objects, their attributes, internal relationships and environment) is also compatible with Frasca's (2001a; 2003a; 2007) theories of games and/as simulations in which the player is one of those interacting elements.

For our purposes (in this chapter) games are dynamic configurative systems of feedback loops. These loops operate between players (if there is more than one), between players and manipulatable game elements, and between game elements (if they affect each other and are not organized as a series of separate and mutually independent items). We could call these three levels transactional, ergodic, and simulative, the ergodic being the only necessary one and thus present in every possible game. This gives us three possible temporal registers: transaction time, configuration time and simulation time, but as we strive for a synthesis, however provisional, we will not follow that path here.

Seeing games as simulations requires that we distinguish between the simulation and its reference system in terms of time. This move gives us model time and reference time. In principle, the relation between the two is partly described by Elverdam and Aarseth's temporal category of representation (including mimetic and arbitrary time). As became evident earlier in this chapter, different events and elements in the simulation have their own temporal specifications, and they are not necessarily all either realistic or arbitrary according to the real- world criterion. The more varied these relations become, the less useful the criterion is in describing the whole game. Therefore the underlying criterion of real world occurrences may have to be broken into several sub-dimensions (at least into speed and duration) as already discussed. The other potential subcategories of order, frequency and simultaneity may also become relevant, if it is important that events in the simulation take place in the same order, as many times, and as closely together as they do in the system being simulated.

As we saw in the previous chapter, it makes sense to separate player rules from gameworld rules. We follow similar logic here and provisionally split model time into player time and gameworld time. The latter is the temporality of the behavior of all the other gameworld elements in the game except the players. Some of these entities can be (to a varying degree) manipulated by the players, while others are beyond their manipulative reach and can only be interpreted. Whether these temporal behaviors can be interpreted or manipulated, they can be specified in terms of repetition, speed, duration, and their simultaneous or successive appearances with other elements. However, this is another path that will not be taken here because it is not necessary to go into greater detail to make the point we are going to make.

At this point we have reference time and model time, the latter further divided into player time and gameworld time. The latter should (for clarity's sake) be divided into two categories as well, to account for the difference between manipulatable elements and other equally dynamic elements beyond the player's manipulation. Still, even this fourfold division is not enough. We need additional categories for game fiction and for the overall invariable temporal structure of the game that is also beyond the player (to the degree the metarules allow that).

Using this approach we will ultimately have six temporal frames (or seven if we separate coordination time from internal time). The first one is related to the game's temporal structure that is beyond the player's configurative action (including Elverdam and Aarseth's internal time and teleology; Zagal-Mateas' coordination time), the second one related to the specifications of the temporal behavior of the non-human agents, objects and entities in the gameworld that the player is not allowed to manipulate and the third one for those he can, the fourth one for the player's own actions, the fifth one for the temporal organization of game fiction (if there is any), and the sixth one for the mimetic accuracy of time (Elverdam and Aarseth's representation).

This multiplicity of different temporalities in digital games concretely demonstrates how much more complicated the issue of time is in games as compared to in stories that are either recounted or presented. This plurality of timeframes also bears witness to a digital game as a complex whole, a sum total of its dynamic parts. In Chapter 4, we started with traditional textual wholes and literary works that were undivided and behaviorally static entities – and here we are at the other end of the complexity scale with dynamic and ergodic systems of parts, wholes, means and ends that can consist of any number of interplaying parts that exhibit dynamic behavior. These observations bring us to the second and final phase of this conclusion, somewhat more critical than the first.

At the center of games as configurative practices is the player's effort to manipulate the other elements in the dynamic system in order to move from the beginning to the winning or other somehow better situation. In short, it is up to the player to produce (cause) the sequences of game events (effects) to close the causal gap between these two positions (initial and final) by using whatever resources he has to the best of his ability. The relation between player actions and game events is by necessity conditional (otherwise there would be no challenges): the purpose success and sometimes also the intention success of the player's actions are not guaranteed.

This primacy of configurative, causal, conditional and functional relations is in stark contrast to the narratological relationships between narrative and story, narrative and narrating, or simply between story and discourse that are of an interpretative nature. The same primacy also constitutes a major theoretical problem or challenge in game studies because theories of art, literature, narrative, and media are for good reasons bound to spatiotemporal concerns. For example, narrative theories only discuss causality as an interpretative ingredient (or enigma) that motivates or explains the succession of events. When both resources and causality are expressed in the configurative realm, these interpretative problems are not helpful to us (they could perhaps be transposed to a more useful shape but that is not our concern here).

This reversal of causal and temporal relations in games compared to their role in narratives points most of all to the necessity of further theoretical work and only secondarily to the main differences between two cognitively and evolutively hardwired forms of cultural expression.[10] However, the most immediate consequence of this reversal in importance and the primacy of conditional, causal, and configurative relations over unconditional, temporal, and interpretative ones is the somewhat limited usefulness of the studies of spatiotemporal relations.

CHAPTER 17

Games as configurative practices: models and metaphors

17.1 Introduction

In the five preceding chapters, we have focused on games and especially digital games: their differences from narratives (Chapter 12), their transmedial ecology and ontology (Chapters 13 and 14), and the rule-based and goal-oriented player effort (Chapters 15 and 16) – among other things. We have also separated games as configurative practices from both interpretative and dominantly interpretative practices, based on the role of the user's ergodic activities in them (either dominant, subservient or non-existent). Before discussing the relations of games to these other practices and ecologies and situating literature and ergodic literature within them, an obvious question needs to be asked: if games and gaming are or form a configurative human practice, what is its (actual and potential) relation to other configurative human practices?

In addition to focusing on games as products (cultural artefacts) forming their own ecology in Chapters 13 and 14 and as processes (the player's rule-constrained and goal-oriented effort) in Chapters 15 and 16, there's also a third articulation, a truly classic and perhaps irresolvable one, to be discussed: the relation of game to world.

17.2 Ludology and the implied player

In formal ludology and game ontology, the question of the relation between game and world has been answered at least in four complementary ways. In Juul's classic game model, only one of its six criteria, negotiable consequences, articulates the game to world dimension. As we saw, that criterion is problematic because it, in principle, repeats the old and questionable idea or ideal of games being separate (unproductive etc.) from the rest of the world, earlier promoted by the classic game scholars Huizinga and Caillois. Sutton-Smith's (1997) probes into the ambiguity of play show the culture- and context-dependent shortcomings of this assumption. After discussing a wide variety of at least partially successful (but mutually clashing) attempts to define play in an equally varied variety of scholarly fields and contexts, Sutton-Smith finally concludes that play "should not be defined only in terms of restricted Western values that say it is non-productive, rational, voluntary, and fun" (Sutton-Smith 1997, 218).

In my early ludology, I also briefly discussed varying degrees of distance between games and the rest of the world in four dimensions:

> [T]he category of static relations implies ready-made relations not to be tampered with. This means that the game is every way closed or separated from the rest of the world. There are alternatives to this: causal, spatial, temporal and functional connections could well exceed the confines of a game ... The dynamic dimension could then be understood as containing various violations of this default separateness of games. (Eskelinen 2001b)

As pervasive games have shown, the temporal and spatial confines and boundaries of the magic circle can be extended to intermingle with the players' and non-players' everyday life. The results, payoffs, and other consequences of the game, be they emotional, physical (injuries), or monetary (loss or gain of resources), can be felt and suffered both long after and outside the game itself and, in principle, events outside the game could influence the game and gameplay.[1] By way of contrast, professionally organized and played games (in national and international leagues, tournaments and cups) are clearly separate from other "real-life" activities both temporally and spatially in the sense that they are played at specific times on specific arenas. In short, the distance varies from game to game, context to context, and definition to definition.

In Frasca's ludology (1999; 2001a; 2003a; 2004; 2007), the point is not the false or misunderstood issue of separateness, but the power of simulations as dynamic representations to critically model the world, the player, and the relation between the two. This power is not a narrative one, and it is here that Frasca's thinking breaks new ground. Without rehashing the famous debate (discussed in previous chapters), suffice it to say that from this perspective the relation of games to the world should be articulated in terms of simulation and model (with real or imaginary references) and not in terms of themes, stories, and other easily detectable surface elements, appearances, and possible similarities. In short, games model dynamic behavior – of players, game worlds, and player to player relations, and thus potentially also of humans, human relationships, societies and social processes and practices (etc.) – instead of simply telling tales about them.

In Frasca's thinking there is a considerable cultural gap between simulations used for various non-ludic purposes (education; decision making; scientific modeling etc.) and the mainstream of representational games taking place in virtual environments inspired by Tolkien and Lucas (modeling monsters and aliens in fantasy environments). In this gap, exist, on the one hand, bestselling and classic games such as *Civilization*[2] and *The Sims*, and, on the other, various small budget serious, independent, and critical games such as *Oil God*, *Darfur Is Dying*, *September 12th*, and *Tekken Torture Tournament*.

Finally, in ludology and game ontology, players are implied players and not real flesh and blood players (Aarseth 2007). Implied players are implied, modeled and constrained by the game structure, and although the players may to a varying degree (and depending on the game structure) play against the structural implications (for example, pursue other goals than the explicitly given or preferred ones, ignore goals altogether, attack other players or socialize with them, commit to grief play, or cheat), they are never entirely free of the constraints set by the game structure. If they were to be free of these constraints then we would no longer be talking about games, but about free play – an activity notoriously hard to adequately define.[3]

Another common move in ludologically informed game research is to see games and gaming as forms of structured play (Salen and Zimmerman 2004) and games as a subset of play. This necessarily foregrounds relations of games to toys, collective and individual improvisations, and other less constrained forms of play. In this way, computer games belong to the ecology of games that belongs to a vague or ambiguous ecology of play that in turn seems to belong to an even vaguer ecology of autotelic activities.[4]

Sometimes, in the second wave of digital game scholarship (assuming that ludologists were the first proper one), the two research objects, real and implied players, are seen to be in a more or less irresolvable conflict with each other – quite probably because they are seen as rival alternatives to each other and not as two legitimate research objects stemming from parallel traditions in the human and social sciences (Aarseth 2007). Although a comprehensive game studies program needs to address both aesthetic and social sides of games and gaming (ibid.), and despite years of premature hype about and several recent pleas for interdisciplinarity (for example Mäyrä 2008), the latter remains an enticing scholarly illusion and a seemingly perpetually delayed goal of the supposedly mature or slowly evolving discipline of game studies. In this situation, it is important to see that the differences in orientations and scholarly backgrounds do not separate supposedly game-centric studies from supposedly player-centric studies[5] (i.e. along the lines supposed by Ermi and Mäyrä 2005 and many others), but concern two entirely different conceptualizations of the player. Regarding the relation of game to world, these two also reflect two different ways of articulation (through real and implied players respectively).

Therefore the rest of this chapter follows these two threads, illuminating not only the relationship of game to world, but implicitly also certain missing links and obscure areas in current game scholarship. First, we'll try to situate games in society and culture as configurative practices capable of modeling other configurative practices, and then we'll take an almost diametrically opposite view informed by social sciences that tend to ignore both rules and implied players.

17.3 The ecology of configurative practices (the power of rules and simulations)

The idea of the ecology of configurative practices goes against seeing games only as parts of representational economies, connecting them to films, drama, cartoons, and written narratives. This orientation towards comparing similarities on the representational surface is discussed in greater detail in the next chapter, but here the points of departure are games in virtual environments consisting of rules, player effort, and gameworld (Aarseth 2004a, 47–48). Whereas the visual appearance of the gameworld may point to certain similarities between games and representational arts, and player effort connects games to ergodic arts (the main similarity being the user's ergodic activity) and therefore to some degree also to performing arts, rules point to an entirely different dimension that has been easy to ignore, as its counterparts are not easily found in the other "media" or arts (if the "rules" of poetic composition are left out of the picture and game rules are not confused with scripts or instructions for more or less improvisational performances), but in scientific, training, and other "serious" or non-entertainment simulations, on the one hand, and various social practices, on the other (hinted at by the non-digital social simulations briefly discussed in Chapter 13). Rules do not translate to other "media" when a game is adapted to other kinds of artefacts or co-created with them to form a series of applications derived from the same intellectual property right (IPR).

Combined with player effort and dynamic representations, rules also display representative powers beyond the static representations of non-ergodic films, novels and the other mainstream media in terms of which most comparisons and ecological insights continue to be made. It is exactly this power of rules and simulation in games that is easily ignored if, on the one hand, representation is equated with narratives, and if, on the other hand, the scope of research questions is limited to those derived from classic game scholarship that was mostly focused on abstract and non-representational games.

Greenblat (1988, 14) defines simulation as "an operating model of central features or elements of a real or proposed system, process, or environment." Two aspects are of primary interest here: time and reduction. Simulations are operational models of larger systems showing the interplay of their major components over time. Therefore, they are dynamic representations that are superb at showing temporal dynamics and change. Common to all simulations is also their simplified and reductive nature compared to the system to be simulated: the features of the latter have to be simplified and some elements of the reference system have to be entirely omitted.

In principle, three broad types of simulation can be distinguished according to the role of the computer: it can do all the work (i.e. take actions and make decisions), some of the work, or none of the work. The first one is called a computer simulation, the second a man–machine ("the computer may simply serve as a high-speed calculator, or it may contain a model or set of models within it which are triggered by the actions of the players"), and the third an all-man simulation (Greenblat and Duke 1975, 13). In the last two cases, there's room for human participants and players, and thus they could be called gaming simulations or simulation games.

In the context of digital game studies, the emphasis on simulation leads to two sets of observation. First, simulations are the object of the player's manipulative actions, and second, the game states are communicated and described to the players by the means of simulation (i.e. dynamic representations). To describe gameplay in Greenblat's terms is to say that the player manipulates the elements and properties of an operating model and triggers responses from that model. Self-evidently, the player cannot manipulate every property of every element every way he wants and not every element allows manipulation. Thus we have to make two additional divisions: the one on the surface between manipulatable and non-manipulatable elements, and the other between the model's division in the first place into interplaying and mutually dependent elements. Both choices (reductive modeling and the limits set to player effort) are inherently rhetorical, political, ethical and ideological once we step out of Tolkien land.

The theoretical primacy of simulation, models, rules (describing how the elements are to be manipulated and how they connect to each other), and gameplay in defining the way games are articulated[6] lead us to the crucial issue of what is modeled and how. As long as what is modeled consists of aliens, monsters, heroes, heroines and other imaginary existents, the question remains latent, but should the model be based on common conflicts in human life and society and the uglier side of human behavior, questions concerning the relations between the behavior of the implied player and its model and between the functioning of the game world and its model become more urgent and interesting.

The behavior of the game system is based on rules, and as we may remember, according to Salen and Zimmerman's common-sense account (2004, 122–125), the rules that limit the player's action are supposed to be explicit and unambiguous, fixed, binding, repeatable, and to be shared by all players. The more we know about the rules, variable outcomes, and player effort in the context of games, the more informed and accurate our comparisons of games and gaming to other constraints and limitations of human action: laws, agreements, etiquette, conventions, instructions, orders, obligations, commands, rituals, and obsessive and compulsive behavior (to name but a few), and the better our chances to design games that simulate these practices. Many of our most important social relations and bonds are based on these constraints that are usually more implicit, multivalent and ambiguous but also less fair, shared and binding than both traditional and digital game rules.

As the examples from social simulation games in Chapter 13 showed, games can be and are sometimes designed to address these differences, usually by foregrounding unfair gameplay and unbalanced gameworlds (Greenblat and Duke 1975; Woods 2004). To some degree, the differences between these two extremes of fair and balanced and unfair and unbalanced illustrate the basic difference between scientific simulations aiming at accuracy and representational games aiming to please by being fair to all participants. The difference is evident in Klabber's (2003) definition of simulation as a combination of different rules (for different players), different resources, and actors (players). Here we can see a readymade continuum running from games to simulations, as the former is conventionally or ideally seen to consist of rules shared by all players and balanced or effectively equal resources to facilitate fair play and equal opportunities (which is not the way to model real-world and interpersonal relationships).

In short, and to return to the theme of the two players, ludology foregrounds the implied player and when appropriate also the critical relation of the implied player's behavior to the behavior of real players outside the game as citizens, consumers, workers, parents, lovers etc. (we could call these referent players or player–models). One could argue that it is only when these two sides effectively clash that the behavior of the real players in the game becomes interesting in a scholarly sense[7] (in other words, interesting to parties other than game designers and game producers, on the one hand, and more or less worried policy makers, parents and popular media, on the other). Be that as it may, the important thing is to emphasize that there are three relationships at play here: between implied players and real players, implied players and referent players, and real players and referent players.

To counterbalance this triple duality, there's also a hierarchy among these three kinds of player and game. As cultural artefacts (descriptions of rules and other major components and their material manifestations such as game boards, dice, cards, and other equipment) the last can exist without players (Aarseth 2007, 1). Rules constrain and create implied players and channel their effort; without understanding what is implied and facilitated by the game structure, real players cannot and do not play the game. This is not to downplay the games' ability to foster communities and provoke interesting behavior beyond the actual gameplay, or to deny the player's ability to use games in surprising and creative ways; it is just to point out that these last activities are grounded in games and game structures. Or to be more precise, there is a difference between game studies and the studies of the uses of games, and if the latter studies entirely cut their ties to the former they may well cease to be game studies. As we shall see, the same danger is also present in attempts to dismiss the constitutive power of rules and focus solely on real players from the perspective of social sciences and social sciences alone.

17.4 Real players

From the social science angle the situation is different, especially regarding rules, players and simulation: players are real players, powers of simulation are ignored, and any focus on rules is routinely denounced as formalism. The results of these common approaches are best expressed in Malaby's (2007) influential and ambitious but ignorant attempt to reconstruct or reinvent game studies "for advancing our understanding of the relationship of games to society" (Malaby 2007, 2). Strangely, Malaby assumes that game studies belong only to social sciences; in his paper, there seems to be no need for game studies in the humanities. Malaby is highly critical of previous game studies, accuses them of formalism and exceptionalism, and proposes a novel approach to games seeing them "as characterized by processes" (ibid.). However, as we shall see a good part of Malaby's criticism is based on his misunderstandings of previous game scholarship.

Malaby (2007, 3) also offers a new definition of games: "A game is a semi-bounded and socially legitimate domain of contrived contingency that generates interpretable outcomes." The problem is that according to this definition games are everywhere and almost every human practice can be conceptualized as a game (turning games into mere metaphors). Any activity that is distinctive enough to be named is semi-bounded (i.e. not completely separated from other activities or separated from them to a varying degree), contingency and attempts to contrive it belong to human life from birth to death, and it is impossible to find outcomes that are not interpretable. The stipulation that games are socially legitimate domains is odd and ahistorical in light of the censorship and bans on a wide variety of games (including chess) and practices of gambling (not to mention the latter's ties to organized crime) ever since the dawn of civilization. In short, Malaby's definition has no descriptive or analytical power, and it explains even less than the exceptionalist claims (about games being separate, safe, and pleasurable) that he (mostly) rightly criticizes.

The problem with Malaby's critique of exceptionalism is at least twofold. First, there's nothing new in this claim, which has been made several times before Malaby, perhaps most elegantly and thoroughly by Brian Sutton-Smith in *The Ambiguity of Play*

(Sutton-Smith 1997). Moreover, it is trivially easy to find examples of practices and consequences that are neither safe nor pleasurable in games (death and permanent physical injuries; loss of wealth, fortune and livelihood in gambling etc.), which makes exceptionalism, i.e. the idea "that games are play and therefore set apart" (Malaby 2007, 4), a useful straw man and a good rhetorical enemy for Malaby's purposes, but nothing more substantial, and given the non-novelty of his position it is rather surprising to see him spend half his paper making a pedestrian case against exceptionalism.

Second, Malaby incorrectly attributes exceptionalism to scholars who have had little or nothing to do with it, especially the ludologists:

> [L]udology at least began with an awareness of the "gameness" of games, and from this conviction recognized that there was something to the *experience* of what is labeled a game that bears attention. In their fascination to draw attention to this mode of experience and make the case for its importance, however, ludologists ultimately fell into the trap of formalism, treating games as special and distinct activities, fundamentally different from everyday life, and further treated this distinctiveness normatively, seeing play as about "fun" or "pleasure" or "enjoyment." (Malaby 2007, 9)

First of all, as we have seen in previous chapters, ludology didn't begin with any idea or focus on the experience of a game, but with locating and theorizing indisputable formal differences between games and other cultural artefacts and means of expression (such as films, drama, toys and written narratives). The experience of games and the relation of games to everyday life were mostly bracketed from consideration and are or were not central to ludological theory.[8] Despite Juul's occasional bow to the traditional idea of games being fun,[9] this normative standpoint is not shared by Frasca (and his work on simulation and serious games) or many other ludologists (Eskelinen, Järvinen). Ironically, Malaby (2007, 19–20) sees Juul as a relative exception to exceptionalism, unlike the other unmentioned ludologists whom he fails to quote.

The depth of Malaby's perhaps understandable misunderstanding of the ludology debate in the humanities is shown in his corresponding comment on the "narratologists" getting "another aspect right, which is that games involve the construction of meaning" (Malaby 2007, 9). Malaby seems to believe that ludologists somehow ignored the construction of meaning, although, in fact, they simply didn't cast it in narrative terms in the first place while admitting the trivial fact that games can be narrativized after the fact.

The situation is not better in the case of Malaby's criticism against formalism, as his argument is based on serious misunderstandings of rules, how they work, and why they are central to games:

> The essential point, then, is that games are grounded in (and constituted by) human practice, and are therefore always in the process of becoming. This also means that they are not reducible to their rules. This is because any given singular moment in any given game may generate new practices or new meanings, which may in turn transform the way the game is played, either formally or practically (through a change in rules or conventions). (Malaby 2007, 11)

As we saw in Chapter 12, there's an overwhelming consensus among game scholars on the importance of rules as a central defining feature of games. As every game scholar knows, new practices and meanings emerge, but this has nothing to do with the fact that there are always rules that constrain the player's actions and to which the player submits. Rules may and do change historically (due to unforeseen and unwelcome results and myriad other factors such as standardization) but at any given moment there are some rules at work and in most cases they work just as Frasca and Salen and Zimmerman have described.

In short then, Malaby's point is naive anti-formalism that he can only ground in vague analogies to various other fields of research such as biology, anthropology of law, or ritual theory (Malaby 2007, 11–12), all of which focus on research objects[10] different from games. To complete the irony, both the ludologists (Juul 2005) and the game designers (Salen and Zimmerman 2004) Malaby mentions in this context have discussed emergence and processes of play in their books. Moreover, as we have seen, in ludology it is not only rules alone but their interplay with player effort and variable outcomes that define a game, and not surprisingly Malaby seems to be unaware of this.

In a short footnote, Malaby adds two more points against rules:

> [T]he rules do not constitute games in and of themselves for another reason: games are governed not only by their rule systems, but also by implicit and shared cultural expectations as well as the material conditions under which they are undertaken. (Malaby 2007, 20)

Material conditions (that Malaby doesn't specify) and cultural expectations are all around us at all times. Still, consider chess: if the players (of whatever gender, class, sexual orientation, ethnicity, and of almost any age) know the rules they can play the game under (almost) any material conditions and with different and even clashing cultural exceptions as long as they share the one basic transcultural expectation of shared and binding rules.

Finally, the novelty Malaby emphasizes, processes, is reduced to four vague forms of contingency in games: stochastic ("pure contingency," explicitly borrowed from MacIntyre 1984), social ("never being certain about another's point of view," also explicitly borrowed from McIntyre 1984), performative ("an action may succeed or fail"), and semiotic ("the unpredictability of meaning that always accompanies attempts to interpret the game's outcomes") (Malaby 2007, 15–16). These issues have been addressed in countless volumes of previous game scholarship, to which Malaby's brief and unspecific descriptions add nothing[11] except perhaps the suggested (and surprising) difficulty he sees in interpretations of the game's outcome (that is usually designed to be very obvious and unambiguous and as such beyond dispute).

In addition to the failure of his new definition of games, Malaby misunderstands the function of rules and the grounding of the ludological formalism in its research objects and repeats the old charges against the form of exceptionalism that only a few scholars admit to. His half-borrowed novelties have already been addressed more thoroughly elsewhere. Especially as unpredictability is at the heart of human experience, one would expect Malaby to offer his social scientist's view on the relation of game contingencies to other human (and inhuman) contingencies. In this respect, Malaby hasn't got much to offer either as he ends up with this statement: "The only difference is that the game presents multiple contingencies in a relatively bounded, explicit, and perhaps more readily graspable form" (Malaby 2007, 17).

Within these ambiguities and vaguenesses Malaby is safely back to the "open-ended" meanings of game, and not surprisingly, the relation between games and other practices becomes familiarly metaphoric in Malaby's conclusion related to his findings in the city of Chania in Greece:

> [T]he different games on which they gambled served as models for their actions in other highstakes arenas of their lives: politics, health, business, and social relations. For example, poker was a fitting model for business (and business for poker), because of their common emphasis on social contingency, the reading of others' intentions and resources ... Discretion and the reading of others are part and parcel of poker and business, but cheating is not acceptable ... In this sense, Greeks viewed these everyday activities as games, and used these characterizations to condone or condemn ethically their own and others' actions with reference to what was allowed in the appropriate game. (Malaby 2007, 18)

There's nothing special or new in this either: games are apt metaphors, perhaps even more so than stories or narratives, for any human activity.

The real problem, however, is that tired metaphors are not models. It is somewhat ironic that ludological research that focuses on rules and dynamic representations (simulations) and maintains that the crucial difference between implied and real players can offer critical views on the games' so far greatly overlooked capability to model human behavior, real societies and social relations, whereas social science approaches to games, by refusing to take game rules seriously, ignoring the power of simulation, and focusing only on real players, can only repeat what has already been said and offer us games as metaphors to spike an open-ended discussion of their unpredictable meanings in a rather limited and conservative setting (that stresses the social legitimacy of games).

In this light, the aspects and worries of formalism and exceptionalism can and perhaps should be recast. The distance (separateness) of games as configurative practices from other configurative human practices depends on how the latter practices are simulated not only in the functioning of the game world but in the rules that constitute the implied players and shape the behavior of real players. If formalism is dismissed from game studies, the most immediate context of play is ignored and bracketed from consideration, and there's nothing left to anchor game studies any longer. As a result, we'd have free floating studies of play leading nowhere except to mutually incompatible case studies, contexts and definitions (as Sutton-Smith's *The Ambiguity of Play* makes more than evident) and studies of player behavior within traditional paradigms of social sciences incapable of separating games from other human activities. If there's a place for game studies, it has to be situated between these two unfruitful extremes.

CHAPTER 18

Transmedial modes and ecologies

18.1 Introduction

In this chapter, we'll look at various discussions and conceptualizations of transmediality and transmedial ecologies from the ludological perspective. The concept of transmediality as formulated and used by Irina Rajewski (2005) and Werner Wolf (2002; 2005) denotes all phenomena that are considered non-specific to individual media. Wolf (2005, 253–254) sees transmediality as one of the two major extracompositional forms of intermediality, and distinguishes it first from the other extracompositional form of intermedial transposition in which "similar contents or formal aspects appear in heteromedial entities but where it is clear ... that one medium acted as an origin in a process of medial transfer." These two are different from the two intracompositional forms of intermediality: plurimediality ("two or more media are overtly present in a given semiotic entity at least in one instance") and intermedial reference. For our purposes, the two extracompostional forms constitute the realm of transmediality as intermedial transpositions presuppose non-media specific elements.

According to Wolf (2005, 253) transmediality can occur on three different levels: "ahistorical formal devices and ways of organizing semiotic complexes," "historical traits that are common to either the form or the content level of several media in given periods," and also on the content level alone (ibid.). The first one of these levels is of obvious interest to us in our attempt to clarify the extent of the modal media ecologies centered around games and stories/narratives. Trans- and intermedial relationships constitute a vast area of research, but in this chapter, the focus is on anchoring some of these practices and devices in specific modes and media ecologies.

However, we cannot take Wolf's system at face value, because digital meta-media complicates Wolf's theories of intermediality in three ways that we have to take into account before moving on with our ecological thinking. To Wolf, media are primarily specified by their underlying semiotic systems (verbal language, music, visual signs etc.) that are conventionally separate carriers of cultural content. The first complication is that each of these separate semiotic systems can now employ several media – as we have seen there's more than one literary medium for written language alone. Second, in non-digital media different kinds of sign were either distinct or fused together (resulting in various hybrids), but not capable of being transformed multiple times back and forth into each other with or without the user's effort. Third, the networked computers' metamedial capacity to imitate and combine (and recombine) the elements of any distinct medium and the whole behavioral (or media-positional) repertoire of these media complicates the situation even further.

In actual scholarly practice, the ideas of transmediality have centered on stories and narratives and their transmission across media. From this perspective, new media and new technologies have expanded the ecology of storytelling to include several digital specimens and in extreme cases also computer games. We have treated narrative as a mode, and seen that games constitute their own mode and ecology, and therefore we can begin by assuming there are both modal and media ecologies (games and narratives being different modes utilizing a variety of media). To better understand the possible interplay of modal ecologies, we'll first draft several ecologies and then try to figure out the basic connections and flows between them, as by definition ecologies are not entirely closed systems.

In the previous chapter, we charted the connections of games with other configurative practices and found two possible forms of connection: metaphors and dynamic models (simulations). Given that many if not all other configurative social practices (i.e. somewhat constrained and regulated and objective-oriented non-trivial human activities) such as business, administration, politics, education, or law (not to mention warfare) are less transparent, fair, safe and balanced and certainly more ambiguous, unequal, unfair and unbalanced than games, dynamic models constitute a more promising way of dealing with their similarities, differences and behavioral dynamics than metaphors that are easily reduced to either ethical pleas for fair play or vague justifications for the lack of fair play.

Given the power of dynamic representations in computer games, we can add them to rules, player effort and variable outcomes as the most important core features of games, in our attempt to connect games and especially digital games to other cultural modes and practices. As in games, variable outcomes[1] logically result from rules and player effort, we may omit them from our reductive draft and focus on three potential game-based ecologies of rules, player effort, and dynamic representations. This is somewhat similar to Aarseth's reduction of games to their core elements: "Any game consists of three aspects: (1) rules, (2) a material/semiotic system (a gameworld), and (3) gameplay (the events resulting from application of the rules to the gameworld)"[2] (Aarseth 2004a, 47–48).

The ecology of rules connects digital games to other kinds of game, simulation (that may or may not allow player/user effort in their execution), and the kinds of sport that are not necessarily considered games. Rules also self-evidently disconnect games from many other cultural artefacts such as films, drama, written narratives, paintings, sculpture, cartoons, architecture and music. In some cases, the latter may have poetic "rules" for composition (as in Dogma films, serial music, or various Oulipian practices in several fields including culinarism) or presentation, but these are more like simple instructions to be followed and neither rules for negotiating challenges, conflicts and adversaries nor rules for the functioning of the artwork (and its parts). Readers, spectators and art lovers are not constrained by rules, but only by conventions that usually vary and clash due to myriad factors (such as the user's prior knowledge, experience and education, all of which contribute to his personal repertoire of applicable and recognized conventions). When games are adapted to films and other types of artefact (comic books, novels etc.) rules are and have to be eliminated from the adaptation.

Player effort (gameplay) leads us in two directions. It ties games to toys and various forms of free or improvisational play that are hard to define and conceptualize (cf. Sutton-Smith 1997).

By way of contrast, it also connects games to various forms of ergodic or "interactive" art and literature and also to theater (such as Augosto Boal's legislative and forum theater), happenings and performances (such as Marina Abramovic's *Rhythm 0*) to the degree they are ergodic. In his massive but qualitatively uneven study of digital performance in the fields of theater, dance, installation and performance art, Steve Dixon, without paying much attention to previous scholarly work in other fields, found four types of poorly and contradictory defined "interactivity" in the appropriation of digital technologies in these fields: navigation, participation, conversation, and collaboration (Dixon 2007, 563). These are easily translated into the user functions of cybertext theory as explorative (navigation), configurative (participation and conversation), and textonic (collaboration and certain types of participation) user functions. In principle, it could be possible to adapt games into ergodic art, cinema or literature and try to maintain some forms of player effort as well as the necessarily variable outcomes. Because ergodic practices are not in the mainstream except in games it is unlikely that such adaptations would flood the market any time soon.[3]

The twofold vibration of games towards freer forms of play and ergodic art constitutes what will henceforth be called ergodic ecology. It will be discussed more thoroughly in the next chapter, which tries to combine insights from ludology and cybertext theory in order to better understand the challenges, poetics, and potentials of ergodic literature (that belongs to the ecology of ergodic arts).

Finally, digital and some non-digital games (LARPs, for example) are part of what could be called representational ecology. Representation is a loaded word and contested concept and therefore some specifications are in order. First, there are at least three kinds of representation: abstract, static and dynamic. Games like *Tetris* and Go exemplify the first kind, which could equally well be termed non-representational, as the pieces and shapes to be manipulated do not represent anything beyond themselves, unlike the usual set of chess pieces (and the standard deck of playing cards) that carry representational residue that some pan-narra-tivists like Murray (2005) and Pearce (2005) have confused with narratives – needless to say without being able to offer viable definitions. The abstract visuality of these games bears some resem-blance to abstract art and film, but these family resemblances have not received the same attention as other, more representational but quite probably equally shallow surface similarities.

Static representations are what games share with film and many other representational media: the moving or still images repre-senting existents and events, fictional or non-fictional, that remain and are intended to remain the same (in terms of order, duration, frequency etc.) from one presentation to the next (discounting various material processes of deterioration and damage in non-digital film). The same is true with static representations in video art, television, paintings, and photographs, and the similarity extends also to non-dynamic and non-ergodic narrative literature (i.e. the kind characterized by static dynamics and interpretative user function). Live drama is slightly different in this respect, as humans and human ensembles are not usually capable of precisely repeating their actions: there are always at least minor variations (variations of pace, timing and intonation, changes of costume or even actors etc.) in representations between any two theatrical performances of the same prewritten play performed by the same group. Greater variations take place in more improvisational forms such as commedia dell'arte. Thus it would seem that in practice the transmediality of stories and narratives takes place in the ecology of (mostly) static representations.

Dynamic representations of events and existents connect games to closed simulations (i.e. those running from start to finish according to given rules without any interventions from human actors or players) and to various forms of generative art that may but don't have to be ergodic. To the degree these dynamic repre-sentations constitute a gameworld to be explored, manipulated or even altered by the player, the similarities between these worlds and static filmic and other representations of unexplorable and non-configurative "worlds" begin to radically diminish, while the differences between fiction and simulation as well as their complex interplay gain more force.

So far we have drafted several lower level ecologies from the perspective of games (especially digital games) and ludology:

ecologies of configurative practices, games, autotelic activities, rules, play and ergodics, and of three kinds of representation. As a system these seven to nine ecologies are remarkably different from what is called transmedia storytelling, which we need to discuss next in order to continue our ecological excursion. This is because transmedia storytelling (Jenkins 2003; 2006) best illustrates limitations inherent in approaches that construct narrative or story ecologies in terms of media and without paying any attention to narratology, the specificity of narrative as a mode and the existence of other modes that cannot be reduced to narrative not to mention actual theories of trans- and intermediality.

18.2 Transmedia storytelling and story-selling

In the view of Henry Jenkins (2003; 2006), who uses a comparative media studies approach, games are part of a larger ecology and economy that for unspecified reasons is called transmedia storytelling. Jenkins' point of departure is the cultural industrial design process and shifts within it from adaptation to co-creation. The former is a process where something (a novel, a cartoon or a movie etc.) is adapted to something else (a movie, a game, a toy etc.) in separate steps. In co-creation, the process is more simultaneous; the point of departure may be a character or a "fictional"[4] world that is then processed in multiple media from cartoons, novels and TV series to games and toys, none of which could be said to be an original on which all subsequent adaptations would be based.

To Jenkins (2003), transmedia storytelling is "the movement of content across media" and collaborative development (within the entertainment industries) of "content that would play well across media." The driving reasons for this business practice are clear:

> The move toward digital effects in film and the improved quality of video game graphics means that it is becoming much more realistic to lower production costs by sharing assets across media. Everything about the structure of the modern entertainment industry was designed with this single idea in mind

– the construction and enhancement of entertainment franchises. (Jenkins 2003)

Jenkins doesn't explain why this industrial logic that applies only to some products (as the vast majority of games, TV series, movies, novels and cartoons continue to exist as standalone products never to be adapted or re-co-created) should be called transmedia storytelling.

Quite typically, Jenkins (2003) doesn't define storytelling, but instead goes on to lament the sad state of cross-media franchises and the poor job they do in producing "compelling transmedial experiences." As a countermeasure, he spells out the ideal form of transmedia storytelling:

> In the ideal form of transmedia storytelling, each medium does what it does best – so that a story might be introduced in a film, expanded through television, novels, and comics, and its world might be explored and experienced through game play. Each franchise entry needs to be self-contained enough to enable autonomous consumption. That is, you don't need to have seen the film to enjoy the game and vice-versa. As *Pokemon* does so well, any given product is a point of entry into the franchise as a whole. (Jenkins 2003)

Finally, transmedial storytelling boils down to shared worlds and characters being the common denominators within the transmedial franchise:

> Transmedia stories aren't necessarily bad stories; they are different kinds of stories. According to Hollywood lore, a good pitch starts with either a compelling character or an interesting world. We might, from there, make the following argument: A good character can sustain multiple narratives and thus lead to a successful movie franchise. A good "world" can sustain multiple characters (and their stories) and thus successfully launch a transmedia franchise. (Jenkins 2003)

Needless to say, according to Jenkins, it is also what the consumers want: "In reality, audiences want the new work to offer new insights into the characters and new experiences of the fictional world" (ibid.).

In Jenkins' later elaboration of the theme in the context of convergence culture (Jenkins 2006), the situation is the same: trans-media storytelling remains a catchphrase with its own rhetorics, far removed from academic discourse, and therefore the way games and narratives are theorized and conceptualized should not be affected by it. Co-creation and adaptation are transmedial practices, but one of the problems with Jenkins' catchphrase is that such practices are not limited to stories. There are many other cultural forms, modes, products, processes and practices that are transmedial, especially if transmediality is described as loosely as Jenkins has described it. Games are and have been transmedial for centuries (if not for millennia) so it is especially problematic to include them in transmedia storytelling without discussing their own circuits of transmediality (i.e. transmedial gaming). A franchise may combine game products and story products that are rarely equally important and successful in either the quantitative (economical) or qualitative (aesthetical) sense.

Therefore, instead of using misleading umbrella terms such as transmedia storytelling, which privileges one possible source of adaptation and one possible element of co-creation, one could use more accurate and neutral terms such as transmedial franchises, transmodal franchises (if the franchise combines narrative products and game products) or quite simply transmedial fictions.

Storytelling can, of course, be defined in a way that suggests it is transmedial (cf. Chatman 1978, 20), but the way Jenkins treats stories creates further problems that remain unsolved and are not even identified in his discourse. The main problem is that Jenkins first reduces storytelling to stories and then reduces stories to characters and fictional worlds, i.e. to the level of existents, and occasionally refers to them simply and neutrally as content. In short, to Jenkins "transmedia storytelling is the art of world-making" (Jenkins 2006, 21). Ultimately, it is about the size and complexity of the world. Necessary information (cues for solving a puzzle, playing a game or understanding a film) can be effectively hidden in the other parts of the franchise, or in the web, or in both real and virtual spaces, to keep the consumers of the franchise interested. However, the obvious problem is with the quality of the experience (keeping the consumers interested for very long periods of time) as Jenkins comes to notice with his prime example of *The Matrix*:

Many film critics trashed the later sequels because they were not sufficiently self- contained and thus bordered on incoherent. Many games critics trashed the games because they were too dependent on the film content and did not offer sufficiently new experiences to players. Many fans expressed disappointment because their own theories about the world of Matrix were more rich and nuanced than anything they saw on the screen. (Jenkins 2006, 96)

As always the holding and other powers of the whole idea are scheduled to be realized at some time in the rhetorical future: "Relatively few, if any franchises achieve the full aesthetic potential of transmedia storytelling – yet" (Jenkins 2006, 97).

Jenkins' shortcomings are useful because they show that common elements in transmedial franchises are not to be situated in stories, but on a still lower or more common level of events and existents (that can equally well be used in stage drama, fictional films, television series, written and graphic novels, and digital and non-digital representational games etc. without any of these being the privileged original to be adapted). The games, books, and feature and animated films in the Matrix franchise constitute an event continuum taking place in a shared world of fiction populated with at least some characters common to the main parts of the franchise (the three feature films). In ecological terms, then, we'd have micro-ecologies of events and existents (characters and settings or worlds moving across both media and modes). This, in turn, points less to the expansion of narrative, story, or "storytelling" ecologies than to their fragmentation and recombination with other ecologies.

18.3 Transmediality and intermediality in formal narratology

To understand that aspect and development better, we need to take a quick look at the basics of narratology. Luckily, there are earlier and more sophisticated accounts of potential transmedialities of stories and narratives that are rooted in problems encountered in narratology and not in the selling imperatives and speculative business opportunities of the entertainment industry. These are most of all related to problems in defining narratives and stories, comparisons made between film, drama and written narratives as well to the expansion of narratology from literary to film studies and beyond. In this train of thought, stories (and their constitutive elements) are the most common transmedial elements that can be adapted from one medium to another and shared between them.

In classical and formal narratology, this view is clearly stated by Chatman: "The transposability of the story is the strongest reason for arguing that narratives are indeed structures independent of any medium" (Chatman 1978, 20). This view is also shared by Genette, with an additional emphasis on narrative as a mode: "The sole specificity of narrative lies in its mode and not is content, which can equally well accommodate itself to a 'representation' that is dramatic, graphic, or other" (Genette 1988, 16). Genette also remarks that there are no specific narrative contents, just "chains of actions or events amenable to any mode of representation" (ibid.).

In this book, we've been using Gerald Prince's definition of narrative as:

[T]he recounting (as product and process, object and act, structure and structuration) of one or more real or fictitious events communicated by one, two or several (more or less overt) narrators to one, two or several (more or less overt) narratees. (Prince 1987, 58)

In the context of transmediality, it has this important consequence: "a dramatic performance representing (many fascinating) events does not constitute a narrative either, since these events, rather than being recounted, occur directly on stage" (ibid.). This is also the most efficient way of distinguishing narrative situations from dramatic situations. Bordwell's "narrative" fiction films are situated somewhere in between narratives and drama, as in films events are either recounted or enacted (Bordwell 1985, 79), although these two options are available in stage drama, too. Novels may also adapt what Jahn (2001) calls a play script mode, making the old mimetic/diegetic–duality a bit more nuanced. Still, the attempts to apply narratology to drama (Jahn 2001; Nünning and Nünning

2002) cannot annul the major differences between written/printed narratives and the performative powers of stage drama and fiction film and their different communicational and presentational structures and machineries. Therefore and quite traditionally, written narratives, drama, and fiction film are the main constituents[5] of the story ecology, within which move the shared elements: "a chrono-logic of events, a set of characters, and a setting" (Chatman 1990, 117).

Instead of listing every possible media for transmitting stories, a futile practice if any (that is bound to repeat media history from the first stone and clay tablets onwards), it is more important to see what happens in adaptations and co-creations within this ecology. Written, animated, and enacted characters are after all very different from one another even though they may utter exactly the same sentences. We well know that both events (constituting a story) and the order in which they are (re)presented (a plot) can be either replicated or altered in these practices and the users are still able to understand that it is, in principle, the same sequence of events, story or plot or both they are witnessing and interpreting. The same applies to the potentially enormous semiotic, experiential and categorical differences between verbal descriptions of places and spaces and the settings in film or on stage. In this respect, transmediality is grounded in the recipient's ability to recognize similar representational patterns in different sign systems – and in his reductive ignorance of the wide variety of the actors' and the whole ensemble's performative and presentational means and devices (in general, the overwhelming difference between script and performance or presentation and between written and embodied communication).

However, the transitions within this familiar ecology are common knowledge by now, easily explainable by the shared patterns of content, user position (interpretative), and behavior of representations (static) within the same mode (story/narrative). However, not every event and existent constitute a story (as performance art has made evident), not every representation is static (as the dynamic, explorable and sometimes also alterable gameworlds have shown), and mere interpretation is not always sufficient (as ergodic art and literature have made clear). The more interesting thing is to see what happens when the supposedly shared elements move between different modes.

18.4 Transitions between modes

Narrativist similarity studies[6] too often either ignore or misunderstand that when bits and pieces of content move across "media" they often change context, function and position, which may affect and usually also affects the modal status of these moving parts. Table 18.1 shows the most common transformations between story and game modes when elements move from (non-ergodic) films to games and vice versa. These transformations are either homomodal (elements retaining their modal status in transformation) or heteromodal (elements changing their modal status in transformation) (Eskelinen 2005). It is important to notice that some transformations between elements are necessarily heteromodal and that there are central elements that are not transposable at all (cf. rules).

In addition to intermodal transformations (between modes) there are, of course, intramodal transformations (taking place within a mode) such as transformations and imitations[7] between narrative texts and adaptations, implementations, and augmentations between games that we have already discussed. Our conceptualization and arrangement of modes differs slightly from traditional notions of mode and especially from Genette's that we used in the previous literary and narratological chapters. In Genette's poetics (cf. 1980; 1982a; 1988; 1992; 1997a), modes are modes of representation and thus drama and narrative are two distinct modes. We agree with this, but need to add three modifications to Genette's system in order to expand and update it to include film and games. First, to make room for films we separate a more general story mode from a more specific narrative mode. Film and drama present but do not narrate stories, except occasionally (cf. voiceover narration, certain speech acts of characters, and intertexts[8] in silent films), and the same applies to cartoons that may include passages of written narration. Second, both narrative and story mode have their own digitally expanded media ecologies as well. Third, games are not modes of (re)presentation like written narratives, stage drama or films, but modes of (human) action characterized by rules, variable outcomes, and player effort.

In terms of intermodal relationships, this doesn't matter much, as long as we understand the difference between the two types of mode (or should we say meta modes) in sorting out dramatizations,

Table 18.1 Examples of intermodal transformations between narrative/story elements and game elements

Element	Transformed to	Type of transformation
episode	cutscene	homomodal
cutscene	episode	homomodal
episode	sub-goal or goal	heteromodal
sub-goal or goal	episode	heteromodal
plot	backstory	homomodal
backstory	plot	homomodal
plot	series of consecutive challenges	heteromodal
series of challenges	plot	heteromodal
story	quest	heteromodal
story	backstory	homomodal
quest	story	heteromodal
backstory	story	homomodal
film character	NPC	homo- or heteromodal
NPC	film character	homo- or heteromodal
film character	player character	heteromodal
player character	film character	heteromodal
film character	adversary	heteromodal
adversary	film character	heteromodal
film setting	dynamic game world	heteromodal
dynamic gameworld	film setting/location	heteromodal

narrativizations, film adaptations, and game adaptations (or ludifications in the absence of better or catchier terms). What matters, however, is that the two meta-modes (of representations and actions) have different relationships to event and existents, i.e. the stuff human life is made of.[9] We have at least two different types of framing that can be applied to events and existents: the art frame and the play frame.

18.5 The tale of two continuums

So far we have been occupying ourselves in theorizing three principal modes, narrative, story and game, and their media ecologies and mutual transmodal relations. We have referred to the existence of other ecologies, and now it is time to take a wider perspective on other modalities and ecologies. As there are neither narratives nor games without events and existents, we might as well begin with everyday events that belong to neither but can give rise to both.

Keeping in mind the audienceless nature of games (everything can be observed by assuming a position of a member of an audience, but in games unlike in drama or cinema audience is not a structurally necessary component), it is not difficult to find theories of actions, activities, and events without audiences in performance theory (in a broad sense). For example, Allan Kaprow wrote about happenings and suggested certain measures and precautions that should be taken, concluding that "it follows that there should not be (and usually cannot be) an audience or audiences to watch a Happening" (Kaprow 1996, 64). In short, there are only participants "interacting" or "transacting"[10] with each other. This is important for our purposes, as it shows that events do not necessarily imply the existence and presence of audiences either in art or in games.

We can schematically construct two preliminary continuums, the first one going from narrative to drama and fiction film and then through performances and happenings to everyday events within the art frame, and the second one from everyday events to classic games (in the sense of Juul's classic game model) in the play frame.

The distinction between drama and performance art reflects the difference between matrixed and non-matrixed performances, as described by Michael Kirby in "The New Theatre":

> The actor functions within subjective or objective person-place matrices. The musician … is non-matrixed. He attempts to be no one other than himself, nor does he function in a place other than that which physically contains him and the audience. (Kirby 1982, 326)[11]

In other words, performers do not project a fictional world or pretend to represent anything beyond themselves. Although fictional worlds and characters are no longer present, there's still an audience watching the performer or performers.

As already mentioned, happenings don't have audiences but only participants; this is a communication structure which finally annuls the structural divide between performers and audience (and also the feedback loop between them). Just as in performance art, fictional worlds and characters are not projected in happenings.

The next step in the continuum concerns what could be called mere *events*. These are similar to happenings, except that these are performed by only one participant (without other participants witnessing the action), for example, Alan Kaprow running or completing some other relatively easily accomplished task. At this point, the only crucial difference between that activity and its everyday counterpart is the existence of the art frame, as long as a recognized artist (like Kaprow) reports, records, and frames his activities as events that still belong to the art frame.

Should the performer fail to do this, or if the performer is not interpreted to be an artist for professional, social, legal or other contextual reasons, then these actions are just everyday actions performed by non-artists: ordinary or extraordinary everyday events and existents, but of course these could be performed with a playful difference and this is exactly what an un-artist (Kaprow 1996, 97–147) does or is supposed to do. In his three papers on the subject Kaprow also traced the tradition of artists using everyday models in their practices of un-art. At this point participatory performances seem to dissolve into situations, operations, structures, feedback loops, and learning processes encountered in our everyday practices and routines, while the un-artist leaving the art frame behind turns into a player–educator opposing both competitive games and exhausted work ethics.

Narratives, performed or presented stories (drama and fiction film), performance art, happenings, events, un-art, and finally everyday playfulness outside the art frame. This continuum could be expressed in negative terms, because once we move along it many familiar and constitutive elements are removed one by one: narrators and narratees, fiction, audience, performers, and explicit, implicit and hidden art frames.

If we move in the other direction, everyday playfulness is only one step away from free play, the different ways of constraining which constitutes the game frame presented in its fullest form in Juul's classic game model. The intermediate steps in the continuum can be constructed from the presence or absence of Frasca's manipulation, grade and goals rules. Whether the rules and roles are self-asserted or given or chosen in the existing game structure also matters.

Certain tensions between various modes and practices of event production, presentation and representation are evident in these two schematic continuums. In the art frame, the users observe and interpret either representations or presentations of events and actions, or become participants in them (in ergodic drama, performances, happenings, events, and Kaprow's everyday un-art). These latter cases have certain similarities to free play, but once equipment, rules and goals are added to it in the play frame these similarities quickly vanish, as they also vanish in the art frame once the audience structures set in.

Second, playing a game is challenging in a way that most happenings, events and un-art are not (the participants do not usually need to have specific skills, or develop and test various tactics and strategies in order to be successful in their actions). Happenings and performances may contain "rules," but from the ludological perspective many of these are more like simple instructions, the execution of which does not constitute a challenge. Both intention and purpose successes are guaranteed in instructions (for the artist or the audience) like "make a soup" (Alison Knowles), "draw the line and follow it"(Naim June Paik), or "touch each other" (Yoko Ono). Their non-challenging and conflict-free everyday nature likens them to more complex scripts or scores for more daring improvisational performances, although the last may in some extreme cases contain elements and possibilities that are or may become dangerous to both performers and audiences (Marina Abramovic's *Rhythm* 0^{12} springs to mind).

However, even in these extreme cases, there is usually a guaranteed temporal passage from start to finish that is accomplishable by following the given instructions, orders, or script, and, in that way, we can still say there is no actual challenge. The situation changes if the instructions for the participants become more transgressive and competitive, for example calling for civil disobedience and legal or illegal action (say, the team that first throws a cake at Rupert Murdoch's face, hacks his phone, sues him successfully for damages or shoots him with a paintball gun wins; see also the Abramovic performance mentioned earlier). The point here is the qualitative, personal, and social nature of the challenges given to players, performers, participants or activists. If games in general (by contemporary western standards) and digital games in particular are characterized by having artificial challenges and conflicts and various "critical" performances, whereas happenings and events are characterized by having no or minimal challenges, there is a grey area between them, a free-floating third option consisting of real and daring personal and social challenges presented to participants, activists, and test subjects in situations outside both art and game frames – in social-psychological experiments, human and animal rights activism, or unorthodox political campaigns (along the lines envisioned by Abbie Hoffman, for example).

Third, there are obvious differences in the arrangement and production of sequences of events:

> A sequence of events enacted constitutes a drama, a sequence of events taking place a performance, a sequence of events recounted a narrative, and perhaps a sequence of events produced by manipulating equipment and following formal rules constitutes a game. (Eskelinen 2004a, 37)

Fourth, differences in embodiment cut across both continuums. Positions vary from the user being a fully embodied existent (a gamer, player, performer, or actor) responsible for producing actions and events, to him merely interpreting and/or manipulating static and/or dynamic representations of events and existents on the screen. Finally, existents may have both functional and fictional aspects. Within the art frame these are for the most part controlled by the presence or absence of matrixes (i.e. fictionality) and audiences (i.e. the functional distribution of roles such as actor, performer, participant or spectator). Within the play frame roles are freely created, selected from a given variety, or strictly prescribed (the player is given a role; he can't select one). Functional roles are defined by rules, goals and player structure, and fictional or matrixed ones, if there are any, by functional roles and the representational options given or left to the player.

The two major transmedial modes (stories and games) are situated at both ends of the continuum. Between action representations (that are either narrated or enacted) and the kinds of action shaped by rules, goals and non-trivial player effort there's a vast area of differently and much more loosely shaped human action in both frames. Coincidently this ergodic or semi-ergodic zone of performances, happenings, events, toys and free or improvisational play is also an area within which the concept or practice of transmediality explains and describes very little. This brings us once again back to the inherent problems in the concept of a medium further complicated by the capabilities of digital media as a meta-medium.

18.6 The problem with media

The major problem at the core of different conceptualizations of transmediality is the fuzzy concept of a medium. In Chapter 2, we argued that a unified digital medium (the kind imagined by Manovich 2001; Murray 1997; and many others) does not actually exist, and in the chapters focusing on games and computer games it become equally evident that there is no medium of the video game (suggested by Wolf 2001 and many others) either. In flawed and vague concepts like transmedia storytelling, the latter component is at least in principle definable in terms of modes, while the former seems to refer to an ever growing variety of gadgets all around the marketplace. Modes (narratives, stories, presentations, performances, and games) are transmedial, and these modes also provide whatever benefit there may be in focusing on transmediality (to see similarities and differences in how these modes are implemented in different media). Even so, at least three kinds of problem haunt the concept of a medium and its appropriate use, especially in the context of the ever expanding, networked and programmable multitude of digital media.

As far back as Chapter 2, we followed Aarseth and moved from media to media functioning; instead of asking what a medium supposedly is and is capable of, it is theoretically more fruitful to ask what a medium does and is capable of doing, without assuming essential differences between media to begin with. This leads to a more accurate grasp of the media space and to recognizing various overlaps in the functioning of different media. In this functional horizon, the explanatory and descriptive powers of transmediality and intermediality (and comparative media studies as well) become very limited, if they are not specified by both modes and media functions. Still, the question remains: what is a medium?

Most discussions in the field of "new media" tend to avoid formal definitions beyond listing the supposedly new features of the new media. Bolter and Grusin (1999) give two definitions of the concept. The longer one (Bolter and Grusin 1999, 273) states it is "the formal, social and material network of practices that generates a logic by which additional instances are repeated or remediated, such as photography, film or television." As Aarseth (2003a, 437) notes this definition "does not address the communi-cational aspects of media, and seems to describe material, artifact producing processes … better than signifying ones." According to the shorter definition (Bolter and Grusin 1999, 65) a medium is "that which remediates." This is not only circular, as Aarseth notes (2003a, 437), but it also underlines the futility of any focus on a medium without taking into account its remediating aspect.

As remediation is also a vaguely defined concept, "the represen-tation of one medium in another" (Bolter and Grusin 1999, 45), it can only lead us back to the interplay of media within which everything is somehow (at least metaphorically) connected (and similar and dissimilar) to everything else, and media scholars can take their rhetorical pick of what to emphasize and foreground at the expense of other equally valid connections. For example, to Bolter and Grusin video games are remediated cinema much more than they are remediated games; similar shortcomings abound in Bolter's (2001) emphasis on hypertextuality and topographic writing in the context of digital literature. Ultimately, such vague connections can be multiplied with no end in digital media that are capable of imitating and simulating analog media and recombining and embedding bits and pieces from any other media. In short, this is what Allan Kay and Adele Goldberg's meta-medium (Kay and Goldberg 2003, 403) does or is capable of doing. In addition to the perspectives provided by modes and functionality (in a cyber-textual sense), this is the third limitation or complication to the applicability and usefulness of the concepts of trans-, inter- and multimediality in this context.

In "Ideology and Innovation," Aarseth theorizes the differences between the analog mass media and computer based communication:

> If the "old" media model consists of a social discourse (say, news) carried out in the physical channel (printed paper, radio, TV), then the digital media model must include something more: the active application that manipulates the signs at the time of use. This level is neither part of the discourse nor the channel, but constitutes a third, rule-based level in-between the other two. (Aarseth 2003a, 419)

This addition or supplement has interesting consequences, as it "places computer-based sign-processes closer to phenomena such as tool-use, rituals, performance, and games than to the analog mass media" (Aarseth 2003a, 419). The discourse/application/channel model is not exclusive to digital communication because it includes "any practice or technology with a manipulative component" (Aarseth 2003a, 421). To specify and break apart the application layer and the manipulation it allows, we'd need to adopt a functional perspective once again, as quite obviously different media will allow, sustain and require also overlapping ways to manipulate the signs. At this point, modes become helpful as one of the basic ways to organize the manipulative dimension.

It is only in the functional framework of several well-defined modalities that the question of transmediality can be fruitfully raised. In addition to the (until now) hegemonic modes of story and narrative, which provide only a partial perspective, we also have the modes of game, performance and presentation (the last two with their ergodic and non-ergodic functional varieties) to consider if we are interested in constructing a fuller and more balanced view of transmediality. From this perspective, it is much more important to further develop comparative game, narrative, story, performance/presentation and ergodic studies without being blinded by the limited and inadequately grounded perspectives of comparative media studies (that can theorize neither modes nor functionality and is haunted by the combinatory and simulative capabilities of the digital meta-medium) and its self-repetitive and self-defeating focus on stories.

The ludological perspective on game ecology is important not only because it adds a major and dominantly ergodic mode to the conceptualizations of modes and transmediality, but also because it foregrounds central elements (such as rules) that cannot be transmedially transported outside the ecologies of games, play and simulations. Furthermore, the ecology of games points to certain limitations in the supposedly all-encompassing capability of computer based communication to simulate, emulate, imitate, replicate and, in principle, also replace its non-digital predecessors. These limitations are first and foremost related to games that can only be played with and within the physical presence of other players. Narrative mode doesn't seem to include similar irreducibility between its digital and non-digital manifestations:[13] the tricks and treats of its cultural inheritance can be reproduced in digital media that also offers new affordances impossible or difficult to implement in non-digital media.

This difference makes transmediality (and any mode- and media-position-blind approach to media) even more shallow than it already is, in the light of sophisticated poststructuralist thinking that foregrounds what is semiotically and materially irreducible and singular in every work of art and process of communication. From that perspective, traditional conceptualizations of transmediality concern, if anything, simple cognitive surface patterns that apply only to the least aesthetically important (re)presentational aspects of art and media.

To this simplicity, we can now add other kinds of simple element and pattern that are not primarily related to (re)presentation or inscription, but to physical and rule-based human action. Alternatively, we could put an end to or raise the stakes for the usefulness of transmediality by foregrounding Aarseth's (2001a,

153) claim that "every structurally different computer game is effectively a new medium." This is because "each game-system requires its own means (components, props, boards, technology) to mediate its behavior to players" (Järvinen 2008, 306). In this situation, transmediality would suddenly cover a handful of old media and around 600000[14] "new" digital game media.

CHAPTER 19

Ergodic modes and play

19.1 Introduction

Previous chapters have demonstrated the ways in which the user in ergodic literature (and art) is more than just a reader or a spectator and yet much less than a game player, although in some cases more capable of affecting and altering the artefact than the latter. This begs the question concerning the relations between various ergodic modes (explorative, configurative, and textonic, each with either personal or impersonal perspective), play in general, and gameplay in particular.

Cybertext theory and game ontology can be combined in several ways, but in what follows our focus is on ergodics. In Aarseth's typology of textual communication, the dividing line between ergodic and non-ergodic literature cuts across user functions. In Chapter 2, we expanded the ergodic side of cybertextuality with two additional dimensions, user position and user objective, and noted that personal perspective implies roleplaying, which was a separate user function in Aarseth's earlier cybertextual typology (Aarseth 1994, 62). User position was designed to account for the possible presence and influence of other users in the realization of an ergodic work and requirements for the user's physical location and bodily mobility. User objective added several alternative objectives to traversal that implies a trajectory that has a given finality: the consulting, completion, winning, and improvisation that typically take place in the contexts of non-fiction, puzzles, games, and play.

In Chapter 5, we discussed modes, distinguished simulative and non-simulative modes, and separated modes of representation (or information) from modes of action. The modes of ergodic action were shown to have several interrelated aspects: control, communication, traversal, existence, and sign production.

In Chapter 11, the five discourse layers of Aarseth's theory (events, progression, negotiation, quasi-events, and construction) were viewed from the perspective of an overall organization of the text. The level of negotiation and its role in the design of a puzzle or a game (to be solved, completed or won) was found to be crucial in determining whether a text is dominantly ergodic.

In Chapter 18, we began to see limitations in mode-centric thinking, despite the fact that modes and functionality are needed as conceptual tools and anchors in any valid construction of transmediality. A somewhat mode-resistant and fuzzy area was located in the realms of play, performance art, and happenings that were situated closer to everyday events and existents than the more structured and constrained modes of action representations (stories, narratives) and modes of rule-based action (cf. games). This borderland is what we'll call in this chapter an ergodic zone. Within the ergodic zone, ergodic literature is a multifaceted field permanently open to other ergodic arts, play, toys and instruments not to mention evolving forms of everyday playfulness. In the rest of this chapter, we examine the relations of ergodic literature to ergodic art and to different forms and value systems of play, before trying to combine cybertext and game typologies.

19.2 Ergodic literature and ergodic art

Ergodic literature and ergodic art share many points of contact and a common history. Egyptian wall inscriptions situated in three-dimensional sacred spaces are among Aarseth's first examples of ergodic literature. Processes of navigation in a gallery space or within an interactive installation are similar to the much less physical exploration of hypertext fiction, although interactive installations and sculptures may also be text based (as in Jenny Holzer's oeuvre), and the genre of locative hypertext narratives just widens the area of the scripton space or furthers the text's spatial dispersion depending on one's point of view. Aarseth's configurative user function (in which the user is choosing or creating at least some scriptons) characterizes practices that have almost become clichés in the art world: multimedia works and installations that merge the images of the users into the audiovisual stream presented to them (offering yet another presentational layer to be narrativized by scholars like Nitsche). Sometimes the users are allowed to make more permanent additions to the artwork either collaboratively or own their own. These practices are clearly textonic in the cyber-textual sense.

There are also borderline cases (or hybrids) between ergodic art and ergodic literature, such as Utterback and Achituv's *Text Rain* (1999), and works that trigger audiovisual output from textual input (such as *Verbarium*) or vice versa. *Text Rain* is a potential intertextual instrument (and as such discussed in the next chapter) that allows users to manipulate falling words and letters that are derived from Evan Zimroth's poem *Talk You* (in the 1993 collection) and catch and arrest them within the areas of a screen whereon their bodily shapes are projected in real time. The letters sometimes form meaningful words and phrases and the partici-pants may try to emphasize that aspect in their playful efforts that are pleasurable in themselves not least because the users may also collaborate and join their bodies and bodily shapes as best they can.

The one obvious difference between ergodic literature and ergodic art, in addition to utilized sign systems, is the physical effort required by most ergodic works of art, which goes far beyond the clicking and typing that are typical of the non-trivial user efforts in ergodic literature. However, as we have seen the difference is far from absolute: nothing prevents ergodic literature from occasionally becoming more demanding in purely physical terms or more directly related to the user's bodily presence, state, or movement if not to skill and strength as well. The sheer physical pleasure of manipulating the letters in *Text Rain* emphasizes the role of the interface in a way that may seem to undermine the literary qualities of the work, and to some degree this is true. By the same token, the more pleasurable the physical manipulation becomes, the closer we are to the realm of the instruments: the sheer ability of mastering them brings joy almost despite or independently of the content or the results of that activity. In this respect, the relationship between the two types (physical and less physical) of ergodic literature resembles the competition between arcade games (played in public places) and console games (played mostly at home) in the 1980s. The former's competitive edge was in more specialized and expensive idiosyncratic interfaces, some of which (such as dance mats) later found their way into private use as well.

Comparisons between the two fields (ergodic art and ergodic literature) are difficult, as ergodic or interactive art is not adequately theorized, and the field is riddled by buzzwords, ideologically fashionable over-interpretations of digitality, and vague conceptualizations of interactivity, a much criticized term that, for example, Dixon (2007) in his extensive and pioneering study of digital performance (in theater, dance, film, and performance art) doesn't seem able to abandon (despite his borrowed criticisms of it). Dixon's four categories of interactivity (2007, 563) – navigation, participation, conversation and collaboration – form a good example of partly acknowledged short-comings. According to Dixon these categorizations are not "exact science" because "degrees of significance and change effected by the user in interactive spaces and performances are judgment calls and matters of opinion" (Dixon 2007, 565).

Still, under digital circumstances it is both pointless and confusing to include, as Dixon does (2007, 587), the omnipresent dialogue between user and software in the category of conversation already containing actual conversations between human users or between them and artificial but personalized entities. These and other conceptual contradictions radically diminish the theoretical value of Dixon's work, and are perhaps best exemplified by his (Dixon 2007, 583) problems with installations where visitors' movement "triggers sensors to activate planned events and programmed sequences and effects." Given Dixon's poorly grounded categorizations that are weakly based on the degree of openness of the system and the level and depth of user interaction (Dixon 2007, 563), he can only end up with the following confusion:

> [I]t is arguable whether the primary interactive paradigm is, according to our continuum, navigation (the course the user

takes), participation (users helping to bring to life the environment's sensory features), conversation (a dialogue between the user and the computer) or collaboration (the user and computer creating art together). (Dixon 2007, 583)

In such cases, cybertextual rigor would be helpful (resulting in this case in the explorative user function), but Dixon is totally unaware of previous scholarship in this area where all arts, including literature, overlap. The whole problem is easily solved by the cybertextual user functions: if the user's movement triggers effects and the movement is not designed to be strictly linear then the user effort is explorative; if the movement becomes part of what is presented back to the user it is configurative; and if the movement can permanently alter the artwork (for example, a record of the user's movement becoming part of the accumulating database) it is textonic.

A related problem concerns the focus on digital media, which seems to inhibit the establishment of more general views on each field. As we noted in Chapter 2, Aarseth's theory is exceptional in its capability to situate any type of text and literature, regardless of its medium, within its heuristic map of media positions. Similarly comprehensive theories do not (yet) exist in other fields, although the concept of the ergodic and the problems in conceptualizing it are common to both ergodic literature and ergodic or "interactive" art.

Despite these and other theoretical shortcomings, there are fruitful comparisons to be made, especially when certain practices seem to lack their counterpart in the other field. One of these is user profiling (or at least an idea of user profiling) affecting the content to be presented, which was employed in interactive films such as *Tender Loving Care* (Wheeler 1999). The idea is quite obvious, but somehow it has not found its way into hypertext fiction or text adventures, although Eastgate's hypertext software StorySpace has a rudimentary answering mechanism (with the options of yes and no) that is potentially connectible to guard fields, and the often used second-person address of text adventures would almost seem to invite such use.

At stake here is the amount and nature of information the system has about the user and how it uses it. Another theme worth rethinking concerns triggers and triggering. In digital performances, the user's movement or some other behavior or quality triggers responses, and needless to say these "triggers" are frequently more physically demanding than and qualitatively different from the mere clicking for information retrieval that is typical of ergodic literature (in addition to the typed dialog and polylog). Given the current diverse range of wireless gadgets and applications capable of exchanging information with one another, it has become possible to gather much more personal bodily grounded information about the user and transmit it to the ergodic system to trigger textual responses. Such pervasive semi- or occasionally ergodic textual environments could surround the reader in his everyday life (and not limit themselves to a specific location) and respond to its patterns and rhythms.

19.3 Sutton-Smith and the ambiguity of play

Although both the user functions of cybertext theory and the forms of interaction in digital performance theory come close to play, play is not among the categories these theories use to describe the interplay between the user and the artifact. Several studies have applied play as a metaphor to theorize the reading process, the relations between readers and texts, or even the games authors supposedly play with their readers (Motte 1995). Caillois' four types of game are also frequently played out in these metaphoric exercises (cf. Ryan 2001a) that can only highlight the difference between play and occasional interpretative playfulness.

Although play is an ambiguous concept, it has been so frequently and contradictorily defined that certain patterns are detectable in its use in different fields of scholarship for a wide variety of purposes. Brian Sutton-Smith (1997) found seven types of play rhetoric in his classic study. Four of these have ancient origins: the rhetorics of fate, power, identity and frivolity (that is also a meta-category reflecting and usually condemning the other six rhetorics), and three have more modern roots: the rhetorics of progress, self and the imaginary (Sutton-Smith 1997, 9–11).

Sutton-Smith (1997, 214) describes these seven rhetorics according to their historical source, particular function, distinctive ludic form and specialized players and advocates as well as their academic and disciplinary contexts. In Sutton-Smith's schema, literature and art are related to the rhetorics of imaginary, a category that usually applies to "playful improvisation of all kinds in literature and elsewhere" (Sutton-Smith 1997, 11). The coordinates of this rhetoric include romanticism (historical source), creativity and flexibility (distinctive functions), fantasy and tropes (specific forms), actors (specialized players), and art and literature (disciplines). Bakhtin, Fagen, and Bateson are listed as primary scholarly advocates of this rhetoric (Sutton-Smith 1997, 215).

The rhetoric of imaginary situates non-ergodic literature and its merely interpretative "mind games" into the cultures and value systems of play, but to find a place for ergodic literature in this scheme is more complicated (although one could speculate on specific ergodic fantasies and tropes). Sutton-Smith doesn't make a distinction between ergodic and non-ergodic art and literature, and therefore we'll have to see to what degree the other rhetorics could illuminate ergodic literature as a play activity. In what follows, we are less interested in the rhetorical aspects (arguments made about a play form) than in the possible forms, functions and player types that ergodic literature could include and adopt – the play practices and ludic forms. Contrariwise, the seven rhetorics are related to the values ascribed to play and therefore the relationship between the values traditionally associated with (non-ergodic) literature have to be rethought in ergodic literature to the degree that the latter is shaped by the forms, functions, and values associated with play.

The rhetorics of power, like the other three ancient rhetorics, "predate modern times and advocate collectively held community values rather than individual experiences" and is therefore "an anathema to many modern progress- and leisure-oriented play theorists" (Sutton-Smith 1997, 10). At first sight, it may be difficult to think of literature outside both progress- and leisure-oriented contexts, but the additional qualifiers help in directing the search. In the rhetorics of power, the ludic forms include skill, strategy, and deep play that have status and victory as their function and in which (professional) athletes are the specialized player type.

Literature could be situated in these ludic forms and functions, in terms of the competition of prestige, fame, fortune and cultural capital among authors in a public arena including literary prizes and contests. Examples of literary contests that test their participants' skill and productivity abound in literary history. They are often related in quantitative terms to poetic composition. In 1677 Ihara Saikaku won one such contest by composing 1600 haikus in 24 hours, and seven years later he is said to have set the ultimate record by composing 23 000 haikus in 24 hours as part of a religious service; that is, Saikaku was able to generate a new haiku every four seconds (Kato 1990, 94).

Saikaku was composing poems that have a strictly formal structure (that was used to judge success and failure); to attribute or impose that kind of activity and requirement on the user would force him to assume the traditional position of an author (that is also one but not the only form of the textonic user function). Such a shift is not what characterizes ergodic literature, despite early hype to the contrary (cf. Bolter 1991; Landow 1992). The power rhetoric concerns not only status but victory, and victory in this context presupposes an opponent and the possibility of loss. The question then becomes what these two presupposed aspects could mean in ergodic literature (or art). The voice in textual adventure games is partly the voice of an opponent, but this opponent doesn't lose (unlike the AI opponent in computerized chess, which is able to lose). The player can lose, at least metaphorically, by not being able to solve the enigma and complete the game. An alternative and more material solution to this problem of loss in single-user ergodic literature would be the concrete loss of the text: the user's singular or cumulative failure triggering the Agrippa effect making that particular text inaccessible to the loser in the future.

The rhetorics of fate is composed of luck and magic as functions, chance as form, and gamblers as players, in addition to mathematics as its disciplinary background and animism and divination as its historical sources (Sutton-Smith 1997, 215). This has several interesting connections to ergodic literature: *I Ching* is, among other things, a book and a procedure for the purposes of divination, and chance is a common factor in both ergodic and non-ergodic literature. Still, in both cases the use of chance and random elements (indeterminate determinability in cybertextual terms) is somewhat limited by the traditional single-reader and user orientations and conventions (discounting MUDs). These conventions are not shared by drama and performance art, which of course can be and have been personalized in more experimental presentations even for only one person (at a time) audiences.

That chance can be fruitfully explored in social relationships was shown by *Surrender Control* (Forced Entertainment 2001). On a textual level it was a series of SMS messages sent to subscribed participants (mostly unknown to one another). The messages consisted of instructions or suggestions (as it was up to each participant whether or not to follow them) that encouraged the participants to take small social risks: "Steal something" (#66), "Get too close to people" (#71), or "Call someone. Tell a lie" (#31). The instructions of *Surrender Control* leave the decision of modes and manners of action (and taking action) to the participant, as only the general outlines of an action to be taken or an event to be performed are given. Although the type of human-to-human inter-action and the kind of persons to do it with were suggested, these constraints were usually related to the participant's life history (including former schoolmates and ex-lovers).

Surrender Control is not a game to be won or a puzzle to be completed. Its suggestions or tasks are not connected to one another, but fully autonomous and self-sufficient. *Surrender Control* cannot be lost either except in the metaphorical and vague terms of the participant's own experience and ultimately in terms of personal values. Depending on the activity of each participant, *Surrender Control* is either a scripted and personalized performance or a linear text made of instructions that stimulates the recipient's imagination even if he chooses not to act according to some instruction or all of them. Similar social risks apply to books like Abbie Hoffman's legendary *Steal this Book* (1989), depending on the method of its acquisition (in principle the book is either stolen or bought). It would be tempting to view instructions (crossing the boundary between individual and social use and between literature and drama or performance) as an ergodic text type par excellence.

The rhetoric of play as identity is usually applied to "traditional and community celebrations and festivals" and functions as "a means of confirming, maintaining, or advancing the power and identity of the community of players" (Sutton-Smith 1997, 10). In addition to community celebrations and festivals the respective ludic forms also include parties and new games[1] (Sutton-Smith 1997, 215). At the heart of this activity are "play forms as forms of bonding, including the exhibition and validation or parody of membership and traditions in the community" (Sutton-Smith 1997, 91). In the existing ergodic literature community creating, confirming and advancing play occurs most of all in MUDs, but also in blogs and social media and in more ephemeral literary formations that are part of what is called alternative reality games such as *Cathy's Book* (Stewart and Weisman 2006), which requires and encourages participants to cooperate and collaborate in order to solve the central or supplementary mystery, cues and clues to which are scattered throughout multiple media.

It is difficult to see in what way the modes, genres and forms of non-ergodic literature could create anything except fan fiction and other specialist communities around them, if and when they could be made ergodic in this way. If the perspective is shifted towards non-fiction the case is different: social media (wikis, blogs, Facebook etc.) creates and provides a fertile ground for ergodic non-fiction or at least hoaxes that pretend to be what they are not to provoke unintentional[2] ergodic responses from the community. In such cases, the user's and user community's ergodic work is unintentional and parallels the role audiences have in Augusto Boal's (1992, 6–16) invisible theater. It may be questionable whether these types of practices reflect the values of "confirming, maintaining, or advancing the power and identity of the community of players" but they certainly relate to and exemplify the aspect of parody Sutton-Smith mentions – an aspect that is compatible with the values of literature as we know it. Examples such as the fake websites of Shawn Rider's *myBall* (2002) in the first volume of the *Electronic Literature Collection* come close to these practices.

The fourth ancient rhetoric of play, frivolity, has its historical origins in work ethics, and is characterized by tricksters, comedians, and jesters as player types, inversion and playfulness as functions, nonsense as form and popular culture as its disciplinary background (Sutton-Smith 1997, 215). In some respects, this rhetoric is well known in ergodic literature, as many ignorant criticisms and comments regard it only as nonsense with futile effects and trivial results replacing whatever value is said to exist in the best traditions of non-ergodic literature. Carnivalization and the inversion of values into nonsense are typical gestures and strategies of the historical avant-gardes as well as their digital successors. Simon Biggs' *The Great Wall of China* (2000) that according to Roberto Simanowski's interpretation (Simanowski 2003) turns Kafka into nonsense would, if it were more ergodic, be a prime example of this.

The modern rhetoric of progress that is associated with juveniles and child's play and games as well as with processes of growth, adaptation, and socialization may therefore seem distant from the usual concerns of ergodic literature. Still, many children's books are mildly or marginally ergodic[3] (with their popup features etc.). To the degree growth, adaptation, and socialization are associated with learning, these processes are not limited to childhood, not even to its extended contemporary western form. Learning to play an instrument constitutes one example of these ludic forms and functions in ergodic literature, and will be taken up again in the next chapter that centers on instrumental texts and textual instruments.

Finally, the rhetoric of self, related as it is to individualism, peak experiences, avant-garde and solitary players, and to leisure, solitary and extreme games, has several potential points of contact with ergodic literature. Some of these can be illustrated by stressing the individual side of *Surrender Control*: within it social contacts and risks were mostly optional and minimal; the persons the participants contacted were not aware of the staging and therefore played their part in the self-serving and self-centered schemes of the participants. Both modernism (multiple focalizations and perspectives) and postmodernism (ontologically clashing and competing fictional worlds) are often understood as reflecting and running parallel to the increasing emphasis upon individuality in western societies, and if that is the case, then extremely personalized ergodic experiences will fit nicely into that continuum – if properly designed of course.

19.4 Ergodic literature and games: the two typologies

Even a superficial comparison between cybertext typology and Elverdam and Aarseth's game ontology reveal not only the same self-corrective idea of an open model, the dimensions of which can be reworked and altered to gain more descriptive and analytical power, but also a crucial difference in underlying schemes, despite the fact that both typologies are slightly biased towards explaining digital specimens.

At the core of cybertext theory is the difference between textons and scriptons, as well as the role of the traversal function in mediating between the two levels and turning textons into scriptons. The difference between the strings of signs as they are in the text and as they are presented to the user has no equivalent in Aarseth's game ontology, although the difference between storage and interface media characterizes digital media in general. Within computer games a similar distinction could be made between game states as they are in the game (textonic game states) and game states as they are (re)presented to the player or players (scriptonic game states). This difference implies the possibility that not all information about the game state is given to the player. This is obviously the case in games of imperfect information such as card games, but the difference has explanatory and heuristic power beyond reformulating the traditional distinction between games of perfect and imperfect information (formulated by Neumann and Morgenstern in 1944).

Several unreliable and perhaps also unfair and unbalanced game designs could be generated from the division between textonic and scriptonic game states. The same division can be expanded to all major game elements, and the resulting differences between rules, goals, challenges, player structures, and virtual and physical spaces as they are and as they are presented to the player include many possibilities not yet frequently implemented in games. Among other things they are related to the conditions under which the difference is revealed or becomes evident to the player, and to the arrangement of gameplay at two levels or dimensions: play in the gameworld and play of the gameworld (i.e. of how it functions). If one is inclined towards locating parallels between art history and game history then perhaps the acknowledged and designed utilization of the difference between these two levels of play could be interpreted to indicate the existence of one possible form of modernism in games.

Elverdam and Aarseth's game typology has 17 dimensions, and results in hundreds of thousands of possible combinations, as compared to the several hundreds resulting from the seven original cybertextual dimensions (even if the two additional parameters of user position and user objective were added, the quantitative difference between cybertextual media positions and combinatory game types would still be significant).

Both typologies include dimensions of time. The category of transience in cybertext's typology has some similarities to the distinction between turn based and real time in single-player games, but the more nuanced categories of haste, interval control, and synchronicity relate mostly to games with more than one player, which is dissimilar to the majority of literary conventions centered on single users unable to affect each other's positions and possibilities. Interval control is therefore comparatively useless or trivial in describing the user's encounter with an ergodic text that is not a game. Still, equivalents of haste (the passing of real time affecting the game state) are frequent in transient texts (or completely synonymous with them if game states are replaced with states of the textual presentation), interactive fiction (where the passing of time may change the state in the simulated world), and MUDs. Moreover, the users of Kac's "avatar"[4] poem *Perhaps* (1998/1999) can act at the same time (synchronicity).

Elverdam and Aarseth's categories of outer time (teleology and representation) are not present in the final cybertext typology (of 1997) although representation is included in its earlier version (Aarseth 1994). In a non-game context, the teleological difference between finite and infinite games (Elverdam and Aarseth 2007, 10) could reflect the difference between *Agrippa* (and other transient texts and textual performances with a fixed duration) and *Book Unbound*.

If the categories of virtual and physical space in Elverdam and Aarseth's game typology are compared to the cybertext typology, then (as we already saw in Chapter 2) the dimensions of perspective (omnipresent vs. vagrant) and positioning (location based, proximity based, or both) are particularly useful or even necessary as additional dimensions to describe texts such as 3D textual installations (e.g., Holzer 1990) that require physical movement from the user and may include sensors detecting the user's position and movement. The same applies even more to locative texts and narratives (see, for examples, Balpe 2010; Borras and Gutierrez 2010).

In computer games, random access and controlled access are related to and depend on both spatial and temporal segmentation of the game and the availability of game elements for manipulation. To some degree, it also depends on the type of the game: in games of progression with linearly presented challenges, access is controlled, while in games of emergence it could be random too, especially if the game space is limited enough (i.e. an arena presentable only on one screen) and all the manipulative devices and their possible objects are available all the time. The dimension of access necessarily grows more complicated when it does not concern access to text, and in video games the dimension should be divided into several sub-dimensions: access to game space, resources, challenges, and actually being able to play the game (without having to wait one's turn or a cutscene to run its course).

Both impersonal and personal (cybertextual) perspectives are in use in games, as not every game requires the player to assume strategic responsibilities as a character. This distinction foregrounds the aspect of roleplay that, as already noted, is not included in the 17 dimensions of Elverdam and Aarseth's game typology. This omission also makes perspective the only cybertextual category that could be directly (i.e. without any modification) added as an extra dimension to the game typology. Likewise both games and ergodic literature contain determinate and indeterminate elements that in the former are primarily related to challenges.

The dimension of links is close to useless in describing games, although Aarseth uses it to describe text adventure games and MUDs in *Cybertext* with the invariable result of finding their links to be conditional. Links are just one possible way of arranging the relations between parts and wholes, in short a way of segmenting and connecting, and there are many other ways of managing that. To understand the logic of segmentation in games we'd have to divide it into several subcategories: causal (into challenges and goals), functional (into given and obtainable resources), spatial (into interconnected game spaces), temporal (into possible periods, rounds, turns etc.), eventual (into playable and merely presented events and actions), and "existential" (into playable and merely decorative existents), just to begin with.

In relation to games, the cybertextual parameter of dynamics is reduced to two values, as there are no games with static dynamics. The applicable division is then between textonically and intra-textonically dynamic games, which to some degree mirrors the distinction between multiplayer and single player games already included in the modified cybertext typology (cf. the parameter of user position), as well as the difference between the two "game" genres of MUDs and text adventures. In video games, it may make more sense to replace strings of signs by game elements in the definition of the dynamics, in which case textonically dynamic games implies that the number and content of the game elements will not remain constant and intratextonically dynamic that there's variation in the content of the game elements presented to the player. However, at this point it seems futile to force further similarities between the two typologies.

The meta-dimensions of player structure (player composition, evaluation, and bond), struggle (challenge and goals) and game state (savability and mutability) are the most interesting meta-dimensions in relation to user functions and ergodicity in the cybertext typology. As we noticed earlier, the question of goals doesn't enter Aarseth's typology of textual communication except via the implicit assumption that the user is always traversing the text. Because we modified that in Chapter 2 by introducing the additional parameter of user objective to shape the user functions, we can leave that as it is.

The presence of challenges and the struggle in general imply the existence of the discourse layer of negotiation that is generally lacking from the types of ergodic literature that are not games. Outside both single- and multi-user games, evaluation seems to be non-existent (beyond occasional comments of the reading-using process in general), but that may change although the idea of a text machine evaluating its user's performance is not backed up by literary conventions.[5] Similarly the meta-dimension of player structure is useful in specifying the user position. Mutability is directly related to the player's resources and therefore it is useful in specifying user positions and to some degree user objectives as well.

19.5 Conclusion

The ergodic side of ergodic literature was originally specified by the parameters of user function and perspective. In the course of this study, we have added several additional parameters to these two: user position and user objective to begin with, which diversified the field to more precisely take into account the presence of other users, the users' spatial and bodily involvement, and most of all the many existing alternatives to traversing a text. Perhaps the most pertinent aspect of this expansion is related to the nature of the user's non-trivial effort: is it work or play or something else altogether? This led us to different modes of action and by necessity to the neighboring fields of games, play and ergodic art. Generally speaking, by combining user functions, user positions (including personal or impersonal perspective), user objectives, different types of feedback loops, and modes of action, the field of ergodics in general and ergodic literature in particular can be described and explained much better and more accurately than by the commonly used but unfocused buzzwords such as interactivity or by the four user functions, as useful as they are.

Aarseth's cybertext model reflects to a certain degree the situation and genre system of the field in the early and mid–1990s. *Cybertext* was written and published before the emergence of ludology and game studies at the turn of the millennium, and in retrospect it is easy to divide the four genres Aarseth discussed at length into two: hypertext fiction and text generators belong to the literary end of the ergodic scale and text adventures and MUDs to the gaming end, which could now be legitimately and fruitfully situated in the field of game studies, too (especially given the close connections between MUDs and MMOGs, on the one hand, and between text adventures and audiovisual adventure and quest games, on the other).

This split necessarily concerns the power relations between interpretative and ergodic user functions: at the literary end the former dominates and at the gaming end the latter. If the field of ergodic literature is divided between literary and game studies, it may at first seem that nothing much has happened since the publication of *Cybertext* and the emergence of the internet. Hypertext fictions and poetry generators are still around, perhaps in a more multimedial shape than before, competing with non-ergodic visual and kinetic texts. Fortunately, they are not all there is, as in the aftermath of ludology and game studies certain new genres and conceptualizations (or would-be genres), most importantly textual instruments and instrumental texts, have also arrived on the scene.

In order to better understand these newcomers, we'll for the last time go back to basics. To Aarseth "a cybertext is a machine for the production of the variety of expression" (Aarseth 1997, 3), and "a mechanical device for the production and consumption of verbal signs" (Aarseth 1997, 21). It consists of verbal signs, a material medium, and the human operator. The ultimate remaining question is what kind of machines these ergodic text machines are or could be, and on what kind of machines they are or could be modeled (or in the case of simulations, what kind of machine is being or could be simulated). Are they toys, instruments, or meta-machines, and are such descriptions more than just heuristic metaphors?

CHAPTER 20

Textual instruments and instrumental texts

20.1 Introduction

In this final chapter, the focus will be on textual instruments and instrumental texts, along with the slowly emerging theories of them that widen the spectrum of ergodic literature and present perhaps the most significant new genre that has begun to take shape since the publication of *Cybertext* in 1997. The discussion about textual instruments and instrumental texts to some degree reflects and parallels the emergence of ludology and digital game studies, and it also has at least an analogous relationship to musical instruments, play and improvisation. In ergodic literature, it signals a possible shift of emphasis from work to play (Moulthrop 2004) and from an overly serious avant-garde to more transparent and ludic communications between the interested parties.

John Cayley was the first to articulate this possibility in the context of ergodic literature (in his artistic presentations at the Digital Arts and Culture conferences in 2000 and 2001) and subsequently the theme has been developed by Cayley himself (2003; 2008), Durand and Wardrip-Fruin (2005), Eskelinen (2004c),

Moulthrop (2003b; 2006; 2008), Wardrip-Fruin (2003; 2007) – Cayley and Moulthrop mainly in interviews and in the paratexts of their ergodic works labeled as instruments. Wardrip-Fruin and Durand have built textual instruments partly inspired by the hypothetical instruments of Mark Bernstein, *Card Shark* and *Thespis* (described in Bernstein 2001; Bernstein and Greco 2004). In 2008, *The Iowa Web Review* published a theme issue on textual instruments edited by Moulthrop.

Despite these developments, it is still unclear whether the proposed concepts are theoretically viable, because, in some cases, discussion around them is haunted by vague metaphors projected onto the already existing genres (such as hypertext fiction), and, in other cases, instrumental texts are confused with textual instruments. Therefore in what follows we try to add some precision to the way textual instruments are theorized.

The key distinction in the area of textual instrumentality is to be made between instrumental texts (capable of playing only one composition that is usually attached to the instrument that plays it) and textual instruments (capable of playing several compositions), according to Wardrip-Fruin's (2007, 231) heuristic suggestion.[1] As a concept, textual instrument is considerably less metaphorical than instrumental text because it has a clear criterion: a capability of playing more than one single attached composition. Instrumental text is a label that lends itself easily to vague analogies between play and ergodic use, and, in some cases, instrumental texts are little more than good old hypertexts in disguise. Therefore, our discussion for the most part revolves around textual instruments and the kind of thinking and theoretization they provoke and require.

20.2 The discussion so far

20.2.1 *Wardrip-Fruin*

Wardrip-Fruin has addressed the topic of textual instruments in a short paper in 2003, more fully in 2007 and 2009, and also in a short paper co-written by David Durand (Durand and Wardrip-Fruin 2005). Wardrip-Fruin and his collaborators have also designed several compositions that illustrate the concepts he has proposed and developed: *Regime Change* (Wardrip-Fruin et al. 2004a), *News Reader* (Wardrip-Fruin et al. 2004b), and, an instrument-in-progress, *Cardplay* (Durand and Wardrip-Fruin 2005).

In his first paper on the subject Wardrip-Fruin provided the following definition: "a textual instrument is a tool for textual performance which may be used to play a variety of compositions" (Wardrip-Fruin 2003, 3). Compositions consist of "a body of text (and/or means of acquiring text) and a set of 'tunings' for the instruments used" (ibid.). The expression "a variety of compositions" comes close to Aarseth's cybertextual variety of expression while providing an interesting variation of the latter. To Aarseth cybertexts are machines and instruments can be seen as a subtype of them.

In Wardrip-Fruin's fullest treatment of textual instruments so far (Wardrip-Fruin 2007, 231–249), he discusses three specific works (*Arteroids*; *News Reader*; *Regime Change*) and foregrounds the concept of n-grams on which his two instruments are based. He also contrasts two major logics for structuring play (with a textual component): graphical and linguistic.[2] He sees the former being applied in many instrumental texts he discusses:

> For *riverIsland* play is primarily through the graphical/physical manipulation of the Quicktime movies, in *Pax* it is the collision detection as characters are caught and clicked; in *New Word Order* the movement of the first-person perspective and collision detection ... and in *Screen* it is the movement of the interactor's body and the collision detection of hitting words. (Wardrip-Fruin 2007, 235)

Wardrip-Fruin's two compositions for textual instruments, *Regime Change* (discussed in Chapter 3) and *News Reader*, "operate using the logic of n-gram statistical models of text (first used in textual play by Claude Shannon)" (Durand and Wardrip-Fruin 2005, 2). From Durand and Wardrip-Fruin's (2005, 3) point of view these instruments "are relatively easy to compose for, but relatively resistant to precise control." This stems from "the aleatoric nature of the automatic processes" and "the size and opaqueness of a statistical model of even a short text" (Durand and Wardrip-Fruin 2005, 2–3).

Generally speaking, the use of n-grams pays attention to "the frequencies of group of symbols rather than only individual symbols" (Wardrip-Fruin 2007, 237). In text generation, the groups of symbols are often syntagms of words (for example, two words following each other constitute a diagram, three words a trigram etc.) that form a basis for mixing two or several texts by indicating the sequences of text to be replaced. To compensate and counter-balance the aleatoric nature of this procedure, it is necessary to use generic, formal or thematic similarities among texts to create more coherence in the outcome, and therefore it is only logical that both *Regime Change* and *News Reader* use non-fictional texts as source texts to be played. *News Reader* is the more coherent [3] because it mixes two live news sources: the *Yahoo! News* RSS feed and alternative news sources found at *Common Dreams* (Wardrip-Fruin 2007, 246–247).

The use of n-grams connects Wardrip-Fruin's instruments to John Cayley's works in the 1990s: "This model (whether called n-grams or Markov Chains) is now widely used in natural language processing and generation, often in combination with other techniques. It has also been used in electronic literature, perhaps most extensively by John Cayley. At least seven of Cayley's works employ 'collocational' word-level digram procedures, including *Book Unbound*" (Wardrip-Fruin 2007, 239). In terms of n-grams, *Regime Change* continues the tradition by moving from two-gram to three- and four-gram generation (Wardrip-Fruin 2007, 243).

In a strict contrast to aleatoric and statistical procedures (and the strengths and weaknesses they exhibit), *Card Play*, Durand and Wardrip-Fruin's instrument-in-progress, is "designed to operate more directly out of human authorship (of texts and rules), with interaction techniques and infrastructural motifs more typical of hypertexts or rule-based artificial intelligence systems" (Durand and Wardrip-Fruin 2005, 3). It also aims to be "a blend of these parallel (non-intersecting) but closely related sets of techniques" (ibid.). From this perspective, textual instruments look like a new genre emerging from two major traditions at the literary end[4] of ergodic and digital literature: text generation (reflecting the AI idea or ideal of an intelligent machine) and hypertext (a simple tool or simple tools for non-linear presentation). (See also Wardrip-Fruin and Harrigan 2004, 165.)

For some reason, Wardrip-Fruin doesn't discuss *The Impermanence Agent* (Wardrip-Fruin et al. 1998–2002) as a textual instrument, although it seems to satisfy the criteria quoted earlier. The bits and pieces taken from net objects the user has recently viewed in a browser are not compositions in the classical sense, but, in principle, they are sources that allow an instrument to produce something (sounds, images, texts). As we noted in Chapter 3, it is possible to play *The Impermanence Agent* by explicitly connecting it to specific compositions (for example by consistently browsing one or several web fictions). Wardrip-Fruin's omission may seem curious as *The Impermanence Agent* clearly played several compositions in its time, but it is also understandable because *The Impermanence Agent* unlike *Regime Change* and *News Reader* had an inbuilt and non-negotiable finality to its process of play. By way of contrast, it could be played again and again. This makes *The Impermanence Agent* a borderline case between instrumental texts and textual instruments, and one could similarly regard *Regime Change* and *News Reader* as additional borderline cases because so far only one composition has been written for each of them.

These three works also illustrate three different basic relations and degrees of openness to source texts: *Regime Change* mixes two given texts (the report of the Warren Commission and the newspaper article on Saddam's fall), *The Impermanence Agent* has only one given text (the story written by Wardrip-Fruin) that is gradually erased by quotes from other texts the user either intentionally or unintentionally selects, and *News Reader* mixes whatever comes up in the news and therefore has no pre-given texts to restrict the interplay of texts.

20.2.2 Cayley

Both Cayley and Moulthrop use musical analogies in drafting and clarifying their ideas of instruments and textual play. Cayley explicitly refers to musical instruments, mixers and sequencers, and distinguishes two kinds of ergodics:

> My point is that we are currently writers trying to build relatively simple textual instruments that are intuitive and, hopefully, both affective and significant when they are played. I mean played as

musical instruments or sequencers or mixers are played. This is ergodic indeed, but still distinguishable from (hard) work or from the type of play in games which is rewarded by winning, by other forms of 'success' or simply by playability. (Cayley 2003, 11)

Cayley is well aware of the problems and complexities involved in thinking using musical analogues. Many doubts are related to rewards and pleasures of play and the skills and learning processes involved in it:

There are, now, a fast-growing myriad of literary object/ event/performances that are like games, like instruments, like automata, like simulations, like mirrors, like environments, and not only do we not quite know how to deal with them – read or play? watch or participate? – we are not sure that giving them the requisite close attention would ever allow us to get back as much (significance and affect) as we get back from more familiar games and instruments and existing cultural (literary) *forms*. Perhaps *riverIsland* is an instrument, but is it as pleasurable or rewarding to learn to play as a guitar? (Cayley 2007)

Rewards and pleasures are related to the problems of finding a proper balance between reading and playing, activities that are usually rewarding in different ways:

To play *riverIsland* like an instrument generates corresponding ambiguities. Playing well might well yield pleasure in your skill as well as some excess of significance and affect, beyond that which is already inscribed within the system of the work, but your playing might also distract you from the underlying configuration of *riverIsland* as something that was composed to be read and appreciated as poetic writing. (Cayley 2007)

In short, the delicate problem is this:

I can configure a poetic environment until it becomes playable, like an instrument, but it will not by dint of this potential become an "instrument" as we currently know them. Its range of expression will be constrained within an extended (and playably extensible) but limited field that is determined by the significance and affect already inscribed within the work, within the poetic environment in this case. (Cayley 2007)

Conventions and acquired skills also play their part, because players have to learn to play their instruments well enough. Cayley is able to put this in a larger scale literary perspective:

Any number of operations may be programmed and applied to the material of language. In a sense the operations associated with print publication and reading are simply one such, historically and culturally significant application, although its operations are not traditionally designed by those artists we call authors or writers. Writers have always been concerned with the publication, the paratextual programming, of their work; some deeply so: artist-poet printers and bookmakers come to mind, along with the poetic traditional developing from Mallarmé. Naturally some writers have gone on to explore the more radical control over textual representation that new media allow (as well as trying to realize theoretically the implications of these innovations). The problem is that there is no predetermined shape to the machines and instruments of textual representation in new media. (Cayley 2003, 11)

20.2.3 Moulthrop

Moulthrop also finds musical analogies useful and stresses the importance of folk instruments because "they do allow you to get in touch with the productive vocabulary very quickly" (Moulthrop 2006, 1). To Moulthrop, the connections between playable instruments and game design are also evident: "You have, with instruments, a text with behavior and temporal dimensions that in some ways map onto the temporal experience and interactive possibilities in game design" (ibid.).

In Moulthrop's case, instruments provide a certain horizon and direction within his oeuvre: "The idea of an instrumental text is part of my continuing movement away from node-link and disjunctive hypertext" and towards "a middle space between literary texts and ludic texts – between interactive fiction, or hypertext fiction, and games" (Moulthrop 2006, 1). This move or movement is partly inspired by Jim Rosenberg's idea of conjunctive and disjunctive hypertexts and also by the spatiality of comics as explored by Scott McCloud (Moulthrop 2006, 2). Equally important in this is also Peter Bogh Anderson's work with non-binary interfaces that is reflected in *Pax* (Moulthrop 2003a) in the following way: "The sprites respond to proximity of the cursor. There are click points. You can move to things and click on them to elicit action. But the process of approaching a sprite changes various states. In future works I'd like to remove the clicks and just work with a grammar of approach" (Moulthrop 2006, 3).

20.3 Predecessors: *Eliza* and *Book Unbound*

Although the concepts of textual instruments and instrumental texts are new, some of the actual works and practices are not. Text generation is a self-evident requirement in both kinds of text and although many early text generators were not ergodic (see Funkhouser 2007, 31–84), some of them were. The famous *Eliza* (Weizenbaum 1966) could be seen as an early instrumental text as it could play or try to play whatever the user decided to bring in contact with it. Still, the problem is that after a few sessions novelties grow thin and the limitations of *Eliza* become more evident and less amusing as the patterns in its responses became too obvious and the Eliza effect (Wardrip-Fruin 2009, 15) sets in.

The tradition of *Eliza* is alive and well, as Mateas and Stern's *Façade* (2002) demonstrates. Instead of replying using questions, the two computer-controlled characters of *Façade* "interpret everything you do as a zero-sum taking sides 'game'" (Stern's private email to Wardrip-Fruin, quoted in Wardrip-Fruin 2007, 220). *Façade* is not a game but an ergodic drama, the playability of which is seriously restricted by the undeniable strengths of its underlying structure: short duration and invariable outcome.

The second crucial step in the history of instrumental texts is John Cayley's *Book Unbound* (1995a), for the very reason of the slow accumulative process within which the user may learn to understand the system better and is rewarded by its responses that grow more personalized if the user is active enough or somewhat consistent in his efforts. *Book Unbound* offers more rewarding forms of resistance and improvement for the user than simple chatterbots like *Eliza* and therefore it takes a much longer time to feel that one has exhausted the work and one's own curiosity; in short, *Book Unbound* invites long-term engagement. An important part in the process of learning to play *Book Unbound* is the reduction of the most annoying kind of indeterminacy: outcomes that seem totally random are the danger that haunts less carefully orchestrated productions of variety of expression.

With *Book Unbound*, the user plays a kind of natural selection by adding the instances he evaluates as the best and most interesting (or simply as good and interesting enough) back into the work's inaccessible database. This reproductive act raises the stakes for the user. If everything goes fine and the subsequent text generations are satisfactory, then that works not only as an incentive to continue the process but also as a reward, because the user can justly feel that he is doing and has learned to do something right. If, contrariwise, the results of the process grow in an unsatisfactory way the user cannot help but think that he's been doing something wrong; under such circumstances it is perhaps more likely that he will start again than that he will blame the work (and the work only) for providing uninteresting outcomes. The longer the process goes on the more personalized the transient but saveable outcomes become, and this gradual appropriation is also similar to what happens when a novice has learned enough and can say with certainty that this is my instrument (both generically and particularly, that is, this kind of instrument is the kind I can play and this particular copy of an instrument is uniquely mine).

It is also helpful that the process of learning to play *Book Unbound* is as fuzzy as learning processes tend to be: the precise behavior and rules of the text generation are not revealed and neither are all textons. The user will quickly know enough to begin (and doesn't have to consult any massive paratext instructing him either before or during play) and will learn more as the process goes on, but will never know everything; the work doesn't become transparent at any point in the teleologically infinite process.

20.4 Instrumental texts on the verge of becoming textual instruments

Although Wardrip-Fruin (2007, 221) labels *Text Rain* (Utterback and Achituv 1999) as playable art the case may not be that simple, because *Text Rain* allows its users to play with letters and words. In any case, Camille Utterback's thinking is important to discussions of playability and instruments because it addresses the issues of interfaces and the user's bodily involvement in play.

Utterback (2004, 218–219) distinguishes between practical and poetic interfaces. The former are about "maintaining the user's sense of control" and therefore "representations on the screen must respond to the user in a logical and predictable way" (Utterback 2004, 218) whereas the latter may explore other possibilities such as questioning "the line between bodies and language by physically putting the user in an unusual 'position' with regards to the words" (Utterback 2004, 219).

Although the examples (including several works of her own) that Utterback describes in her article are not illogical and unpredictable, they still illustrate the differences in bodily involvement and the manipulation of texts. These differences (roughly between texts that require only average hand and eye coordination and the rest that demand more extensive bodily involvement from the user) are important not only in the general theoretization of ergodic literature, but also in understanding textual instruments and instrumental texts. In *Text Rain* (Utterback and Achituv 1999), which responds to "a wide variety of human gestures and motions," there is "no wrong way to interact" with the piece (Utterback 2004, 221). Once the user understands the correlation of her or his bodily projection and behavior of the text (letters need to be stopped and gathered to be read) the rest is easy and follows the logic of the user's or users' movements. Similar simple and effective correlations between the user's body and the behavior of the text characterize Utterbeck's other examples, from *The Legible City* (Shaw 1989) and its partial inversion in Utterback's *Vicissitudes* (1998; described in Utterback 2004, 224–226) to *As Much as You Love Me* (Kruglanski 2000; described and discussed in Kruglanski 2007, 82–83 and in Utterback 2004, 225–226), which use, among other things, the user's vertical movement up and down the ladder and a forcefeedback mouse to embody common metaphors (such as up and down for states of mind) and in most cases offer the user a non-complicated presence in both physical and virtual space.

As important as these kinds of interface are, their nature is also almost diametrically opposed to Wardrip-Fruin's approach: "However, a textual instrument need not be like a prepared piano. The direct selection of text, rather than manipulation of a non-linguistic device, can be its interface" (Wardrip-Fruin 2003, 3). By the same token, there are significant similarities in Utterback's and Wardrip-Fruin's thinking: "Understanding at a gut level how a textual instrument's probability spaces function for a given composition is part of learning to play that piece" (ibid.). The major differences are located in the relationship between the instruments' affordances and the possible textual outcomes that doesn't have to be "one-to-one at all levels" (ibid.) as they seem to be in Utterback's examples that are not textual instruments but instrumental texts. Nevertheless, Utterback's instrumental texts *Text Rain*, *Vicissitudes*, and *See/saw* (Utterback and Chapman 2001) could easily be converted into textual instruments playing many other compositions than those they are currently attached to.

The usual "critical" approaches to works such as *Text Rain* write it off as merely or almost frivolous.[5] However, *Text Rain*'s source text, Evan Zimroth's poem "Talk, you" (1993), is about bodies and language and thus there is a thematic connection between the text and the user's configurative behavior.[6] This is not to say *Text Rain* is complicated or that it could not be made more complicated in terms of both bodily and textual requirements.

Similar thematic-ergodic connections are potentially all around us to be discovered and implemented in instrumental texts and textual instruments (hypothetically between exercise mats and novels about sports, alcometers and Bukowski's oeuvre, or Bluetooth vibrators and pornography). This plenitude of almost readymade interface media for networked textual instruments along with developments in ubiquitous, wearable and otherwise ever present digital technology puts even more emphasis on the potential of textual instruments.

20.5 Real and hypothetical textual instruments of Jim Andrews and Mark Bernstein

Jim Andrews' *Arteroids* (2001–) clearly satisfies the criteria of a textual instrument as multiple texts can be composed for it and played by it. *Arteroids* is repurposing the well-known arcade game *Asteroids*; the game's mechanics are left intact, and the players shoot and explode different kind of objects: words and syntagms that produce literary special effects that become more meaningful if the player is aware of certain avant-garde aesthetics including lettrism and sound poetry. Andrews' paratext (Andrews 2005) links *Arteroids* primarily to the tradition of cut-ups but in the context of textual instruments it is relevant in three other respects.

First, because it is like intelligent machinima, but unlike machinima it retains the game mechanics (making it a game modification and not a non-game). Second, because it uses an already existing system and turns it first into an instrumental text and then with *Word for Weirdos* a textual (or literary) instrument that can play other texts than the ones originally selected by Andrews. Third, because it is well-balanced. *Arteroids* has three modes of engagement; in addition to game and play modes the user can switch them off to enter what could be called a literary mode and concentrate only on the texts the system otherwise plays with. *Arteroids* is rich in intertextuality and in commenting on experimental literary traditions but also very playable in its flexibility. Its metarules allow users to decide how clearly it presents the source texts and how much time there will be for the reader to both read and play. This solution achieves the balance between playing and reading by leaving it to each user to decide and try out according to their idiosyncratic preferences. Instead of trying to achieve playability by other and perhaps more complicated and difficult ways, it retains the guaranteed playability of an arcade classic, and adds literary content on top of that mainly in the form of quotes and excepts from other texts – a move that turns its borrowed game mechanics into new forms of commentary.

Still, this borrowed interactivity, to use Orit Kruglanski's term (Kruglanski 2007, 77–79), doesn't really solve the issue. The non-reading player (NRP) can choose to ignore the bits and pieces of sound poetry (by turning the audio off) and also ignore the splintering and exploding words to simply focus on enjoying the borrowed game mechanics. Although it is unlikely that such users are in the majority (because such players would be better off by playing the original arcade classic), they still demonstrate the potential independence of game mechanics in relation to the flow or shape of signs to be interpreted as poetry. Similarly, the non-playing reader (NPR) can avoid or minimize game-related challenges. In this respect, *Arteroids*[7] is not a conceptual fusion of a game and poetry, but instead a user-friendly compartmentalized hybrid of the two. One can speculate whether the result would be different if the audio track were used only for poetry, freeing the user's hands and eyes for playing the game.

Mark Bernstein's two systems exist as descriptions and the present author is unaware of any literary compositions written for them. As systems they are described by Bernstein and Greco (Bernstein 2001; Bernstein and Greco 2004) and discussed by Stern (2004) and Durand and Wardrip-Fruin (2005). Bernstein and Greco (2004, 171) call these systems sculptural hypertext systems, as they remove "unwanted connections" from what they call a tangle. In *Card Shark*, the user is dealt seven cards (or nodes) that may "specify constraints on the context in which they appear" (ibid.). The key constraint for the user's progress is the following rule:

> The constraints for each of the player's cards are evaluated. Cards whose conditions are not satisfied are disabled; the reader sees at most a brief title and an indication of what conditions need to be satisfied for the card to be seen. (Bernstein and Greco 2004, 172)

This seems to be a more complicated (but also somewhat less elegant) way of introducing conditional links and judging from Bernstein and Greco's (2004, 171) hypothetical examples (i.e. constraints that specify that certain nodes need to be read early in the process or not at all and that characters are introduced before they are treated otherwise) the constraints and modifications of the context may simply work towards creating more coherence for those who lament the supposed lack of it in hypertext fiction. *Thespis* "extends the core idea of *Card Shark*" (Bernstein and Greco 2004, 175) and ultimately both systems "present alternative approaches to hypertext" (Bernstein and Greco 2004, 179).

However, these alternative approaches do not seem to have materialized or been realized since the publication of Bernstein's first paper. This may reflect to some extent a generic stagnation of hypertext fiction and poetry and also that the distance between the two genres and communities of hypertext and "interactive" fiction remains as significant as it has been for the last two decades, precluding hybrids and crossovers between them. In cybertextual terms, Bernstein's new systems remedy the static dynamics of *StorySpace* hypertexts by introducing intratextonic dynamics (one of the key characteristics of "interactive fiction" in addition to personal perspective), but the overall design is still dominated by the usual questions concerning how to connect fragments, conjunctively or disjunctively (Rosenberg 2001), and how to present them to the user, sequentially or simultaneously.

In the context of textual instruments, the most interesting aspect of *Thespis* is its theatricality: "Each actor moves across the bounded, two-dimensional space that represents the stage" (Bernstein and Greco 2004, 175). Only one of these represents the reader and the other agents are computational structures that select actions "that are likely to improve their happiness"(ibid.). These autonomous actors are not there to present a puzzle and help the reader in solving it, but to provide "the *appearance* of intentionally and individuality" (ibid.). This appearance is not necessarily adversarial either, and therefore the friction between actors and the user could be turned in directions other than competitive. One way to increase this dynamic is to go beyond the idea of the reader missing action (Bernstein and Greco 2004, 175), which doesn't happen in static hypertext fiction, and let the user learn to control, affect or manipulate (to a varying degree) the other actors or a majority of them.

Generally speaking, Bernstein as well as Moulthrop and Durand and Wardrip-Fruin's *Cardplay* seem to share common intentions: either to break away from stagnated traditions or to make them more dynamic. This is best expressed by Moulthrop's search for a middle space between "interactive fiction, or hypertext fiction, and games" (Moulthrop 2006, 1). What these three genres and modes have in common (always possible exceptions aside) is that unlike play they are or imply terminable processes with clear finality: interactive fictions are most of all puzzles to be solved, games are competitions to be won, and hypertext fiction is usually a totality of static nodes to be read in its never changing entirety (its only variable feature being the presentation order of its nodes). Play is more interminable, there's no clear finality, and in a way that is even more challenging to literary tradition play is enjoyable self-expression. In ergodic terms, the differences are not primarily situated in user functions, but in user objectives, discourse levels, and the differences between anamorphic and metamorphic texts and processes. The distance between interpretative reception and ergodic work may well be smaller than the one between ergodic work and play, especially if the latter is also taken to be self-expression. As musical instruments clearly are machines for self-expression, the inspiring analogue between them and textual instruments and more generally playable ergodic literature merits another look.

20.6 The musical analogy

On closer inspection, the obvious analogy between more or less hypothetical textual instruments and existing musical instruments is complicated and breaks down in an interesting way. The aspiring musician learns to master an instrument either by playing increasingly difficult compositions or by using the mastered instrument for gradually more advanced improvisation. Several instruments can play the same composition (separately or together), some instruments such as piano can be played by more than one person at the same time, and several different instruments are usually required for a proper public performance of most classical and modern compositions. Equivalents of all these fundamental characteristics are lacking in the field of literature.

Playing a musical instrument is not only an open-ended learning process, but also a process characterized by certain given constraints, especially if the instrument is used for playing a composition. The musician needs to internalize not only the general cultural conventions of performance (given that the use of instruments is usually both solitary and social), but first and foremost learn the manipulative rules of the chosen instrument with the typical goal of as faultless a performance of a prewritten composition as possible. Still, musical notation is not exact except in its programmable forms, and therefore human instrumentalists always have room for variation in their performative interpretation. This performative aspect is necessarily very sensitive to the player's embodied skills: there are countless small bodily differences that result in a great variety of different performances or "interpretations" of exactly the same composition. In principle, keyboard and mouse could be tuned until they were as responsive as a proper musical instrument, in which case the usually insignificant differences in timing and strength (among other factors) would yield a variety of textual, visual or auditive outcomes.

Playing for fun, improvisation (individual or collective), and varying well-known compositions require skills that usually take quite some time to develop. In ergodic literature, this learning period is likely to cause problems for motivation, as reading a poorly constructed text or textual outcome again and again before something interesting or challenging begins to appear is not rewarding at all (except from the writer's patient point of view). A related problem is the possible repertoire that becomes available after a certain adequate level of skill is reached. In music, thousands of compositions are available to be played by instrumentalists who have sufficiently mastered their instruments and that is one of the crucial motivational factors that encourages instrumentalists to continue learning. In ergodic literature, mastering an instrument that is, in principle, capable of playing (or at least resulting in) several compositions gives many fewer rewards to the player-in-progress. In short, what would be the point of learning to play an instrument if the learned skill would not be useful for decades?

Western music shares a basic notational system, on top of which electronic and digital composers and compositions have added an extensive layer of additional parameters. This kind of precision and the resulting comparability is by necessity and tradition lacking from literature, ergodic or not, although at least the former is usually accompanied by precise enough instructions of what to do. In the classical age, the concept of poetics could be interpreted to function in a way comparable to musical notation, but the revival of prescriptive poetics in movements like the OuLiPo constitutes only a small subsystem within the literary field as we know it. Nevertheless, it could serve as one possible point of departure, especially if the procedures and operations the group developed and studied were transformed from poetic creation to the functioning of a literary medium and the methods of play and reception that would open up the Oulipian corpus to variable outcomes. In short, what lies ahead in that area is the ludification or ergodication of Oulipian practices and playtexts (Motte 1995). To take only one example, Wardrip-Fruin's n-gram instruments are in Oulipian terms substitutions at the level of syntagms. Many other possible ways of combining operations and linguistic objects remain available, such as larding, which is addition at the level of sentences.

Instruments can be used in highly unpredictable ways, and even destroyed as part of the performance (as Harpo Marx and Jimi Hendrix have entertainingly shown), but these extremes only serve to emphasize that the instrumentalist–player is supposed to control the instrument. In some respects, the possible shift of control from the author or the text to the user–player is diametrically opposed to positions various literary avant-gardes prefer (because the user is supposed to do all the hard work in deciphering the text and its more or less concealed relation to traditions it is set to change or ridicule), although an end-player using text machines for enjoyment and as his or her means of expression may seem the apotheosis of many worn-out ideals of the historical avant-gardes that aimed at freeing the recipient and erasing the differences between art and life. The potential for the player's self-expression is probably the point at which textual and musical instruments are almost diametrically opposed to each other. *Arteroids* and its *Word for Weirdos* provide one possible solution because the player may write or choose the text and then use the instrument to play with it. In this model, the authors are responsible for the instrument and its "tunings" and it is up to the players to find suitable texts for the machine. This kind of division of labor is also implicit in *Text Rain* and *Screen* (Wardrip-Fruin et al. 2002–), as one may ask what exactly would be lost in these two instrumental texts if they also used other texts. The separation of interfaces and manipulative devices from the texts to be manipulated is to some degree similar to the separation of composers from craftsmen building and tuning musical instruments for yet another group of people to play.

Control, at least to some degree, presupposes precision and predictability in the feedback loop between the player and the instrument. Fully or excessively random instruments would be abandoned quickly because they do not offer the possibility of developing and improving one's mastery and control of the instrument. The problem is that in ergodic and generative literature it is easy to generate variation using random and semi-or quasi-random procedures. Contrary to this, the aim of providing the player with interesting and intelligent responses that are more predictable and determinate than unpredictable and indeterminate requires heuristic and precise analysis of the texts the player is supposed to play with the instrument. This is potentially a point at which literary theory and practice draw close to each other.

Literary tradition contains at least five easy dialectics that could be adapted as flexible frames for the functioning of an instrument: the text as an object and a process, the work and the oeuvre, the text and the intertext, the reader's and the text's control over reading, and the maintenance and destruction of the text. The task and pleasure of the reader-user-player-instrumentalist would be to maintain, break or (re)create the balance between these oppositional poles. The instruments could also be tuned by theories that are precise enough; in addition to the Oulipian corpus there are many other almost readymade candidates ranging from Freud's case history of Schreber[8] to the particularities of the traversal function in cybertext theory. All these theories are more useful or instrumental for building textual instruments than instrumental texts, as the former should be able to handle any given text and not just the one that comes with the system.

Instruments also inevitably raise the perhaps uncomfortable question of skills and differences in skills: every instrument is not for everyone and the differences among players are both obvious and irreducible. The same is, of course, true with any other skill including reading, but this is also something that is usually concealed in literary discussions: among myriad other cultural differences (in gender, class, ethnicity etc.) the differences of skills are delegated to the realm of education and treated as educational (and not aesthetic) problems in relation to whatever is considered to be adequate in terms of contemporary literacy.

Finally, electronic and digital (or virtual) musical instruments that are not limited by the constraints of analog instruments could form a starting point for tunings and designs of textual instruments, because programmable instruments could be modeled by each other and also embedded in each other, in for example the way Toni Dove's interactive film *Artificial Changelings* (1998) used the software of David Rokeby's *Very Nervous System* (1986–1990) to mediate between images and the user's bodily movement (Dixon 2007, 591). This option of borrowed, embedded, and re-appropriated instruments is for some reason missing from the literary field. Highly sophisticated virtual instruments are in extensive use in electronic and digital music, and to convert some of these for textual production (even as a side effect of the foregrounded production of music) would immediately supply many affordances ranging from precise ways of controlling and combining oral and written language to an extensive vocabulary of temporal manipulation (Eskelinen and Kuitunen 2013).

20.7 Conclusion: dimensions and directions

As we have seen, the metaphors and heuristics of play and instruments move in at least four different directions: music and musical instruments (*riverIsland* and *Under Language*), child's play and bodily improvisation (*Text Rain*), arcade and card games (*Arteroids*, *Card Shark*, *Card Play*), and drama and performance (*Surrender Control*, *Thespis*, *Façade*). One could perhaps add another potential metaphor to those four: medical and scholarly instruments that extend our perceptive capability to things not seen or otherwise grasped without them. Medical instruments and especially modest everyday medical devices (thermometers and other meters measuring blood pressure or pulse) could be used to integrate the user's varying bodily states into play with texts.

As we saw, the ergodic "genre" of textual instruments is in its infancy, existing mostly in the form of theoretizations and speculations. The textual instruments that exist usually have only one composition currently attached to them, with the notable exception of *Arteroids* and its user-friendly extensions. In addition to these, several instrumental texts could be converted into textual instruments, most easily by changing the currently flowing or raining texts to some other texts. It seems then that we have reached a certain critical edge that constrains and prevents any academic endeavor such as this one from going much further into the subject. Nevertheless, certain general observations can be made and certain dimensions and directions discerned to conclude this chapter.

It may well be that the problems and challenges play and textual instruments present to literary theory and practice are tied to our basic long duration (in Braudel's sense) assumptions and presuppositions of literature. Some of these were touched on in the chapters that discussed transtextuality, the textual whole, and the interplay of text types. It is likely that successful textual instruments utilize other kinds of hyper-, inter-, meta-, and architextual relation than those that have been so far recognized, and they do not subordinate their inner and outer dynamics to traditional notions of textual wholes. Such texts may supplement themselves from the outside, vary not only their content but their form, structure and behavior, and allow their parts and phases more autonomy and autonomous development than has hitherto been realized or understood to be possible.

In addition to these inherited and implicit cultural constraints, several pragmatic choices are becoming more visible. As *Arteroids* demonstrates, the vast variety of readymade game mechanics and game structures are there to be repurposed and appropriated or simply filled with different kind of content. The variety of almost readymade devices is not limited to games (as our references to digital musical and medical instruments showed), but game structures self-evidently guarantee that the instrument is and remains playable. *Text Rain* underscores the importance and potential of involving the user's body and bodily pleasures in the suggested play, and *Vicissitudes*, among many other instruments relying on audio, shows another way to combine texts and bodily movement. The general importance of audio and human (or inhuman) voice in delivering the text may well lie in the way that it frees the player's eyes for other purposes than reading. *Book Unbound* and Cayley's ambient aesthetics (Cayley 2004c) foreground long-term personalized processes that allow meditative presences and absences of the player who doesn't have to stay continuously (fully) alert. *riverIsland* and its transliteral morphs create a vocabulary of transitional stages that play with textual co-presences and their legibility. *News Reader* is free of pre-supplied texts and is therefore on the verge of almost complete separation of instruments from compositions; composers and craftsmen that design and build musical instruments are usually two different breeds and if that institutionalized difference is repeated in the field of literature it would be up to each reader–player what and what kind of texts to play with the instruments the author–designers created. The pioneering efforts of Cayley, Moulthrop, and Wardrip-Fruin in this respect all point to more dynamic textual structures than those the current generic and experimental templates include. Should we ask what the play they are after is about, all we can do is risk one final hypothesis.

In earlier chapters, we saw that cybertext theory includes and perhaps balances two major dynamics of the text (cf. the parameters of dynamics and transience) and the user (cf. the parameter of user function). If these are translated into the language of rules, the former come close to gameworld rules and the latter to manipulation rules. However, there is a third alternative provided by metarules. In digital games, these affect the settings of the other rules and they are not supposed to be the target of the gameplay. In broad cultural terms, this may be because games are supposed to be fair, but as we all know literature is perhaps the best aesthetic instrument to deal with the unfair, the uncanny, and the unbalanced. Consequently, one could suggest that textual instruments should allow the players to play not only according to manipulation rules and gameworld rules but also about them, through metarules that they may learn to tweak and affect for their amusement and enlightenment.[9]

NOTES

Chapter 1

1 In *Cybertext* Aarseth represents his theory as an extension to literary theory, challenges the primacy of narrative by introducing ergodic discourses, studies both literature and games, and presents a heuristic theory of media that shifts the focus from what a medium supposedly is to what it actually does. In short, the book more offers much more than perspectives on ergodic literature.

2 Co-incidentally *Cybertext* (Aarseth 1997, 103–5) includes a schematic model of internal structure similar to Wardrip-Fruin's model.

3 "In art and literature we may have to configure in order to be able to interpret whereas in games we have to interpret in order to configure and proceed from the beginning to the winning or some other situation." (Eskelinen 2001)

Chapter 2

1 It is important to notice that the relation between textons and scriptons is arbitrary in digital media and not trivial as in non-digital (projector/screen) cinema. That's the "essence" of its unique dual materiality, which stems from the (historical) separation of the storage medium from the interface medium (Aarseth 1997, 43).

2 The model is not closed, as the parameters of the cybertext typology can be supplemented, changed, and removed, or made more detailed should the evidence or need arise.

3 The all important links of hypertext theory form only one of the seven dimensions, and it is exactly this broader view that is valuable, as it gives us more to think of than simple link and node-structures. Consequently, it doesn't make much sense to contrast links with

the "computational" as Hayles (2001a) does, because they are both included in Aarseth's model. Hayles' own theoretical contribution (albeit not her only one), cyberlliterature, then becomes just a simplified version of Aarseth's cybertext.

4   The theories of audiovisual media are far from reaching equally comprehensive and inclusive conceptualisations and models, despite several in-depth media-archaeological studies from Ceram 1965 to Huhtamo 1996, Manovich 2001, and Zielinski 1999 and 2006 and their interest in the history of machines for seeing and hearing.

5   The concept of ergodic literature cross-cutting a wide variety of media is also able to signal an end or at least a well-grounded alternative to the use of such unfocused, muddled, and overtly hyped concepts as interactivity. The distinction between ergodic and non-ergodic literature is clear and pragmatic and much easier to verify and work with than the myriad more or less insufficient and contradictory definitions of agency and interactivity.

6   Cf. chapter 12 in McHale's *Postmodernist Fiction* (1987).

7   To my knowledge this deduction and the statistical method behind it has not been questioned in sometimes heated discussions around *Cybertext*.

8   This is not to say that a medium doesn't matter, as there probably are also other than historical differences in the range of media positions that different media can occupy. Seen in this light the typology could be applied to pinpoint media specificities in much greater accuracy than N. Katherine Hayles' (2002, 29–33) media specific analysis currently does.

9   There are three obvious sources for additional textons (Eskelinen 2000): the text itself (as in Cayley's *Book Unbound*), the user (as in most MUDs), or an outside text or texts (as in Wardrip-Fruin's *The Impermanence Agent*).

10 Bootz's description of cybertext theory is not entirely accurate as the latter also includes "a schematic model of internal structure" that we already discussed above.

11 In his early paper on computer games (Aarseth 1998 [1995], 85–6) Aarseth proposes a category of user position.

12 See Parlett 1999, 21.

13 It is different to be able to skip scriptons at will (tmesis) and to necessarily and involuntarily miss some of them.

14 Five second intervals would make transient time the dominant

mode of time, whereas five minute intervals between the program's interventions would very likely make *Hegirascope* seem intransient.

15   In this holographic poem substantives turn into (or are seen to turn into) adjectives and vice versa relative to the spectators' perspective affected by his movement.

16   *Agrippa*'s (Gibson 1992) accompanying art book was intended to include fading images executed in "disappearing" ink. Exposure to light or air would have made the images gradually vanish, but due to technical problems Dennis Anspaugh's idea was never concretised. Even if such fading ink were used and applied to words the transient process would have been irreversible – a severe limitation of transient possibilities readily available in digital media.

17   Aarseth's model is descriptive and focused on what the existing genres (hypertext fictions, text adventures etc.) do and not on what they could do, which is our "poetic" focus in this chapter.

18   This is typical of heuristic models in general and is not to be considered a defect. Aarseth's model has more than enough analytical and explanatory power compared to its theoretical alternatives.

19   It may be important to note that in cybertext theory permanent scriptons do not imply static dynamics. Although one could argue that printed signs are materially permanent (they don't move or morph or change their position on a page or disappear except through material deterioration and damage) the way some digital signifiers obviously are not, that difference is of no importance to cybertext theory (Aarseth 1997, 65–70). Printed game books such as *The Money Spider* (Waterfield and Davies 1988) have intratextonic dynamics because the reader is not supposed to read the same strings of signs every time, although the strings of signs as such are as permanent as the static scriptons in *Moby Dick*.

20   Interval control is one of the categories of internal time in Elverdam and Aarseth's game typology (Elverdam and Aarseth 2007) that will be discussed in chapters 14 and 16.

Chapter 3

1   If textons are involved it is only because they are identical to scriptons; i.e. the classic theories move back and forth in the codex corpus within which the difference between textons and scriptons doesn't usually become important.

2 This type bears no resemblance to the hypertextuality theorised a decade later by Landow and Bolter. The relation of Genette's concept to Ted Nelson's ideas of hypertextuality, already relatively well-known at the time of the publication of Genette's *Palimpsests* (1982), is more complex. If actual and potential nelsonian systems such as *Xanadu* or *ZigZag* (see Lukka and Ervasti 2001 for details) would contain and archive every subsequent modification of every text ever included in them, they could be described as hypertextual machines also in Genette's sense. Throughout this chapter, however, we'll use Genette's concept.

3 See Aarseth 1997, 65.

4 As opposed to autographic sequels written by the same author.

5 In order to see the full scope of changed relationships between and within texts we should free ourselves from the confusion promoted by the old-school hypertext theory (cf. Landow 1992) that saw links embodying the post-structuralist ideas and conceptualisations of intertextuality. Obviously, links can be used to make explicit references and transclusions will work as direct quotations, if for some obscure reason we wish merely to emphasize, foreground or boost the traditional notions of intertextuality. However, it should be equally obvious that although links have been too often confused with intertextuality, there are both intertextual relations that cannot be shown by links, and various uses of links that have nothing whatsoever to do with traditional intertextuality. Every traditional notion of intertextuality is ultimately dependent on the unpredictably varying interpretative and transpositional skills of the readers and this dimension can neither be reduced to links nor fully expressed in them. On the other hand, the links forming concrete connections (instead of mere references) between online hypertexts are already potentially very different from their distant print relatives, as unlike the latter they are not merely interpretative and they could also be timed, changed, conditioned, chained, concealed, randomized and layered for complex effects the tradition knows nothing about.

6 That can be obtained from Wardrip-Fruin et al. 2002.

7 Given the ambiguity in Genette's definitions of hypertextuality (concerning only an earlier or another text) we can have at least two interpretations of the hypotext. It can be either a text published before (such as the newspaper article that is to be transformed in *Regime Change*) or a previous text published as a part of the machine transforming it (such as Wardrip-Fruin's original story in *The Impermanence Agent*). In this chapter we'll use the latter

interpretation without necessarily resorting to Genette's (1997a, 52) hypothesis of an allographic ad-hoc hypotext.

8 In a mesostic poem a vertical phrase or word intersects the middle of horizontal lines.

9 In Genette's terms described earlier in this chapter.

10 "If texts are laid out in a regular grid, as a table of letters, one table for the source and one table for the target, to morph transliterally from one text (one table of letters) to another, is to work out, letter-by-letter, how the source letters will become the target ones." (John Cayley; http://www.shadoof.net/in/intext01.html)

11 The horizontal texts can transform to vertical texts but not to other horizontal texts and the same logic applies to the vertical texts.

12 Of course a print volume could in thousands of pages record and reproduce every single step in the 512 transformation processes in *riverIsland*, but such a copy wouldn't be either transient or ergodic.

13 Typing yes or no hardly constitutes an intertextual let alone a hypertextual event.

14 The dimensions of user position and user objective are omitted, as the main purpose of this table is simply to visualize the general point made in the discussion of different behavioral transformations.

15 There is an obvious difference between the Oulipian practices that necessarily involve previous texts, such as perverbs, and those that don't, such as lipograms. See also Genette's (1997b, 39–53) discussion of Oulipian practices and Roubaud's (1998, 41) dismissive comment on it.

16 If the text is programmed to vary its expression and/or to supplement it from the outside, there's no reason why this variability couldn't sometimes affect also the text's architextual determinants (genres, modes, discourse types,) although I'm not aware of any actual examples of such mode or genre shifters.

17 This could be interpreted to be the case with Quoneau's *Exercices de style* (1947). Still, its 49 texts are stylistic variations of each other without any one of them being specified as a hypotext. Moreover, none of them could be said to be a prior text, unlike Wang's texts in *riverIsland* and Wardrip-Fruin's original story in *The Impermanence Agent*.

18 This behavior of *The Impermanence Agent* is related mainly to intertextuality, but it could be turned into hypertextual "mode" too if the user were persistent and patient enough to limit his browsing to only one or two sites.

Chapter 4

1 With the exception of their transient time, various kinetic literary works on video and film share the same values.

2 Some critics (cf. Douglas 2001; Gardner 2003; Mangen 2007) have conducted small-scale studies on how hypertext fictions are being read, but that's about all there's to it. We know next to nothing about how text generators such as *Book Unbound* or textual instruments such as *Regime Change* and *The Impermanence Agent* are being used. To make matters worse, some reader-response scholars cannot even understand the basic concepts characterizing how their newly found research objects function and what kind of textual behavior their empirically studied readers have to face: "Empirical study of readers underlines the inadequacy of Eskelinen's characterization of literary texts as »static, intransient, determinate«: readers show not only considerable variation between their readings (pointing to the indeterminacy of the literary text), but also much flexibility within readings in the perspectives taken from one episode to the next." (Miall 2003) Miall's category mistakes are all the more astonishing because he is "knowingly" participating in the cybertext debate without realising that Aarseth's determinability (and mine) has nothing to do with the always and already variable interpretations of readers, which are not news to anyone. See also Schäfer 2010 for the problems of applying reader-response theories to literary objects on and beyond the screen.

3 Needless to say it is not reducible to any of these dimensions.

4 Certain artists' books may complicate the process but cannot deny complete access to readers persistent enough.

5 Recently Wardrip-Fruin's (2009) three effects have shed new light upon the relation between textual surfaces and processes.

6 See http://toccobrator.com/classic.html for details.

7 We come back to these and other assumptions in chapters 8 and 16 that are more specifically devoted to time in narratives and games.

8 As opposed to interpreted content.

9 This happens through the mediation of the user's browsing activities, but the user is not in the position to directly add textons as he is in *Book Unbound.*

10 This possibility was discussed in more detail in the context of transtextuality.

11 That perhaps mirrors a common control structure (repeat/while).

12 According to Aarseth's definition (1994, 51), non-linear texts don't present their strings of signs in one fixed (temporal or spatial) sequence because of the shape, mechanisms or conventions of the text.

13 In other words, two or several simultaneous appearances or disappearances of signs are presented on the reading surface.

14 As always there are borderline cases. William Poundstone's *Project for Tachistoscope* (2005) utilizes subliminal effects in presenting a looped Flash-narrative one word at a time. Although the work is non-ergodic and strictly sequential, the positioning, size and very short duration of each word accompanied with visual effects and the audio track very effectively undermine the user's ability to piece together a semantically valid story. On the other hand, it is not impossible and after a few additional reading-viewings the task could or perhaps should be completed. From the theoretical perspective adapted in this study, *Project for Tachistoscope* is a fine example of spatio-temporal sequencing and transient time. Its aesthetics of disturbance and its paratextual explicitness correlating concrete poetry to manipulative advertisments bring to the fore the questions of misappropriation and possibly malign cultural contexts of literary media. One may be tempted to ask whether we need separate machines for the reception of such works. In Poundstone's case, however, a simple video recorder would do to slow down the flow of scriptons.

15 Of these discourse levels, see Aarseth 1995, 141 and 171–7.

16 Pattern poetry is Dick Higgins' term for pre–20th century visual poetry (Higgins 1987).

17 There's no upper limit to the number of possible scriptons *Eliza* may produce, but the user can read all that is presented to him in the session both initiated and terminated by him. The user will soon experience the Eliza effect (Wardrip-Fruin 2009, 32–8) that affects his approach to scriptons and how to play with them.

18 Perhaps ergodic work should be divided into non-strategic and strategic forms.

19 Here too we have an epistemological problem. How do we know there will be no resolution at some distant point in the future? This is just one example of many new and intertwined epistemological and ontological problems not to be found in modernist and postmodernist fiction.

20 Perhaps one should distinguish between text-based and link-based schools of hypertext readers and scholars. To the latter the proof of the much hyped inexhaustibility of hypertext fiction is ultimately

grounded in the devastating number of possible paths through the text. Such readers are probably more familiar, and certainly more at home, with mainstream fiction than experimental texts with altering perspectives and multiple fragmented story lines (and other standard tricks of the trade). The latter types of fiction already disrupt and complicate the reader's cumulative gathering of knowledge and validity of the hypothesis he makes; as each new segment, sequence or node has to be interpretatively connected to the hypothesized whole one could argue that the order in which these segments, sequences or nodes are read shouldn't matter too much.

21 We could add conventions from audiovisual media to the list. For example simple transient texts such as *The Dreamlife of Letters* could be seen as textual movies. This type of domestication should work for those users that are not familiar with video and other non-digital kinetic poetry.

22 Should we want to cybertextually update Barthes' variety of pleasures, we may have to add (given the communication and control aspects inherent in cybertext theory) several ergodic "perversions" to the scene beginning with voyeurs and exhibitionists exploiting the possibilities of multi-user communication and sadists and masochists overtly interested in the control of the feedback loops.

Chapter 5

1 This opposition between narrative and ergodic texts is one of the key subtexts in the debate between ludologists and narrativists that we'll pay close attention to in chapter 12.

2 Aarseth (1994) divides cybertexts into determinate and indeterminate ones.

3 As ergodic texts are not a novelty introduced by the emergence of digital media, but existed well before the technologies of paper and print (*I Ching*), one could imagine that they would already have been recognized and conceptualised as a text type or a discourse mode, but that doesn't seem to be the case.

4 Therefore ergodic literature is a mixture or a cross-section of two transmedial modes of cultural expression: literature and ergodics.

5 Thus we are not trying to construct digital genres. Of these attempts and their inherent problems see Block (2010) as well as Glazier (2002), Stefans (2003) and Funkhouser (2007).

6   They also represent both classical and post-classical narratology.

7   Definitions of argument seem to be the least problematic and they can well do without references to and discussions about narrative. The status of description is more complex: to some scholars it is eternally subservient to narrative and only an aspect of it (Genette 1982) or a common surface phenomena but not an independent text-type (Fludernik 1996); to others description is a text type in its own right, one that needs to be emancipated from the tyranny of narrative (Chatman 1990; Hamon 1981).

8   In the last section of *The Architext* (pp.80–5) the whole range of architextuality is schematised to include theories of genre, modes, forms, themes, discourses, figures and styles.

9   In many cases the ergodic nature of the text is communicated to the user by explicit instructions. Under such circumstances the latter text-type then serves ergodics. In some cases such as *Surrender Control* (Forced Entertainment 2001) the whole text consists of instructions sent to the user and the action based on these SMS messages constitutes the flexible and individualised ergodic part of the text.

10 We'll later try to theorise modes of user action into categories that are more precise than the foursome of the explorative, configurative, textonic and role-playing ones.

11 Genres do not usually exist in their pure state, they are easily mixed and parodied and evolve in time, there's usually no consensus of what the defining features of each genre are or how many genres there are in the first place, and different interest groups (scholars, publishers, booksellers, authors, readers, fans, and journalists to begin with) use their own and only partly mutually compatible criteria.

12 Although each of these is specifiable by the other cybertextual variables.

13 For some reason the meta-genres in Fludernik 1996 are called macro-genres in Fludernik 2000.

14 Fludernik (2000) speculates on the possibility of eliminating the level of macro-genres from the model and reducing it to only two levels of genres and discourse modes. As the purpose of the constructed macro-genres is to order genres into manageable categories, the loss may not be great even if Fludernik (2000) laments the position of literary scholars amidst conflicting genre definitions and intuitions leading to different expectations and experiences. She writes (2000): "Why is it so much more important to literary scholars that they

can 'prove' a text to be narrative rather than, say, lyric? Perhaps this is the case because there are so many poems or prose texts that defy categorisation, that force readers to decide whether to read them as narrative rather than as poetry? Because we read literary texts quite differently when we read them as narratives rather than as poems or essays." One could ask how pressing the problem actually is. Most texts respond well to generic and modal expectations (hybrids included), and those that don't most definitely require much more specific, detailed and complex decisions and strategies from the reader than simple choices between reading them as narratives, poetry or essays. In many cases the most interesting and interpretatively demanding challenges are not related to the text-types or macro-genres or their interplaying combinations, but to the underdeveloped or undermined theories of the primary text-types. The main problems with the French New Novel (a sub-genre of novel) are not necessarily related to the question of its major text-type (is it narrative or description?) or to the interplay of narrative and description, but to contemporary theories of narrative and description that lack explanatory and descriptive power when applied to the novels of Robbe-Grillet, Butor or Sarraute. This situation has created what could be called a pseudo text type or a supplementary text type of anti-narrative as a kind of waste basket for the "experimental" texts that can't be conveniently situated in the traditional triangle of narrative, description and argument/commentary.

15 Fludernik argues for a qualitative difference between proper narratives and narratives that occur in conversation, because according to her natural narratology, narrative is primarily related to experientiality (what isn't or wouldn't be related to it?) and not to the temporality of events – an idiosyncratic oddity we'll address in more detail in chapter 6.

16 To quote Fludernik (2000): "Conversation has been proposed as a meta-genre to account for the prominence of interactivity in the oral language. In written texts, there are not many such interactive genres. On the level of discourse mode, the textual manifestation that most closely corresponds to interaction is dialogue, a prominent surface element in narrative."

17 Chatman uses capitalized words to refer to the class of text-types and lower case for individual "surface" examples of those types and we'll follow his practice in this paragraph.

18 Chatman (1990, 73) admits this possibility in his analysis of Resnais' *Mon Oncle d'Amérique*.

19 Chatman introduces exposition but writes it off as a combination of description and argument.

20 This problem is further discussed and theorised in the subsequent chapters on narratology.

21 Riddles could be elevated to the status of text-type: they can be presented by descriptive and narrative passages that serve them (as they must both contain and conceal the necessary cues needed to solve the riddle).

22 See Virtanen 1992.

23 Based on Fontanier's (1968) classic work.

24 These syntactic types of progression on the level of words (and not meaning) could be compared to semantic progression as one possible criterion to distinguish between discourse modes in linguistics. Carlotta S. Smith (2002) distinguishes five discourse modes, narrative, report, description, argument and information based on the kind of textual entities they introduce and their either temporal or atemporal progression.

25 In Cybertext (Aarseth 1997, 90–1) these "syntactical" figures are supplemented by semantic figures (tropes) such as aporia and epiphany in the context of the hypertext novel and later also by graphic computer games, although the ultimate global epiphanies are very different in these two cases (completion and "winning" in adventure games and something much less defined in hypertext fiction).

26 In Aarseth's text selection poetry (*Agrippa; Book Unbound; Calligrammes, Cent Mille Millard de Poèmes*) already occupies every value of every variable except personal perspective, thus displaying a much wider range of media positions than narrative prose. Moreover, there seems to be no conflict between ergodics and poetry regardless of how the latter is to be conceptualised (as a mode, a genre or a reflective meta-genre): ergodic poetry is poetry.

27 A hypothetical new genre to be discussed in chapter 20.

Chapter 6

1 With classical narratology of the 1960s and 1970s, the print-orientation is self-evident and justifiable, but with later and mostly cognitively oriented post-classical narratology in the 1990s (cf.

Fludernik 1996, Herman 1999, Jahn 1999, Ryan 1991) the exclusion of narratives in digital media is more suspicious, especially given the claims for universality and generality the advocates of these narratologies routinely made. *Narratologies* (Herman 1999) includes several papers by prominent post-classical narratologists, but only Marie-Laure Ryan (1999) ventures near computers and digital media – but only to borrow four promising metaphors from them (virtuality, windows, recursivity and morphing).

2 Needless to be said, the existence of a relatively large group of texts without a text-type undermines the general validity of the text-type approach, which could as well be reduced to classifying texts according to two meta text types: classifiable (and unproblematic) and unclassifiable (and too difficult).

3 Such as, say, ergodic and descriptive layers and functions that may or may not dominate them.

4 There are notable exceptions such as Koskimaa 2000 and Gunder 2004. Early hypertext theorists made all kinds of claims about the novelty of hypertext narratives, but they were not narratologically informed or focused. Typically they resembled George P. Landow's (1992, 101) argument that hypertext "calls into question ideas about plot and story current since Aristotle." As Aarseth (1996, 94) dryly notes, "Aristotelian ideas of story and plot have been contested since Horace (…) so hypertext is in any case not a radically unprecedented critique of Aristotelian concepts."

5 In this they have surprisingly much in common with their classical counterpart.

6 The all too evident historical contradiction or paradox is that while narrative experiments have continued from modernism to postmodernism to hypertext fiction and beyond, their ties to narratological research seem to have been severely severed roughly in parallel to other triumphs of the narrative turn.

7 According to Goody (2007) fictional narratives are not well understood or accepted in certain oral cultures.

8 We'll return to this point later in chapter 11.

9 The fabula/sjuzet pair was developed by the Russian Formalists; perhaps the most influential discourse/story distinction was promoted by Chatman 1978; among many others Pavel (1986), Ryan (1991), Ronen (1994), and Dolezel (1998) have theorised discourses in relation to possible worlds they accommodate; and Herman (2002) has stressed the importance of story worlds instead of stories.

10 The cognitive or cognitivist concepts such as frames, scripts and preference rules may to some degree explain certain features of everyday oral communication, but to apply them to fictional literature mostly free of the constraints and conventions of everyday communication constitutes a leap of faith, which is not backed up by studies of actual reception and cognitive processing of complex literary texts.

11 Quite tellingly the title of chapter 7, in which Fludernik tries to integrate postmodernist and experimental narratives into her model, is Games with tellers, telling and told. One could ask whether ludification (turning texts and reading processes into gaming and playing) isn't a suitable candidate for another form of naturalisation. It would also be difficult to deny the connection of games and playing to experientiality

12 In everyday communication it makes sense to figure if and how the teller knows the tale, but one of the time-tested wonders of narrative fiction is that this question doesn't have to arise and doesn't have to be answered either.

13 This implies a value judgment or at the very least an explicit choice to be made between the preferences of ordinary and professional readers.

14 There's a thin line separating canonized modernism and standard postmodernism from their more experimental forms. Within modernism the said distinction can be said to exist between *Ulysses* and *Finnegans Wake* and within postmodernism, maybe, between *Gravity's Rainbow* and the more spatially or materially (i.e. drawing from the tradition of artists' books) oriented work of Raymond Federman or Daniliewski's *The House of Leaves*.

15 The concept of narrativity could also be challenged by redefining it as the maximum use of recognizable narrative patterns, devices or means; i.e. the depth, range and variety of narrative techniques used. This model contains a similar idea of a lower threshold of narrativity, but it doesn't make a U-turn at the face of an extremely varied use of an extensive narrative vocabulary, i.e. there is no upper threshold that would be independent of the readers' skills, capabilities and aesthetic preferences.

16 What is worth telling is far from the neutral concept that it is supposed to be. It depends upon and varies according to how the act of telling is conducted, the expectations of readers, and the inferences they are capable of making (including the dimensions of allegory, parody and travesty to name only a few).

17 Presumably then also the conventions of the genre are included in the readers' reality when they read fantasy or deliberately anachronistic postmodernist narratives in which it is quite possible for Abe Lincoln (the former U.S. president) to answer the phone.

18 Which begs the question concerning theoretical progress; i.e. are we not yet past the 1920s? The explanatory power of Herman's scripts dramatically decreases in the face of *Finnegans Wake* and *Nightwood*.

Chapter 7

1 The distinction between hetero- and homodiegetic positions is not always absolute (Genette 1988, 102–5), and in some cases of free indirect discourse the voices of narrators and characters may be impossible to tell apart.

2 In my opinion it is hard to overlook Ping's dystopian feel, created by its broken syntax and a very limited freedom of movement and expression allowed to its protagonist.

3 This seems to be Fludernik's suggestion, although she doesn't analyse Stein's texts from that perspective.

4 As also other text-types (description, commentary, instruction) and material arrangements (such as binding, layout, and typography) contribute to the complications in the construction of fictional worlds, one could ask whether in addition to expanded narratologies we also need more perspective theories of the novel, capable of taking into account the complex interplay of text types and material foundations in postmodernist fiction.

5 As such, various postmodernist problems and dead-ends in story construction are not much of a challenge, as there's no theoretical need to assume that simple and coherent stories should be constructed or that such stories should serve as a criterion for narrativity.

6 Needless to say textonic and intratextonic dynamics, indeterminate determination, transience, personal perspective, conrolled access, ergodic user functions and even links could be organised to create epistemological and ontological problems unknown to McHale's three books on postmodernism. The reader and the user may have to ask questions such as "to which work does this part belong?", "how many new embedded narrative levels are there this time and for how

long?", "is the existence of that narrator dependent on the behavior of this character?" or "will I ever see this passage again?" just to name a few new possibilities.

7 In Genette's tripartite narratological model, both mood and tense concern the relations between narrative and story, while voice concerns the relationship of narrating to both narrative and story (Genette 1980, 32).

Chapter 8

1 On the other hand Bordwell states that screen time or duration is part of the film's stylistic system and not of its narrative system: "Fabula duration and syuzhet duration are not embodied in the film's stylistic system, but a third sort of duration is. We can call this *screen* duration, or 'projection time.'(...) Since screen duration is ingredient to the very medium of cinema, all film techniques – mise-en-scène, cinematography, editing and sound – contribute to its creation." (Bordwell 1985, 81–2) Although Bordwell uses the terms of fabula and syuzhet time reminiscent of the Russian Formalists the distinctions he makes within the aspects of order, duration and frequency are derived from Genette (except for his own additions of course).

2 For earlier formulations of this idea see Eskelinen 1998 and Eskelinen and Koskimaa 2001.

3 In Eskelinen 1990 the reader is given instructions not to read certain passages of the novel after their designated expiration dates. See Koskimaa 2000, 44 for further details.

4 The printed material accompanying *Agrippa* was planned to utilize vanishing ink. See http://agrippa.english.ucsb.edu/ for further details of the project.

5 In the early years of cinema screen durations did vary because certain presentation mechanics required a human technician to manually maintain the presentation speed as consistently as possible. See Zielinski 1999 for details.

6 Because of the extra material necessarily affects at least one of the three temporal aspects of order, duration and frequency.

7 As noted before, reading time and system time can equally well be used in non-narrative texts and for non-narrative purposes, which means they are not narrative categories in themselves.

8 Herman's revision is based on Uli Margolin comments on Herman's chapter in progress. According to Herman (2002, 213) Margolin argues that temporal elements could be ordered fully, partially, multiply, and randomly.

9 Here non-linear refers to texts that do not present their signs in one fixed order, and linear refers to those that do (Aarseth 1994, 51).

10 Cf. Aarseth 1994 and 1997, Koskimaa 2000, Rau 2000 and Gunder 2004.

11 This seems to be largely a Scandinavian or more broadly European phenomenon, as the most prominent American hypertext theorists (cf. Bolter 1991, Landow 1992 and Douglas 1994) seem to rely on less sophisticated theories of narrative lacking necessary explanatory power, i.e., theories that from the Genettean perspective belong to the pre-history of narratology.

12 In Genette's model (1980, 48), anachronies (analepsis and prolepsis) have two kinds of specifications, extent and reach. The former is about the story time covered by the anachrony and the latter about the distance between successive segments of the text. Needless to say, the latter loses much of its use value in hypertext fiction, while the former becomes more important, as it is one possible key to figuring out the order of the events in the story (as it is not tied to the current presentation order but to the content of the segment whether it happens to be a prolepsis, analepsis or neither in a particular actual discourse).

13 Such replacements and supplements may affect the aspects of duration and frequency as well.

14 As *Reagan Library* is a web fiction, this arrangement can be circumvented by the reader re-entering the text from another location and starting the same cycle of textual supplementation from the beginning.

15 It should also be noted that the effects of the textual supplements in *Reagan Library* are not limited to only one narratological category. The fact that the successive versions often give fuller accounts of the events affects (slows down) the speed of narrative and also necessarily complicates the task of figuring out the order of narrated events.

16 Genette (1980, 95) schematizes them as follows (NT denotes narrative time and ST story time): pause (NT=n, ST=0), scene (NT=ST), summary (NT<ST) and ellipsis (NT=0, ST=n). Chatman's stretch would be NT>ST.

17 If all dialogue and polylogue were included only in audio files, then the duration of a scene would be exactly measurable, including the

already mentioned speeds of pronunciation and the possible dead spaces in the conversation.

18 In this context, kinetic includes also texts with immobile words and letters that function like slide-shows (such as Hegirascope) and automatically replace segments of text with other segments.

19 It is possible to construct an object the kind of which Liestol describes. In such a case what the reader reads in his first reading will constitute the whole text that is available to him in subsequent readings (and all the unread nodes will vanish or become inaccessible to him forever), or if one wants to serialize the experience, then the maximum length of reading will always be dictated by the length of previous reading.

20 In *Hegirascope* the conceptual difference between parts and phases would roughly correspond to two possible ways of using it: explorative (i.e. actively navigating it within the given temporal constraint) and interpretative (not navigating and allowing the text to present itself in 30 second intervals).

21 Instructions are not effective as users can ignore them at will. Print narratives cannot effectively control reading time whereas digital narratives can be programmed to effectively control reading time.

22 Print narratives can set conditions to reading too, but readers can easily ignore them. In principle programmed conditions could be hacked and subverted, but that requires more advanced (and relatively rare) skills than simply ignoring instructions.

23 These constraints are unlike the more famous constraints developed and tested by the OuLiPo, as the group's efforts concern textual production and not reception – a theoretical limitation or blind spot that could easily be remedied.

24 These constraints can coincide with both interpretative and ergodic user functions and with both transient and intransient time, as the constraints only require that the reader tries to adapt his reading practice to suit or meet the text's behavior whether or not he can influence it.

25 This arrangement not only puts more cognitive stress on the reader, but it also emphasises distinctions among readers, as reading fast now becomes an asset much like reaction speed in games.

26 As a point of comparison John Cage's composition *ASLSP/Organ 2* (1987) is planned to be performed as slowly as possible for 639 years from 2000 to 2639. For further details see http://www.as-slow-as-possible.com/johncageproject.htm

27 Moulthrop's oeuvre seems to progress from first sabotaging narrative order (in *Victory Garden*) to sabotaging duration and speed (in *Hegirascope*), frequency (in *Reagan Library*) and finally simultaneity (in *Pax*).

28 In light of cybertext theory, linguistic units should be divided into textons and scriptons and operations combined with traversal functions and media positions.

29 Also the order and simultaneity of change could be included. The latter was briefly discussed earlier in this chapter.

Chapter 9

1 Adding more information doesn't necessarily increase coherence, as in principle it could equally well decrease it, but in *Reagan Library* it does.

2 The main focus of this chapter is not to discuss the merits of different theoretical views on distance and focalization, but to construct a model capable of describing and explaining the ways of regulating narrative information inherent in digital media.

3 The narrative of thoughts is always reduced to either speeches or events. (Genette 1988, 63)

4 Genette also discusses Barthes' *effect de reel's* (see Barthes 1989) contribution to creating the mimetic illusion.

5 Obviously narrative distance is the topic here, along with the relation of the states of character's speech to it. Thus in addition to Genette's three-part and McHale's seven-part gradation there is also a state with no distance; i.e. when there's only the character's discourse, as in dialogue novels such as *La Celestina* (1499).

6 Later Genette (1988, 56–7) is in favour of Brian McHale's (1978) more complex seven-part gradation, the details of which don't concern us here.

7 Roughly, as a narrator is not necessarily omniscient even if he knows more than a character. Therefore Susan Lanser (1981, 224) and William Nelles (1997, 81) propose to call zero focalization free focalization instead. Genette's (1988, 73–4) own revision of zero focalization makes it equivalent to "variable, and sometimes zero focalization."

8 Or more precisely a confusion "between the question of *who is the character whose point of view orients the narrative perspective?* and

the very different question of *who is the narrator?*" (Genette 1980, 186)

9 Although both global knowledge and unlimited access to information characterize the typical case of zero focalization, the traditional omniscient narrator, these two dimensions should not be confused with each other.

10 One could perhaps use the basic aspects of tense to further specify the changes and shifts in variable and multiple internal focalizations, i.e. their order, duration and frequency.

11 The problem with this move is the risk of falling back into the confusion between mood and voice that Genette's model manages to avoid.

12 Chatman's solution to the problems of point of view and focalization (1990, 143–8) is to divide the area into four narrative functions: slant ("the narrator's attitudes and other mental nuances appropriate to the report function of discourse"), filter ("the much wider range of mental activity experienced by the character in the story world – perceptions, cognitions, attitudes, emotions, memories, fantasies, and the like"), center ("the presentation of a story in such a way that a certain character is of paramount importance") and interest-focus (some character's "interest point of view").

13 The difference between the expressed world and the reference world and the distance between them is somewhat limited as a theoretical point of departure. The latter may be easy to establish in modernist narratives, but with ontologically oriented postmodernist fiction there may be an array of expressed worlds in conflict from which it is impossible to deduce the reference world. Marie-Laure Ryan (1991, 1) presented a similar model based on the difference between the textual actual world and the textual reference world, and quite logically had to exclude postmodernist fiction from the realm of narrative, as it could have seriously undermined the descriptive and analytical power of her model.

14 Ruth Ronen has also discussed relations between narration and focalization emphasizing that "focalization pre-determines narration." (Ronen 1994, 180) This claim is based on the idea that focalizers and focalized fictional objects are on the same ontological level: "focalization is inseparable from the focalized object." (Ronen 1994, 176). However, as Raine Koskimaa points out, "it is difficult to see how focalization can predeterminate narrating, since, after all, it is the narrator who is responsible for the choice of the focalizer." (Koskimaa 1999, 137)

15 We could add two more levels (the one between two or several

users and the other between narrative and narrating – a dimension recognised, but to some degree overlooked by Genette as we shall see in the next chapter), but for the following discussion the first three will be sufficient.

16 Information should not be confused with the user's interpretation of it.

17 This has nothing to do with the reader's interpretations of narrative. Omniscience simply means that the reader has access to the whole text, i.e. that every bit of information is presented to him.

18 In the table below, however, the distinction is between complete and incomplete access to scriptons.

19 In chapter 8 several ways of regulating system time and reading time were introduced and these may also become relevant in this context, further specifying the temporally limited access to narrative text.

20 See Koskimaa (2000, 44) for further discussion.

21 Situating *Agrippa* depends on how to interpret the time given to read it – is it sufficient for reading the whole text or not?

22 That doesn't change even if the pages were to be read in more than one order.

23 They may of course pretend to address us (as in Calvino's *If on a winter's night a traveler*), but we still can't reply to them or discuss with them.

Chapter 10

1 Narrative meta-situations discussed here should be distinguished from the narrative situations that are combinations of the values of the main parameters of mood and voice (see Genette 1988, 128–9).

2 As we saw in chapters 3 and 4.

3 Some narratologists prefer to call metadiegetic levels and narrators hypodiegetic instead.

4 For example, by extradiegetic narrators intruding in the diegetic universe or by diegetic characters' intrusions into the metadiegetic world. This movement can go in the other direction as well: characters may search for and encounter their authors, or a character may be assassinated by a character in a novel he is reading.

5   Possible as it is also possible that the timeframe remains the same during the metalepsis.

6   Technically it is possible to instruct the reader to rip off pages from a book, which eventually would decrease the number of narrative levels in it, given that there's more than one to begin with.

7   Not to mention the well-known printed and unbound narrative of Marc Saporta (*Composition No. 1*), although it doesn't seem to play with narrative levels the way discussed here.

8   The last option (unlimited) refers to texts where new narrative levels are constantly generated each time the reader begins a new session with the text. As such it is an extreme case of texts with variable levels, in which there's no upper limit to the number of levels generated.

9   The number of scriptonic narrative levels either equals the number of textonic narrative levels (t=s) or is less than it (t>s).

10 Of course there's no theoretical upper limit to the number of times these shifts may occur in any direction.

11 Todorov's time of reading is not similar to our conceptualisation of reading time in chapter 8.

12 Genette's (1988, 14) nonfictional order from story to narration to narrative is not of interest here for two reasons. The temporal complexity of fictional narratives is greater than nonfictional narratives (see Cohn 1999), and it is exactly the construction of the pretended narrative situation in fiction that is at the core of any competent theoretisation of the narrative voice.

13 In Margolin's (1999, 165) cognitivist view, "literary narrative – and especially the narrating voice's discourse offers us models of the human mind at work as it constructs different internal representations (cognitive maps) of dynamic situations."

14 As insights derived from modal logic and theories of possible worlds have been applied to fiction since the mid–1970s (Pavel 1975; Eco 1978) the approach is far from new. It is usually oriented towards semantics, which explains its absence from formal narratologies and presence in thematic or story-oriented ones (such as Ryan 1991).

15 These categories and several others are already included in Keir Elam's dramatological model (1997 [1980], 189–90).

16 Genette convincingly argues against the concept of implied author as an actual agent: "(...) a narrative of fiction is produced fictively by its narrator and actually by its (real) author. No one is toiling

away between them, and every type of textual performance can be attributed only to one or the other, depending on the level chosen." (Genette 1988, 139–40)

17 This term is used synonymously with text adventures.

Chapter 11

1 We will come back to trans- and intermediality from a considerably broader perspective in chapter 18, after concluding the subsequent section (chapter 12 to 17) on games.

2 Usually the impulse for transmediality comes from literary narratologists and not from theatre, drama or film scholars, perhaps because the latter are not either as keen or as ignorant as to neglect the performative and medium-specific aspects in their area of expertise.

3 Presumably the same machinery is at the disposal of non-narrative film makers too.

4 Many if not all of these sequences of events also have Chatman's (1990, 9) precious "chrono-logic", a doubly temporal logic of the presentation of events and the events presented – for instance in a simulation presenting the next 20 years of the potential effects of the world-wide food crisis, global warming and armed conflicts on an average Western middle-class family in one hour.

5 Another fatality in this equation is that story is the content plane of narrative and as such ultimately the reader's or the spectator's interpretative construct. To make matters even worse, human beings are cognitively capable of constructing stories from any event or chain of events or projecting a story on any event. However, events can be arranged in many other configurations as well, including performances and games. Moreover, already Mandler (1984) saw fundamental differences among event, scene and story schemas.

6 Later in the context of MUDs Aarseth (1997, 157) adds two more discourse planes to this scheme: quasi-events and construction.

7 This is compatible with Aarseth's statement that the intriguee "represents an immanent position (...) that must be (re)constructed by the implied user, and not by the voice of the event narrator." (Aarseth 1995, 142)

8 The ergodic voice's suggestions present another difference between

ergodic and narrative discourse, as in the former the user can test the suggestion and alter the course of his traversal because of that.

9 Additionally and following our modal definition of narrative, we could also argue that adventure games are dialogues between the ergodic voice and the user and thus of dramatic and not narrative mode. However, even if the dialogue is interpreted as drama or dramatic, it still serves the user's ergodic goal of solving the puzzle or mystery.

10 To complicate matters somewhat, the two schemes are repeated also in a later paper (Aarseth 1999), with additional differences concerning the user's time, which doesn't matter in traditional theories of narrative – but as we already saw in chapter 8 that could easily change. When Aarseth (1999) repeats the latter scheme, including the three kinds of representation, he uses it to sum up the difference between narrative and ergodic modes. The modal focus as such is compatible with our approach in this chapter.

11 Aarseth (1997, 94) uses the unfortunate metaphor "game of narration" to describe *Afternoon*, which after all is not a game, as it lacks explicit rules and goals, not to mention that the user doesn't encounter opponents in his traversal.

12 In chapter 5 we discussed ergodics and ergodic literature in relation to text-types, modes, and genres, and suggested several ways to make cybertext theory and typology more nuanced.

13 Of course this doesn't mean that games could not or do not include and embed narrative elements, just that the ergodic game elements are more central and important than them; so to speak, they rule. Much of the narrativists' confusion, to be discussed in more detail in the next chapter, stems from their misreading of the ludologists' position. When the former stated that games are not narratives, the latter thought it meant games could or should not include narratives.

14 Based on this conclusion we could argue that textonically and intratextonically dynamic literature (with or without ergodic user functions) is potentially as important as ergodic literature.

Chapter 12

1 Compared to the theoretical and conceptual advances made by ludologists and post-ludologists in these and many other research areas, the narrativist side has little to show. Consequently we know

much more about digital games than we did a decade ago, when the discussion was centred around and still constrained by unfounded narrativist assumptions.

2 The progress away from narratively oriented studies of games towards issues more native to games is clearly visible if one compares the proceedings of six major international academic conferences on digital games: the first one in Copenhagen in 2001, its successor in Tampere in 2002 (Mäyrä 2002), and the first four Digra conferences in 2003, 2005, 2007 and 2009.

3 This subtheme will resurface again in chapter 18.

4 Michael Mateas (2002) proposed the term "narrativist" in order to refer more precisely to a scholar who uses "narrative and literary theory as the foundation upon which to build a theory of interactive media." Aarseth describes the ideology of narrativism in less benevolent terms: "This is the notion that everything is a story, and that story-telling is our primary, perhaps only, mode of understanding, our cognitive perspective on the world. Life is a story, this discussion is a story, and the building that I work in is also a story, or better, an architectural narrative. Ironically, most proper *narratologists*, who actually have to think about and define narratives in a scholarly responsible and accurate way are not guilty of this overgeneralization. But among anthropologists, business people, technologists, visual artists, media theorists, and other laypersons, this ideology – or what Alan Rauch once fittingly called *story fetishism* – is strong and uncontested." (Aarseth 2004, 49)

5 According to Google's scholar service (scholar.google.fi) as of July 2011 both papers had been quoted in more than 200 papers and books. Given that, a full explication of the debate could easily fill this entire book.

6 Frasca to game rhetoric and serious games (2007), Juul to the interplay of rules and fiction (2004b) and casual games (2010), Jenkins to convergence culture (2007), and Eskelinen to game ecology (2005) and cybertext poetics (2004 and this study), while Aarseth has continued his engagement with game ontology. Moreover, engagement in the debate from the ludologists' side was a secondary, yet necessary issue to begin with, as the main focus of ludological research was understandably elsewhere.

7 Based on this more or less innocent and amateurish misinterpretation one could indeed conclude that the debate didn't take place.

8 Probably the second most common misquote from the same

paragraph is the syntagm "to annihilate for good the discussion of games as stories, narratives, or cinema" somehow misread to mean that the way games use cinematic elements should not be studied: "Any 'annihilation' (Eskelinen 2001a) of a discussion of moving image features in video games would be misleading. At the same time, any approach based predominantly on film theory risks remaining detached from game specifics. Instead, the place between the two poles is seen as the most fruitful area for the argument." (Nitsche 2008, 122). In retrospect it is hard to understand why abandoning the silly idea that computer games are a new but so far unidentified species of interactive narrative or cinema should preclude a discussion of moving image features in video games. I'm glad it doesn't, although Nitsche's probes into video game space are seriously compromised by his untenable definition of narrative.

9   This lack of basic and necessary definitions should be recognized as the most important self-defeating feature in the variety of narrativist positions. The degree to which they are not defined is a reliable indicator of the existence of non-academic practices.

10   Jenkins' position is indeed an intermediary one as it is situated between academic and non-academic positions.

11   Or one half, as she defines narrativity but not narrative.

12   And certainly not the kind Murray (1997) theorises with her four loose defining qualities: for instance *Tetris*, one of the strangest objects ever to be narrativized, is neither encyclopaedic nor spatial in Murray's sense.

13   As I stated in my response to Jenkins: "If we study games and narratives as bodies of information, elementary differences multiply again. According to the well-known phrase of David Bordwell, narration is 'the process whereby the film's sjuzet and style interact in the course of cueing and constraining the spectator's construction of the fabula'. In games there are other kinds of dominant cues and constraints: rules, goals, the necessary manipulation of an equipment, and the affect of possible other players for starters. This means that information is distributed differently (invested in formal rules for example), it is to be obtained differently (by manipulating the equipment) and it is to be used differently (in moving towards the goal)." (Eskelinen 2004b)

14   Jenkins (2004, 122) also argues that "games fit within a much older tradition of spatial stories" which goes against basic facts of cultural history: for instance the oldest astragals (forerunners of dice) date back to prehistory. (Eskelinen 2004b) Jenkins' error (that he shares

with many other proponents of narrativism) is another instance of the same ahistorical fallacy – the inability to see that computer games are the newest newcomers in the millennia long history of games.

15 She also states that her answer to the first question is positive.

16 This is a sign that there's a strong consensus about the role of rules among both narrative and game scholars.

17 Obviously the redefining game could be played in both directions. By simply defining narratives as games of interpretation the issue could be most economically settled.

18 The two omitted points are not related to the ludological position adopted in this book but to Juul's theoretisation of game time, which will be addressed in the chapter that discusses temporality and causality in games.

19 Because in narratology the narratee is different from the implied reader and the real reader, and in accordance with this generally accepted division, the narratee is also different from the implied player and the real player.

20 These "right" sequences are typical of games of progression and not of games of emergence. See Juul 2004b, 72–9 for these two broad types of games.

21 The lack of a definite point of ending also indicates the presence of open series of events. Also, even in games such as *GTA: San Andreas* that have an overall goal, there are plenty of other activities the player may choose to pursue. See Flanagan 2005 for players that simply want to drive around in the game world.

22 To some degree Ryan seems to be aware of the role different definitions play in the debate as she writes: "It may turn out in the end that the quarrel between ludologists and narrativists (...) revolves around the scope of the term 'narrative' than around the nature of games, for I am not aware of any narrativist claiming that games are the same thing as novels or movies." (Ryan 2006, 200) As Ryan and most other narrativists do not provide even working definitions of games, it is absurd to claim that there's no disagreement around the nature of games, and if the narrativist side implicitly agrees with the definitions of games provided by the ludologists (and their predecessors) as well as with their understanding of the nature of the games, they should perhaps stop disagreeing with the ludologists. It is also very different to see the differences among games, novels, and films in terms of ludology than it is to see the differences, as Ryan does, only in terms of narrative and narrativity.

23   Film scholars used to have a hard time seeing the difference between computer games and interactive cinema in the early 2000s, as anthologies such as *Screen/Play* (King & Krzywinska 2002) rather mercilessly show. Surprisingly, that beginner's blindness is not yet a blast from the past as Jan Simons's more recent paper (2007b) and book (2007a) have difficulties in telling apart even ordinary films and games. In his paper Simons quotes my joke, "Luckily, outside theory, people are usually excellent at distinguishing between narrative situations and gaming situations: if I throw a ball at you, I don't expect you to drop it and wait until it starts telling stories." (Eskelinen 2004) and comments: "If there is still anybody waiting, it must be for Eskelinen to explain the point of this stab at narratology. Narratologists will be happy to explain to him the difference between the act of throwing a ball and the act of *recounting* that (f)act."

Very well. It is evident that Simons gets neither the joke nor the basic narratological fact behind it, probably because his approach is the punchline to that joke: it constantly confuses the act with the recounting of the act – something that competent narratologists and ludologists do not do.

This is evident in his comment on Frasca: "According to ludologists, the major difference between games and narratives is that the former address 'external observers' who apprehend 'what has happened,' whereas the latter require 'involved players' who care about 'what is going to happen'" (Frasca, 2003b). Reader-response researchers and film theorists have argued time and again that readers and film spectators experience events narrated in novels and films as if they occur in the present, and anyone who has ever seen a Hitchcock movie knows that film spectators are very much concerned about "what is going to happen." (Simons 2007b)

The simple point Simons misses (in addition to tellingly confusing the former and the latter in the above quote) is that the spectator of a Hitchcock film cannot influence what happens in the movie, whereas the player both can and has to affect what happens in the game. Simons conflates the spectator's interpretative activity with the player's extanoematic activity over and over again in his paper, but the origins of this category mistake seems to be in his book on Lars von Trier's "game cinema": "The presumed distinguishing feature of games usually boils down to the actions and input required from the player (...) However, since narrative of any interest is also shaped by non-trivial actions of the protagonist, the term 'ergodic' is applicable to narratives as well. Game theorists beg to differ, because, in their view, the non-trivial shaping actions should come from the player. The difference between a narratologist and a ludologist seems to be that the former is interested in a chain of events from the point of view of a lurker, whereas the latter seeks to study it from the point of view of an involved player." (Simons 2007a, 182)

For my part I have neither space nor cruelty to continue commenting on Simons' continuous chain of category mistakes (confusing metaphorical models with dynamic simulations and mind games with game artifacts etc.), as almost every chapter in this book shows how much the differences he overlooks matter. After all, all he asked me to do was to explain a joke that, thanks to him, is now less of a joke than it was 10 years ago.

24 When scholars from social sciences and cultural studies feel compelled to give their views on games and narratives, they tend to overemphasize the role and the meaning-making processes of real players at the expense of implied players constrained and empowered by the actual game structures. See chapter 17 for further discussion of the differences between real and implied players.

25 Theoretically because it confuses narratives, narrativity and meaning, and pragmatically because it ultimately contains only one all-important dimension: the degree of narrativity that is not connected to game specific features.

Chapter 13

1 Juul compares the definitions of Huizinga (1938), Caillois (1958), Suits (1978), Avedon and Sutton-Smith (1971), Crawford (1982), Kelley (1988), and Salen and Zimmerman (2004). Salen and Zimmerman also compare Huizinga, Caillois, Suits, Crawford and Avedon and Sutton-Smith – and in addition Parlett (1999), Abt (1970), and Costikyan (1994).

2 Similar definitional features of games are to be found in dictionary definitions of game as well: "Any contest undertaken for recreation or prize, played according to rules, and depending on strength, skill, or luck to win."(*The New International Webster's Comprehensive Dictionary of the English Language* 1999, 519).

3 Juul (2004b, 31–2) later specifies that games have fixed rules – a stipulation that leads to unnecessary borderline cases to be discussed below.

4 One could discuss the lack of the player to player dimension in the model, but given the existence of single-player games that dimension would not work as a criterion for all games.

5 For instance in the famous case of Dynamo Kiev playing soccer against a German "elite" team and refusing to lose despite the deadly consequences of that decision. See Duncan 2001 for further details.

6 One could argue that it could be played without real bullets, but on the other hand the rules of the game underline the necessity of using real bullets.

7 We'll be discussing Frasca's definition in greater detail in chapter 15 on the gaming situation.

8 This is also compatible with the usual emphasis on the voluntary nature of play in many definitions (for instance in Aarseth, Smedstad and Sunnanå 2003, 43).

9 This outcome could be avoided by applying Salen and Zimmerman's (2004, 80) definition stressing the artificial nature of conflict in games, but that in turn contradicts certain well-known historical facts such as Roman games and Sutton-Smith's conclusion quoted above.

10 This doesn't mean that the negotiable and non-negotiable consequences should be dismissed in game studies or that cultural and social contexts of games should not be studied, but simply that this criterion doesn't work well as a part of game definitions that aim to be as universal and general as possible.

11 Playing soccer with friends (instead of anonymous opponents) usually decreases the likelihood of getting injured.

12 That may lead to what one could call a Simonsian fallacy, as discussed in the previous chapter.

13 For some reason neither Juul nor Salen and Zimmerman discuss this model in their comparative approach to game definitions.

14 I'm quoting from the on-line version of Crawford's book and therefore cannot give references to page numbers. All quotes are from the section titled "Computers" in chapter 4.

15 Crawford sees computers as game technology and not as game media or a game medium. This is compatible with Aarseth's insistence that computers are not a medium but a highly flexible material technology: "It cannot be repeated often enough that the computer is not a medium, but a flexible material technology that will accommodate many very different media." (Aarseth 2004, 46) As we shall see, this perspective has certain consequences for the concept of transmediality.

16 See Greenblat and Duke 1975 and Woods 2004.

17 Needless to say telecommunication networks around us have multiplied during the three decades since Crawford's pioneering

book, and if we were to follow W.J. Mitchell's (2003) insights on networks scaling up and receivers and transmitters scaling down, we could easily see that the advantages this process offers already go far beyond enabling games with huge numbers of players. In addition to mobile gaming and trans-reality games that are capable of connecting, combining, embedding and intertwining virtual and physical playgrounds in ever more complex ways, there are other networks working at closer range that could, among other things, easily transmit the information about the state of the player's body (pulse, blood pressure etc.) to the game system – thus adding an extra element to be played with that has been lacking from most if not all kinds and types of commercial games and sports so far. Advanced communication networks could also be used to disrupt the magic circle from the outside by letting real-time real-life information change and affect the behavior of the game elements (rules, obstacles, resources, player positions etc.) in a crucial way while the game is being played.

18 Crawford discusses PC-games, not console games.

19 This single-player orientation could be seen as an anomaly or a novelty in the history of games and game technologies.

20 Media is here put in quotation marks given what was said about game technologies earlier in this chapter.

21 We'll discuss this distinction more fully later in this chapter.

22 In contrast to relationships between digital and non-digital works of literature and film, the case of games is more complicated, as the realm of digital games is not just an extension of the realm of non-digital games. In other words, while digital literature and film include all the possibilities of print literature and non-digital film, digital games do not contain all the possibilities of non-digital games. In other words, films and books can be digitally implemented whereas only a subset of non-digital games can be digitally implemented, and others can only be adapted.

23 Woods also has further suggestions for creating unbalanced world with misinformed players: "Players can be interacting with slightly differing game worlds, might have access to only a limited number of areas or might be subject to conflicting influences from within the simulated system itself. A player's words may be distorted, their sight restricted, their appearance to other players modified; indeed, they may not even be visible to other participants within the game." (Woods 2004)

24 Juul adds physical laws to the list in sports, but I find it to be slightly misleading. While physical laws influence the players' performances,

it is up to the players and/or the referee to uphold the rules (of how and what to perform).

25 The following list is far from being exhaustive.

26 This is a typical relation in many games that have simplified versions for children or novices.

27 For real and possible examples see Lundgen and Björk's (2003) description of computer augmented games.

28 The distinction between a hypogame to be adapted or implemented into a hypergame is modified from Genette's hypo- and hypertext (1997, 5). A hypergame is a systematic transformation or imitation of a previous hypogame. In many ways the distinction between implementation and adaptation resembles Genette's hypertextual distinction between imitations and transformations discussed in chapter 3.

29 This would test the validity of the concept of adaptation even more than digital sport games and simulations. Mechanical hockey and football games constitute a clearer borderline case and so do table-top sports (or more accurately coaching games) such as *Strat-O-Matic* (a major forerunner of fantasy sports) that utilizes cards and dice in its non-digitalized form.

30 This opens up the possibility for improved versions of board and card games that lift the restrictions inherent in physical boards and cards and replace them with programmable and more malleable virtual boards and cards. Such games would be augmented implementations mentioned above. See Peitz, Eriksson and Björk 2005 for augmented board games. Sports could also be augmented by using digital technology, for example by gathering and evaluating information about the athlete's body (blood pressure, pulse, etc.)

31 A whole defined as the sum total of game states.

32 Manipulation rules describe how the simulation functions, ludus rules determine the winning conditions, and meta-rules concern the extent to which players can alter the rules. Rules will be discussed in more detail in chapter 15.

33 Narrative is in quotation marks as the circulating element in these conceptualisations is usually not narrative but story or plot. Moreover as we have already seen narratives also have their own transmedial ecology.

Chapter 14

1   In this book the terms digital games and computer games refer to all programmable games (i.e. that include computers). These include PC-, console and mobile games. The term video game is used for the most part synonymously with digital and computer games except when the reference is to text-based games.

2   The reasons for the exclusion of narrative from their model are worth quoting: "Elements and components required for the analysis of interaction within the game are, in our opinion, way more invariant than the themes, characterization, narration or audio-visual style of games and thus they are explicitly left out from this treatise." (Björk and Holopainen 2003, 2)

3   This is yet another example of the counterproductivity of the narrativists redefining game. In their zeal to include computer games, narrativists propose definitions that would lead to counterintuitive results when applied to forms and practices generally thought to be non-narrative.

4   The paper also discusses the locus of manipulation (the number of the entities the player manipulates) and the difference between indirect and direct manipulation ("the manipulation is mapped directly to the input device") (Zagal et al 2005, 10). The first of these dimensions was already discussed in the previous chapter, but we'll be returning to the issues of manipulation in the context of the gaming situation in the next two chapters.

5   We'll use the latter model, as it is a modified and revised version of the former.

6   To take three examples: Both Crawford (1982) and Myers (1990) list six genres, that is, relatively few compared to Wolf's (2001) 42 genres. What is common to all these and many other ad hoc lists is their total or almost total disconnectedness from the millennia-old problems and definitions of genre. Wolf mentions a couple of insignificant papers on film and Hollywood genres, but ultimately ends up by classifying game genres on the basis of "the interactive experience" (Wolf 2001, 42) and comes up with inherently dysfunctional genres such as adaptations and gambling. Crawford is entirely non-academic, making distinctions based on skills (such as strategy versus action). Myers' main references are to Frye and Aristotle but he confuses "the game sequence" with the latter's plot structure that he later uses as one of the three determining factors of genre, alongside confusingly articulated text materials and player

interactions. For instance the values in the latter category consist of the following four: discover, learn, manipulate and test.

7 The earlier model contained the meta category of rules that is not included in the revised model. Elverdam and Aarseth don't explicitly explain the omission. Aarseth, Smedstad and Sunnanå (2003, 53) divide the rule dimension into the presence or absence of topological, time based and objective based rules while stating that "rules are the most central element of game, yet are notoriously hard to categorize, since it would then be easy to make a new game that breaks the categorisation." (ibid.) One may ask whether the same doesn't apply to many other dimensions in the typology as well – or typologies in general. Our discussion in the previous chapter already resulted in several sub-dimensions of rules that could be used in classifying games. We'll continue discussing rules in the next chapter.

8 In this respect it is somewhat ironic that the paper of Aarseth, Smedstad, and Sunnanå was presented at the DIGRA 2003 conference and the paper of Fernández-Vara, Zagal and Mateas at the DIGRA 2005 conference. The latter doesn't mention the former, while repeating one of the distinctions it discussed and abandoned and noting the possible difference in the dimensionality of movement and representation.

9 In another paper by the GOP scholars the differences between these layers of game space are explained as follows: "Consider an example using a familiar game such as *Space Invaders*, but with a twist. Let's imagine that the invaders are not flat two dimensional sprites but rather are beautifully rendered in 3D. At the representational level, we could argue that this version of *Space Invaders* is 3D. On another level, we observe what is happening in the game. The invaders march across the screen from left to right and also, down towards the player. All their actions occur in a two dimensional plane. *Space Invaders* has a Two Dimensional Gameworld. The player, however, can only move his spaceship from side to side. The space of movement for the player is only one dimensional. Thus, we say that *Space Invaders* has One Dimensional Gameplay." (Zagal et al 2005, 11)

10 As every model, typology or selection always and inevitably reflects the needs, perspectives and objectives of the scholars, this is not a critique of Elverdam and Aarseth's model. In addition to the elegance and precision of its definitions, this typology's strength is in its open-endedness that allows improved typologies to be constructed.

11 Avedon finds eight types of interaction patterns: "a) Intra-individual—action taking place within the mind of a person or action involving the mind and a part of the body, but requiring no

contact with another person or external object. b) Extra-individual—
action directed by a person toward an object in the environment,
requiring no contact with another person. c) Aggregate—action
directed by a person toward an object in the environment while in
the company of other persons who are also directing action toward
objects in the environment. Action is not directed toward each
other, no inter-action between participants is required or necessary.
d) Inter-individual—action of a competitive nature directed by one
person toward another. e) Unilateral—action of a competitive nature
among three or more persons, one of whom is an antagonist or 'it'.
Interaction is in simultaneous competitive dyadic relationships. f)
Multi-lateral—action of a competitive nature among three or more
persons, no one person is an antagonist. g) Intra-group—action of
a co-operative nature by two or more persons intent upon reaching
a mutual goal. Action requires positive verbal and non-verbal
interaction. h) Inter-group—action of a competitive nature between
two or more intra-groups." (Avedon 1971, 424–5)

12 "Competition is an ingredient in most games; the question here is how
intense is the competition and what creates this intensity." (Gump, Redl
and Sutton-Smith 1971, 410) The authors then divide competition
factors in five sub-dimensions: a) Centrality of Winning and Losing; b)
Goal Directed vs. Opponent Directed; c) Self Enhancement vs. Defeat
of the "other"; d) Team vs. Individual Competition, and e) Interference
with Participants by Participants. (ibid.)

13 The losing end is divided in four subgroups: loss of possessions,
implications that one is inadequate skillwise, implication that destiny
is against one, and loss of dignity. (Gump, Redl and Sutton-Smith
1971, 414)

14 Here too the authors separate four subcategories: one winner; one
winner and seconds and thirds; several winners; and all win but the
loser. (Gump, Redl and Sutton-Smith 1971, 414) This dimension could
be integrated into Elverdam and Aarseth's category of evaluation.

15 Here the authors distinguish between game play rewards and
punishments and game end rewards and punishments. They also
state that "This is a consideration of the *extent* to which the
reward and punishment idea gets into the game as opposed to the
kinds of pleasure-pain content." (Gump, Redl and Sutton-Smith
1971, 414)

16 This dimension is comparatively self-evident and the authors see
its relevance related to "position an adult game leader may have to
assume." (Gump, Redl and Sutton-Smith 1971, 417) The reference
to an adult results from one of the possible uses of the model:

"determining which games are suitable for the needs and capacities of different groups of children." (Gump, Redl and Sutton-Smith 1971, 408)

17 Gump, Redl and Sutton-Smith (1971, 415) divide obstacles in the following three groups: 1) Beyond the participant obstacles that have two sub-groups, 1a) opponent produced and/or manipulated obstacles and 1b) impersonal obstacles, and 2) "Tied-to Person" obstacles. The latter are handicaps that restrict function, for instance in blindfold games.

18 This is more than a thousand times more than the 576 textonomical positions or genres in Aarseth's cybertext typology.

19 The problems of genre do not equally affect every major game technology discussed in the previous chapter. For instance board game scholars Murray (1952), Bell (1960 and 1969) and Parlett (1999) divide their field into four or five game groups or "genres".

20 Lars Konzack's (2002) model for game analysis is yet another well-defined point of departure for the pursuit of game genres, with its seven interplaying layers of hardware, program code, functionality, gameplay, meaning, referentiality, and socio-culture. The nature of these layers necessarily requires interdisciplinary game scholarship – which I cannot provide on my own. Similarly Aki Järvinen's thorough treatment of the complexities in theorizing game genres (2008, 304–33) comes up with the following ten genre nominators: game components, game environments, rule sets, game information, game mechanics, game system behavior, game theme, game interface, game context and game rhetorics or style. None of these promising points of departure promise the relative simplicity we find in film and literary genres.

Chapter 15

1 As Juul (2004b, 55) rightly notes, rules are not only limitations but affordances as well, because they set up potential actions. Limitations provide frames within which affordances guarantee variation.

2 Although some players are able to hack and many others to mod the game, these activities result in either a completely new game or a game variation.

3 The players in this and other chapters are for the most part implied and not real "flesh and blood" players (see Aarseth 2007, 1–3), the

relations of which are discussed in chapter 17 in the context of game research theories and approaches.

4 Configurative action is the dominant one, as it consists of the player's efforts to close the non-trivial gap between the beginning and the winning (or more valued) situations. This configurative action may often require and include both explorative and constructive action, which are sub-types of configurative action in this context.

5 Given the ergodic and other cybertextual difficulties previously discussed.

6 These differences in the necessity of these five major game elements could have been used as an additional comparative transmedial dimension in chapter 13.

7 Järvinen's theme rules are here included in Juul's information rules (themes being one possible topic of information).

8 Philosophies of action don't carry as far, as they tend to stay on a very general level, and are usually limited to "analyses of actions performed by one agent."(van Dijk 1977, 185) Action consists of agents, acts or act-types, intentions, purposes, modes (manner and means) and context (spatial, temporal, circumstatial). Agents and their positions (specified by player structures) as well as spatiotemporal circumstances are preliminary covered by the game typologies discussed in chapter 14, and the act-types describe what the game mechanics explicitly allow (such as kicking, flying, jumping, shooting, dancing etc.) and constitute the player's basic action repertoire. This leaves us with intentions, purposes, and modes that are useful in specifying gameplay as a relation between player actions and game events. If this relation is to be understood in terms of modalities we have several almost ready-made dimensions to consider: deontic (prohibition/permission/obligation), epistemic (knowledge/certainty/doubt), doxastic (belief/disbelief/ignorance), alethic (possibility/impossibility/necessity), axiological (good/bad/indifferent) and boulomaeic (desire/wishes/preferences). In a more inclusive and comprehensive treatment each rule type should be discussed in these six dimensions as well as in relation to their basic functions discussed in chapter 13.

9 As we saw in the context of social simulation games, the status of metarules may change in this respect (for example when some players or teams are given the right to change in-game rules while the game is still on).

10 Nevertheless, information rules regulate this evaluation and how much of it is delivered to the player (for example by visible and

continuously updated scores or as information about remaining "lives" or "health" or other resources) and when (in the boxing match running the full 3 or 15 rounds, it is only after their performance that the contenders come to know the final score and the winner).

11 Of course self-expression is not limited to ignoring or playing against explicit goals and preferences, as any virtuoso or otherwise stylised way of goal-abiding playing makes evident.

12 Another way to express this is to say there is a difference between game states as they are in the game and game states as they are presented to the players.

13 In games with final teleology one or several specific intention successes (specified by goal and grade rules) are also purpose-successes (for example scoring the winning goal or killing the final monster), but on other occasions (earlier in the game) intention and purpose successes are not equal.

14 As Juul (2007) demonstrates, there isn't much room for alternative action in *Scramble* and by extension other arcade games, and if the player pursues that path the game is simply over much faster than it would be if the player "obeys" the grade rules.

15 This is because relatively few games are organised around continuously repeated and swiftly punished and rewarded micro level actions.

Chapter 16

1 Instead of explicitly revising my previous model here I will simply present a new model by combining insights from various sources including my old model.

2 In the context of Juul's theoretical framework this move makes sense for two reasons. First, it is crucial to show this incoherence, as it also points to a feature that is specific to or at least typical of games: players can easily tolerate and accept this incoherence and it doesn't ruin the game for them. Secondly, no time will be wasted investigating whether another kind of theory of time would be needed to better explain the newly found temporal incoherence.

3 In fact equivalents of play time are common to many other conceptualizations of game time and can also be found in Aarseth (1999) and Eskelinen (2001a and 2001c) to begin with.

4 This concept of event time is derived from Eskelinen 2001a and should not be confused with Schechner's event time.

5 If it were measured in pseudo-time, for example in the number of specific actions the player is able or allowed to take, then we would find more distortions of the 1:1 ratio between play time and fictional time. In *Civilization III* rounds become shorter and shorter in terms of fictional time: in the beginning several hundred years of fictional time pass quickly whereas in the last rounds the same number of actions advances fictional time by only a year. This in turn could lead us to study the rhythm or tempo of games instead of the speed of isolated actions and events.

6 In short, fictional time moving forward is just a convention that could be broken as easily as it is broken in any other fiction. The significance of such practices in games is a different matter and is dependent on the role fictional time plays in them. Fictional time can be entirely unspecific, decorative and more or less disconnected from the rest of the game, or it may be and become a primary target of the player's manipulative efforts. At the heart of this matter is the varying significance and insignificance of both play time and fictional time in games, which is very different from the constitutive role of discourse and story times in narratives.

7 Micro-level observations would lead to cataloguing temporal specifications of every game component – hence the preference for the top-down approach. As Zagal and Mateas put it: "Videogames execute on a computational infrastructure, in which the fundamental state changes are the billions (on contemporary hardware) of computational state changes happening per second. Describing events at this granularity would achieve maximal precision, but be incredibly onerous. Further, players cannot perceive events at the level of individual instruction execution; such an analysis would fail to provide a description of game time relevant to players and designers." (Zagal and Mateas 2007, 517)

8 We don't discuss that typology in this chapter, as the typology of Elverdam and Aarseth is an improved version of it.

9 Elverdam and Aarseth almost say as much: "Haste describes whether the passage of external time alters the game state. Synchronicity describes whether simultaneous player action is allowed. Finally, interval control determines whether a player has control of the game time (or time cycles within the game)." (Elverdam and Aarseth 2007, 6)

10 In the digital era of deep remixability everything can be combined with everything else while the real dilemma is our asymmetrical

understanding of the things to be mixed – despite the recent progress in digital game studies we still know a lot more about narratives and interpretative practices than about games and configurative practices.

Chapter 17

1 To take a purely hypothetical example: you're playing *Return to Camp Wolfowitz*, a massively multiplayer war crimes simulation, and the daily or hourly body count in Iraq broadcasted in your local news media will determine what kind of atrocities you can commit against unarmed civilians in the game within the next few hours.

2 This doesn't mean that history matters much in the game: in order to win in *Civilization* the player doesn't have to take the game's modelling of "real" history seriously except as a game environment to be manipulated and interpreted.

3 In this respect Sutton-Smith's *The Ambiguity of Play* (1997) reads like an encyclopaedia of clashing attempts to define play. Probably the only way to make sense of them is to treat them as rhetorical devices as Sutton-Smith does.

4 Complex relations among different ecologies, economies, and activities will be discussed in the next chapter. In "Explorations in game ecology" (Eskelinen 2006) digital game ecology was situated within the larger ecology of games (board games, card games etc.) situated within play ecology (toys, instruments, games, sports, role-play, performance) that was itself situated within recreational ecology (sex, drugs, music, dance, play, culinarism etc.). The paper also distinguished between content, entertainment, media and modal ecologies. (Eskelinen 2006, 99)

5 Juul's *Casual Games* (2010) shows the undeniable benefits of studying games and players together.

6 More generally, taking into account systems and models and not limiting ourselves only to the problems of work and text does not mean that the problems and articulations of the latter two have vanished or been solved beyond discussion. Quite simply their relations are now being articulated in the framework of systems and models in a strictly literal and not merely metaphorical sense.

7 See Montola 2010 for "extreme" LARP examples that bring games a little bit closer to the well-known social-psychological experiments of Milgram (1974) and Zimbardo (2008). The importance of the latter two to critical forms of game studies is in their exploration of

the limits of roleplay and obedience to rules. Probably the ultimate critical game fostering critical play (Flanagan 2009) would be some as yet unforeseen combination of ubiquitous and wearable digital technologies, LARP aesthetics, Augusto Boal's invisible and legislative theatre (Boal 1992, 6–30), and social-psychological experiments measuring the distance between real players and their socially pressured and ethically compromized referents.

8 Or at least to the first wave of ludologists (Frasca; Juul; Eskelinen; Järvinen) and game ontologists (Aarseth) associated with them.

9 Moreover fun, enjoyment and pleasure carry so many connotations that we may need psychologically and psychoanalytically oriented game research to sort them out.

10 For example, within the scope of the humanities, literature and film are not accompanied by explicit and binding rules governing the behavior of the material artefact and the recipient's interpretative engagement. Because of these differences in the empirical objects of research one can then "paradoxically" remain a post-structuralistically and phenomenologically informed anti-formalist in the former fields while adapting a formalist position in game studies.

11 Such as the following quote describing social contingency: "This is the unpredictability of never being certain about another's point of view (and often, resources), and is a key component of games such as chess, poker and countless other games." (Malaby 2007, 16) Or this one describing performative contingency: "Here the issue is the execution of an action by a participant, an action that may succeed or fail. This kind of unpredictability plays a significant role in athletic contests, but also is the core of many action-oriented computer games." (Malaby 2007, 16) Regarding chess and poker a better term would be strategic unpredictability as the opponent's strategy is what is not known in games as different from each other as chess (a game of perfect information) and poker (a game of imperfect information). The possibility of failing action is hardly limited to athletic contests and "many action-oriented computer games" as Malaby claims. If he means trivial action such as moving one's piece on the game board, many athletic contests include that kind of action (athletes usually manage to run 100 meters for example), and if not, then players may also fail in poker in their non-trivial attempts to bluff. Either way, Malaby's interpretations and examples fail. It is not for nothing that the original Russian formalists called themselves specifiers and not formalists.

Chapter 18

1 As we saw in the narratological section and in chapter 10 particularly, variable outcomes could also result from the system's non-ergodic behavior.

2 Not every material/semiotic system constitutes a representational game world, as card and dice games have shown, and the same observation applies also to most game boards and playgrounds.

3 It is equally hard to find adaptations between the genres of hypertext and interactive fiction.

4 It could well be argued after Aarseth (1994, 78–9) that game worlds are combinations of fiction and simulation, hence the quotation marks.

5 There are other specimens in this ecology, such as comic books, radio plays, and television series to name a few.

6 Studies that promote the idea that intertextual resonances, broad cultural archetypes or generic recognition not to mention the all time banality of the player's experience are somehow narrative elements connecting games and narrative fiction films. For a typical example of this type of reasoning or declaration, see King and Krzywinska 2002, 24.

7 This distinction as well as the one between intra- and intermodal transformations is derived from Genette 1997a.

8 I.e. the texts between silent episodes to the degree they include narration and not merely announce places, dates or characters' names.

9 Quite amusingly, the typical arguments used for seeing narrative as both discursive and cognitive mode (organizing our temporal existence and our knowledge of the world etc.) could be said about play and games as well, and with either the same or a significantly much lesser amount of cognitive-cultural-evolutionary speculation: game is a fundamental way of organizing human experience and a tool for constructing models of reality (variation, plans, goals, challenges, rules, strategies, adversaries, interaction, play testing, simulation); games allow human beings to come to terms with the temporality of their existence (making sense of and playing with what could happen; the futility of goals and competition); game is a particular mode of thinking that relates to the concrete and particular as opposed to the abstract and general (manipulation of concrete and particular objects as a form of mediatation to see a bigger picture); game creates and transmits cultural traditions

(rituals, sport, nationalism) and builds the values and beliefs that define cultural identities (fair play); game is a vehicle of dominant ideologies and an instrument of power (see the chapters on the rhetoric of power in Sutton-Smith 1997); game is an instrument of self-creation (zen practices, professional sports); game is a repository of practical knowledge (embodied skills, training games); game is a mold in which we shape and anticipate our future; game, in its fictional form, widens our mental universe beyond the actual and the familiar and provides a playfield for thought experiments; game is an exhaustible source of education and entertainment; game is a mirror in which we discover what it means to be human and play widens that horizon towards other mammals and some birds. (See Ryan 2005, 345 for the narrative variants of this non-exhaustive list)

In short, the already available evidence of cross-cultural similarities in gaming (Roberts et al 1959; Roberts and Sutton-Smith 1962; Chick 1998) as well as animal play (Fagen 1981) and its evolutionary roots going back approximately 65 million years (Sutton-Smith 2005) should make us realize that games and play are at least as deeply rooted in evolution and human cognition as our narrative abilities the cognitive and evolutive study of which is still far too speculative and rudimentary.

10 "Interaction" takes place between actors and audience and transaction between actors. (Elam 1980, 87–92) The latter obviously doesn't exist if there's only one actor or if the performance consists of two or more compartmentalized performances by different performers. The difference between compartmentalized and non-compartmentalized performances was introduced in Kirby 1982. Compartmentalized parts do not affect each other within the overall structure of the presentation.

11 It should also be clear that I'm not reducing theatre here to the most boring theatre of words, as there is a huge continuum and variety of ergodic and non-ergodic theatre and performance art and matrixed and non-matrixed performances.

12 "So in *Rhythm 0* in the Galleria Studio Mora in Naples in early 1975, she decided to do nothing and see what the audience would do to her instead. For six hours, Abramovic simply stood still and allowed herself to be manipulated by the public in any way they chose, using any of the seventy-two items laid out on a table, which included a fork, a bottle of perfume, sugar, an axe, a bell, a feather, chains, needles, scissors, a pen, a book, honey, a hammer, a saw, a lamb bone, a newspaper, grapes, olive oil, a Polaroid Camera, a rosemary branch, a mirror, a rose, lipstick, a large gold

necklace, a bowler hat, and a pistol (and a bullet). (Westcott 2010, 73–6)

13 This is not the case with poetry, thanks to Eduardo Kac's (2003) biopoetry.

14 The approximate number of game ontologically grounded "media positions" in Elverdam and Aarseth's (2007) typology.

Chapter 19

1 See de Koeven 1978 for these collaborative and communal "counter-culture" games.

2 Unintentional in the sense that these responses then become parts of the ergodic work that may also at some point become non-ergodic again (for example when the hoax is seen through or publicly exposed to be a hoax or documented and published as one).

3 See McGaffery and Nichol 1992, 165–89 for examples.

4 *Perhaps* is a 24-letter poem for 24 synchronous users (each one controlling the movement of one letter).

5 Educational and ideological conventions are a different matter. One may imagine an ideologically motivated need for ergodic Bibles or Little Red Books that record the way they are read and evaluate, reward and punish their users.

Chapter 20

1 Wardrip-Fruin later abandoned this distinction in *Expressive Processing* (Wardrip-Fruin 2009, 409), but without denying its usefulness: "I'm also abandoning an earlier terminological distinction (...)between 'instrumental texts' and 'textual instruments' (...) But the distinction between the ideas is still present here, simply without the confusingly similar terms."

2 He also drafts two other logics of simulation and discourse. (Wardrip-Fruin 2007, 249)

3 *Regime Change* uses the report of the Warren Commission and a newspaper story about Saddam's fall.

4 In contrast to "interactive fiction" and MUDs at the gaming end.

5 The way Matt Gorbert treats it in his response is illuminating also in

this respect, because among the self-defeating, unimaginative, story-centric, and avant-garde-blind questions he asks are the following: "Given these observations about simplicity of interaction and brevity of content, a question presents itself: using a simple, familiar physical interaction which maintains the user's sense of control, how far can the complexity of the content be pushed? Is there a necessary correlation between simple interaction and simple content? Or is it possible to create a body-centric interactive piece with the storytelling capacity of an epic novel or a play? In *Text Rain*, for instance, what would be the appropriate interaction for progressing to a new body of text? How might one 'turn the page' or choose a different 'chapter'? (...) If these pieces are like the haiku of the genre, how might we go about creating the Homer?" (Gorbert 2004, 221–2)

6 The connection between thematics and the type of ergodic activity is another addition to the variety of transtextual relationships. Similar connections could also exist between formal arrangements (such as the shape of a concrete poem) and required ergodic activity.

7 *Arteroids* has already gone through several development cycles, and its future prospects include multi-player modes that lead to yet another relatively unexplored frontier in textual instruments – and in E-poetry, despite such forerunners as Eduardo Kac's *Perhaps* (1998/1999), in which each of the 24 simultaneous users moved their "own" word on the screen.

8 "Delusions of jealousy contradict the subject, delusions of persecution contradict the verb, and erotomania contradicts the object. But in fact a fourth kind of contradiction is possible – namely, one which rejects the proposition as a whole." (Freud 1981 [1911], 203) Needless to say this systematization and mechanism could be situated or embedded as a parergon in all four scenes and schemes of writing and textual production: sender/receiver, signifier/signified, text/intertext, and textons/scriptons.

9 See Eskelinen 2007, 200–3 for further suggestions.

BIBLIOGRAPHY

Aarseth, Espen 1991. *Texts of Change. Towards a Poetics of Nonlinearity*. Bergen: University of Bergen.
—1994. "Nonlinearity and Literary Theory". In *Hyper/Text/Theory*, edited by George P. Landow, 51–85. Baltimore, MA: Johns Hopkins University Press.
—1995. *Cybertext. Perspectives on Ergodic Literature*. PhD diss., University of Bergen. http://ask.bibsys.no/ask/action/show?pid=r00016654&kid=forskpub.
—1997. *Cybertext. Perspectives on Ergodic Literature*. Baltimore, MA: Johns Hopkins University Press.
—1998 [1995]. "Dataspillets diskurs." In *Digitalkultur og nettverkskommunikasjon*, 75–98. Bergen: Espen Aarseth.
—1999. "Aporia and Epiphany in *Doom* and *The Speaking Clock*: Temporality in Ergodic Art." In *Cyberspace Textuality*, edited by Marie-Laure Ryan, 31–41. Bloomington and Indianapolis: University of Indiana Press.
—2001a. "Allegories of Space." In *Cybertext Yearbook 2000*, edited by Markku Eskelinen and Raine Koskimaa, 152–71. Saarijärvi: Research Center for Contemporary Culture.
—2001b. "Computer Game Studies, Year One." *Game Studies – The International Journal of Computer Game Research*, 1, 1. www.gamestudies.org/0101/editorial.html (5 July 2011).
—2003a. "We All Want to Change the World: The Ideology of Innovation in Digital Media." In *Digital Media Revisited*, edited by Gunnar Liestol, Andrew Morrison, and Terje Rasmussen, 416–39. Cambridge, MA: MIT Press.
—2003b. "Playing Research: Methodological Approaches to Game Analysis." Paper presented at the Digital Arts and Culture Conference in Melbourne, May 2003. http://www.cs.uu.nl/docs/vakken/vw/literature/02.GameApproaches2.pdf (30 July 2011).
—2004a. "Genre Trouble: Narrativism and the Art of Simulation." In Wardrip-Fruin and Harrigan (eds) 2004, 45–55.
—2004b. "Quest Games as Post-Narrative Discourse." In Ryan ed. 2004, 61–90.

—2006. "Narrative Literature in the Turing Universe." In *The Novel, Volume 2*, edited by Franco Moretti, 839–67. Princeton and Oxford: Princeton University Press.

—2007. "I Fought the Law: Transgressive Play and the Implied Player". *In Situated Play*, Proceedings of the Digra 2007 Conference. http://www.digra.org/dl/order_by_author? publication=Situated%20Play (5 July 2011).

Aarseth, Espen, Solveig Marie Smedstad, and Lise Sunnanå 2003. "A Multi-Dimensional Typology of Games." In *Level Up – digital games research conference proceedings*, edited by Marinka Copier and Joost Raessens, 48–53. Utrecht: Utrecht University Press.

Abt, C. C. 1970. *Serious Games*. New York: Viking.

Altman, Rick 1999. *Film/Genre*. London: British Film Institute.

Amerika, Mark 1997. *Grammatron*. http://www.grammatron.com/ (5 July 2011).

Andrews, Jim 2001. *Arteroids*. www.vispo.com/arteroids (5 July 2011).

—2005. "Games, Po, Art, Play, and Arteroids 2.03." www.vispo.com/arteroids/onarteroids.htm (5 July 2011).

Ankerson, Ingrid and Megan Sapnar 2006 [2001]. *Cruising*. In *Electronic Literature Collection, Volume 1*, edited by N. Katherine Hayles, Nick Montfort, Scott Rettberg and Stephanie Strickland. http://collection.eliterature.org/1/works/ankerson_sapnar__cruising.html (5 July 2011).

Anonymous. *The Celestina. A Fifteenth-century Spanish Novel in Dialogue*. Translated by Lesley Byrd Simpson. Berkeley and London: University of California Press, 2006 [1499].

Aspnes, James 1989–90. *TinyMUD*. A multi-user dungeon that ran on a unix machine at Carnagie Mellon University from August 1989 to April 1990.

Avedon, Elliott M. 1971. "The Structural Elements of Games." In *The Study of Games*, edited by Elliott M. Avedon and Brian Sutton-Smith, 419–26. New York: Wiley.

Avedon, Elliott M. and Brian Sutton-Smith 1971. *The Study of Games*. New York: Wiley.

Bal, Mieke 1983. "The Narrating and the Focalizing: A Theory of Agents in Narrative." *Style* 17: 234–69.

Balpe, Jean-Pierre 2004. *Fictions (fiction)*. Installation. http://www.maisonpop.net/spip.php?article366.

—2005. *Fictions d'Issy*. Locative text installation.

—2007. "Principles and Processes of Generative Literature. Questions to Literature." In Gendolla and Schäfer (eds) 2007, 309–17.

—2010. "A Town as a Novel. An Interactive and Generative Literary

Installation in Urban Space." In Gendolla and Schäfer (eds) 2010, 331–44.

Barthes, Roland 1975 [1973]. *The Pleasure of the Text*. Translated by Richard Miller. New York: Hill and Wang.

—1977. *Image-Music-Text*. London: Fontana.

—1989. "The Reality Effect". In Roland Barthes, *The Rustle of Language*, 141–8. Berkeley and Los Angeles: University of California Press.

Bartle, Richard 2003. *Designing Virtual Worlds*. Indianapolis: New Riders.

Beckett, Samuel 1995a [1966]. "Ping". In Beckett 1995b, 193–6.

—1995b. *The Complete Short Prose 1929–1989*. Edited and with an Introduction and Notes by S. E. Gontarski. New York: Grove Press.

Bell, Robert 1960. *Board and Table Games I*. Oxford: Oxford University Press.

—1969. *Board and Table Games II*. Oxford: Oxford University Press.

Bénabou, Marcel 1998 [1986]. "Rule and Constraint." In *OuLiPo – A Primer of Potential Literature*, edited by Warren J. Motte, Jr., 40–7. Normal, IL: Dalkey Archive Press.

Bense, Max 1962. *Theorie der Texte*. Cologne: Kiepenhauer & Witsch.

Bernstein, Mark 2001. "*Card Shark* and *Thespis*: Exotic Tools for Hypertext Narrative." In Proceedings of the 12th ACM Conference on Hypertext and Hypermedia", edited by Hugh Davis, Jane Yellowlees Douglas, and David G. Durand, 41–50. New York: ACM Press.

Bernstein, Mark and Diane Greco 2004. "*Card Shark* and *Thespis*: Exotic Tools for Hypertext Narrative." In Wardrip-Fruin and Harrigan (eds) 2004, 167–82.

Biggs, Simon 2000. *The Great Wall of China*. www.littlepig.org.uk/wall/wall.htm (7 July 2011).

Björk, Staffan and Jussi Holopainen 2003. "Describing Games. An Interaction-Centric Structural Framework." Proceedings of DiGRA 2003 Conference. http://www.digra.org/dl/order_by_author?publication=Level%20Up%20Conference%20Proceedings (5 July 2011).

Björk, Staffan, S. Lundgren, and Jussi Holopainen 2003. "Game Design Patterns." Proceedings of DiGRA 2003 Conference. http://www.digra.org/dl/order_by_author?publication =Level%20Up%20Conference%20Proceedings (5 July 2011).

Block, Friedrich W. 2010. "How to Construct a Genre of Digital Poetry."In Gendolla and Schäfer (eds) 2010, 391–402.

Boal, Augusto 1992. *Games for Actors and Non-actors*. London: Routledge.

Bogost, Ian 2006. *Unit Operations. An Approach to Videogame Criticism*. Cambridge and London: MIT Press.

Bogost, Ian and Nick Montfort 2009. *Racing the Beam*. Cambridge, MA, and London: MIT Press.

Bolter, Jay David 1991. *Writing Space*. Hillsdale, NJ: Erlbaum.

—2001. *Writing Space*, 2nd edn. Mahwah, NJ, and London: Erlbaum.

Bolter, Jay David and Richard Grusin 1999. *Remediation. Understanding New Media*. Cambridge, MA: MIT Press.

Bootz, Philippe 1996. "Poetic Machinations". *Visible Language*, 30, 118–37.

—2003. "Hypertext: Solution/dissolution." Translated by John Cayley. In *Cybertext Yearbook* 2002–2003, edited by John Cayley, Markku Eskelinen, Loss Pequeno Glazier, and Raine Koskimaa, 56–82. Saarijärvi: Research Center for Contemporary Culture

—2006. "Digital Poetry: From Cybertext to Programmed Forms." In *Leonardo Electronic Almanac*, 14, 5–6. http://leoalmanac.org/journal/vol_14/lea_v14_n05–06/pbootz.html (30 July 2011).

—2007. "Unique-reading Poems: a Multimedia Generator." In Kac ed. 2007, 67–75.

Bordwell, David 1985. *Narration in the Fiction Film*. Madison: University of Wisconsin Press.

Borràs Castanyer, Laura and Juan B. Gutierrez 2010. "The Global Poetic System. A System of Poetic Positioning." In Gendolla and Schäfer (eds) 2010, 345–61.

Burgaud, Patrick-Henry 2002. "French E-poetry. A Short/Long Story." In *Dichtung Digital*, 23. http://www.brown.edu/Research/dichtung-digital/2002/05–25-Burgaud.htm (5 July 2011).

Cage, John 1987. *ASLSP/Organ 2*. Composition/performance.

Caillois, Roger 1979 [1961]. *Man, Play, Games*. Translated by Meyer Barash. New York: Schocken Books.

Calvino, Italo 1973 [1969]. *The Castle of Crossed Destinies*. Translated by William Weaver. New York and London: Harcourt Brace.

—1981. *If on a Winter's Night a Traveller*. Translated by William Weaver. New York: Harcourt Brace.

Carr, Diane, David Buckingham, Andrew Burns, and Gareth Schott 2006. *Computer Games: Text, Narrative and Play*. Cambridge: Polity Press.

Cayley, John 1994. *The Golden Lion*. London: Wellsweep.

—1995a. *Book Unbound*. London: Wellsweep.

—1995b. *The Speaking Clock*. London: Wellsweep.

—2001. "In the Event of Text." In *Cybertext Yearbook 2000*, edited by Markku Eskelinen and Raine Koskimaa, 86–99. Saarijärvi: Research Center for Contemporary Culture.

—2003. "From Byte to Inscription." *The Iowa Web Review*. http://iowareview.uiowa.edu/TIRW/TIRW_Archive/tirweb/feature/cayley/cayley_interview.pdf (7 July 2011).

—2004a. "Literal Art: Neither Lines nor Pixels but Letters." In Wardrip-Fruin and Harrigan (eds) 2004, 208–17.

—2004b. *overboard*. http://programmatology.shadoof.net/index. php?p=works/ overboard/overboard.html (7 July 2011).

—2004c. "Overboard. An Example of Ambient Time-based Art in Digital Media." *Dichtung Digital*, 2, 2004. http://dichtung-digital.mewi. unibas.ch/2004/2-Cayley.htm.

—2006 [1999]. *windsound*. In *Electronic Literature Collection*, *Volume 1*, edited by N. Katherine Hayles, Nick Montfort, Scott Rettberg, and Stephanie Strickland. http://collection.eliterature.org/1/works/cayley__windsound.html (5 July 2011).

—2007. "Beyond Codexspace: Potentialities of Literary Cybertext." In Kac ed. 2007, 105–25.

—2008a. *riverIsland QT. Iowa Review Web*, 9, 2 (theme issue on Instruments and Playable Text, guest edited by Stuart Moulthrop). http://research-intermedia.art.uiowa.edu/tirw/vol9n2/artworks/riverisland/riverislandQT.html (5 July 2011).

—2008b. *riverIsland*. http://research-intermedia.art.uiowa.edu/tirw/vol9n2/johncayley/php (5 July 2011)

Ceram, C. W. 1965. *Archaeology of Cinema*. New York: Harcourt Brace.

Chatman, Seymour 1978. *Story and Discourse*. Ithaca, NY: Cornell University Press.

—1990. *Coming to Terms*. Ithaca, NY: Cornell University Press.

Chick, Garry 1998. "Games in Culture Revisted. A Replication and Extension of Roberts, Arth, and Busch (1959)." *Cross-Cultural Research*, 32, 2, 185–206.

Cohn, Dorrit 1999. *The Distinction of Fiction*. Baltimore, MA, and London: Johns Hopkins University Press.

Copier, Marinka and Joost Raessens (eds) 2003. *Level Up* – Proceedings of Digital Games Research Conference 2003. University of Utrecht: Utrecht.

Cortazar, Julio 1966 [1963]. *Hopscotch*. Translated by Gregory Rabassa. New York: Pantheon Books.

—1994 [1968]. *62: A Model Kit*. Translated by Gregory Rabassa. London and New York: Marion Boyars.

Costikyan, Greg 1994. "I Have No Words and I Must Design." In *Interactive Fantasy*, 2. Also available at http://www.costik.com/nowords.html (5 July 2011).

Crawford, Chris 1982. *The Art of Computer Game Design*. http://www.vancouver.wsu.edu/fac/peabody/game-book/Coverpage.html (20 January 2009).

Crowther, William and Don Woods 1976. *Adventure*.

Culler, Jonathan 1975. *Structuralist Poetics*. London and New York: Routledge.

Danielewski, Mark Z. 2000. *The House of Leaves*. New York: Pantheon Books.

De Koven, Bernard 1978. *The Well-Played Game*. Garden City, NY: Doubleday.

Dixon, Steve 2007. *Digital Performance*. Cambridge, MA, and London: MIT Press.

Dolezel, Lubomir 1973. *Narrative Modes in Czech Literature*. Toronto: University of Toronto Press.

—1998. *Heterocosmica: Fiction and Possible Worlds*. Baltimore, MA: Johns Hopkins University Press.

Douglas, Jane Yellowlees 1994. "How Do I Stop This Thing?: Closure and Indeterminacy in Interactive Narratives". In *Hyper/Text/Theory*, edited by George P. Landow, 159–88. Baltimore, MA: Johns Hopkins University Press.

—2001. *The End of Books or Books without End? Reading Interactive Narratives*. Ann Arbor: University of Michigan Press.

Douglas, Jane Yellowless and Andrew Hargadon 2004. "The Pleasures of Immersion and Interaction: Schemas, Scripts, and the Fifth Business." In Wardrip-Fruin and Harrigan (eds) 2004, 192–206.

Dove, Toni 1998. *Artificial Changelings*. http://www.medienkunstnetz.de/works/artificial-changelings/ (5 July 2011).

Drucker, Johanna 1995. *The Century of Artists' Books*. New York: Granary Books.

Duncan, Andy 2001. *Defending the Honour of Kiev*. London: Fourth Estate Ltd.

Durand, David and Noah Wardrip-Fruin 2005. "*Cardplay*, a New Textual Instrument." http://pear.hcmc.uvic.ca:8080/ach/site/xhtml.xq?id=175 (7 July 2011).

Eco, Umberto 1978. "Possible Worlds and Text Pragmatics." In *Versus*, 19/20.

Elam, Keir 1980. *The Semiotics of Theatre and Drama*. London: Routledge.

Elverdam, Christian and Espen Aarseth 2007. "Game Classification and Game Design: Construction through Critical Analysis." *Games and Culture 2007*, 2, 3–22.

Ermi, Laura and Frans Mäyrä 2005. "Fundamental Components of the Gameplay Experience: Analysing Immersion." In the Proceedings of Digra 2005 conference. http://www.digra.org/dl/db/06276.41516.pdf (5 July 2011).

Eskelinen, Markku 1990. *Semtext*. Helsinki: Tammi.

—1998. "Omission Impossible: the Ergodics of Time." Paper presented at the the Digital Arts and Culture Conference, Bergen, Norway,

November 1998. http://cmc.uib.no/dac98/papers/eskelinen.html (30 July 2011).

—2000. "Cybertext Palimpsests." Paper presented at the Digital Arts and Culture Conference, Bergen, Norway, August 2000.

—2001a. "The Gaming Situation." In *Game Studies*, 1, 1. www. gamestudies.org/0101/eskelinen (7 July 2011).

—2001b. *Kybertekstien narratologia*. (Cybertext narratology) Saarijärvi: Research Center for Contemporary Culture.

—2001c. "Cybertext Theory and Literary Studies, A User's Manual." In *Electronic Book Review*, 12. http://www.altx.com/ebr/ebr12/eskel.htm (5 July 2011).

—2004a . "Towards Computer Game Studies". In Wardrip-Fruin and Harrigan (eds) 2004, 36–44.

—2004b. "Response to Henry Jenkins." http://www. electronicbookreview.com/thread/firstperson/astragalian (5 July 2011).

—2004c. "Six Problems in Search of a Solution." *Dichtung Digital*, 3/2004. http://dichtung-digital.mewi.unibas.ch/2004/3-Eskelinen.htm (19 October 2011).

—2005. "Explorations in Game Ecology, Part 1". *Forum Computerphilologie* 5/2005. http://www.computerphilologie. uni-muenchen.de/jg05/eskelinen.html (7 July 2011). Also in *Jahrbuch für Computerphilologie 7*, edited by Georg Braungart, Peter Gendolla and Fotis Jannidis, 93–109. Paderborn: Mentis (2006).

—2007. "Six Problems in Search of a Solution. The Challenge of Cybertext Theory and Ludology to Literary Theory". In *The Aesthetics of Net Literature. Writing, Reading and Playing in Programmable Media*, edited by Peter Gendolla and Jörgen Schäfer, 179–209. Bielefeld: transcript Verlag.

—2012 (forthcoming). *Interface 3*. Provosoft: Helsinki. Eskelinen, Markku and Raine Koskimaa 2001.

Eskelinen, Markku and Raine Koskimaa 2001. "Discourse Timer– Towards Temporally Dynamic Texts." In *Dichtung Digital*, June 2001.

Eskelinen, Markku and Kimmo Kuitunen 2013 (forthcoming). "Interface 4: A Game Plan for a Textual and Musical Instrument."

Eskelinen, Markku and Ragnhild Tronstad 2003: "Video Games and Configurative Performances." In Wolf and Perron (eds) 2003, 195–220.

Fagen, Robert 1981. *Animal Play Behaviour*. New York: Oxford University Press.

Fernández-Vara, Clara, José Pablo Zagal, and Michael Mateas 2005. "Evolution of Spatial Configurations in Videogames." Proceedings of DiGRA 2005 Conference: Changing Views – Worlds in Play. http://www. cc.gatech.edu/~jp/Papers/Spatial_configurations.pdf (30 July 2011).

Firstenberg, Allen 1995. *The Unending Addventure*. www.addventure. com/addventure/ (5 July 2011).

Flanagan, Mary 2005. "Troubling 'Games for Girls': Notes from the Edge of Game Design." In DiGRA 2005 conference proceedings. http://www.digra.org/dl/order_by_author?publication=Changing%20 Views:%20Worlds%20in%20Play (5 July 2011).

—2009. *Critical Play*. Cambridge, MA, and London: MIT Press.

Fludernik, Monika 1996. *Towards Natural Narratology*. London: Routledge.

—2000. "Genres, Text Types, or Discourse Modes? Narrative Modalities and Genetic Categorisation." In *Style*, 34, 2, 274–92. http:// findarticles.com/p/articles/mi_m2342/is_2_34/ai_68279076 (5 July 2011).

Fontanier, Pierre 1968 [1821–30]. *Les Figures du Discours*. Paris: Flammarion.

Forced Entertainment 2001. *Surrender Control*. http://www.timetchells. com/projects/works/ surrender-control/ (7 July 2011).

Frasca, Gonzalo 1999. "Ludology Meets Narratology: Similitude and Differences between (Video)games and Narrative." In *Parnasso*, 3/1999, Cybertext Special Issue, edited by Markku Eskelinen and Raine Koskimaa, 365–71. http://www.ludology.org/articles/ludology. htm (30 July 2011).

Frasca, Gonzalo 2001a. *The Videogames of the Oppressed*. MA Thesis, Georgia Institute of Technology.

—2001b. "Ephemeral Games: Is It Barbaric to Design Videogames after Auschwitz?" In *Cybertext Yearbook 2000*, edited by Markku Eskelinen and Raine Koskimaa, 172–82. Saarijärvi: Research Center for Contemporary Culture.

—2003a. "Simulation versus Narrative: Introduction to Ludology." In Wolf and Perron (eds) 2003, 221–35.

—2003b. "Ludologists Love Stories too: Notes from a Debate that Never Took Place." In Copier and Raessens (eds) 2003, 92–9.

—2004. "Videogames of the Oppressed: Critical Thinking, Education, Tolerance, and Other Trivial Issues." In Wardrip-Fruin and Harrigan (eds) 2004, 85–94.

—2007. *Play the Message. Play, Game and Videogame Rhetoric*. PhD diss., IT-University of Copenhagen. http://www.powerfulrobot.com/ Frasca_Play_the_Message_PhD.pdf (30 July 2011).

Frawley, William. 1992. *Linguistic Semantics*. Hillsdale, NJ: Erlbaum.

Freud, Sigmund 1981 [1911]. "Psychoanalytic Notes on an Autobiographical Account of Paranoia." In *The Pelican Freud Library, Vol. 9*, edited by Angela Richards, 138–223. London: Penguin.

Fuller, Matthew ed. 2008. *Software Studies. A Lexicon.* Cambridge, MA, and London: MIT Press.

Funkhouser, C. T. 2007. *Prehistoric Digital Poetry: An Archaeology of Forms, 1959–1995.* Tuscaloosa: University of Alabama Press.

Gardner, Colin 2003. "Meta-Interpretation and Hypertext Fiction: A Critical Response." *Computers and the Humanities,* 37, 33–56.

Gendolla, Peter 2010. "No Preexistent World." In Gendolla and Schäfer (eds) 2010, 365–90.

Gendolla, Peter and Jörgen Schäfer (eds) 2007. *The Aesthetics of Net Literature.* Bielefeld: transcript Verlag.

—(eds) 2010. *Beyond the Screen.* Bielefeld: transcript Verlag.

Genette, Gérard 1980 [1972]. *Narrative Discourse. An Essay in Method.* Translated by Jane E. Lewin. Ithaca, NY: Cornell University Press.

—1982a. "The Frontiers of Narrative." In Genette 1982b, 126–44.

—1982b. *Figures of Literary Discourse.* Translated by Alan Sheridan. New York: Columbia University Press.

—1988 [1983]. *Narrative Discourse Revisited.* Translated by Jane E. Lewin. Ithaca, NY: Cornell University Press.

—1992 [1979]. *The Architext: An Introduction.* Translated by Jane E. Lewin. Berkeley and Los Angeles: University of California Press.

—1993 [1991]. *Fiction and Diction.* Translated by Catherine Porter. Ithaca, NY: Cornell University Press.

—1997a [1982]. *Palimpsests. Literature in the Second Degree.* Translated by Channa Newman and Claude Doubinsky. Lincoln and London: University of Nebraska Press.

—1997b [1987]. *Paratexts.* Translated by Jane E. Lewin. Cambridge: Cambridge University Press.

—1997c [1994]. *The Work of Art. Immanence and Transcendence.* Translated by G. M. Goshgarian. Ithaca, NY, and London: Cornell University Press.

—2005. *Essays in Aesthetics.* Lincoln and London: University of Nebraska Press.

Gibson, William 1992. *Agrippa: A Book of Dead.* New York: Kevin Begos.

Glazier, Loss Pequeno 2002. *Digital Poetics:The Making of E-Poetries.* Tuscaloosa: University of Alabama Press.

Goody, Jack 2006. "From Oral to Written: An Anthropological Breakthrough in Storytelling." In *The Novel, Volume I,* edited by Franco Moretti, 3–36. Princeton and Oxford: Princeton University Press.

Gorbert, Matt 2004. "Response." In Wardrip-Fruin and Harrigan (eds) 2004, 218–22.

Greenblat, Cathy 1988. *Designing Games and Simulations. An Illustrated Handbook*. London: Sage.

Greenblat, Cathy and Richard Duke 1975. *Gaming – Simulation. Rationale, Design and Applications*. New York: Wiley.

Grusin, Richard 2005. "Remediation." In Herman, Jahn and Ryan (eds) 2005, 497–8.

Gump, Paul, Fritz Redl, and Brian Sutton-Smith 1971. "The Dimensions of Games." In *The Study of Games*, edited by Elliot M. Avedon and Brian Sutton-Smith, 408–18. New York: Wiley.

Gunder, Anna 1999. "Berättelsels spel: Berättärteknik och ergodicitet in Michael Joyce's Afternoon, a Story." *Human IT*, 3, 3, 27–127.

—2004. *Hyperworks. On Digital Literature and Computer Games*. PhD diss., Uppsala University.

Hamon, Philippe 1981. "Rhetorical Status of the Descriptive." *Yale French Studies*, 61, 1–26.

Hayles, N. Katherine 2001a. "Cyberliterature and Multicourses: Rescuing Electronic Literature from Infanticide". *Electronic Book Review*, 11. http://www.electronicbookreview.com/thread/electropoetics/interspecial (5 July 2011).

—2001b. "What Cybertext Theory Can't Do." *Electronic Book Review*, 12. http://www.altx.com/EBR/RIPOSTE/rip12/rip12hay.htm (5 July 2011).

—2002. *Writing Machines*. Cambridge and London: MIT Press.

—2007. "Electronic Literature: What is It?". http://eliterature.org/pad/elp.html (5 July 2011).

—2008. *Electronic Literature. New Horizons for the Literary*. Notre Dame, IN: University of Notre Dame Press.

Heise, Ursula 1997. *Chronoschisms. Time, Narrative, and Postmodernism*. Cambridge: Cambridge University Press.

Herman, David ed. 1999. *Narratologies: New Perspectives on Narrative Analysis*. Columbus: Ohio State University Press.

Herman, David 2002. *Story Logic. Problems and Possibilities of Narrative*. Lincoln and London: University of Nebraska Press .

Herman, David, Manfred Jahn and Marie-Laure Ryan (eds) 2005. *Routledge Encyclopedia of Narrative Theory*. London and New York: Routledge.

Higgins, Dick 1966. "Intermedia." *Something Else Newsletter*, 1.

—1982. "Some Poetry Intermedia" in Kostelanetz ed. 1982, 414–15.

—1987. *Pattern Poetry. Guide to Unknown Literature*. Albany: State University of New York Press.

Hoffman, Abbie 1989 (1971). *Steal this Book*. In *The Best of Abbie Hoffman*, edited by Daniel Simon and Abbie Hoffman, 187–339. New York: Four Walls Eight Windows.

Holzer, Jenny 1990. *Untitled (The Last Room)*. Installation, 44th Venice
    Biennale.
—1993. *I am Awake at the Place where Women Die*. Electronic
    Installation.
Huhtamo, Erkki 1996. *Elävän kuvan arkeologia*. Jyväskylä:
    YLE-opetuspalvelut.
Huizinga, Johan 1950 [1938]. *Homo Ludens*. Boston, MA: Beacon
    Press.
Ikonen, Teemu 2003. "Moving Text in Avant-Garde Poetry. Towards a
    Poetics of Textual Motion." In *Dichtung Digital, Scandinavian Special
    Issue*, edited by Markku Eskelinen. http://www.brown.edu/Research/
    dichtung-digital/2003/4-ikonen.htm (5 July 2011).
Ingold, Jon 2006 [2001]. *All Roads*. In *Electronic Literature Collection,
    Volume 1*, edited by N. Katherine Hayles, Nick Montfort, Scott
    Rettberg, and Stephanie Strickland. http://collection.eliterature.org/1/
    works/ingold__all_roads.html (5 July 2011).
Jackson, Shelley 1995. *The Patchwork Girl*. Cambridge, MA: Eastgate
    Systems.
Jahn, Manfred 1996. "Windows of Focalization: Deconstructing and
    Reconstructing a Narratological Concept." *Style*, 30, 2, 241–67.
—1999. "'Speak, Friend, and Enter': Garden Paths, Artificial Intelligence,
    and Cognitive Narratology." In Herman ed. 1999, 167–94.
—2001. "Narrative Voice and Agency in Drama. Aspects of a
    Narratology of Drama." *New Literary History*, 32, 659–79.
—2005. *Narratology: A Guide to the Theory of Narrative*. English
    Department, University of Cologne. http://www.uni-koeln.de/~ame02/
    pppn.htm (5 July 2011).
Jakobson, Roman 1971 (1935). "The Dominant." In *Readings in Russian
    Poetics: Formalist and Structuralist Views*, edited by Ladislav Matejka ja
    Krystyna Pomorska, 105–10. Cambridge, MA, and London: MIT Press.
Järvinen, Aki 2003. "Making and Breaking Games: a Typology of Rules."
    In Copier and Raessens (eds) 2003, 68–79.
—2008. *Games without Frontiers. Theories and Methods for Game
    Studies and Design*. PhD diss.,University of Tampere. Acta Electronica
    Universitatis Tamperensis 701. http://acta.uta.fi/teos.php?id=11046 (5
    July 2011).
Jenkins, Henry 2003. "Transmedia Storytelling". *Technology Review*,
    January 15, 2003. http://www.technologyreview.com/Biotech/13052/
    page1/ (5 July 2011).
— 2004a. "Game Design as Narrative Architecture." In Wardrip-Fruin
    and Harrigan (eds) 2004, 118–30.
—2004b. "Henry Jenkins Responds in Turn." http://www.
    electronicbookreview.com/thread/firstperson/well-syuzheted (5 July 2011).

—2006. *Convergence Culture*. New York and London: New York University Press.

Johnson, B. S. 2007 [1969]. *The Unfortunates*. London: Picador.

Jost, Francois 1983. "Narration(s): en decà et au delà." *Communications*, 38, 192–212.

Joyce, James 1988 [1939]. *Finnegans Wake*. London and Boston, MA: Faber & Faber.

Joyce, Michael 1990 [1987]. *Afternoon, a Story*. Cambridge, MA: Eastgate Systems.

—1995. *Of Two Minds*. Ann Arbor: University of Michigan Press.

Juul, Jesper 1998. "A Clash between Game and Narrative." Paper presented at the Digital Arts and Culture Conference, Bergen, Norway, November 1998. http://www.jesperjuul.net/text/clash_between_game_and_narrative.html (30 July 2011).

—1999. *A Clash between Game and Narrative*. MA Thesis, University of Copenhagen. www.jesperjuul.dk/thesis (5 July 2011).

—2000. "What Computer Games Can and Can't Do." Paper presented at the DAC 2000 conference in Bergen, August 2000. http://www.jesperjuul.net/text/wcgcacd.html (30 July 2011).

—2001. "Games Telling Stories? A Brief Note on Games and Narratives." In *Game Studies*, 1, 1. http://www.gamestudies.org/0101/juul-gts/ (5 July 2011).

—2004a. "Introduction to Game Time." In Wardrip-Fruin and Harrigan (eds) 2004, 131–42.

—2004b. *Half-Real: Video Games between Real Rules and Fictional Worlds*. PhD diss., IT-University of Copenhagen.

—2005. *Half-Real*. Cambridge, MA, and London: MIT Press.

—2007. "Without a Goal." In *Videogame/Player/Text*, edited by Tanya Krzywinska and Barry Atkins, 190–203. Manchester: Manchester University Press. http://www.jesperjuul.net/text/withoutagoal/ (5 July 2011).

—2009. "Fear of Failing: the Many Meanings of Difficulty in Video Games." In *The Video Game Theory Reader* 2, edited by Mark J. P. Wolf & Bernard Perron, 237–52. New York: Routledge 2009. http://www.jesperjuul.net/text/fearoffailing/ (5 July 2011).

—2010. *Casual Games*. Cambridge, MA, and London: MIT Press.

Kac, Eduardo 1992. *Astray in Daimos*. http://www.ekac.org/allholopoems.html (5 July 2011).

—1995. *Holopoetry: Essays, Manifestos, Critical and Theoretical Writings*. Lexington: New Media Editions. www.ekac.org/holopoetrybook.pdf (5 July 2011).

—1996. "Key Concepts of Holopoetry." In *Experimental-Concrete-Visual. Avant-Garde Poetry Since the 1960s*, edited by K. David

Jackson, Eric Vos, and Johanna Drucker, 247–57. Atlanta, GA, and Amsterdam: Rodopi.

Kac, Eduardo 1998/1999. *Perhaps.* http://www.ekac.org/perhaps.html (5 July 2011).

—2003. "Biopoetry." In *Cybertext Yearbook* 2002–2003, edited by John Cayley, Markku Eskelinen, Loss Pequeno Glazier, and Raine Koskimaa, 184–5. Saarijärvi: Research Center for Contemporary Culture.

Kac, Eduardo ed. 1996. *New Media Poetry. Visible Language*, 30, 2.

—2007. *Media Poetry. An International Anthology.* Bristol and Chicago: Intellect.

Kaprow, Allan 1996. *Essays on the Blurring of Art and Life.* Berkeley: University of California Press.

Kato, Shuichi 1990. *A History of Japanese Literature, Vol. 2.* Tokyo: Kodansha International .

Kay, Allan and Adele Goldberg 2003 [1977]. "Personal dynamic media." In *The New Media Reader*, edited by Wardrip-Fruin and Montfort, 393–405. Cambridge and London: MIT Press.

Kelley, David 1988. *The Art of Reasoning.* New York: W.W. Norton.

King, Geoff and Tanya Krzywinska (eds) 2002. *ScreenPlay. Cinema/Videogames/Interfaces.* London and New York: Wallflower Press.

Kirby, Michael 1982. "The New Theatre." In *Avant-Garde Tradition in Literature*, edited by Richard Kostelanetz, 324–40. Buffalo, NY: Prometheus Books.

Klabbers, Jan 2003. "The Gaming Landscape. A Taxonomy for Classifying Games and Simulations." In Copier and Raessens (eds) 2003, 54–67.

Klevjer, Rune 2002. "In Defence of Cut Scenes." In Mäyrä ed. 2002, 191–202.

Knoebel, David 1999. *The Wheels.* http://home.ptd.net/~clkpoet/wheels/index.html (5 July 2011).

Knowlton, Jeff, Naomi Spellman, and Jeremy Hight 2002. *34 North 118 West: Mining the Urban Landscape.* Locative Narrative.

Konzack, Lars 2002. "Computer Game Criticism: A Method for Computer Game Analysis." In Mäyrä ed. 2002, 89–100.

Koskimaa, Raine 1999. "Possible Worlds in Literary Theory." *Poetics Today*, 20, 1, 133–8.

—2000. *Digital Literature. From Text to Hypertext and Beyond.* PhD diss., University of Jyväskylä. http://users.jyu.fi/~koskimaa/thesis/thesis.shtml (30 July 2011).

Kostelanetz, Richard ed. 1982. *The Avant-Garde Tradition in Literature.* Buffalo, NY: Prometheus Books.

Kristeva, Julia 1980. *Desire in Language. A Semiotic Approach to*

Literature and Art. Translated by Alice Jardine, Thomas Gora, and Leon S. Roudiez. New York: Columbia University Press.

Kruglanski, Orit 2000. *As Much as You Love Me*. Art Installation.

—2007. "Interactive poems." In Kac ed. 2007, 77–84.

Landow, George P. 1992. *Hypertext. The Convergence of Contemporary Critical Theory and Culture*. Baltimore, MA: Johns Hopkins University Press.

—1997. *Hypertext 2.0. The Convergence of Contemporary Critical Theory and Culture*. Baltimore, MA: Johns Hopkins University Press.

Landow, George P. ed. 1994. *Hyper/Text /Theory*. Baltimore, MA: Johns Hopkins University Press.

Lanser, Susan 1981. *The Narrative Act: Point of View in Prose Fiction*. Princeton: Princeton University Press.

Liestol, Gunnar 1994. "Wittgenstein, Genette, and the Reader's Narrative of Hypertext." In *Hyper/Text/Theory*, edited by George P. Landow, 87–120. Baltimore, MA: Johns Hopkins University Press.

Lindley, Craig L. 2003. "Game Taxonomies: A High Level Framework for Game Analysis and Design." In *Gamasutra*, October 3, 2003. http://www.gamasutra.com/features/20031003/lindley_01.shtml (5 July 2011).

Lukka, Tuomas and Katariina Ervasti 2001. "GZIGZAG. A Platform for Cybertext Experiments." In Eskelinen and Koskimaa (eds) 2001, 141–51.

Lundgren, Sus and Staffan Björk 2003. "Game Mechanics: Describing Computer-Augmented Games in Terms of Interaction." Proceedings of *TIDSE* 2003, 45–56. http://citeseerx.ist.psu.edu/viewdoc/summary?doi=10.1.1.13.5147 (7 July 2011).

MacIntyre, Alistair 1984. *After Virtue*, 2nd edn. Notre Dame, IN: University of Notre Dame Press.

Malaby, Thomas 2007. "Beyond Play: A New Approach to Games." In *Games and Culture*, 2, 2, 95–113. http://papers.ssrn.com/sol3/papers.cfm?abstract_id=922456 (5 July 2011).

Mandler, Jean 1985. *Stories, Scripts and Scenes: Aspects of Schema Theory*. Hillsdale, NJ: Elbaum.

Mangen, Anna 2006. *New Narrative Pleasures?: A Cognitive-phenomenological Study of the Experience of Reading Digital Narrative Fictions*. Trondheim: Norwegian University of Science and Technology.

Manovich, Lev 2001. *The Language of New Media*. Cambridge, MA, and London: MIT Press.

Margolin, Uri 1999. "Of What Is Past, Is Passing, or to Come: Temporality, Aspectuality, Modality, and the Nature of Literary Narrative." In Herman ed. 1999, 142–66.

Mateas, Michael 2002. *Interactive Drama, Art and Artificial Intelligence*.

PhD diss., Carnegie Mellon University. http://www–2.cs.cmu. edu/~michaelm/publications/CMU-CS–02–206.pdf (5 July 2011).

Mateas, Michael and Andrew Stern 2002. *Façade.* Ergodic digital drama.

Mathews, Harry and Brotchie, Alistair (eds) 1998. *The OuLiPo Compendium.* London: Atlas Press.

Mäyrä, Frans 2008. *Introduction to Game Studies: Games in Culture.* London: Sage.

—ed. 2002. *Computer Games and Digital Cultures Conference Proceedings.* Tampere: Tampere University Press.

McGaffery, Steve 1973. *Carnival. The First Panel 1967–1970.* Toronto: Coach House Press. http://archives.chbooks.com/online_books/ carnival/ (7 July 2011).

—1977. *Carnival: The Second Panel 1971–1975.* Toronto: Coach House Press.

McGaffery, Steve and B. P. Nichol 1992. *Rational Geomancy. The Kids of the Book-Machine. The Collected Research Reports of the Toronto Research Group 1973–1982.* Vancouver: Talon Books.

McHale, Brian 1978. "Free Indirect Discourse: A Survey of Recent Accounts." *PTL*, 3, 2.

—1987. *Postmodernist Fiction.* New York: Methuen.

—1992. *Constructing Postmodernism.* London: Routledge.

—2004. *Obligation towards a Difficult Whole.* Tuscaloosa: University of Alabama Press.

McMahon, F. F., Donald E. Lytle, and Brian Sutton-Smith (eds) 2005. *Play: An Interdisciplinary Synthesis.* Lanham, MA: University Press of America.

Melo e Castro, E. M. de 2007. "Videopoetry." In Kac ed. 2008, 175–84.

Memmott, Talan 2000. *From Lexia to Perplexia. In Electronic Literature Collection, Volume 1,* edited by N. Katherine Hayles, Nick Montfort, Scott Rettberg, and Stephanie Strickland. http://collection.eliterature. org/1/works/memmott__lexia_to_perplexia.html (5 July 2011).

Miall, David 2003. "Reading hypertext. Theoretical ambitions and empirical studies." *Forum Computerphilologie*, 3. http:// computerphilologie.uni-muenchen.de/jg03/miall.html (7 July 2011).

Milgram, Stanley 1974. *Obedience to Authority. An Experimental View.* New York: Harper & Row.

Mitchell, W. J. 2003. *ME ++. The Cyborg Self and the Networked City.* Cambridge, MA, and London: MIT Press.

Montfort, Nick 2005. *Twisty Little Passages. An Approach to Interactive Fiction.* Cambridge, MA, and London: MIT Press.

Montola, Markus 2010. "The Positive Negative Experience in Extreme Role-Playing." Paper presented at Nordic Digra 2010 Conference,

Stockholm, Sweden, August 2010. http://www.digra.org/dl/
db/10343.56524.pdf (30 July 2011).

Morrissey, Judd 2005 [2000]. *The Jew's Daughter.* In *Electronic Literature Collection, Volume 1*, edited by N. Katherine Hayles, Nick Montfort, Scott Rettberg, and Stephanie Strickland. http://collection.eliterature. org/1/works/morrissey__the_jews_daughter.html (7 July 2011).

Motte, Warren 1995. *Playtexts.* Lincoln and London: University of Nebraska Press.

—ed. 1986. *OuLiPo – a Primer of Potential Literature.* Normal, IL: Dalkey Archive Press.

Moulthrop, Stuart 1991. *Victory Garden.* Cambridge, MA: Eastgate Systems.

—1995. *Hegirascope.* https://pantherfile.uwm.edu/moulthro/hypertexts/ hgs/ (30 July 2011).

—1997. "No War Machine." In *Reading Matters. Narrative in New Media Ecology*, edited by Joseph Tabbi and Michael Wutz, 269–92. Ithaca, NY, and London: Cornell University Press.

—1999. *Reagan Library.* In *Electronic Literature Collection, Volume 1*, edited by N. Katherine Hayles, Nick Montfort, Scott Rettberg, and Stephanie Strickland. http://collection.eliterature.org/1/works/ moulthrop__reagan_library.html (7 July 2011).

—2003a. *Pax. An Instrument.* https://pantherfile.uwm.edu/moulthro/ hypertexts/pax/ (30 July 2011).

—2003b. "About Pax." https://pantherfile.uwm.edu/moulthro/hypertexts/ pax/about.htm (30 July 2011).

—2004. "From Work to Play: Molecular Culture in the Time of Deadly Games." In Wardrip-Fruin and Harrigan (eds) 2004, 56–69.

—2006. "Interview with Stuart Moulthrop by Noah Wardrip-Fruin." In *The Iowa Web Review.* http://mural.uv.es/mopasa/articulo1 (31 July 2011).

—2007. *Under Language.* http://research-intermedia.art.uiowa.edu/tirw/ vol9n2/artworks/underLanguage/index.htm (5 July 2011).

—2008. "Some Joyces, not an Eco." In *The Iowa Web Review.* http:// research-intermedia.art.uiowa.edu/tirw/vol9n2/ (5 July 2011).

Murray, H. J. R. 1952. *A History of Board Games Other than Chess.* Oxford: Oxford University Press.

Murray, Janet H. 1997. *Hamlet on the Holodeck.* New York: Free Press.

—2004. "From Game-Story to Cyberdrama." In Wardrip-Fruin and Harrigan (eds) 2004, 2–11.

—2005. "The Last Word on Ludology v Narratology." Preface to Murray's keynote at DIGRA 2005 Conference. http://www.lcc.gatech. edu/~murray/digra05/lastword.pdf (5 July 2011).

Musarra, Ulla 1986. "Duplication and Multiplication. Postmodernist Devices in the Novels of Italo Calvino." In *Approaching*

Postmodernism, edited by Douwe Fokkema and Hans Bertens, 135–55. Amsterdam and Philadelphia, PA: John Benjamins Publishing Company.

—1987. "Narrative Discourse in Postmodernist Texts: The Conventions of the Novel and the Multiplication of Narrative Instances." In *Exploring Postmodernism,* edited by Matei Calinescu and Douwe Fokkema, 215–31. Amsterdam and Philadelphia, PA: John Benjamins Publishing Company.

Myers, David 1990. "Computer Game Genres." *Play and Culture,* 3, 286–301.

Nabokov, Vladimir 1962. *Pale Fire.* New York: Weidenfeld & Nicholson.

Nelles, William 1997. *Frameworks. Narrative Levels and Embedded Narrative.* New York: Peter Lang.

Nelson,Theodore Holm 1993 [1981]. *Literary Machines.* Sausalito, CA: Mindful Press.

Nitsche, Michael 2008. *Video Game Spaces.* Cambridge, MA, and London: MIT Press.

Nünning, Ansgar and Vera Nünning (eds) 2002. *Erzähltheorie transgenerisch, intermedial, interdisziplinär.* Trier: WVT.

Olsen, Lance 2005. *10:01.* In *Electronic Literature Collection, Volume 1,* edited by N. Katherine Hayles, Nick Montfort, Scott Rettberg, and Stephanie Strickland. http://collection.eliterature.org/1/works/olsen_guthrie__10_01.html (5 July 2011).

Osthoff, Simone 1994. "Eduardo Kac – The Aesthetics of Dialogue." www.ekac.org/intervcomp94.html (31 July 2011).

OuLiPo Laboratory. Texts from the Bibliothèque Oulipiènne. 1995. Translated and edited by Harry Mathews and Ian White. London: Atlas Press.

Parlett, David 1999. *The Oxford History of Board Games.* Oxford and New York: Oxford University Press.

Pavel, Thomas 1975. "Possible Worlds in Literary Semantics." *Journal of Aesthetics and Art Criticism,* 34, 2, 165–76.

—1986. *Fictional Worlds.* Cambridge, MA: Harvard University Press.

Pavic, Milorad 1988 [1984]. *Dictionary of the Khazars.* Translate by Christina Pribicevic-Zoric. New York: Knopf.

—1990. *Landscape Painted with Tea.* Translated by Christina Pribicevic-Zoric. New York: Knopf.

Pearce, Celia 2005. "Theory Wars: An Argument Against Arguments in the so-called Ludology/Narratology Debate." In Proceedings of DiGRA 2005 Conference: Changing Views – Worlds in Play. http://www.digra.org/dl/order_by_author?publication=Changing%20Views:%20Worlds%20in%20Play (5 July 2011).

Peitz, Johan, Daniel Eriksson, and Staffan Björk 2005. "Augmented

Board Games – Enhancing Board Games with Electronics."
www.digra.org/dl/db/06278.47142.pdf (31 July 2011).

Perloff, Marjorie 2002. *21st-Century Modernism*. Oxford and Malden,
MA: Blackwell.

Poundstone, William 2005. *Project for a Tachistoscope*. In *Electronic
Literature Collection, Volume 1*. Edited by N. Katherine Hayles, Nick
Montfort, Scott Rettberg, and Stephanie Strickland. http://collection.
eliterature.org/1/works/poundstone__project_for_tachistoscope_
bottomless_pit.html (7 July 2011).

Prince, Gerald 1981. *Narratology*. Berlin: Walter de Gruyter & Co.

—1987. *The Dictionary of Narratology*. Lincoln and London: University
of Nebraska Press.

Quoneau, Raymond 1947. *Exercices de style*. Paris: Gallimard.

—1962. *Cent Mille Milliards de Poèmes*. Paris: Gallimard.

—1998. *100,000,000,000,000 Poems*. Translated by Stanley Chapman.
In Mathews and Brotchie (eds) 1998, 15–33.

Rajewski, Irina 2005. "Intermediality, Intertextuality, and Remediation: A
Literary Perspective on Intermediality." In *Intermédialités*, 6, 43–64.

Rand, Ayn 1936. *Night of January 16th*. Chicago: Longman.

Rau, Anja 2000. *What you Click is What you Get? – Die Stellung von
Autoren und Lesern in interaktiver digitaler Literatur*. PhD diss.,
Johannes Gutenberg-Universität Mainz.

—2001. "Reload –Yes/No. Clashing Times in Graphic Adventure Games."
Paper presented at the Computer Games and Digital Textualities
Conference, Copenhagen, March 2001.

Rider, Shawn 2002. *myBall*. In *Electronic Literature Collection, Volume
1*, edited by N. Katherine Hayles, Nick Montfort, Scott Rettberg, and
Stephanie Strickland. http://collection.eliterature.org/1/works/rider__
myball.html (5 July 2011).

Rimmon-Kenan, Shlomith 1983. *Narrative Fiction: Contemporary
Poetics*. London: Methuen.

Robbe-Grillet, Alain 1976. *Topologie d'une Cité Fantôme*. Paris: Minuit.

—1996 [1963]. *For a New Novel*. Translated by Richard Howard.
Evanston, IL: Northwestern University Press.

Roberts, John M., Malcolm J. Arth, and Robert R. Busch 1959. "Games
in Culture." *American Anthropologist*, 61: 597–605.

Roberts, John M. and Brian Sutton-Smith 1962. "Child Training and
Game Involvement." *Ethnology*, 1: 166–85.

Rokeby, David 1986–90. *Very Nervous System*. http://homepage.mac.
com/davidrokeby/vns.html (5 July 2011).

—1995. "Transforming Mirrors: Subjectivity and Control in Interactive
Media." In *Critical Issues in Digital Media*, edited by Simon Penny,
133–58. Albany: SUNY Press.

Ronen, Ruth 1994. *Possible Worlds in Literary Theory*. Oxford: Oxford University Press.

Rosenberg, Jim 1993. *Intergrams*. Cambridge, MA: Eastgate Systems.

—1996. "The Structure of Hypertext Activity." Proceedings of the seventh ACM Conference on Hypertext, 22–30. http://www.well.com/ user/jer/SHA_out.html (5 July 2011).

—2001. "And *And*: Conjunctive Hypertext and the Structure Acteme Juncture." In Hypertext 2001: Proceedings of the Twelfth ACM Conference on Hypertext and Hypermedia, 51–60. New York: ACM. http://www.well.com/user/jer/aachsaj.pdf (31 July 2011).

Roubaud, Jacques 1967. *E.* Paris: Gallimard.

—1998 [1991]. "The Oulipo and Combinatorial Art." In *The Oulipo Compendium,* edited by Harry Mathews and Alistair Brotchie, 37–44. Translated by Harry Mathews. London: Atlas Press.

Ryan, Marie-Laure 1991. *Possible Worlds, Artificial Intelligence and Narrative Theory*. Bloomington and Indianapolis: Indiana University Press.

—1999. "Cyberage Narratology: Computers, Metaphors, and Narrative." In Herman ed. 1999, 142–66.

—ed. 1999. *Cyberspace Textuality*. Bloomington and Indianapolis: University of Indiana Press.

—2001a. *Narrative as Virtual Reality*. Baltimore, MA: Johns Hopkins University Press.

—2001b. "Beyond Myth and Metaphor: The Case of Narrative in Digital Media". *Game Studies*, 1, 1. www.gamestudies.org/0101/ryan (5 July 2011).

—2003. *Narrative across Media*. Baltimore, MA: Johns Hopkins University Press.

—2005. "Narrative." In *Routledge Encyclopedia of Narrative Theory,* edited by David Herman, Manfred Jahn, and Marie-Laure Ryan, 344–8. London and New York: Routledge.

—2006. *Avatars of Story*. Minneapolis and London: University of Minnesota Press.

Salen, Katie and Eric Zimmerman 2004. *Rules of Play. Game Design Fundamentals*. Cambridge, MA, and London: MIT Press,

Saporta, Marc 1962. *Composition No.1*. Paris: Seuil.

Schechner, Richard 1988. *Performance Theory*. London: Routledge.

Shaw, Jeffrey 1989. *The Legible City*. http://www.medienkunstnetz.de/ works/the-legible-city/ (7 July 2011).

Sicart, Miguel 2009. *The Ethics of Computer Games*. Cambridge, MA, and London: MIT Press.

Simanowski, Roberto 2003. "Aleatoric as Enlightment. Simon Biggs Deconstruction of a Kafka Text." In *Cybertext Yearbook 2003*, edited by John Cayley, Markku Eskelinen, Loss Pequeno Glazier, and Raine Koskimaa, 120–8. Saarijärvi: Research Center for Contemporary Culture.

Simons, Jan 2007a. *Playing the Waves. Lars von Trier's Game Cinema.* Amsterdam: University of Amsterdam Press.

—2007b. "Narrative, Games and Theory." *Game Studies*, 7, 1. http:// gamestudies.org/0701/articles/simons (31 July 2011).

Smith, Carlotta S. 2003. *Modes of Discourse. The Local Structure of Texts.* Cambridge: Cambridge University Press.

Stefans, Brian Kim 2000. *The Dreamlife of Letters.* In *Electonic Literature Collection, Volume 1*, edited by N. Katherine Hayles, Nick Montfort, Scott Rettberg, and Stephanie Strickland. http://collection.eliterature. org/1/works/stefans__the_dreamlife_of_letters.html (5 July 2011).

—2003. *Fashionable Noise.* Berkeley, CA: Atelos.

Stern, Andrew 2004. "Response." In Wardrip-Fruin and Harrigan (eds) 2004, 167–73.

Sternberg, Meir 1978. *Expositional Modes and Temporal Ordering in Fiction.* Baltimore, MA, and London: Johns Hopkins University Press.

Stewart, Sean and Jordan Weisman 2006. *Cathy's Book.* Philadelphia, PA, and London: Running Press.

Strand, Randi 1992. *Norisbo.* Original Artwork. Described in Aarseth 1995.

Strehovec, Janez 2001. "The Moving Word." In *Cybertext Yearbook 2000*, edited by Markku Eskelinen and Raine Koskimaa, 100–16. Saarijärvi: Research Center for Contemporary Culture.

—2003. "Attitudes on the Move. On the Perception of Digital Poetry Objects." In *Cybertext Yearbook 2002–2003*, edited by John Cayley, Markku Eskelinen, Loss Pequeno Glazier, and Raine Koskimaa, 39–55. Saarijärvi: Research Center for Contemporary Culture.

Suits, Bernard 1987. *The Grasshopper.* Toronto: University of Toronto Press.

Sutton-Smith, Brian 1997. *The Ambiguity of Play.* Cambridge, MA, and London: Harvard University Press.

—2005. "Evolutionary Resonances for Play." In McMahon, Lytle and Sutton-Smith (eds) 2005, 1–7.

Tisselli, Eugenio 2010. "Narrative Motors." In *Regards Croisés*, edited by Philippe Bootz and Sandy Baldwin, 1–10. Morgantown: West Virginia University Press.

Todorov, Tzvetan 1966. "Les Catégories du récit littéraire". *Communications*, 8, 125–51.

—1977 [1971]. *The Poetics of Prose.* Translated by Richard Howard. Oxford: Blackwell.

Tronstad, Ragnhild 2004. *Interpretation, Performance, Play & Seduction: Textual Adventures in Tubmud.* Ph.D diss., University of Oslo.

Utterback, Camille 2004. "Unusual Positions – Embodied Interaction with Symbolic Spaces." In Wardrip-Fruin and Harrigan (eds) 2004, 218–26.

Utterback, Camille and Romi Achituv 1999. *Text Rain*. www.camilleutterback.com/textrain.html (5 July 2011).

Utterback, Camille and Adam Chapman 2001. *See/Saw*. www.camilleutterback.com/seesaw.html (5 July 2011).

Van Dijk, Teun 1977. *Text and Context. Explorations in the Sematics and Pragmatics of Discourse*. London and New York: Longman.

Virtanen, Tuija 1992. "Issues of Text Typology: Narrative – A Basic Type of Text?" *Text 12*, 2, 293–310.

Walker, Jill 1999. "Piecing Together and Tearing Apart: Finding the Story in 'Afternoon'." *Proceedings of Hypertext '99*, 111–17. New York: ACM Press.

Wardrip-Fruin, Noah 2003. "From Instrumental Texts to Textual Instruments". www.hyperfiction.org/talks/dac03.pdf (5 July 2011).

—2007. "Playable Media and Textual Instruments." In Gendolla and Schäfer (eds), 211–53.

—2009. *Expressive Processing. Digital Fictions, Computer Games, and Software Studies*. Cambridge, MA, and London: MIT Press.

Wardrip-Fruin, Noah, Adam Chapman, Brion Moss, and Duane Whitehurst. 1998–2002. *The Impermanence Agent*. http://www. noahwf.com/agent/index.html (5 July 2011).

Wardrip-Fruin, Noah and Brion Moss 2002. "The Impermanence Agent: Project and Context." In *Cybertext Yearbook 2001*, edited by Markku Eskelinen and Raine Koskimaa, 14–59. Saarijärvi: Research Center for Contemporary Culture.

Wardrip-Fruin, Noah, et al. 2002. *Screen*. CAVE Work.

—2004. *News Reader*. http://turbulence.org/Works/twotxt/nr-index.htm (5 July 2011).

Wardrip-Fruin, Noah and Pat Harrigan (eds) 2004. *First Person. New Media as Story, Performance and Game*. Cambridge, MA, and London: MIT Press.

Wardrip-Fruin, Noah, David Durand, Brion Moss, and Elaine Froehlich 2004. *Regime Change*. In *Electronic Literature Collection, Volume 1*, edited by N.Katherine Hayles, Nick Montfort, Scott Rettberg, and Stephanie Strickland. http://collection.eliterature.org/1/works/ wardrip-fruin_durand_moss_froehlich__regime_change.html (5 July 2011).

Waterfield, Robin and Wilfred Davies 1988. *Money Spider*. London: Penguin.

Weizenbaum, Joseph 1966. *Eliza*. Computer program.

Westcott, James 2010. *When Marina Abramovic Dies. A Biography*. Cambridge, MA, and London: MIT Press.

Wolf, Mark J. P. ed. 2001. *The Medium of the Video Game*. Austin: University of Texas Press.

Wolf, Mark J. P. and Bernard Perron (eds) 2003. *The Video Game Theory Reader*. London: Routledge.

Wolf, Werner 2002. "Intermediality Revisited. Reflections on Word and Music Relations in the Context of a General Typology of Intermediality." In Suzanne M. Lodato, Suzanne Aspden, and Walter Bernhart (eds), *Word and Music Studies: Essays in Honor of Steven Paul Scher and on Cultural Identity and the Musical Stage*, 13–34. Amsterdam and Atlanta, GA: Rodopi.

—2005. "Intermediality." In Herman, Jahn and Ryan (eds) 2005, 252–6.

Woods, Stewart 2004. "Loading the Dice: The Challenge of Serious Videogames." In *Game Studies*, 4, 1. http://gamestudies.org/0401/woods/ (5 July 2011).

Zagal, José P. and Michael Mateas 2007. "Temporal Frames: A Unifying Framework for the Analysis of Game Temporality." In Situated Play, Proceedings of DiGRA 2007 Conference, 516–23.

Zagal, José P., Michael Mateas, Clara Fernández-Vara, Brian Hochhalter, and Nolan Lichti 2005. "Towards an Ontological Language for Game Analysis." Proceedings of DiGRA 2005 Conference: Changing Views – Worlds in Play. http://ir.lib.sfu.ca/handle/1892/1591 (7 July 2011).

Zagal, José P., Clara Fernández-Vara and Michael Mateas 2008. "Rounds, Levels, and Waves. The Early Evolution of Gameplay Segmentation." In *Games and Culture*, 3, 2, 175–98.

Zielinski, Siegfried 1999. *Audiovisions. Cinema and Television as Entr'actes in History*. Amsterdam: Amsterdam University Press.

—2006. *Deep Time of the Media. Toward an Archaeology of Hearing and Seeing by Technical Means*. London and Cambridge, MA: MIT Press.

Zimbardo, Philip 2008. *The Lucifer Effect. Understanding How Good People Turn Evil*. New York: Random House.

Zimroth, Evan 1993. *Dead, Dinner, or Naked*. Evanston, IL: TriQuarterly Books.

Films

Duchamp, Marcel and Man Ray 1926. *Anemic Cinema*.

Sharits, Paul 1966. *Word Movie*.

Vertov, Dziga 1929. *A Man with a Movie Camera*.

Wheeler, David 1999. *Tender Loving Care*. (Interactive Film)

Games

Akella 2000. *Sea Dogs*. Bethesda Softworks.

Atari 1980. *Missile Command*. Atari.

Blizzard Entertainment 2004. *The World of Warcraft*.

Capcom 2003. *Viewtiful Joe*.

Counterstrike Team 2000. *Counter-Strike*.

Cyan 1993. *Myst*. Broderbund.

Cyan 1997. *Riven*. Broderbund.

Electronic Arts 2002. *FIFA 2002*. Electronic Arts.

Firaxis Games 2002. *Civilization III*. Infogrames.

First Star 1984. *Spy vs. Spy*.

Frasca, Gonzalo 2001c. *September 12th, a Toy World*. http://www.
   newsgaming.com/games/index12.htm (31 July 2011).

Gamson, William A. 1966. *SIMSOC*.

ID Software 1999. *Quake III Arena*. Electronic Arts.

Lionhead Studios 2001. *Black & White*. Electronic Arts.

Mateas, Michael and Andrew Stern 2000. *Façade*.

Maxis 1989. *Sim City*. Electronic Arts.

Maxis 2004. *The Sims 2*. Electonic Arts.

Mechner, Jordan 1997. *The Last Express*. Broderbund.

Nintendo 2002. *Animal Crossing*. Nintendo.

Nintendo 2003. *Warioware Inc*. Nintendo.

Number None Inc. *2008*. *Braid*. Microsoft Game Studios.

Pazhitnov, Alexei 1985. *Tetris*. Spectrum Holybyte.

Persuasive Games 2006. *The Arcade Wire: Oil God*. http://www.
   persuasivegames.com/games/ game.aspx?game=arcadewireoil (31 July
   2011).

Remedy 2001. *Max Payne*. Take 2 Interactive.

Rockstar Games 2001. *Grand Theft Auto III*. Rockstar Games.

Rockstar Games 2004. *Grand Theft Auto: San Andreas*.

Saber Interactive 2007. *TimeShift*.

Sega 1982. *Pengo*. Sega.

Shirts, S. Garry 1969. *StarPower*. Simulation Training Systems.

Sierra Online 1987. *Space Quest 1*. Sierra.

Stern, Eddo and Mark Allen 2001. *Tekken Torture Tournament*. Game
   performance/ custom hardware.

Strat-O-Matic 1968. *Strat-O-Matic Football*.

Taito 1977. *Space Invaders*.

Take Action 2006. *Darfur is Dying*. http://www.darfurisdying.com/ (31
   July 2011).

Verant Interactive 1999. *EverQuest*. Sony Online Entertainment.

INDEX